PROPERTY RIGHTS

PROPERTY RIGHTS

Cooperation, Conflict, and Law

Edited by

Terry L. Anderson and Fred S. McChesney

PRINCETON UNIVERSITY PRESS

PRINCETON AND OXFORD

LIBRARY OF CONGRESS CATALOGING-IN-PUBLICATION DATA

Property rights : cooperation, conflict, and law / edited by Terry L. Anderson and
    Fred S. McChesney.
        p. cm.
    Includes bibliographical references and index.
    ISBN 0-691-09997-9 (alk. paper) — ISBN 0-691-09998-7 (pbk. : alk. paper)
        1. Property.   2. Property—Economic aspects.   3. Property—Social aspects.
    I. Anderson, Terry Lee, 1946–   II. McChesney, Fred S., 1948–
    K720 .P763 2003
    346.04—dc21   2002025136

British Library Cataloging-in-Publication Data is available

This book has been composed in American Gothic and Sabon

Printed on acid-free paper. ∞

www.pupress.princeton.edu

Printed in the United States of America

10 9 8 7 6 5 4 3 2 1

CONTENTS

FIGURES AND TABLES

ACKNOWLEDGMENTS

This book reflects the editors' long-held belief that a basic text on property rights was long overdue. Each of us had, separately, considered filling that gap with a book of his own. Competing demands for time and the growing realization that other scholars were specializing in subtopics of the general subject, however, increasingly counseled the approach represented in this volume. We identified the topics that we thought were crucial to a basic text and then sought the scholars who were best qualified to deal with each topic. Our goal was a volume that captured the benefits of comparative advantage and specialization while presenting a comprehensive and integrated text. Thanks to the team effort, we accomplished our mission.

It is appropriate to acknowledge the debts we incurred along the way. Terry Anderson wishes to thank his mentors at the University of Washington, especially Douglass C. North, who got him thinking about property rights before most young economists had heard of the field. He owes special thanks to his close friend and coauthor, P. J. Hill, for the many hours spent in the office or on horseback discussing the intricacies of property rights. He also appreciates support from Marty and Illie Anderson for supporting his position as Senior Fellow at the Hoover Institution.

Fred McChesney is particularly indebted to Louis De Alessi for introducing him to the subject of property rights economics and to his teachers at the University of Virginia and University of Miami Law and Economics Center who advanced his understanding of the subject. In addition to De Alessi, they include Kenneth Clarkson, Henry Manne, Donald Martin, and Roland McKean. Jean-Pierre Centi and Jacques Garello offered the chance to lecture on property rights twice in the Diplôme d'Études Approfondies program at the Université d'Aix-Marseille III, an opportunity that was exceptionally valuable for developing the overall approach to the book.

Mostly, of course, we are indebted to the authors here, who endured the usual ignominies inflicted by editors demanding yet another clarification and worse, yet another rewrite. We hope that their adherence to our demands added positive value to their already high level of scholarship. Special thanks are owed David Haddock, who (in addition to his own chapter) provided countless valuable suggestions throughout the book. There is no question that our adherence to his suggestions added much to our introductions to each section. We note with sadness the passing of Edwin West following his writing of the first chapter. Eddie was a path-breaking scholar, but more, a delightful colleague and cherished friend.

Property Rights: Contract, Conflict, and Law would not have seen the light of day without the assistance of the Hoover Institution at Stanford University and of PERC—The Center for Free Market Environmentalism in Bozeman, Montana. Thanks to the leadership of John Raisian, director of the Hoover Institution, we were able to pursue this project. People too numerous to mention at Hoover helped us organize a working conference where the chapters in this volume were first aired and where we benefited from the suggestions of many other scholars and practitioners. At PERC, Michelle Johnson painstakingly kept track of progress on each chapter, inputted and formatted changes, and made sure the authors and editors met deadlines. Without her management, we would still be working on a first draft.

Finally, we thank Peter and Kirsten Bedford, idea venture capitalists who supported this project through the Hoover Institution. Peter and Kirsten understand that a free society depends on the rule of law, of which property rights are an integral part, and are supporters of Hoover's property rights initiative. They are unique in their willingness to make an investment in developing ideas that will bear fruit mainly for future generations. Thus, we dedicate this volume to Peter and Kirsten Bedford.

THE ECONOMIC APPROACH TO PROPERTY RIGHTS

The institution of property — ownership and control of assets — is as old as humankind. In every society, even the former Soviet Union, individuals have had rights to own at least some property. Property rights have evolved, not just in complex industrial societies where individuals own everything from personal automobiles to shares of giant corporations, but also in American Indian societies, where individuals owned personal property like bows and arrows, tipis, and horses. To be sure, not all members of society share equally in ownership and control of assets and, in some instances, some persons may be denied ownership rights altogether. But property rights for some people, at least over some assets, have prevailed at all times and in all places.

This volume examines the reasons for the ubiquity of property rights, by which we mean the formal or informal rules that govern access to and use of tangible assets such as land and buildings, and intangible assets such as patents and contract rights. By this definition, clearly the deed to land or the title to a car constitutes a property right. Less formal, but no less important, are property rights to personal property such as clothing or jewelry, although these rights are not recorded with any agency.

Property is often called a "bundle of sticks" because it actually is made up of multiple rights. In its most complete form, ownership of property gives its owner the right to derive value from the asset, to exclude others from using it, and to transfer the asset to others. As discussed by Yoram Barzel in chapter 2, however, property rights may be less complete, allowing an owner to derive only some value from an asset, exclude only some people from using it, or transfer only certain uses for a specified time period.

Government institutions can play an important role in defining and enforcing property rights through the courts and the state's police power. Because government today is nearly ubiquitous, it is conventionally viewed as an inextricable part of any system defining and enforcing property rights.

But government involvement, though often useful, is not necessary for creating or enforcing rights. As discussed in chapter 3 by Thráinn

Eggertsson, informal and even formal property rights exist without governmental involvement. When a person occupies a seat in a movie theater, it is considered his for the duration of the movie without a police officer monitoring each aisle. If a dispute over claims to the seat arises, the theater operator would typically settle it himself, using familiar and generally accepted rules such as "first-come first-served," the subject of Dean Lueck's chapter 8, rather than calling on the government.

This perspective may surprise some readers, because a paramount government role in creating and enforcing property rights is usually taken as given. Neither the fact nor the desirability of that role is necessarily to be disputed. This volume strives, however, not to take government as given, but to show why and how the governmental role emerges. To employ social-science terms, government thus is treated here as endogenous, not exogenous. That is, its existence and functions in a property rights regime are not merely posited, but treated as subjects for investigation and explanation in a general model of property rights delineation.

As will be shown, the role of government emerges as a function of the difficulties of private definition and enforcement of property rights. Therefore, in the early chapters of this book, government appears on stage only fleetingly, as the spotlights focus more on private actors. Beginning in parts III and IV, however, and increasingly thereafter, government actors (politicians, bureaucrats, judges) play increasingly important roles. In the end, an analysis proceeding from private to governmental action furthers an understanding of what government should and can do. It is often the institution best suited to define and enforce property rights, but not always.

THE ECONOMIC PERSPECTIVE

This volume analyzes the emergence and importance of property rights from an economic perspective.[1] Economics emphasizes that life is a series of choices among alternatives, choices required because we face limits.[2] There is only so much time, so much money, so much land, so much oil, and so forth.

To some, this general definition of an economic perspective may be surprising. If economics is about choices people make, then economics must be claiming it can study nearly everything about life. And so, indeed, it does. Of course, economists routinely analyze prices, products, and markets. But economists also analyze things such as love and marriage, drug addiction, altruism, terrorism, capital punishment, and practically any other phenomenon about which human beings make choices, which is virtually everything in life.

In other words, it is not the substance, but the methodology of economics that defines economic science and distinguishes it from other social sciences.[3] Economic methodology, including that applied to property rights, builds on four basic postulates, presented here. At the heart of all four is an insistence on the individual as the unit of analysis (so-called methodological individualism). The economist "commences with individuals as evaluating, choosing, and acting units. Regardless of the possible complexity of the processes or institutional structures from which outcomes emerge, the economist focuses on individual choices" (Buchanan 1987a).[4]

If the individual is the basic unit of analysis, economics insists that constructs such as classes (à la Marx), government, the firm, society, and similar abstractions are only useful analytically to the extent they specify how individual preferences and actions are agglomerated. A class, a government, or a society does not make choices. Not being animate entities, none can act except through the decisions of individuals capable of choosing. True, economists talk about the firm (Barzel, chapter 2) or the government (McChesney, chapter 9), but only as a shorthand summary for how the myriad individuals within these institutions act. This is not to say that individuals always act individually; certainly collective action takes place. But collective action can only be a manifestation of individual preferences and actions shaped by constraints and conditioned by rules for aggregating individual preferences and actions.

Using the individual as the unit of analysis, this volume (like most of economics) aspires to be positive, referring to what individual actors do, not what they should do under some notion of morality or civic virtue. Positive analysis seeks to describe what does happen in the world and predict what will happen, not to prescribe normative rules for making the world a different (perhaps better) place. To analogize, the distinction between positive and normative is seen in newspapers, where one finds both sports news (positive) and editorials (normative). This is not to say that economics ignores issues important to morality and virtue; its analysis of actions such as addiction and altruism was noted earlier.[5] But economic analysis ordinarily treats such things as it does other subjects, as phenomena to be explained. That is the spirit animating the analysis of property rights in this volume.

THE FOUR BASIC POSTULATES

Building on the individual as the basic unit of positive analysis, four postulates guide the economic analysis of property rights.

Postulate 1: Individuals choose under conditions of scarcity; no one has as much of the world's riches as he would like.

As already noted, economics begins with the fact that choices are made subject to constraints. Because resources are limited, we must choose which of our unlimited desires to satisfy, meaning we must make trade-offs. In a world of scarcity, one use of an asset precludes another and, thereby, generates an opportunity cost (as discussed, for example, by Bruce Yandle in chapter 10). The cost of breathing clean air, building houses, or irrigating crops is measured in terms of the alternative uses that are foregone. Land occupied by a house cannot provide grizzly bear habitat. Water used for irrigation cannot provide a free-flowing stream in which fish can spawn.

Postulate 2: Individuals act rationally to pursue their self-interest by continually adjusting to the incremental (marginal) benefits and incremental (marginal) costs of their actions.

Methodological individualism presumes that individuals are rational. By rational we mean that people have well-defined preferences and act systematically to maximize the amount of those things (tangible or intangible) that satisfy those preferences, subject to the cost of achieving satisfaction. An individual's maximization of his satisfaction does not necessarily imply selfishness. Even a person satisfied with what he had for himself would want more for his family, his friends, the members of his church or club, or others. Human desires (including desires to see others better off) are limitless.

But resources are not limitless. Rational maximization therefore requires individuals to weigh the benefits and costs that their choices entail, asking what additional gains there are from additional amounts of a good or service and what must be sacrificed (foregone) to obtain the gains. This does not mean that individuals always measure perfectly and never make mistakes. In fact, making mistakes bears out the assumption of rationality: information is costly to obtain (scarce), so rational actors will never have perfect information when they make their choices.

In the analysis of property rights that follows, the rationality postulate is particularly important in thinking about why and how property rights evolve. Because resources are scarce (have alternative beneficial uses), rational actors employ resources to define and enforce property rights as long as the benefits of using resources in that way exceeds their costs. If the marginal benefits of defining and enforcing rights are greater than the marginal costs, do it. More dynamically, if the cost of acting falls (rises), do more (less) of it.

The process of rational wealth maximization described by postulate 2 applies to all individuals, not only those in modern capitalistic economies. It is well accepted that the owner of a firm must compare the additional revenue from extra production with the additional resource cost if he is to maximize profits. It is sometimes claimed that such rational calculation does not apply to people in developing economies or nonwestern cultures. Trosper (1978, 503) notes, for example, that explanations of economic differences between American Indians and whites have frequently rested on supposed differences in values. His evidence shows, however, that Indian ranchers are no less efficient and no less interested in profiting than their non-Indian counterparts. Trosper concludes, "The theory of the 'optimizing' [i.e., rational maximizing] peasant is now ascendant in economic development theory, because more facts are consistent with it. . . . People of diverse cultures make allocation decisions similarly." Where there are differences in Indians' output and efficiency, those differences are best explained by the different structures of property rights (Anderson and Lueck 1992). The empirical evidence that Louis De Alessi summarizes in chapter 4 of this volume illustrates this point more generally.

Postulate 3:   Scarcity and rational behavior result in competition for resources, and societal rules govern how this competition proceeds.

Rational maximization of one's satisfaction in the face of resource scarcity means that individuals will compete to own resources conducive to their personal welfare. People will invest time and effort vying with others to determine who gets how much of the resource, and under what conditions. In the case of movie theater seats on opening night, one must arrive early to take first possession (as Lueck's chapter 8 discusses). With an open access fishery, fishers will race to catch fish before someone else takes them (Gordon 1954).

The competition for open access resources is costly because the same time and effort spent competing for resources could be expended in other ways. Less obviously, competition for resources may degenerate into violence, as David Haddock explains in chapter 7. Whatever the type of cost, rational individuals invest in defining rights up to the point where the incremental benefits of competing for resources equal the cost of doing so.

The fact that competition is costly means that individuals may benefit collectively from defining rules to govern competition for resources, choosing those rules that lower the overall costs of resource competition. Individuals might collectively agree, for example, that violence or threats of violence will not be recognized as a way to define property rights. As a way to reduce the costs of violence, rules can be agreed upon privately. For example, there is no statute that requires airline passengers to respect the right of the first passenger who puts his suitcase in the overhead bin to use that space during the flight. Such a rule presumably is preferable to a might-makes-rights system whereby the biggest and strongest passenger takes what he wants, regardless of the desires of others.

Where the number of people competing for a resource is small and the group is homogeneous, there is a greater incentive to minimize wasteful competition for property rights by contracting, rather than warring, over property rights (as discussed in chapter 6 by Gary Libecap). Privately contrived and enforced rules may not work best in all situations, however. Increasing group size and heterogeneity at some point may produce the Hobbesian jungle, where life is "nasty, brutish and short." Externally imposed rules, embodied in explicit laws or ordinances, then may become preferable to private solutions in minimizing conflict over resources.

Explaining the evolution of rules governing competition for rights has been a major task for economists and lawyers studying property. Rather than taking property rights as exogenous, economic and legal scholars recognize that rules which evolve are produced by rational individuals willing to devote effort to defining and enforcing property rights, as long as the marginal benefits to them of doing so exceed the marginal costs. Institutional entrepreneurs recognize that establishing property rights or redefining the rules that determine who benefits from scarce resources can be just as valuable as producing a better mousetrap. Terry Anderson and P. J. Hill discuss this issue in chapter 5.

> *Postulate 4*:   Given individual rationality and self-interest, a
> system of well-specified and transferable property rights
> encourages positive-sum games with mutual gains from trade.

Competition for the use of scarce resources can result in conflict or cooperation, depending on the system of property rights. If property rights are not well defined and enforced, the incentive to take by threat or violence increases, with the predictable results that resource owners will invest less in developing their property or even keeping it up (Tullock 1967). Likewise, if property rights are not transferable, those who might place a higher value on a scarce resource will have little option to negotiate over it, relative to the incentives to take it by theft or resort to government (Epstein 1985a). On the other hand, if property rights are well defined, enforced, and transferable, owners can trade their rights with others, making all parties better off.

The potential for gains from trade is revealed by many comparative studies that show economies with greater economic freedom — secure and tradable property rights defended by the rule of law — outperform other economies. For example, in economies with higher levels of economic freedom, per capita gross domestic product grew approximately 2.5 percent, as compared to a 1.5 percent decline in economies with less economic freedom between 1980 and 1994 (Gwartney, Lawson, and Block 1996). Keefer and Knack (1997) report similarly that the absence of a secure rule of law diminishes rates of economic growth. Norton (1998) not only finds that growth rates are higher in countries with more secure property rights, but that environmental quality is better. As Norton (1998, 51) puts it, "the specification of strong aggregate property rights appears to have an important place in improving human well-being."

THE ROAD AHEAD

The four postulates stated above guide the discussions of the law and economics of property rights that follow. In part I, Edwin West surveys early political economists' work on property rights. West concludes that while some economists (Adam Smith and David Hume, for example) understood the nexus between property rights, freedom, and growth, early economic thinkers were more concerned with establishing the normative bases for private property. Doubtless in part because of the embryonic state of economics itself, positive (descriptive) analysis of property rights was little studied.

That neglect disappeared in the mid-twentieth century when the role of property rights within business firms, particularly large corporations, was increasingly scrutinized. In chapter 2, Yoram Barzel presents a critical précis of how this literature has developed in the past twenty-five years. It is no exaggeration to say that the property rights revolution in economic thinking has completely revised the way in which the modern corporation is analyzed. Disappearing among lawyers are earlier notions of the corporation as a "creature of the state." So is the previously central idea among economists that the firm is defined by its production function and cost curves. Both lawyers and economists now view corporations as creatures of an interconnected web of contracts that establish property rights among the contracting parties (managers, investors, lenders, workers, and so forth).

Part II of this volume establishes the modern property rights approach, departing from the "tragedy of the commons." In chapter 3, Thráinn Eggertsson distinguishes open access and common property from private property, measuring distinctions among the three according to a group's ability to govern itself and to exclude outsiders. Among groups with different characteristics, different forms of property are desirable; no one form of property rights is optimal in all settings. However, with the growth of population and related changes, private property (permitting the exclusion of nonowners) tends to become more desirable. As Eggertsson concludes, "when exclusion and governance are absent, economic agents lack the incentive to economize in the use of resources, maintain their quality, and invest in their improvement." Whether private property truly is superior to other ownership forms is an empirical proposition. In chapter 4, Louis De Alessi continues Eggertsson's theme by summarizing the many empirical studies in particular settings where private and nonprivate property rights coexist, and so can be compared. Overwhelmingly, the studies document the positive impact that property rights have on resource stewardship, human cooperation, and wealth, when the economic conditions for the emergence of private rights are fulfilled.

If private property is generally a superior institution (but not always, Eggertsson cautions), the rules by which property is defined and enforced are important to understand. Part III considers the evolution of property rights. In chapter 5, Terry Anderson and P. J. Hill introduce the institutional entrepreneur as an evolutionary force in defining rights. Property rights evolve as rational individuals devote effort (time and money) to defining and enforcing their claims to scarce resources. Whether individuals by themselves can escape the tragedy of the commons depends largely on their ability to contract among themselves for exclusion and governance. In chapter 6, Gary Libecap develops the factors that determine whether private contracting for property rights is feasible. Libecap demonstrates that in many historical and contemporary settings, cooperation among private individuals to define and enforce rights has indeed occurred. Enforcing contracting for property rights is not costless, as David Haddock explains in chapter 7. He develops the crucial point that force underlies all enforcement. This does not mean that force is always exercised, because its exercise is a zero-sum, if not negative-sum, game. Haddock explains why a party with an absolute advantage in the use of force will not control all resources simply because devoting effort to enforce rights has opportunity costs in other productive activities.

Part IV develops the potential for collective action or government to establish and enforce property rights in situations where individual action might fail. Dean Lueck discusses how first possession rules determine who will be excluded from open access resources and how those rules can limit the dissipation of resources in the race to get property rights. In this regard, first possession rules represent a quasi-contractual solution to defining rights.

Fred McChesney in chapter 9 introduces government as the collectively sanctioned agency with a monopoly on the legitimate use of force. Government may be the cheapest definer and enforcer of property rights in some situations, but it is naive to assume that government, with its monopoly on force, will perform optimally. Although governments can help define and enforce property rights, the same governmental force is available to redistribute wealth from one group in society to another. Hence, McChesney raises the fundamental dilemma of political economy: how can collective coercive power be harnessed to enforce property rights and the rule of law, without abuse of that same power to disrupt rights?

In part V, the focus shifts to conflicting uses of private property (so-called externalities) and the possibility of government intervention in resolving those conflicts. In chapter 10, Bruce Yandle reviews the work of English economist A. C. Pigou, the influential advocate of government command-and-control policies to resolve conflicting property uses. Yandle contrasts Pigou's solution with that of Ronald Coase. Pigou's reliance on government regulatory fixes for externalities ignored the role of private property rights. Coase, on the other hand, showed how private property and bargaining over contending uses could resolve conflicts, as long as transaction costs were not prohibitive. In chapter 11, Harold Demsetz challenges the twin notions that transaction costs are different from other production costs and that transaction costs create market failure. Typical of his path-breaking analyses of property rights (1964, 1966, 1967), Demsetz argues here that externalities could be eliminated if the firms generating them simply merged, but that such integration entails other costs. Hence, if firms fail to integrate to eliminate externalities, this suggests that the costs of eliminating the externalities outweigh the benefits and, so, are of no economic relevance.

In addition to externalities, private property, once defined, may be incompatible with the production of public goods. Public goods — tangible things like roads, dams, and national defense, or intangibles such as scenic views and orderly development of urban space — are often said to require government taking of land or land use zoning. Part VI considers those claims. In chapter 12, Richard Epstein discusses the reasons eminent domain procedures may be necessary to allow the government to produce public goods and overcome holdout problems. Epstein also discusses the pernicious results that can come from this power. Similarly, in the volume's concluding chapter 13, William Fischel uses zoning as an example of how the coercive power of government can be harnessed to overcome free riding, but how this process can also go astray. Especially at the local level, zoning becomes a way to rearrange and clarify property rights. When done at the local level where exit from zoning rules is less costly, zoning may remove some spillover effects. However, even when the costs and benefits of changing property rights through zoning inure to local people, there is a possibility that zoning will result in the type of rent seeking described by McChesney in chapter 9.

CONCLUSION

Much of the literature on property rights — and this volume is no exception — relies on economic history for its lessons. Especially on the frontier, whether it be the United States of the nineteenth century or Brazil today, different resource endowments, new technologies, and a lack of property rights provide fertile opportunities for institutional innovation. Often, government is largely absent or even nonexistent, meaning that solutions to defining and defending property must arise from private, contractual ordering. Historical episodes therefore furnish ideal natural laboratories to observe the phenomena analyzed in this volume.

The focus on history should not be taken to mean that the model developed in this volume is any less applicable to modern property rights settings. From the open access of the oceans to the far reaches of space, new frontiers where property rights have not been established offer new applications for the law and economics of property rights. Issues that arose concerning property rights on the high seas the late nineteenth century (Ellickson 1991) are relevant in the twentieth century (Clarkson 1974), and for the same reasons. The same open-access problem arises in the privacy of our homes when the telemarketing firm invades our private time. (See the introduction to part III for an elaboration of this problem.) With the accelerating growth of populations, issues of the relative importance of private versus governmental solutions to property rights problems take on increased urgency. We hope this volume stimulates scholars to expand the approach presented here, ultimately finding new applications and solutions to problems that, at their core, are ones of property rights.

ENDNOTES

1. There are, of course, other approaches. See, for example, Dietze (1971). Most of these other approaches, however, are normative rather than positive, a distinction discussed in this Introduction.

2. This emphasis is consistent with perhaps the most celebrated definition of economics, that of Lionel Robbins: "Economics is the science which studies human behavior as a relationship between ends and scarce means which have alternative uses" (1935, 16). For other discussions of economics' domain, see Kirzner (1976) and Buchanan (1979).

3. See, for example, Enthoven (1963, 422):

[T]he tools of analysis that we . . . use are the simplest, most fundamental concepts of economic theory, combined with the simplest quantitative methods. . . . The economic theory we are using is the theory most of us learned as sophomores. The reason Ph.D.'s are required is that many economists do not believe what they have learned until they have gone through graduate school and acquired a vested interest in the analysis.

4. This 1987 article is the lecture Buchanan delivered in accepting the 1986 Nobel Prize in Economic Science.

5. Works combining economic and religious thinking appear frequently. See, for example, Dean and Waterman (1999).

PART I

INTRODUCTION

The idea that property rights might themselves be a distinct and explicit area of economic inquiry is relatively recent. In classical economics, well-defined and secure property rights were typically assumed to exist, not analyzed or explained. As noted by Steve Pejovich (1972, 310), one of the first modern economists writing about property rights: "A student of economics discovers early that the entire body of the standard theory of production and exchange is built upon the assumption of private property rights over resources."

With their presence simply assumed, property rights are usually exogenous rather than endogenous in economic analysis. However one might judge Karl Marx's economic writings in other respects, he accurately criticized the economics of his day for ignoring issues of property:

> Political economy proceeds from the fact of private property, but it does not explain it to us. We have presupposed private property . . . [Private property] is explained from external circumstances. As to how far these external . . . circumstances are but the expression of a necessary course of [human] development, political economy teaches us nothing. (Marx [1844] 1959, 68–69)[1]

For example, although a system of secure and transferable property rights implicitly underpins Adam Smith's famous "invisible hand," *The Wealth of Nations* ([1776] 1976a) discusses only fitfully how property rights condition behavior, how they evolve, or how they are protected.[2]

Economists did little work on the actual reasons for and consequences of property until the late nineteenth century. Other disciplines—Marx himself was more a philosopher and sociologist than an economist—had more to say about the positive economics of property.[3] Belatedly, however, economists discovered the importance of property rights as a discrete intellectual domain. With the work notably of Coase (1960), Demsetz (1964, 1966, 1967), and Alchian (1958, 1965b), a general approach began to emerge, focusing on fundamental property rights questions. What is the nature of property? Why and how do property rights evolve? Why are different forms of property ownership observed at different times and in different places? What are the respective roles of private contracts and public law in defining and enforcing property rights? How well do these alternative systems perform? These are the questions addressed by the authors in this volume.

History of Economic Thought

From antiquity, the institution of property has stimulated considerable thinking by moral and legal philosophers, theologians, and others. In his *Politics*, for example, Aristotle writes: "Let us consider what should be our arrangements about property: should the citizens of the perfect state have their possessions in common or not?" Deciding finally that property should be owned privately but made accessible for use by all, Aristotle criticized Plato who, in *The Republic*, argued that property should be communal both in ownership and in use.

As Edwin West discusses in chapter 1, neither Aristotle's nor Plato's answers resolved the issue for good. The normative question, whether individuals should own and use property privately, was for centuries posed and debated by economically minded thinkers. Returning to the classical Greek philosophers, early church thinkers wrestled with Aristotle's question until Thomas Aquinas established the Church's definitive position, one that found private property legitimate within a grander system of natural law. With the rise of Protestantism, that position was reexamined.

It is at this point that West picks up the story. Enlightenment scholars such as John Locke continued to ponder the normative basis for property, as did the nineteenth-century Utilitarians. Locke's defense, not just of private ownership but also of private use, was enormously influential. If a man owns his own labor, as all must concede he should, should he not own the fruits of that labor? By definition, ownership of a thing must include the right to use that thing and to retain the gains from that use.

West indicates how influential Locke's perspective remained a century later in *The Wealth of Nations*, the first great work of economics. Not only did Smith, like Locke, view property within a larger system of natural rights dictated by natural law, both saw the institutions of property and government as self-reinforcing. Private property created a role for government in defending property, and the existence of government to enforce property rights stimulated further creation of property.

From this notion of the property–government relationship flowed Smith's famous assignment to government of three major tasks: national defense, administration of justice, and "certain public works." The role of the first two functions in protecting property is obvious, but the importance of the third, public works, is not so obvious in a property rights framework. As noted in part VI of this volume, creation of public goods today is frequently (perhaps ordinarily) seen as requiring government interference with private property, not its advancement. West's chapter elucidates what Smith meant by "certain public works."

West argues that, for Smith, the public works with which government should concern itself are projects such as road building, things that in principle could be performed by private firms amassing large sums of investor capital—what would come to be called public corporations (which of course are privately owned). But in Smith's time, such public corporations could be established and operated only by government fiat and regulation, a system Smith decried and wanted abolished. Thus, the "certain public works" that Smith urged upon government were free incorporations that actually would entail enlargements of private property rights in England.

Locke and Smith's belief in the importance of private ownership and use was shared by David Hume, West continues. But it was vigorously challenged by the Utilitarians, the most famous of whom were Jeremy Bentham and John Stuart Mill. As West discusses, the Utilitarians reduced the desirable role of private property in society, favoring instead greater government direction of resources. Mill's position was similar to that of Aristotle, arguing for private ownership but communal use. Mill differed from Aristotle, however, in that a central government would dictate what communal use would be, rather than leaving questions of use to the disaggregated communal users themselves, as Aristotle would have done.

Jeremy Bentham added a patina of science to the idea that government direction of property would be superior to individual decisions. With Bentham's "felicific calculus," units of pleasure and pain could be measured, meaning the measurer would be able to define institutions that yielded the greatest happiness to the greatest number. Doing so meant the measurer must have the ability to force others to comply with the ultimate configuration of rights dictated by the calculus, and so the ultimate measurer must be the government. Indeed, property itself was impossible without government. Bentham defined property as

> the expectation of deriving certain advantages from a thing. . . . Now this expectation, this persuasion, can only be the work of law. I cannot count upon the enjoyment of that which I regard as mine, except through the promise of the law which guarantees it to me. . . . Property and law are born together, and die together. Before laws were made there was not property; take away laws, and property ceases. (Bentham 1882, 111–13)[4]

If property is subsidiary to government and law, it would follow that the law can refuse to define property or to redefine it as it chooses, to achieve maximal happiness.[5] In his infamous advocacy of torture, Bentham came close to denying the essential core of the Lockean system that every man owns his own body. To Bentham, torture was one way for government to use the "felicific calculus" to produce the maximum good for the greatest number. One commentator summarizes:

> [T]here is [for Bentham] no natural harmony of interests such as the one that Adam Smith had postulated. . . . Instead, the task falls on government to produce an artificial harmony of interests by means of legislation. To Bentham, it was the function of legislation and of the science treating of it to establish a system of punishments and rewards that would induce individuals to pursue actions leading to the greatest happiness of the greatest number. (Spiegel 1971, 341)

PROPERTY RIGHTS AND THE FIRM

The Benthamite perspective is normative, as was that of almost all those writing in an economic vein that West discusses. Positive economic analysis of property began to move from the background to the foreground of economic and legal thinking with the publication in 1932 of a book co-authored by a lawyer and an economist. Adolph Berle and Gardiner Means' *The Modern Corporation and Private Property* created a sensation upon its publication, and it remains topical to this day.[6] For the first time since Marx, and to a greater extent than found in Marx, notions of property were identified as central to an understanding of economics and law.

The essence of the modern corporation, according to Berle and Means, was the separation of ownership from control. Allegedly, property rights to firms were splintering, as those who nominally owned the firm (shareholders) no longer effectively owned it. Those who ran the firm (directors and officers) in fact were the apparent beneficiaries of the rewards generated by assets that they did not own. Shareholders nominally owned firms, but were forced to share the fruits of their property with those who actually controlled (managed) it without ownership. Berle and Means summarized:

> There has resulted the dissolution of the old atom of ownership into its component parts, control and beneficial ownership. This dissolution of the atom of property destroys the very foundation on which the economic order of the past three centuries has rested. Private enterprise, which has molded economic life since the close of the middle ages, has been rooted in the institution of private property. Under the feudal system, its predecessor, economic organization grew out of mutual obligations and privilege derived by various individuals from their relation to property which no one of them owned. Private enterprise, on the other hand, has assumed an owner of the instruments of production with complete property rights over those instruments. (Berle and Means 1932, 8)

Comparison to Smith's hopes that government would permit "certain public works" is inevitable. Smith believed that a property-minded government would end the system allowing private incorporation only by government permission and would allow liberal incorporation as a means of amassing capital on a scale necessary to undertake large public works. That system had in fact emerged in the first part of the twentieth century; it was that system that Berle and Means described. But allegedly, large corporate firms, emerging as the dominant form of business at the time Berle and Means wrote, were increasingly a device whereby one group, managers, could use shareholder property to advance their own interests, not the interest of shareholder-owners. The rationale for private property seemed undermined by ownership of an increasingly important sort, corporate shares.

It would be difficult to overstate the acclamation given to the Berle–Means book when it was published. Reviewers likened it, in its insights and expected importance, to *The Federalist* papers and *The Wealth of Nations*.[7] The reasons why it is hardly read today are less important than the impetus it gave to others to think more carefully about property rights within the firm. In a survey article, Armen Alchian (1965a) noted that several of the phenomena by which managers seemed to profit at shareholders' expense stemmed from the fact that many firms were profit-regulated. Economists' profit-maximization paradigm did not apply to these firms (or their owners) in the first place, because firm owners did not enjoy the right to the full fruits of ownership.

More fundamentally, Alchian noted, economists were committing what would today be called the "nirvana fallacy" in analyzing the division between property ownership and property control in large corporations. Berle and Means focused only on the costs of having specialized management distinct from investors, costs registered in terms of managers pursuing their own goals (bigger offices, nicer furniture, better computers) rather than maximizing investor profits. But these costs (today, we would call them agency costs) have their benefits. The chief executive officer can run a company at a greater profit than can the thousands of shareholders. Further, it may cost shareholders more to detect and punish managerial agency costs than shareholders would save. The costs identified by Berle and Means, that is, are not inconsistent with what property owners knowingly would choose to incur, because owners still are better off.

The Berle–Means book spawned an entire literature in economics and law, examining the nature and implications of property rights in firms. Even today, though, many issues are not fully resolved, as discussed in chapter 2 by Yoram Barzel. Some progress has been made. As Barzel and Kochin (1992) observed a decade ago, until about 1960, the definition of the firm was technological, not economic. The firm was defined by its production functions and input prices, which together determined cost curves.[8] Barzel explains here that it no longer suffices to define firms in terms of their cost-determined production functions, as that approach ignores fundamental property rights issues. "The production function is an elegant description of how inputs relate to output," he writes, "but its simplicity comes at the cost of overlooking organization and monitoring, factors related to ownership." He points out that modern analysis of the firm has focused on issues such as the relative transaction costs of contracting through firms versus markets, the nature of team production in the firm, and other questions concerning property rights and the corporate firm.[9]

An essential insight of the Barzel chapter is the relationship between theories of the firm and property rights within the firm. Responding to the question of why firms exist, Coase's seminal article (1937) focused on differences in transaction costs between organizing production in a firm as opposed to the market. But, Barzel notes, organizing production in firms means that someone will own the assets needed to produce, as opposed to renting or hiring them through markets. The extent of the firm defines the extent of asset ownership, and vice versa.

Even this perspective may be too limiting. Ownership itself is not monolithic. It arises from contract, and contracts can be written to give a few, many, or all of the fruits of property in various combinations to the different contracting parties. If Art pays Betty for the possession and use of her car for the next year, who "owns" the car? If Carol sells a life estate in her real property to Dan for his life, with the remainder interest to Dan's daughter, Eve, subject to a reversion to Carol if Dan is ever convicted of a crime, who owns the real estate? Barzel's point is that if the firm is distinguished from the market by its ownership of certain assets, ownership is in turn a creature of contract. For some purposes, then, it is more helpful to define the firm in terms of the contracts that make it up.

The focus on contracts leads Barzel to consider a related phenomenon. Ownership (as opposed to contract) is especially problematic for labor inputs, which cannot be fully owned, either in law or in fact. As Barzel notes, even if human beings legally could be owned as slaves, the owner would not thereby secure what he really seeks, maximum possible output from the slave. When slavery was legal, the problem of shirking by slaves was manifest from the fact that their ownership still required costly use of overseers to secure the expected labor inputs — just as shareholders must oversee their managers, despite management's contractual obligation to maximize shareholder profits.

In effect, Barzel raises anew the problem raised by Berle and Means and illustrates its basic property rights origins. Firm owners understand the benefits and costs of separating the ownership from the control of their property, the firm. But their legal rights (what the law gives them) are less important to them than their economic rights (the extent to which they expect to benefit from what they own). Full legal ownership is not as valuable as is incomplete (but more profitable) part-ownership that is defined contractually. To put Barzel's discussion in Lockean terms, even if a slave legally does not own his own body, economically he always owns a part of it, because the costs of eliciting full value from the slave exceeds the benefits of doing so.

ENDNOTES

1. For a discussion, see Pejovich (1972).

2. Today, likewise, sophisticated economic models implicitly assume that the owners of resources have the right to keep the fruits of their use.

3. Marx was an admirer of Proudhon, the French philosopher-sociologist opposed to institutions of private property.

4. For a highly critical appraisal of Bentham, see Roberts and Stratton (2000).

5. Toward the end of his life, in a conversation with his biographer, Sir John Bowring, Bentham lamented the performance that government had actually turned in, at least when measured against Bentham's notion of what constituted the greatest good for the greatest number: "I was, however, . . . a great reformist; but never suspected that the people in power were against reform. I supposed they only wanted to know what was good in order to embrace it" (Atkinson 1969, 23).

6. See, for example, several papers analyzing the Berle–Means book in the June 1983 issue of *The Journal of Law and Economics*.

7. For further discussion of the reception accorded the book, see McChesney 1988, 235–40.

8. "The traditional view, still dominant in textbooks, is based on two major assertions: I. That factor prices and technology determine the optimal size of the production unit, and II. that the production unit as determined in I is the firm. Under competition a firm's size is simply the size of the production unit that minimizes average cost" (Barzel and Kochin 1992, 24).

9. For one economist's summary of the literature, see Williamson (1981); for a useful summary from a legal perspective, see Wolfson (1984). Important contributions to the literature, several of them discussed in Barzel's chapter, include Coase (n.s. 1937), Alchian and Demsetz (1972), Jensen and Meckling (1976, 1979).

CHAPTER ONE

PROPERTY RIGHTS IN THE HISTORY OF ECONOMIC THOUGHT

From Locke to J. S. Mill

Edwin G. West

This chapter proposes to acquaint the reader with the historical background of the concept of property rights and several surrounding controversies by reviewing early work on property by economists and philosophers (with an emphasis on the former). The survey focuses on significant contributions from the seventeenth to the nineteenth centuries, setting the stage for the subsequent chapters that reflect more recent thinking. The first section of this chapter offers a critical assessment of the seventeenth-century work of John Locke which, to this day, has provoked the most intensive discussion and controversy.[1] The second section identifies the Lockean natural law or natural rights influence on the writings of Adam Smith, the eighteenth-century father of economics. The third section analyzes Jeremy Bentham's hostile criticism of the Locke and Smith views on property and Bentham's preference for his own philosophy of Utilitarianism, which can be summed up as the principle of the "pursuit of the greatest happiness." In addition, the third section examines the practical attempt of Bentham's disciple, Edwin Chadwick, to achieve egalitarian legislation. The fourth section focuses on the remarkably influential Utilitarian (and egalitarian) writer John Stuart Mill, and explores the connection between him and the "scientific socialists," including Marx and Engels. The final section offers the main conclusions.

JOHN LOCKE

When John Locke's *Two Treatises of Government* first appeared in 1690, nothing could have shocked the ruling classes more. Hitherto, property had been viewed as something exclusively created by government. Locke maintained that it was, instead, the source of government. As a consequence, "Government has no other end but the preservation of property" (Locke [1690] 1991, 329). The message, in other words, was that property and property rights existed prior to government. To what extent Locke's proclamation was in support of the English Revolution of 1688 is a matter of debate. In his preface, he expressed the hope "to establish the throne of our great restorer, our present King William . . . , to justify to the world the people of England, whose love of their first and natural rights with their resolution to preserve them, saved the nation, when it was on the very brink of slavery and ruin" (Locke [1690] 1991, 46).

Locke's reference to "natural rights" so early in his treatise symbolized his central thrust. To understand fully Lockean natural rights, it is first necessary to examine the arguments of his chief adversaries, the supporters of absolute monarchy. Their position was represented in Sir Robert Filmer's celebrated *Patriarcha*, published in 1680. As Filmer believed that the relation between King and subject was the same as that between father and child, it followed logically that individual property could be granted only by the crown. It was this argument that Locke firmly rejected. God, he insisted, had not bestowed property rights on the monarchy exclusively. Locke maintained not only that private property existed previous to government, but it was also upheld by natural law and the doctrine of natural rights.

Locke's pregovernment "state of nature" was not a "state of war," in striking contrast with the position of an earlier philosopher, Thomas Hobbes ([1651] 1914). Men became acquainted with the law of nature through their reason. Mistakes might be made, especially since it was potentially rancorous for each and all individuals to do their own policing of their individual property rights. It was dangerous, in Locke's words, that "every Man hath a right to punish the Offender, and be Executioner" of this law (Locke [1690] 1991, 272). Men will consequently find it practical to consent to a social contract forming a government that is primarily a trustee for its citizens. At the same time, there was the possibility that governments might err, so that, on occasion, they too should be subject to appropriate discipline. "If government is bound by the Law of Nature, then deviation by the rulers from the tenets of this law was sufficient grounds for their overthrow" (Valcke 1989, 943). This right of revolution in Locke's view was justified because private property was antecedent to, or independent of, government.

Locke's moral philosophy sees man's evolution in terms of conquering his surrounding nature. At first, his appropriation of land stems from a need for basic subsistence and survival. Eventually, however, private property also expresses man's ability to reason and to develop his personality. Locke places such heavy emphasis on economic production that one is tempted to look for a connection to the mercantilism of his time. Mercantilism urged the encouragement of exports and discouragement of imports, with the purpose of increasing relative economic power over one's neighbors.

In the section *Of Property*, Locke ([1690] 1991, 286) maintains that "God . . . has given the Earth to the Children of Men, given it to mankind in common." The use of the phrase "in common" might at first sight suggest elements of collectivism, what today would be called commonly owned or communally owned property. Some interpreters understand Locke's common ownership to mean the absence of ownership, or open access property owned by no one or thing. "That which is common is not ownership" (Valcke 1989, 957). As for Locke's natural rights, these range from the broad and philosophical, to the narrow and materialistic. Among the former are the rights to one's own life and liberty. The latter relate to rights to produce not only useful consumer goods but also concomitant producer-goods. The main example of a producer-good was improved land, as explained in section 27 of Locke's *Second Treatise* ([1690] 1991, 287):

> Though the earth, and all inferior Creatures be common to all Men, yet every Man has a Property in his own Person. This no body has any Right to but himself. The Labour of his Body, and the Work of his Hands, we may say, are properly his. Whatsoever then, he removes out of the State that Nature hath provided, and left it in, he hath mixed his Labour with, and joyned to it something that is his own, and thereby makes it his Property. It being by him removed from the common state Nature placed it in, hath by this labour something annexed to it, that excludes the common right of other men.

Some writers interpret Locke as saying here that mixing a man's labor with an external object results in an extension of his personality, moving one step further toward human self-realization. Two centuries later, Karl Marx would extend this proposition radically to claim that capitalism "alienates" and dehumanizes its workers because markets obliged them to part with their output, output that was a revered extension of their personalities. Locke would not have approved of this interpretation of his argument.[2]

In the passage quoted above, Locke offers a normative theory of the creation of property rights. Also in section 27 of his *Second Treatise* ([1690] 1991, 288), Locke amplifies and qualifies his theory of appropriation, or creation of property, as follows, "For this labour being the unquestionable Property of the Labourer, no Man but he can have a right to what that is once joyned to, *at least where there is enough, and as good left in common for others*" (emphasis added). For several scholars, this so-called Lockean "proviso" has obscured his general argument, and much has subsequently been written in attempts to fully understand it. One common and obvious question has been whether unqualified appropriation of a resource by one worker interferes with the liberty of others. Nozick (1974, 174), for instance, observes: "A process normally giving rise to a permanent bequeathable property right in a previously unowned thing will not do so if the position of others no longer at liberty to use the thing is thereby worsened." It has been this last word, "worsened," that has been the main focus in the appropriation debate.

Narveson (1991, 3) raises the query, "worsened compared with what?" He reviews what he finds to be at least five interpretations of Locke's proviso, and contends that those who interpret it to mean that the individual worker-appropriator is thereby causing others to have less, in the sense of depriving others of something, are wrong on two counts. First, there is an implicit assumption that there is a fixed or finite quantity of a potential resource such as land. This static view is erroneous because once people own land, they proceed to land clearance, ditching, fertilizing, and irrigating. More dynamically, then, ownership results in expanded resources for everyone: "they [the owners] transform what is less useful into what is more so, thus increasing resources . . . And secondly, what he 'deprives' others of isn't a 'good.' It is merely a chunk of the material world, awaiting someone who will turn it to good use" (Narveson 1991, 13).

Much of the Lockean discussion relates to normative (as distinct from positive) analysis. Locke was particularly absorbed with morality and "justice issues." The focus of much modern deliberation, in contrast, is on positive analysis such as the question of how property rights *emerge* in practice, regardless of the reasoning of moral philosophy. The chapters that follow in this volume are essentially positive. Nevertheless, justice remains important. As Lueck observes in chapter 8 of this volume, "Locke's theory of property remains a powerful defense of individual rights." More particularly, Locke's defense of rights "remains more or less consistent with real-world application of the rule of first possession."

ADAM SMITH

Adam Smith's *The Wealth of Nations* was, and remains, a powerful work of economic science rather than philosophy. Nevertheless, there has been considerable debate about how much of Smith's work is infused with Locke's Natural Law/Natural Rights tradition.[3] It is easy to point to Smithian quotations reminiscent of Lockean language. Consider, for instance, Locke's opposition to idleness in society and his belief that active production is conducive to human development. This is also suggested in Smith's statement that "[m]an was made for action, that he may call forth the whole vigor on his soul, and strain every nerve in order to produce those ends which it is the purpose of his being to advance. Nature has taught him that neither himself nor mankind can be fully satisfied with his conduct . . . unless he actually produced them" (Smith [1759] 1976b, 106).

A more striking Lockean sentiment appears in Smith's moral championship of the rights of employees and employers to produce mutually agreed-upon labor contracts. To hinder a man from employing his labor howsoever he desires without injury to his neighbor, Smith insists, is a violation of the "most sacred property." Indeed, "[t]he property which every man has in his own labour, as it is the original foundation of all other property, so it is the most sacred and inviolable" (Smith [1776] 1976a, I. xc, 12, 138).

In his "Lecture on Justice," part of a series of lectures given at Glasgow University in the early 1760s, Smith made one important distinction in Locke's reasoning: he confined natural rights to the rights to liberty and life, whereas the right to property was an acquired right depending on the current disposition of society. "The rights which a man has to the preservation of his body and reputation from injury are called natural . . ." (Smith 1896, 401). Smith's separation of natural rights from the rights to property are further expressed in the following quotation from his Glasgow lectures:

> The origin of natural rights is quite evident. That a person has a right to have his body free from injury, and his liberty free from infringement unless there be a proper cause, nobody doubts. But acquired rights such as property require more explanation. Property and civil government very much depend on one another. The preservation of property and the inequality of possession first formed it, and the state of property must always vary with the form of government. (Smith 1896, 401)

Smith's placement of liberty in the category of natural rights is significant because what he calls "natural liberty" pervades the whole of *The Wealth of Nations*. He condemns all legislation that interfered with free individual trading, but such freedom to trade affected the incentive to create and maintain property. Due to the existence of continuous markets, prices were being kept reasonably stable and, thus, incentives to further capital (or property) accumulation, were emerging. Capital accumulation, in turn, encouraged further divisions of labor (specialization) and these resulted in sustained technological progress.

So far, it seems that several of Smith's arguments echo John Locke's reasoning, although Smith's separation of natural rights from property rights was a substantial modification. The duties of government reported by both writers reveal striking similarities. Just as Locke argued that "Government has no other end but the preservation of property"

(Locke [1690] 1991, 329), Smith maintained that "Till there be property there can be no government, the very end of which is to secure wealth and to defend the rich from the poor" (Smith 1896, 291).

Economists now attempt a full rationale of Smith's position as follows: Even where property rights exist independent of government, there are significant costs in defining and protecting them. Anderson and Hill (chapter 5) call these "transaction costs" and provide illuminating examples. McChesney (chapter 9) identifies the role for government as justified by its lower costs of defining and defending rights. Adam Smith observed that property rights always require the ability to exclude others (nonowners): "It is only under the shelter of the civil magistrate that the owner of that valuable property, which is acquired by the labour of many years . . . can sleep a single night in security" (Smith [1776] 1976a, 710). Several other contributors to this volume, however, would qualify Smith's argument that property can survive only via the protection of government.

Beyond this, others would point out that government can typically lower the costs of defining private rights only because of its monopoly on the use of force. This being so, it may be naive to believe that such government monopoly is always used for the public good (McChesney, chapter 9). Ultimately the justification of government is an empirical matter, a point that is repeatedly made by Smith's historical case studies. Consider, for instance, his empirical analysis of slow economic growth in China. In Smith's words:

> In a country too, where, though the rich or the owners of large capitals enjoy a good deal of security, the poor or the owners of small capitals enjoy scarce any, but are liable, under the pretence of justice, to be pillaged and plundered at any time by the inferior mandarins, the quantity of stock employed in all the different branches of business transacted within it, can never be equal to what the nature and extent of that business might admit. In every different branch, the oppression of the poor must establish the monopoly of the rich, who, by engrossing the whole trade to themselves, will be able to make very large profits. (Smith [1776] 1976a, 112)

Smith's view that a central duty of the sovereign was the preservation of property via a proper legal framework is emphasized in the following passage:

> When the law does not enforce the performance of contracts, it puts all borrowers nearly upon the same footing with bankrupts or people of doubtful credit in better regulated countries. The uncertainty of recovering his money makes the lender exact the same usurious interest which is usually required from bankrupts. Among the barbarous nations who over-ran the western

provinces of the Roman Empire, the performance of contracts was left for many ages to the faith of the contracting parties. The courts of justice of their kings seldom intermeddled in it. The high rate of interest, which took place in those ancient times, may perhaps be partly accounted for from this cause. (Smith [1776] 1976a, 112)

In all, there were three duties of the sovereign according to Smith:

1. Protection against invasion by other countries
2. The duty of protecting as far as possible every member of society from the injustice and oppression of every other member, that is, the duty of establishing an exact administration of justice
3. The duty of erecting and maintaining certain public works and certain public institutions, "which it can never be for the interest of any individual, or small number of individuals to maintain because the profit could never repay the expense to any individual or small number of individuals . . ." (Smith [1776] 1976a, 688).

The natural law (rights) tradition is located most clearly in the second of these three duties. As for the third, Smith has been criticized by libertarians for outlining a positive (public works) role for government that went further than upholding justice and protecting property. Duty number 3, in fact, has been described as representing the philosophy not of natural law/rights but of Benthamite Utilitarianism which instructs government to supersede the market in many areas.

Such criticism is off-target. Smith's argument with respect to the third duty is commonly misunderstood and must be evaluated in its eighteenth-century context. In particular, the arguments involve the role of government in allowing large-scale stockholder-owned firms to exist. Smith's discussion of the third duty clearly shows his increasing awareness of the advantages of the extension of limited liability. There was a growing need at the beginning of the industrial revolution for "instrumentality" in carrying on a large business. There was, in other words, a general demand for more legal variety in the structure of property rights. To merchants and entrepreneurs, the commercial advantages from incorporation were becoming obvious: continuity of existence, management independent of that of stockholders, ease of suit against third parties or against stockholders, transferable shares, unlimited divisibility of the equities, and the distinct limitation of liability for a company's debts and for those of its shareholders.

Traditionally, the major ways that a corporation (company) could be created were (1) by judicial interpretations of the common law, or (2) by the king's charter. This area of royal (and later parliamentary) discretion to create new property rights substantially explains Smith's discussion of public works under the head of the "third duty of the sovereign"; and indeed, it was traditionally the sovereign's responsibility long before that of legislatures. Most of the corporations formed from 1485 to 1700 were created exclusively by royal charter rather than by parliamentary charter. The Russia Company (1555), the East India Company (1600), and the Hudson's Bay Company (1670) were originally chartered directly by the crown without benefit of Parliament. Charters, or equivalent letters patent, were granted by the crown in pursuance of special statutory authority, for instance, as in the case of the Bank of England (1694) and the London Assurance Company (1720).

Later, the additional sanction of Parliament was increasingly demanded to accompany privileges created by the crown. In the latter half of the eighteenth century, incorporation by special act became more common for utilities such as canal and water companies. Charters and private acts of incorporation usually included special provisions regulating the activities of the organization in question. It is arguable that the nature of the complex procedure necessary to secure incorporation would have been viewed by Smith as another hindrance to private business freedom. His third duty of the sovereign, therefore, could have been seen by him, not as an instruction to government to undertake discretionary and utilitarian economic intervention, but rather as a demand for the enlargement of the whole legal framework and, therefore, the area of natural liberty, a demand that was consistent with natural law tradition.

In the late eighteenth century, special deliberation was called for in deciding how to satisfy the increasing needs of new projects that required large sums of capital. It was in such a context that Smith expounded the sovereign's third duty. This was a time when the joint-stock organization was widely suspect after the calamity of the South Sea Bubble of 1720. We now know that the great shortcoming in that period lay not so much in the joint-stock system itself as in the way it was then applied and the need for more experience with it. In any case, the disaster had more to do with government failure than market failure. Holders of government bonds were allowed to exchange them for stock in the new South Sea Company, which had been given a monopoly of British trade with the islands of the South Seas.

Before 1720, there was insufficient appreciation of the dangers of ambitiously selling new bonds to raise capital beyond the amount necessary for the operation of any given undertaking. The collapse of the South Sea Bubble led promptly to the Bubble Act of 1720. It was a restrictive piece of legislation passed by a government showing signs of panic, many members of government having themselves been ruined by the collapse of the bubble. Writing fifty-six years later, Smith, in effect, was requesting the authorities to relax their attitude. The most appropriate policy was to "clear the decks" for the exercise of more business liberty, especially in the sense of allowing the creation and spread of new legal instruments.[4]

There is an interesting parallel between Smith and Frank Knight ([1924] 1997) on the subject of incentives. Harold Demsetz' essay (chapter 11) reminds us of the famous article by Knight criticizing Pigou's contention that the existence of external costs demands government imposition of a corrective tax. The context of the debate was a scenario containing two roads, one of which is superior and the other inferior (in terms of congestion, road surface, and so on). Pigou argued that drivers would make excessive use of the superior road and ignore the consequent additional congestion cost (i.e., the external cost). This situation allegedly calls for a government tax on the use of the superior road. The optimal tax would be large enough to reduce congestion on the superior road. Knight argued that Pigou neglected the issue of road ownership. Demsetz points out in his chapter that once the tax is imposed, decisions made by resource owners are clearly shown to eliminate potential externalities. In other words, the private owner of the superior road can charge an appropriate toll for its use. Because ordinary economic reasoning shows that such a toll will exactly equal Pigou's ideal government tax, the latter becomes superfluous.

Adam Smith anticipated Knight's analysis. Smith treats roads under "the third duty of the sovereign," based on the need for what he called "public works." When it came to the issue of who should pay for them, Smith insisted that the greater part of the public works can be self-financing. "A highway, a bridge, a navigable canal, for example, may in most cases be both made and maintained by a small toll upon the carriages which make use of them . . ." (Smith [1776] 1976a, 724). In the same way, other public works were already being supplied by joint-stock firms in the areas of banking, insurance, canals, and bridges. Although Smith classified public works as those which it "would not profit an individual or small number of individuals" (Smith [1776] 1976a, 723), eventually, he argues explicitly, it would profit a *large* number of individuals, organized in for-profit joint-stock enterprises. It is clear, therefore, that, like Frank Knight, Smith did not neglect the issue of resource ownership and the incentives it creates. If he had done so, it is likely that, like Pigou, he would have assumed central government was the only route to the provision of public works.[5]

It is useful, finally, to refer to a common belief that Smith disliked large joint-stock enterprises. What he mainly criticized was the frequent habit of governments in attaching a monopoly of trade to the grant of joint-stock status. The South Seas Company was one example, but there were several others. In contrast, enterprises such as the Hudson's Bay

Company (without the monopoly privilege), met with his unqualified approval. His opinion of joint-stock companies in domestic activities was also favorable, as was his whole discussion of the need for "public works" (the sovereign's third duty), properly understood. Indeed, this led to Adam Smith's recommendations to allow joint-stock enterprises in the "public works" of banking, canals, water supply, roads, and bridges. Such enterprises would not only have much-needed access to large capital markets, they would also be able to avoid ambiguous title to their property.

Some economists might object to the foregoing treatment of Smith as it presents him as a doctrinaire believer in extreme laissez-faire. The most influential support for this critique has been the much-quoted conclusion of Jacob Viner (1958, 213) that "[T]he modern advocate of laissez faire who objects to government participation in business on the ground that it is an encroachment upon a field reserved by nature for private enterprise, cannot find support for this argument in the *Wealth of Nations*." In contrast to Viner, we shall find ourselves asking whether one hitherto private activity should be "nationalized" because it is reserved by nature for the provision by the public sector. At this stage, the need for definitions abound. What, for instance, is meant by "nature"? How do we recognize private enterprise? What denotes "laissez-faire"? What is market failure? What is government failure? To neglect to begin to answer these questions is to risk descending to the vague language of popular rhetoric. The fact remains that in his treatment of "public works," in most cases, Smith's prescriptions for new public works was via extension of private provision by way of public companies enjoying new privileges of joint stock and limited liability.

THE BENTHAMITE REVOLUTION

John Locke's natural law/rights system of thought and his conviction that private property existed prior to law received hostile criticism from Jeremy Bentham in his *Theory of Legislation*, first published in 1795, five years after the death of Smith. He protested that the advocates of natural law and natural rights, such as John Locke and his followers, had advanced no proof. Their systems, moreover, varied unpredictably in content. Natural rights were dangerous metaphors ("nonsense on stilts") based on capricious and subjective feelings. The only true conception of right, Bentham insisted, was one that was based on "real laws." Property, which involves a guarantee of security of possession into the future, cannot exist without government: "Property and law are born together and die together" (quoted in Paul 1979, 50). And property in the real world can change following alterations in law. To assert dogmatically a natural right in property would be to claim that government had no freedom to tax it without the consent of the owners.

Lockean followers would probably answer that Bentham was confusing the concept of right with the concept of power. Accordingly, Jonathan Macey observes:

> Merely because the government or some other organization has the raw power to take away my wealth, or my ability to earn wealth, does not mean that it has the right to do so. . . . Thus, a state's mere exercise of its power to deprive citizens of their property rights does not mean that these rights do not exist. The idea of natural rights refers to those rights that human beings possess by virtue of their status as human beings. (Macey 1994, 186)

This observation emphasizes that natural law is based on some version of morality.

Despite his dismissal of the natural rights theory of government and property, Bentham was not averse to interjecting his own system of morality, a system that describes not only what we do, but what we ought to do. In Bentham's words:

> Nature has placed mankind under the governance of two sovereign masters, pain and pleasure. It is for them alone to point out what we ought to do, as well as to determine what we shall do. On the one hand the standard of right and wrong, on the other the chain of causes and effects are fastened to this throne. (quoted in Paul 1979, 52)

Bentham's ultimate principle, the pursuit of the greatest happiness, implied the need for equality of material possessions, an objective that Bentham himself tried initially to keep within bounds, but which in the hands of followers such as J. S. Mill eventually inspired an intellectual, if not political, revolution. The predictability of enjoyment of property into the future that Adam Smith had urged on behalf of his free market vision, faced a frontal challenge.

Bentham's happiness principle spawned a substantial catalogue of what he called his "agenda" for government intervention. His list was based on a cost-benefit analysis of each individual issue. If the expected increase in benefit (happiness) was greater than the expected increase in cost (pain), then government should undertake the project, and not otherwise. On this principle, he approved of government aid in the construction of canals, railways, hospitals, and public workhouses. Despite Bentham's complaint that the doctrine of natural law/rights advanced no method of proof, his own principle of utility (greatest happiness) failed also in this respect. He was defensive as well on the question of how the legislators were to be selected. And once selected, where were they to obtain the precise information concerning the propensities of given projects to bring happiness or pain? These questions will be addressed in more detail when we examine further the property implications of Benthamite Utilitarianism.

The fruition of Utilitarianism can best be seen in the works of Bentham's disciples, Edwin Chadwick and John Stuart Mill. Chadwick was Bentham's last secretary and became one of the most influential Utilitarian policy makers in nineteenth-century England, covering such areas as poor law revision (1834), health and sanitation (1840s), and railway regulation (1860s). He introduced his own principle of competition, and it provided an indicator to his penchant for sweeping regulations. There are, Chadwick insisted, "conditions of competition which create inevitable waste and insecurity of property, which raise prices and check improvement, which engender fraud and violence, and subject the public to irresponsible monopolies of the worst sort" (quoted in Crain and Ekelund 1976, 152).

The waste that Chadwick wanted to eradicate appeared at first to be associated with natural monopoly, a situation where a single firm is the least-cost producer. This market structure, however, was often assumed rather than demonstrated. His typical reform plan was to allow competition "for the field," with a government-run auction for the right to produce, and the winning bidder agreeing to undertake centralized contract management of the whole industry or service. One of Chadwick's immediate examples was the postal service. Efficiency improvements, he argued, stemmed from awarding an exclusive contract to the successful bidder, an arrangement that, he argued, reduced transaction costs, excess capacity, and uneconomic overlapping (duplication). The reformed, nationalized undertaking would not be run by government personnel, however, because, Chadwick insisted, government was incapable of direct management. The alternative he favored was public ownership together with a "special executive commission" to run these undertakings.

On the subject of efficient resource allocation, Adam Smith focused on private resource ownership and the useful incentives that accompanied it. Bentham, in contrast, asserted that public (i.e. government) ownership was more desirable. But public ownership was a vague concept and rarely did it receive full definition or analytic rigor. Within a collectivity, one's share of public assets is not likely to be exactly the same as other individual citizens. Even if such shares were initially equal, the question arises about the rules of collective decision making. Does public ownership mean that priority is to be given to the preferences of the median voter, bearing in mind that individual preferences will vary across the population of voters?

More important is the question of the influence of government employees. De Alessi (chapter 4, this volume) emphasizes that "government employees with authority to manage government-owned resources, like government regulators, have incentive to manage them in response to political pressures, bribes, and their personal preferences." None of those considerations accompanied Chadwick's recommendations of public ownership and "special executive commissions." As Buchanan (1978, 3) has observed, Britain's nineteenth-century Benthamite Utilitarianism "provided idealized objectives for government policy to the neglect of institutional structure."

One example affords an insight into Chadwick's general policy approach. The London cab market, he declared, displayed wasteful excess capacity because, at any one time, at least one-third of the cabs were unemployed. Therefore, instead of continuing to allow inordinate competition within the field, London needed competition for the whole field (i.e., the whole cab market). Central contract management would be appropriate, as would another "special executive commission." It has since been shown that unoccupied cabs actually lower the full costs of operation by reducing waiting time (Crain and Ekelund 1976, fn 19). Chadwick's recommended competition for the whole field was, therefore, inappropriate. No less important, and more pertinent to the present essay, was the expected damage from Chadwick's policy to the property rights of individual cab owners, a subject that did not figure much in his deliberations. To be fair to Chadwick, his concept of competition for the whole field has subsequently attracted serious attention by economists (see Demsetz 1968). Dominant firms are prevented from earning great monopoly profits whenever there is a constant threat of "competition for the whole field" from outsiders.

JOHN STUART MILL

In contrast to Smith's rejection of a large redistribution function of government, John Stuart Mill gave it pride of place. In so doing, he attacked the whole foundation of Smithian political economy, including the role of property. Focusing on economic methodology, Mill drew a sharp distinction between positive and normative issues. The laws of production (such as the law of diminishing returns), Mill emphasized, were inexorable (positive economics), whereas, in contrast, the laws of distribution were malleable according to society's disposition (normative economics). Prevailing divisions of the national produce should be subjected to the Utilitarian tests for maximum happiness. The latter objective was clarified by the Utilitarian creed, which implied not simply the greatest happiness but "the greatest happiness of the greatest number." Since each individual had an equal claim to happiness, he also had an equal claim to the means of happiness. This assertion implied the need for the collectivization of property and income of all kinds.

One new element in the writings of the Utilitarians was an enthusiasm for the contemporary spread of a democracy based on simple majority voting. This, too, had profound implications for property rights. It was well known, even in Mill's time, that democracy often encouraged transfers to special interests. Since, in effect, these interests are given the right to determine the disposition of wealth created by others, property rights are correspondingly attenuated. In contrast, Adam Smith's efficiency-generating "invisible hand" system depended upon the existence of private property rights that were stable and well defined. In addition, Smith assumed the natural liberty of all participants to choose what they believed were the best suppliers, employers, and employees.

Utilitarianism ignored these crucial Smithian conditions. In several instances, the emergence of Benthamite government suppliers resulted in the crowding out of private suppliers, to the detriment of the latter's property rights. Consider, for example, Mill's argument ([1848] 1969, 953) that government can provide better education than that supplied in private schools that were freely selected by parents:

> Now any well-intentioned and tolerably civilized government may think, without presumption, that it does or ought to possess a degree of cultivation above the average of the community which it rules, and that it should therefore be capable of offering better education and better instruction to the people, than the great number of them would spontaneously demand. Education, therefore, is one of those things which it is admissible in principle that a government should provide for the people.

In this passage, use of "well-intentioned" and "tolerably civilized" to describe government illustrates the increasing faith in reformed democracy that in the mid-nineteenth century Mill hoped was arriving.

It must be said that of all the economists discussed herein, none have exceeded Mill in the intellectual energy devoted to the question of property and in the search for possible and reasonable social policies toward it.[6] Among all the classical economics writers, Mill was the first to include in his major work two whole chapters on the subject of private property. The chapter starts with a noncontroversial, Lockean approach that recognizes in each person a right to the exclusive disposal of what individuals have "produced by their own exertions, or received either by gift or by fair agreement, without force or fraud, from those who produced it" (Mill [1848] 1969, 218). Each person, however, is not entitled to the whole produce because capital as well as labor have contributed to production; and capital, Mill makes clear, is the consequence of saving and abstinence.

In his fuller definition of property, Mill contended that although it involves, among other things, a legitimate right of bequest, or gift after death, "the right of inheritance, as distinguished from bequest, does not" (Mill [1848] 1969, 221). Mill here began to inject his Utilitarian value judgments as to how the wealth of recently deceased persons should be disposed of. The two chief beneficiaries, he contended, were (1) relatives, even distant ones, and (2) the state. Mill insisted that "in a majority of instances the good not only of society but of the individuals would be better consulted by bequeathing to them a moderate, [but not] a large provision" (Mill [1848] 1969, 224). To the extent moderate bequests meant there was money left over, the state should take the residue. Mill expressed an implicit claim to know the "good" of society plus that of individuals, and to determine what is a desirably "moderate" bequest to children in individual cases. It seems apparent that his position was colored by the new enthusiasm for governments run by persons well versed in and motivated by Bentham's maximum happiness doctrine.

Mill conceded that bequest is one of the attributes of property. "All the reasons, which recommend that private property should exist, recommend *pro tanto* this extension of it. *But property is only a means to an end, not in itself an end* (Mill [1848] 1969, 226, emphasis added). Mill preferred a restriction, not on what one might bequeath, but on what anyone should be permitted to acquire by bequest or inheritance (Mill [1848] 1969, 227). Bequests should not be allowed to enrich one individual beyond a certain maximum, "which should be fixed sufficiently high to afford the means of comfortable independence" (Mill [1848] 1969, 228).

Mill ends his chapter with some searching questions concerning the justification of property in land:

> When the "sacredness of property" is talked of, it should always be remembered, that any such sacredness does not belong in the same degree to landed property. No man made the land. It is the original inheritance of the whole species. Its appropriation is wholly a question of general expediency. When private property in land is not expedient, it is unjust. (Mill [1848] 1969, 233)

It is important to remember that Mill was writing in 1848, when the Irish Potato Famine was fresh in his mind. Ownership of land had caused suffering, he complained, not only because of the incompetence of some landlords but also due to an improper legal framework. The main example of the latter was the continuation of primogeniture (the legal requirement that the eldest son inherit his father's estate), a practice against which, like Adam Smith, Mill objected. The system of land ownership had reduced welfare, Mill protested, because many proprietors were not improvers of the land. Moreover, they frequently granted the liberty of cultivation "on such terms as to prevent improvements from being made by any one else" (Mill [1848] 1969, 231). Much of this inefficiency was due to the institution of primogeniture. "When the land goes wholly to the heir, it generally goes to him severed from the pecuniary resources which would enable him to improve it, the personal property being absorbed by the provision for younger children, and the land itself often heavily burthened by the same purpose" (Mill [1848] 1969, 231).

The logic of such an argument would suggest a solution, not in the crude form of land nationalization, but in amending the constitution to reduce or end the practice of primogeniture. This was the strategy of Adam Smith. While Mill might be seen as arguing implicitly in the same direction, he proceeds to spend much time condemning the character of existing landlords. "The community has too much at stake in the proper cultivation of the land . . . to leave these things to the discretion of a class of persons called landlords, when they have shown themselves unfit for the trust" (Mill [1848] 1969, 234). If Mill was intimating that there was another class of persons more suitable to the task, he did not explicitly suggest any.

Mill's approach contrasts with John Locke's "proviso." Locke claimed, "For this labour being the unquestionable Property of the Labourer, no Man but he can have a right to what that is once joined to, at least where there is enough, and as good left in common for others" (Locke [1690] 1991, *Second Treatise*, Section 27, 288). Narveson's 1991 interpretation of Locke assumes that, when individuals obtain pieces of land, they improve it and so actually expand resources. In this way others benefit, at least in the long run. Mill would not have accepted this claim. From the very nature of the case, he insisted, "whoever owns land, keeps others out of the enjoyment of it." Whereas the Narveson interpretation of Locke takes it for granted that those who "join their labour" with the land will proceed to improve it, Mill was not convinced and demanded advance proof. To him it was axiomatic "that property in land should be interpreted strictly, and that the balance in all cases of doubt should incline against the proprietor" (Mill [1848] 1969, 234). In the case of land, he emphasized, "no exclusive right should be permitted in any individual, which cannot be shown to be productive of positive good" (Mill [1848] 1969, 235). Notice that Mill was adopting non-Lockean language in his Benthamite assumption in the previous sentence that rights to land had to be "permitted" by government.

As for the postulated leading causes of the devastating Irish famine, several do not stand up to scrutiny.[7] But Mill's explanation does not stand up, either. Why were Irish farmers incompetent, as Mill claimed? At the risk of digression, some further discussion of the Irish Potato Famine is appropriate.

In his book *Why Ireland Starved* (1983), Joel Mokyr restates the issue as "Why was Ireland poor?" In emergencies, the poorest have no cushion of modest savings to help them purchase other foods (imported or otherwise). This is not an academic point. It is true that the disease, caused by the fungus *Phylophthora Infestans*, spread alarmingly beginning in 1845 and decimated the crucial potato crop. Yet the same blight also "struck Belgium, the Netherlands and Scotland with little demographic effect. The underlying problem, whatever it was had already driven Ireland to an extremity of poverty. Therefore why indeed was it so poor?" (Bethell 1998, 243–44). It is noteworthy that conditions in Ireland had deteriorated so much, even prior to the famine period, that some landlords as well as tenants had already become impoverished.

Having first attributed Ireland's problem to overpopulation, economist Thomas Malthus, identified another and more important clue: "There is indeed a fatal deficiency in one of the greatest sources of prosperity, the perfect security of property; and till this defect is remedied, it is not so easy to pronounce upon the degree in which the redundant capital of England would flow into Ireland with the best effect" (Malthus [1836] 1951, 349–50). The lack of "security of property" had several causes. One was "the chronic guerrilla war between tenants and landlords" (Bethell 1998, 252). Added to that violence and resulting lack of secure property rights was the profound and continuous religious hostility between Catholics and Protestants.

Another, more important factor was the stifling restrictions on manufacturing imposed by a protectionist English government, which prevented the Irish from realizing the full value of their property. Adam Smith had already warned about this in a letter to Henry Dundas in November 1779. The letter is quoted in full by Viner (1965, 350–52). Speculating on what the Irish Parliament had meant when speaking of a "free trade," Smith observed:

> They may perhaps understand by it no more than the power of exporting their own produce to the foreign country where they can find the best market. Nothing can be more just and reasonable than this demand, nor can anything be more unjust and unreasonable than some of the restraints which their Industry in this respect at present labours under. They are prohibited under the heaviest penalties to export Glass to any Country. Wool they can export only to Great Britain. Woolen goods they can export only from certain Ports in their own Country and to certain Ports in Great Britain.
>
> They may mean to demand the Power of importing such goods as they have

occasion for from any Country where they can find them cheapest, subject to no other duties and restraints than such as may be imposed by their own Parliament. This freedom, tho' in my opinion perfectly reasonable, will interfere a little with some of our paltry monopolies. Glass, Hops, Foreign Sugars, several sorts of East Indian goods can at present be imported only from Great Britain.

They may mean to demand a free trade to our American and African Plantations, free from the restraints which the 18th of the present King imposed upon it, or at least from some of those restraints, such as the prohibition of exporting thither their own Woolen and Cotton manufactures, Glass, Hatts, Hops, Gunpowder, etc. This freedom, tho' it would interfere with some of our monopolies, I am convinced, would do no harm to Great Britain. It would be reasonable, indeed, that whatever goods were exported from Ireland to these Plantations should be subject to the like duties as those of the same kind exported from England in the terms of the 18th of the present King.

. . .

Whatever the Irish mean to demand in this way, in the present situation of our affairs I should think it madness not to grant it.

The fact that Smith's warnings were not heeded and that Ireland was left to flounder economically with emasculated property rights substantially answers the question: Why was Ireland poor? In turn, it helps explain why it compared so badly with other countries that were stricken with the same potato blight. In short, "the country was already destitute and on the brink of starvation, needing only the potato blight to trigger the catastrophe" (Bethell 1998, 256). After 1790 hopes for improvement rested on the planned Act of Union, and it led to the hope that the discrimination hitherto practiced by England against Irish industry would cease. "The reality, however, was very different" (Woodham-Smith 1968, 15).

Understanding the true, property-based reasons for the Irish famine is important, for many have drawn incorrect conclusions from the episode. Mokyr (1983, 294) observes:

Ireland was a principal reason why the young science of economics abandoned its steadfast adherence to the sanctity of private property and free enterprise and realized that under certain circumstances, Adam Smith's invisible hand transformed itself into a claw capable of holding the economy in a deadly grip of poverty.

The facts above show, on the contrary, that in Ireland at the time of the famine, property rights were not observed with sanctity. For political reasons the conditions of Adam Smith's free enterprise model were not allowed to operate.

Mill wrote at a time when different varieties of socialism were appearing throughout Europe. Indeed, his *Principles* were published in the same year, 1848, as Marx and Engels' *Communist Manifesto*. The *Manifesto* contained the radical pronouncement that "the theory of the Communists may be summed up in a single sentence: Abolition of private property" (Marx and Engels [1848] 1962, 47). Probably the most incendiary of all declarations was that of Proudhon ([1840] 1994, 211), who protested: "What is property? It is theft."[8] Marx and Engels denounced private property as exclusively a product of capitalism, claiming their analysis to be "scientific socialism." In diametric opposition to John Locke, they asserted that prior to capitalism, there had been no private property in land. According to Pipes (1999), however, Marx and Engels constructed to their own satisfaction a theoretical model of early society and then described — with minimal recourse to either anthropology or history, of which they were largely ignorant — how property might have evolved. The scheme was abstract, although the injection of a vocabulary drawn from economics, sociology, and psychology gave it the appearance of being more scientific than previous theories. The Marx–Engels view was rooted not in empirical evidence but in the Romantic vision of the "brotherhood of mankind . . ." (Pipes 1999, 52). Such a vision contemplates the nonexistence of private property and, therefore, the public ownership of land and other assets. But when one adds the political structure that fosters the "dictatorship of the proletariat" espoused by Marx and Engels, in a framework that is supposed to be democratic, it is difficult to obtain a clear and convincing picture of how the alternative to private property would function.

Conclusion

Ryan (1989, 229) observes that "a crucial question to be asked of any system of property rights is whether it favors political stability and political liberty." To a large extent this question looks for answers that are sociological. In our review of the treatment of property and property rights in the history of economic thought, it is Smith and Hume who stand out as having emphasized most the relationship between freedom and property (capital) accumulation. To Smith, these items together constituted a necessary condition for new divisions of labor that resulted in lower prices and in technological progress via invention and innovation. The mercantilist system that Smith was attacking was one of politically imposed preferences that slowed productivity by robbing property rights of much of their proper (undistorted) functions. In contrast, well-respected property rights placed in a clear and secure legal setting, together with guaranteed liberty, were sufficient to set the wealth of nations on a course for almost perpetual growth. In Smith's words ([1776] 1976a, 42):

> All systems either of preference or of restraint, therefore, being thus completely taken away, the obvious and simple system of natural liberty establishes itself of its own accord. Every man, as long as he does not violate the laws of justice, is left perfectly free to pursue his own interest in his own way, and to bring both his industry and capital into competition with those of any other man, or order of men. The sovereign is completely discharged from a duty, in the attempting to perform which he must always be exposed to innumerable delusions and for the proper performance of which no human wisdom or knowledge could ever be sufficient; the duty of superintending the industry of private people, and of directing it towards the employments most suitable to the interest of the society.

A relationship between property rights and liberty is also to be found in Locke, although it is not as defined as in Smith. Locke's perspective was more that of moral philosophy than political economy or sociology. Locke wished to defend the liberty of citizens against the despotism of absolute monarchy. He aimed also to elevate liberty to a natural right. The latter stemmed from natural law, which, in turn, is based on the reasoning of free people. The writings of Adam Smith suggest the natural law approach of Locke, especially Smith's reference to labor as the "most sacred property."

With the Utilitarians of the nineteenth century, the emphasis on the sanctity of natural rights changed almost completely. They seem undisturbed that taxation beyond some minimum was a strong potential eroder of the value of property owned by those taxed. The revolutionary change in sentiment was expressed clearly in John Stuart Mill's separation of the laws of production from the laws of distribution. The distribution of wealth via taxation, Mill asserted, was a matter of discretionary human institution. "The things once there, mankind, individually or collectively can do with them as they like" (Mill [1848] 1969, 200). The flaw in this statement is that the political distribution of "the things once there" would be a serious brake on the things being there in the future. Investment, after all, is a function of its expected net (after-tax) proceeds.

With Mill, connections between property rights and liberty became ambiguous. Instruction to voters to use taxation to do as they wished with the fruits of other people's investments would have been seen by Locke and Smith primarily as an invasion of others' rights. The same can be said of Chadwick's arbitrarily appointed "special executive commissions" to run his nationalized undertakings. Crowning the whole

Utilitarian program was its liberty-threatening subjection of all individuals to instructions about how to achieve maximum happiness.

It is true that the natural law tradition that the Benthamites attacked was itself based on some deep notions of human equality. Natural law equality was not, however, the equality of wealth or income that Mill had in mind. To John Locke, it was equality of access to appropriate natural rights, and so ultimately benefit from, natural resources. To Adam Smith, it was the equality of all to enter the market system. Both Locke and Smith saw equality in terms of opportunity to prosper, not in terms of the final prosperity people achieve. The implication in both Locke and Smith is that some eventual inequality would ensue, at least for a time. And if this was a problem, what was the solution? For Smith, the constant incentive of workers to improve their property (i.e., their labor power) could, to a large extent, be relied on to improve things more than could government intervention.

Griswold (1999) concludes that Smith (unlike the Utilitarians) was skeptical of the state's ability to organize a plan of redistribution that would be fair and efficient. Smith saw the problem partly as one of the state's inadequate knowledge of the particular circumstances that determine each person's opportunities. Because one family, for instance, will be more responsible than another in preparing its offspring for the labor market, some inequality is unavoidable. With regard to the state's possible efforts to redistribute in favor of the deserving, Griswold (1999, 252) interprets Smith as emphasizing: "Assessing in a consistent manner who the deserving are, and just what they are due, lies beyond the ken of the legislator or statesman." In any case, the self-interest of the bureaucrat in siphoning off for himself much of the income intended for redistribution would itself block suitable action to achieve equity or precise commutative justice.

Some admirers of Adam Smith may be sensitive to the presence of religious language and concepts in his work, and especially in his adoption of the theocentric principles of natural law. Pufendorf, one of Smith's mentors on this subject, started with the proposition that reason alone shows us that man may live in society successfully only if basic rules are observed and that these included protection of property rights. But to go further than reason alone, Pufendorf urged, the question of what determines whether actions are right or wrong can only be settled by law, and the basic natural law presupposes the will of a superior. "Natural law binds by virtue of the divine will. . . . Since God created our nature and fitted us with the capacities that make social life possible, it must be His will that we should live in society and observe those rules that are necessary for the existence of social life" (Simmons 1989, 225).

The part of natural law that obliged individuals to do good things for society allowed it to increasingly take on the appearance of a basically Utilitarian society. Smith's friend, David Hume, went as far as to remove God from his whole conception of natural law. He offered a justification for rules of justice and property based on convenience or utility. This could have opened the door for the Benthamites, although Hume's position was ultimately not compatible with theirs. It is easy to conjecture, nevertheless, that Adam Smith, who seemed less in haste to remove God from his total view of society, would have been disturbed by the Utilitarians' confident replacement of God's will by Bentham's will: secular salvation via the simple principle of maximum happiness.

Endnotes

I wish to acknowledge constructive comments from my colleagues Keith Acheson, Ron Bodkin, and Steve Ferris.

1. Modern developments of the Lockean argument are reviewed by Dean Lueck (chapter 8, this volume).

2. And neither would Adam Smith who held that humans have a natural propensity to "truck, barter and exchange."

3. Lord Robbins (1952) expressed the contrary view that Smith's *The Wealth of Nations* was instead largely in the mold of Utilitarianism.

4. Although the issue of limited liability drew most attention in the middle of the nineteenth century, Smith was ahead of his time in his comments on the central principle. He discussed it thoroughly, for instance, when comparing joint-stock companies with private partnerships ("copartneries" in Smithian language). Apart from the nontransferability of shares in a partnership, Smith explained, it differed from the joint-stock company in that "each partner is bound for the debts contracted by the company to the whole extent of his fortune. In a joint-stock company, on the contrary, each partner is bound only to the extent of his share" (Smith [1776] 1976a, 740). Smith also acknowledged the principle of limited liability in his observation that the greater part of the proprietors of the joint-stock companies received annual dividends and enjoyed "total exemption from trouble and from risk, beyond a limited sum" (Smith [1776] 1976a, 741). This facility encouraged many people to become adventurers in joint-stock companies who would not otherwise hazard their fortunes in a private partnership.

5. Note that Smith's public works are not what economists call public goods because the price system does not break down and exclusion is possible.

6. It is true that the results of Mill's lengthy deliberations were often blurred by his adherence to doctrinaire Utilitarianism. However, his overall quest for the truth was genuine. His was a wide-ranging, multidisciplined approach that referred not only to economics but also to sociology, history, and recorded custom.

7. *The Times* believed that "the Celt is less energetic, less independent, less industrious than the Saxon" (quoted in Bethell 1998, 245). Others were con-

vinced that overpopulation was the root of the problem, a proposition that has been subsequently discredited (Bethell 1998, 246). Mill's position reflected the classical economists' "laws" of population and rent. Finally there was the conviction that the main cause was Ireland's lack of natural resources.

8. It should be noted that Marx and Proudhon were vehemently opposed to each other (Bethell, 1998, 114).

CHAPTER TWO

PROPERTY RIGHTS IN THE FIRM

Yoram Barzel

Transaction cost analysis does not end with the development of rights. The same considerations that determine when an asset will move from the public domain into private hands also suggest the organizational framework under which the asset will be exploited. Because the most valued uses of an asset usually require the cooperation of other asset owners, property rights—even when developed—are not independent of transactions involving others.

One important form of organization within which cooperation takes place is the business firm. Using the organizational structure of the firm, owners of such capital goods as buildings, machinery, and human labor cooperate to produce higher-valued goods. Since firms may involve many individuals, economists have been interested in analyzing questions related to the size and scope of firms. What determines the size of the firm? Why is it that some businesses are very large in size, while others are much smaller? And what determines the scope of a firm—the range of activities the firm engages in? Why does Ford assemble both passenger vehicles and commercial trucks, yet not produce gasoline?[1] The development of property rights theory has its roots both in questions related to the origin of property rights, and in the organizational forms asset owners use to exploit their assets.

I begin by arguing that the received neoclassical model of the firm is both inadequate to explain the world we observe and is internally inconsistent. The history of this critique began with Coase's (1937) "The Nature of the Firm," and a summary of this seminal work follows my own analysis. Coase's original work left out important details, and authors working within the same line of thought developed models to address these gaps. I summarize those I consider the most important.

I then turn to Cheung's (1983) critique of the fundamental distinction introduced by Coase—that of transactions occurring either within the firm or across markets. Cheung contends that it is not possible to measure the limits of the firm when many transactions do not fall clearly into one category or another. While I am sympathetic to this criticism, nonetheless I present a newer line of thought reaffirming the possibility of boundaries to the firm. This newer analysis has its roots in Coase's other definitive work, "The Problem of Social Cost" (1960). I argue that the firm is defined by property rights considerations—particularly in the role that equity capital plays in guaranteeing the actions of asset owners operating within the confines of the firm.

THE NEOCLASSICAL FIRM

The received model, as presented in leading price theory textbooks, descends from Walras ([1874, 1877] 1954). The model includes consumers, commodities, and prices, and it is extended to include production by firms. In the Walrasian world, price information is available at zero cost, and property rights are well defined and costlessly enforced. Organization does not matter in such a world. Individuals can do whatever firms do, at the same cost. The attempt to superimpose organization in a Walrasian world is, at best, trivial, and more likely to result in internal inconsistencies.

This model begins with consumers who fully own collections of endowments. Consumers may increase their utility via trade. Under certain specified conditions, a set of prices exists at which consumers will voluntarily engage in trade, and the resulting distribution of commodities will be Pareto Optimal. Commodities are entirely owned; before a sale one party owns a commodity, and after sale the other does. There is no theft between trading partners nor uncertainty about the characteristics or price of the good.

As the model is extended to include production, a model of the firm is developed. Production transforms some goods into others, a production function describing the technological relationship between inputs and outputs. Given input prices and a well-behaved production function, it is possible to determine the cost of any particular output. The minimum cost of producing each quantity of a good traces out the cost curve for the good. The U-shaped cost curve in the Walrasian world (where average costs at first decline, then rise) results from the characteristics of the underlying production function, especially of the scale of its capital equipment. The cost function is the dual of the production function—to have one is to have the other. Given the U shape and some added assumptions, the cost function is a model of the firm. Competition drives the price of each good to the minimum average cost.

Recall the questions we ask of our model of the firm. What limits the size of the firm? What limits the scope of its actions? What activities are considered to be within the firm? In the Walrasian model, the average cost curve tells us the size of the firm in units of output. It also tells us which combination of inputs will be purchased in order to produce this quantity of output. A firm's scope is determined analogously.[2]

Capital goods produce a stream of services over time. Firms that convert resources into goods may acquire the assets, use them for the duration of interest, and resell them across the market. This story leaves the firm as the exclusive owner of both capital goods and consumed commodities. All businesses would then own their own buildings and equipment. The limit of the firm could be defined by the list of assets and commodities it currently possesses, and its size by the size(s) of its capital goods.

Even if this model of the firm worked well for commodities, capital assets are problematic. The foregoing description would seem to ignore the important role of human resources within the firm. Absent slavery, labor services are generally rented, as are the services of a host of more conventional capital assets. Walrasian analysis, then, must be extended to allow for the transfer of services from assets, without the transfer of assets themselves. Assets may be owned by different parties, and the services they produce may be transferred independently of the asset itself.

Under this model of the firm, it does not seem important whether the firm itself or some other entity owns a capital asset. Commodities destroyed in the productive process would certainly have to be owned by the firm, in the same way that commodities destroyed in consumption would have to be owned by the consumer. But in the case of capital assets, it is the services provided by a capital asset that are destroyed. The service a capital asset provides may be purchased (rented) without purchasing the asset itself. The efficient firm must locate a piece of equipment needed to produce its output next to where it operates, but it need not own it. Ownership per se does not matter. This means that the production function will not specify what, if any, capital inputs will be owned by a firm. Since this is the case, the size and scope of the cost-minimizing firm, as measured by the combination of commodities and capital assets, is indeterminate.

Even more troublesome to duality is the labor factor. The production function, among other things, implies a derived demand for labor services in efficiency units. What invariably enters the cost function, however, is the hourly wage. The hourly wage could reflect efficiency only if there were one-to-one correspondence between efficiency and hours without any supervision. Unsupervised, utility-maximizing workers whose wages are set independent of their contribution to production would tend to produce nothing, let alone commit the efficient level of effort.

The cost function derived from the production functions is, at best, inadequate. The production function is an elegant description of how inputs relate to output, but its simplicity comes at the cost of overlooking organization and monitoring, factors related to ownership. If we are trying to discover the limits to the firm—what it will own and produce—we must include within our model more complex assumptions concerning price and quality information and the ownership status of assets (beyond the distinction that a party either owns an asset entirely, or does not own it at all).[3]

THE TRANSACTION COST NATURE OF THE FIRM

In "The Nature of the Firm" (1937), Ronald Coase initiated the movement away from the production function view of the firm. He switched the unit of analysis from the quantity of a good produced by a firm, to the number of transactions conducted within it. In creating this distinction, he also created transaction cost analysis.

For Coase, production may take place at either the direction of managers of a firm or the direction of the market. A manager must make decisions concerning activities in which the firm will engage. Managers face the option of either buying the output from another party or producing it in-house. A firm that creates a good by using resources it controls is engaged in a transaction within the firm. If, instead, it purchases the good from another party, it is engaged in an across-markets transaction.

How will a manager decide whether to produce a good or buy it? Coase's answer was based on cost. In the Walrasian world, a manager considering buying an input would costlessly know its price and exact qualities. But for Coase, the Walrasian assumptions do not hold. A manager must spend resources transacting with other parties. These are the costs of using markets to organize the production of inputs. Coase presumed that these costs are rising on the margin, and a manager would eventually find some transactions for which it is less expensive to produce the input within the firm.

The firm also incurs costs of organizing the production of inputs. A manager must direct workers as to which goods to produce, using which technology. These managerial costs would rise on the margin and, here too, a manager would eventually find it less costly to incur the transaction cost of purchasing it instead of the managerial costs of producing it within the firm. Production is efficient when the total cost of another transaction—including transaction and managerial costs—are equal through the market or in-house production.

The advantages of this framework—comparing costs of using markets to cost of monitoring production within the firm—is that it explicitly recognizes the importance of such factors as accounting and legal costs, agency costs, time spent monitoring workers, and the expense of verifying the characteristics of goods purchased from other firms. It provides a logical boundary to the firm. Coase's 1937 paper, however, lacks detail as to what counts as a transaction cost. Why does the cost of using the market rise on the margin? Given the importance of these costs — Coase's real insight — what are their natures?

TEAM PRODUCTION

Other authors have developed models explaining the alternative costs of firms using markets versus producing in-house. One such argument is by Alchian and Demsetz (1972). They argue that firms will buy inputs across markets, unless team production is an important element in the production process. Given the Walrasian assumption of perfect information when purchasing inputs, it would not matter if a firm buys the output of a worker or pays the worker for his time. But for some productive processes, measuring the amount of output produced by a worker, and so his optimal value, is prohibitively expensive.

Consider Alchian and Allen's (1977, 202) example of a fishing boat. The number of fish produced by a fishing boat will vary with the efforts of each member of the crew. If any member reduces his effort, fewer fish will be caught. Paying the crew based on the number of fish caught by each member — their marginal contribution — would be equivalent to the Walrasian example of an across-market transaction. But how would the owners of the boat determine how many fish each crewmen caught? If the production technology involves many crewmen working with one large net, then it would be expensive to measure how many fish were produced by any given crewman.

Alchian and Demsetz (1972) argue that with team production, where the output contribution by each owner of labor services (worker) is not separable, each will be paid for his input (hours) contributed to the productive process. Because workers' pay will be only based on the time they transfer to their employers, they have an incentive to shirk. Managers will then have to monitor workers to ensure that the time for which they are paying yields output.

With transaction costs — in this case prohibitively expensive measurement costs of marginal output — the manager supervises workers' effort and pay them for their time. The manager's reward is the residual; the difference between the value of output and the pay for inputs. This explanation falls within Coase's original distinction between production carried out across markets or within firms because of alternative costs of measuring output versus measuring inputs.

Measurement Cost

Barzel (1982) proposes a related explanation for why the transaction costs of using markets to organize production may exceed the bureaucratic costs of a vertically integrated firm.[4] Suppose that the vertical steps involved in making a dress consist of the production of cloth, the cutting of cloth, the sewing of the cut sections, and the retailing of the completed product. In a world with only across-market transactions, every worker sells his output across a market and none are rented or paid by the hour. Every purchaser of inputs, then, will have to verify that each input he purchases corresponds to the contracted specifications regarding quality and quantity. In the Walrasian world, this measurement is inconsequential, because it is performed at zero cost.

I assume, however, that measurement is costly. When the stages in dress making are performed by separate firms, each purchaser of inputs risks losses by not measuring. If the cutter of cloth does not measure the quality of cloth he purchases, the producer of cloth will gain from producing lower quality specimens. If the cutter does not engage in measuring the quality, the sewer may do so, and refuse to pay the high-quality price for the low-quality pieces. The problem is compounding; the retailer must measure the quality of the cloth, the quality of the cutting, and the quality of the sewing, even though the person engaged in sewing previously measured the quality of the cloth and the quality of the sewing.

This repeat measurement is, in the Coasean sense, a transaction cost. If each quality of cloth were accurately priced, measurement would not be a relevant aspect of market transactions. But given some expense in measurement, the market may be a more expensive institution for organizing production than the firm, with its bureaucratic costs. In the example, a dress retailer could hire a cloth maker, cutter, and sewer, and pay each for the time they spent in their respective trades. Given that their payment varied with the number of hours worked, the incentive to produce lower-quality goods is reduced, as is their incentive to measure the upstream inputs into their productive tasks. Each worker's incentive to produce any output is reduced, creating the need for monitoring. There is then a tradeoff between the cost of measuring output at each stage of production and the cost of measuring effort (monitoring workers). Given a cost-minimizing firm, the lower-cost process will dominate.

The team production model and the measurement costs model both explain how alternative payment schemes (using inputs instead of output) result in differing costs of using the market instead of using firms to organize production. In these models the wage contract and the allocation of the residual seem to be the defining characteristics of the firm.

Little has been said about property rights and ownership up to this point, other than the assumption that it is not possible to separate the productive effort of a worker from the worker himself. Workers are rented, not purchased, and it is not possible to buy the effort of workers.[5]

EXPROPRIABLE QUASI RENTS

Williamson (1975) and Klein, Crawford, and Alchian (1978) propose similar models in which considerations of ownership over physical assets determine the scope of the firm.[6] Although sunk costs are irrelevant for future decision making, they define "quasi rents," which is a payment that investors expect to receive as future compensation when incurring the cost. Quasi rents are important for ownership because they may be appropriable.

To take a standard example of an asset with appropriable quasi rents, oil pipelines are expensive to install and have little salvage value. Once installed, the cost of transporting oil in them is substantially lower than with the alternative land-based transport. Pipelines would be developed only if owners expect to receive a premium at least as large as the quasi rent above the marginal cost of transporting oil.

Any firm considering constructing a pipeline must have assurances that it will receive its quasi rents. One option is signing a long-term contract specifying the price at which oil transportation services will be sold. Both Williamson (1975) and Klein, Crawford, and Alchian (1978) assert that in some cases it is prohibitively expensive to write a contract that protects quasi rents. In these circumstances, either that asset will not be constructed or it will be owned by another party otherwise capable of capturing the rents.

This, then, is a theory of vertical integration. The vertically integrated firm will own multiple assets that are related through the holdup problem. The limits of the firm will depend on the number of assets with these characteristics. Most importantly, this relates the idea of cost to ownership. A firm that is vertically integrated in this manner will have a cost advantage over its rivals. So in this way, ownership arrangements are determined by cost, and cost is determined by the pattern of ownership.

These models of the firm explain why maximizing individuals would select one institution over another. Yet these explanations seem only partial at best. A theory of the firm would empirically identify the size and scope of any given firm, and lead to refutable implications as to when they change. Unfortunately there has been little empirical verification of these theories. It is difficult to pin down which model best describes why Ford Motor Company has its current size and make-up. Is there some element of team production that makes the measurement of marginal output prohibitively expensive? Ford performs some operations in-house, including the assembly of parts into autos, but purchases parts from other firms. Is there something about assembly that makes repeat measurement especially expensive? Does the assembly process involve assets with substantial sunk costs?

CONTRACTS VERSUS FIRMS; CHEUNG'S CRITIQUE

Cheung (1983) raises serious doubt as to whether the firm and market are in fact alternative institutions. Unless we are able to distinguish the boundaries of the firm, we cannot describe whether a transaction occurred in the market or the firm. If this is so, then our theory of the firm lacks falsifiability and is, therefore, pointless.

Consider piece work, which Cheung analyzes extensively. In the Coasian analysis, if a worker is paid for his output, then the buyer of that output is not his employer, but his customer. The transaction between them is in the market and not the firm. But if the worker is paid by the hour, the transaction is within the firm. Cheung notes that it is often the case that actual contractual arrangements fall somewhere in between. Payments may take the form of an hourly wage plus a per-unit payment, as is often the case with salespeople, who receive both commissions (based on their performance — their output) and an hourly wage. Are salespeople employees or suppliers?

Managers, in deciding how to organize the next transaction, consider the costs of alternative contracts — payments based on one of many margins. The distinction between payments for output (market transactions) and payments for inputs (within the firm) is too limiting to describe the variability in contractual practice that we observe. Cheung notes that many factory workers in Hong Kong are paid a fixed amount for every unit of output they produce. Their product is standardized and easily counted, and it is relatively inexpensive to find a price that equates marginal cost with derived demand. An hourly contract where payment does not change with output would fail to sufficiently motivate these workers.

For other processes, however, workers receive payments by the hour. Two reasons seem to account for paying workers by the hour. First, in the case of team work, assessing the marginal contribution of a worker may be difficult. Second, as output becomes less standardized, it becomes increasingly difficult to find a price that ensures that workers receive their opportunity cost. Under these circumstances, firms are increasingly likely to pay by the hour — and save the cost of searching for the correct price. As previously noted, though, this also eliminates the incentive to perform any work, thus requiring monitoring.

Now as Cheung observed, in transactions occurring within the same factory, payment for some workers is based on inputs (time), while for others payment is based on output. Does it make sense to claim that if a wage contract is used, the transaction occurs within the firm, but if an output (piece work) contract is selected, the transaction is instead between two firms (across the market)? Cheung's response is to view the firm as a nexus of contracts without clear boundaries. He proposes that we instead focus on alternate contractual forms.

The Problem of Social Cost

In "The Problem of Social Cost," Coase (1960) directed us to the conditions under which property rights matter. For the limiting case when transaction costs are zero, Coase demonstrates that the identity of the owner of an asset is irrelevant to the asset's use. The usefulness of the idea (dubbed "The Coase Theorem" by George Stigler) is in understanding why ownership does matter as we introduce differing transaction costs.

Up until this point, I have left both the definition of property rights (and its relation to ownership) and transaction costs unspecified. The Coase Theorem brings these two concepts to the fore and, in doing so, forces additional precision in the use of these terms. It also implicitly calls for the distinction between economic (property) rights and legal (property) rights.

Following Alchian (1965b) and Cheung (1969), I propose the following definitions: *Economic rights* reflect the ability, in expected terms, to benefit from a good or service. Benefit refers to either the utility received by direct consumption, or the utility derived via exchange for other goods or services. The economic right to an asset is generally less than the present value of the goods and services produced by means of that asset. An apple tree in my front yard may produce a certain number of bushels of apples per year. My economic rights over that tree are less than the value of these apples as long as school children passing by take apples without compensating me.

Legal rights are the rights that the state recognizes as those of a particular individual or set of individuals. It is clear that the benefits the two kinds of rights delineated are not the same. The apples stolen by school children are legally mine, but are not part of my economic rights because it is not economical for me to prevent the theft. Likewise, the benefit I receive from the view of my neighbor's rose garden is not legally mine. My neighbor could build a fence, and the state would prevent me from removing it. But given the cost of fencing, I have economic rights to my neighbor's roses.

Transaction costs are the resources used to establish and maintain economic rights. This definition is consistent with the Coase Theorem. If transaction costs are zero, then property rights are perfectly well established and maintained. Coase's cattle-grazing rancher cannot impose any cost on the wheat-raising farmer without paying compensation. As transaction costs become positive (and significant) the Coase Theorem will fail to apply—the rancher will impose the cost of cattle on the farmer, for the farmer will find it too expensive to enforce his rights over the asset.

These definitions of property rights and transaction costs clarify the importance of the Coase Theorem in explaining both ownership and contract patterns. Given positive transaction costs, the relation between ownership and residual claimancy emerges. The party with the most control over the variability in the value of the asset must become the residual claimant for the asset to be used efficiently. Stated differently, economic agents only behave efficiently if they bear the cost or receive the benefit of their action. As we expect parties to select contractual forms that maximize the value of their interaction, observed contracts should allocate residual claimancy to minimize dissipation. Consider, for example, one of the transactions analyzed by Cheung—painting the eyes on a doll. As long as the rate at which the worker may paint is constant, a piece rate or the corresponding hourly wage result in the same cost-minimizing outcome.

But if this is a new process, then neither the factory manager nor the worker is likely to know what piece rate will equate the worker's income to his opportunity cost. If a piece rate is selected, the worker will bear the variability resulting from the error in setting it. An hourly wage eliminates the variability born by the worker, transferring it entirely to the factory owner. We expect that the party with the most control over the variability would become residual claimant (though in the case here I do not know who that should be). Surely there are sources of variability in this transaction other than that associated with selecting a piece rate price. One other source, for example, is the worker's effort level. As the cost of monitoring the worker's effort increases, the wage contract becomes increasingly inefficient, making it more likely that we will observe contracts with marginal payments for output.

Cheung's analysis is more than a reaction to Coase's distinction between markets and management. It is an attempt to reconcile "The Nature of the Firm" (1937) with "The Problem of Social Cost" (1960). Let me summarize the central insight of Coase's "The Problem of Social Cost" paper, and how Cheung applied this to "The Nature of the Firm."

Given the zero transaction cost assumption of the Walrasian model, the ownership of an asset is irrelevant to its efficient use. Without transaction costs, property rights are well-defined and enforced, which implies that all imposition of costs on one party by another result in full compensation. Ownership is irrelevant to resource allocation.

Cheung extended that fundamental Coasean insight to observe that within a single firm, alternative contracts for different types of transactions are related to transaction costs. Given zero transaction costs, resulting, for example, from perfect observation of the workers' effort levels, there is no difference between paying workers by the hour or by the piece. The firm is unnecessary, and the transaction boundaries within or between firms are arbitrary. A plumber you hire by the hour is not viewed as your employee. On the other hand, a person you hire to clean your home and pay a fixed amount per cleaning is considered your employee. The waiter at your favorite restaurant probably receives both an hourly wage plus tips — payments both by the input (time) and output (quality of service). Is the waiter working for the customer or the restaurant?

Prior to Cheung, a transaction was defined to have occurred either in the firm or across a market, depending on whether it was a wage contract or output contract. Cheung questions this test of the firm's boundaries. Real firms use different contracts with their employees, depending on the attributes of the transaction. Some transactions involve only marginal payments for output, some involve only payments that vary with time, and others combine the forms. Given this continuum of contracts, defining the limits of the firm using the distinction between paying by wage or by output must be arbitrary. The received theory lacks empirical sufficiency — the theoretical units cannot be uniquely matched with something measurable. Cheung suggests that we instead analyze the manner in which contracts change as attributes to the transaction vary in either value or measurement cost.

Transaction costs, therefore, have important implications for property rights in the firm. As explained, the firm's owner will be the one with claims to the (variable) net residuals of the firm. But when transaction costs are not zero — allowing, for example, a worker to provide less than the specified effort, different contracts assign residual claimancy to alternative parties, which increases or decreases their incentive to impose costs on their partners in the transaction. When property rights are viewed as economic rights, ownership becomes a less categorical concept.

THE SIZE AND SCOPE OF THE FIRM

In the remainder of this chapter, I advance a theory that explains why firms exist, and identify factors that delineate their boundaries (Barzel and Suen 1995; Barzel 1997). While I believe Cheung's critique of previous property rights explanations, including my measurement-costs argument, is correct, I offer an additional component to the theory of the firm that seems free of that critique.

I have argued (Barzel 1987), following Coase and Cheung, that efficient contracts will assign residual claimancy to the party with the greatest control over the variability in outcome. Often there are multiple sources of variability in outcome, and each transactor may have an incentive to shirk and blame the resulting decrease in value on random fluctuations. For example, in fixed rental contracts between tenant farmers and landowners, the farmer has an incentive to use farming practices such as overgrazing or failing to rotate crops that excessively transfer the value of the land into marketable output. Landowners under the same contract have an incentive to provide inefficiently low levels of such inputs as fences and drainage ditches — factors that will be depreciated by the farmer. The choice of contract form, however, can lessen each party's incentive to shirk. For example, a share contract, where the farmer and landowner split the output, lessens the severity of each of the above problems. The optimal contract minimizes the sum of these dissipations subject to the costs of contracting.

One major exception to the principle that the efficient contact will assign residual claimancy to the party with the most control over the outcome occurs when the participants' wealth is not adequate to enable them to bear the full costs of residual claimancy, even though they are the parties with the most control over their outcome. Herein lies an explanation for why firms exist. Further argument produces an operational theory of the firm.

Consider the pilot of a commercial passenger airline. If the pilot is to bear the full consequences of his actions in providing piloting services, he must be able to compensate for all of the damage he may cause. Yet, in extreme cases, the pilot may cause losses, for example, by destruction of the aircraft, that far exceed his personal wealth. The pilot may have the most control over the variability in outcome — by performing such actions and flying only when sober — yet the pilot probably is not sufficiently wealthy to guarantee his performance. Given that he will not bear the full consequences of his actions, he has an incentive to take courses of action that increase the likelihood of adverse results. For example, he may not be paying perfect attention at all times to his flying, nor sleeping a full eight hours before every flight.

Although this example is extreme, the problem is general. Sometimes workers' resources may be insufficient to replace defective work and, more importantly, to compensate for the damage that defective work may cause. In a number of industries, independent workers purchase bonding—insurance guaranteeing their actions—but this market trans-action does not solve the contracting problem, for it is the insurer, not the worker, that pays for damages. When an independent worker's out-put is backed by a bonding agency, he will accrue any cost savings from haste or risky production, and the bonding agency will pay for any damages this work may cause. The worker is then not the residual claimant to his actions and, therefore, will have more incentive to shirk.

One solution to this contracting problem is for parties with sufficient capital to guarantee the workers actions. This guarantee and the capital assets backing it define the limits of the firm. It is equivalent to insur-ance, except that the firm will also enter into contracts that alter the incentive of the worker to create this damage. When a firm hires a worker by the hour, the firm both receives the benefits and bears the cost of substandard or risky work. The firm has become more of the residual claimant, and the worker's incentive to perform negligently has been reduced since his pay does not decline if he takes additional time to produce higher-quality goods.

This is not to imply that we are returning to the definition of the firm as a collection of wage contracts. In this conception, the firm's basic feature is not the wage contract per se, but rather the guarantee of the worker's output, backed by the firm's capital assets. Cheung points out that the managers of a firm may determine that rewarding a worker's contribution by the piece is more profitable than paying him an hourly wage. Cheung does not explain, however, why such a worker would not operate independently. The answer could be that the worker cannot guarantee the quality of the product, and the firm assumes this task. In the case of painting the eyes on a doll, the firm-employer may, for ex-ample, guarantee to the wholesaler that the paint is not toxic. Indeed, it may provide the worker with the paint to assure itself the worker did not select the cheaper, perhaps toxic, paint.

The guarantee function is subject to both economies and disecon-omies, that together contribute to the determination of the size of the firm. Economies of scale result from the same amount of equity capital backing multiple transactions that are not highly correlated in outcome. If there is a remote chance that a pilot will crash a jet, causing $50 million in damage, the airline company employing the pilot must have $50 million available to back the particular flight. But because the cor-relation of several flights crashing at the same time is less than one, an increase in the number of flights will require less than a commensurate increase in the capital backing each flight.

The diseconomies to scale in this guaranteeing function result from the firm owners' decreased control over the firm's activities. The man-agers of such firms are constrained by the capital owners, but these constraints are of the nature of wage contracts. This limits managers' incentive to fully monitor other employees. In the largest firms, the managers controlling the firms have very small ownership stakes and are, therefore, less likely to act as residual claimants to their own actions. Larger firms can guarantee a larger number of transactions per dollar of equity, but at a higher cost of monitoring. A balance between these costs will determine firm size.

Many components of this model of the firm are measurable and lead to a falsifiable theory. For example, changes in the equity capital of a firm should in principle be observable. Likewise, firms engaged in businesses with differing levels of risk should have different debt-to-equity levels. As the firm's transactions become subject to lower risk of adverse results (or the possible adverse results become less costly), the same equity capital can guarantee a larger number of transactions, and we should observe firms expanding the number of transactions backed by their capital.

CONCLUSION

Production function theory, claiming to be dual to cost theory, has been proposed as an explanation of why firms have a particular size and scope. The core of this theory is that certain assets must be used together to minimize the average cost of production. Using assets together, however, is not a theory of the firm, as illustrated by any transaction where one factor owner buys the services of another.

Coase proposed that firms and markets are alternative organizational arrangements. Transactions may occur by using either institution, and the limit to the size of any particular firm is the ability to conduct the same transaction at a lower cost by using the market. Since nonmarginal payments based on inputs rather than on outputs lead to shirking, absent other considerations, markets should provide lower cost production than management within the firm. Yet a large amount of economic activity occurs within firms.

Team production, sunk costs, and multiple measurement have all been proposed as theories of the firm and seem to have some explanatory power. However, none seem entirely satisfactory, if the criteria by which they are judged is the ability to explain a significant proportion of the variation we observe in firm size and scope. Cheung, in applying the Coase Theorem to the distinction between markets and firms, argues that we have created a false dichotomy and that we should analyze a range of contractual forms, none of which are uniquely linked to the organization of the firm.

I am sympathetic to this criticism, yet I contend that a more comprehensive analysis of residual claimancy may lead to an operational theory of the firm. The firm is a set of contracts whose variability is contractually guaranteed by common equity capital. If a transaction includes this guarantee, then it occurs within the firm and it is part of the scope of the firm. Any given transaction may have multiple attributes subject to variability in outcome, but only those elements guaranteed by the firm's equity capital are included within the firm.

Costs determine the size and scope of the firm. However, these are not engineering or production costs independent of ownership considerations. Property right analysis identifies what costs are relevant when analyzing changes in the boundaries of the firm. Without property rights analysis, economic theory must be silent as to the factors that change the firm.

ENDNOTES

Thanks to Timothy Dittmer for his extensive help in preparing this paper.

1. These questions are of more than academic interest. Difficulties with the conventional (nonproperty rights) economic theory of the firm corresponded to a series of antitrust court rulings in the 1950s and 1960s. These rulings have severely curtailed certain types of seemingly wealth-enhancing business activities. Reacting to these rulings and the economic logic behind them which they viewed as erroneous, scholars developed many of the current transaction cost theories.

2. If the production of one good decreases the cost of producing another, then the two products will be produced by the same firm because the complementarity in production will reduce the average cost for each.

3. Stigler (1968, 71–94) used the "survivor test" to measure efficient size. His main conclusion is that there is a wide range of optimum sizes: "[T]he long-run marginal and average cost curves of the firms are customarily horizontal over a long range of sizes." This finding undermines the usefulness of the economies of scale argument in explaining the size of particular firm.

4. An input supplier is considered to be upstream to an input purchaser, and the two are considered vertically related.

5. Slavery is a case where workers were purchased, not rented. But slaves required overseers, implying monitoring was an important element of slavery. Slavery is an important illustration of why property rights matter. A slave will work at a different output rate, as opposed to the rate he would choose as an independent business owner. This implies that purchasing a slave does not imply purchasing all of the attributes of an asset. You may purchase the physical body of a slave, and some of his work effort, but you will not be purchasing all of his attributes valuable in production.

6. Grossman and Hart (1986) also offer a model of the firm based on asset ownership notions. I critically discuss this model in other articles.

PART II

INTRODUCTION

> We may well call it "the tragedy of the commons," using
> the word "tragedy" as the philosopher Whitehead used
> it: "The essence of dramatic tragedy is not unhappiness.
> It resides in the solemnity of the remorseless working
> of things."
>
> —Garrett Hardin (1968, 1244)

Two thousand years after Plato and Aristotle examined fundamental issues of private property, many of the same questions are still posed. Ackerman (1975, 1) notes that the study of property begins with contemporary questions like, "Why should one person exclude the world? Why not simply declare that all things are owned in common, that whenever anyone wants to use something he can do so?" After all, the air is free. In all but a few countries, people are free to have as many children as they like without purchasing that right or obtaining permission.

But costless access and free permissions are the exception for things of much value. For the most part, even in an era when one still can download music off the Internet without paying for it, persons eager to use something usually must either buy the right or rent permission from an owner. The ability to exclude nonowners is a fundamental branch in the bundle of sticks that make up private property rights.

In the two chapters in this section, Thráinn Eggertsson and Louis De Alessi examine the rationale for exclusion. Both chapters contrast individual private property with communal property and with governmental property, and contrast those three ownership forms with resources that are effectively unowned (that is, in open access). Often there is terminological confusion among those concepts; commentators lose sight of the distinction between communal and government property, for example. Government property is regulated by bureaucrats with neither private rights to the property's benefits nor private obligations to bear its costs, which typically accrue to the public treasury or to some noncontrolling third party. In contrast, those who regulate the use of communal property are its direct beneficiaries and are directly liable for its costs.

As Eggertsson explains, access to communal property is limited by the group in control of the commons, as in the case of a common area (e.g., the party room) in a privately owned apartment building. Open access, however, refers to assets for which there is no limit on access, such as a city street; anyone who wishes can use the asset. A resource is in open access if there is no limit on who can use it or how or if theoretical limits are unenforced. Complete open access is rare, but some resources come quite close (Haddock and Kiesling 2001). It is the problems that arise with the lack of exclusion that promote efforts to define private or communal property rights and enforce them against access by those without rights.

OPEN ACCESS AND SCARCITY

The rationale for rules that define who will be excluded and who will be included (and how) emerges strikingly in settings where private property is not the norm (Lepage 1985). In the movie *The Gods Must Be Crazy*, a bushman clan enjoys a seemingly idyllic existence in the Kalahari Desert. Game is plentiful and arable land exceeds what clan members can cultivate. Then one day a pilot passing overhead tosses an empty Coke bottle out the window. To the bushmen the mysterious bottle must be a gift from the gods, so at first they simply venerate it. But practical uses are gradually discovered. Children invent games using the bottle; it proves useful for crushing grain. Soon, many bushmen clamor simultaneously to use the lone, god-given bottle. As competing demands for the bottle increase, clan members begin to fight over it. The elders are aghast. The clan has never known internal violence, even dispute, over access to game, land, or other resources.

The situation portrayed raises two fundamental questions. First, why is there friction over use of a bottle but nothing else? Meat and crops are essential for survival. Bottles, though useful, are not; bushmen had subsisted for centuries without them. The answer is that the bottle is scarce relative to the bushmen's demand for it, while (in the movie at least) other resources are not.[1]

Second, how can the bushmen resolve the problem of scarcity (i.e., how to choose among competing desires to use the bottle) and especially how can they end the struggle within the formerly peaceful clan? Struggling to use an asset is a substitute for using the time productively, and so is costly (Libecap, chapter 6; Haddock, chapter 7). One way to end the bushmen's costly struggle is to destroy the source of the friction itself, the solution chosen in the movie: the clan elders delegate one bushman to return the gift to the gods by throwing it over the edge of the earth.

But that solution has obvious drawbacks. It is costly to dispatch a productive clan member on a long and perilous journey. More important, destroying the asset leaves the clan poorer than if they could discover a peaceful way to use the bottle. In most societies, including real-world bushman clans (Thomas 1958), some other way is sought to regulate use of scarce assets so that the benefits of the gods' largesse are preserved while the costs of dispute are controlled.

Private property offers one way to achieve those net benefits. Suppose that some bushman or a group of bushmen were accorded ownership of the bottle, with ownership embracing a right to exclude others from its use. That solution is the one typically chosen, in both greater and lesser developed societies. Studies of primitive cultures

> reveal common tenure to be quite rare, even in hunting and gathering societies. Property rights in some form predominate by far, and, most important, their existence may be easily explained in terms of the necessity for orderly exploitation and conservation of the resource. . . . Speaking generally, we may say that stable primitive cultures appear to have discovered the dangers of common-property tenure and to have developed measures to protect their resources. Or, if a more Darwinian explanation be preferred, we may say that only those primitive cultures have survived which succeeded in developing such institutions. (Gordon 1954, 134–35)

OPEN ACCESS — NOT COMMONS

Gordon (1954) first addressed the distinction between private property resources versus open access resources, which raised the specter of a "tragedy of the commons," as biologist Garret Hardin later named it.[2] Eggertsson shows in chapter 3 how an understanding of open access resources leads to a general investigation of property rights (individual or communal) that exclude some uses. Under plausible circumstances, Eggertsson explains, a society's failure to establish an appropriate scheme of property rights can result in extinction of the resource, even extinction of a society that depends on it. Eggertsson's analysis of fishing rights in Iceland makes clear that the tragedy of open access is no mere textbook problem.

Examples of over-exploitation of other open access resources are ubiquitous. Historically, the near extinction of the American bison is well known. The species ultimately was saved because a few ranchers began to confine live animals on private land, removing them from open access (Lueck 2001). The problem persists today for other species. Poaching of geese, deer, sheep, and other species on public land has reached "epidemic proportions" according to authorities, "wiping out" some local populations (Slocum 1987, 1). The problem is fueled by poachers' perception that the wildlife taken is unowned. As one poacher put it: "I haven't done anything I'm really ashamed of. To me, if I steal from someone, that is bad. But the good Lord put that game out there" (Slocum 1987, 16). Likewise, small bird populations in Europe are dwindling despite legal protection, because the birds are perceived to belong to no one (Hudson 1990, A1). (The model developed here is more general than fishing, bison, and poaching. It has been used, for example, to analyze the effects of different ownership forms of hospitals.[3])

To see why exclusion is important, consider a resource such as fish that can be harvested but subsequently renews itself. Imagine fish inhabiting a lake that anyone can use. Assume for simplicity that catching the fish requires a boat, and that those on each boat are equally adept at fishing. Despite the equal fishing abilities there would be decreasing returns to fishing, because each new boat catching fish makes catching more difficult for those already on the lake—anything taken by one boat would be gone. Those on the original boats would have to remain longer on the lake and search its more difficult reaches. Most would simply return to shore with fewer fish if a new boat embarked. That implies that the average and marginal catch would go down with entry.

Table II.1 illustrates that impact. On a given day, as the number of boats (column 1) increases, initially the number of fish caught (column 2) gradually increases from 0 to 55. Each additional boat up to the tenth increases the total catch, but the marginal increment (column 3) falls as the number of boats rises. Indeed, an eleventh boat would add nothing to the total.

How many boats would in fact embark each day? To answer, one must know the value of fish relative to the cost of catching them. Suppose that consumers value an additional fish by $10, the price that each fish fetches in the market. Thus a $10 marginal value of fish to consumers would be identical to a $10 marginal revenue per fish that is earned by a boat. As for the cost of catching fish, the economic costs of any endeavor are opportunity costs. Consequently, when a boat embarks, its costs are the value of whatever output the same inputs would have produced in some off-lake endeavor. Suppose that is $65 per day.

Table II.2 shows the net value of the lake's fishery (column 8) to be the total revenue value that can be derived from the fishery (column 5) net of total cost of exploiting the resource (column 4). That net value is greatest if four boats embark. Adding a fourth boat increases revenue, the value that consumers place on an additional fish, by $70, which is more than the $65 value of the fourth boat's inputs had they been used in a different pursuit. In contrast, adding a fifth boat would increase the value of the fish taken by only $60, which is less than the $65 opportunity cost. The net value of the fishery increases so long as the margi-

TABLE II.1
No. of Boats v. No. of Fish Caught Per Day (Marginal Fish)

(1) Boats	(2) Fish caught per day		(3) Change in fish caught per day (marginal fish)
0	0		
		$\longrightarrow$	10
1	10		
		$\longrightarrow$	9
2	19		
		$\longrightarrow$	8
3	27		
		$\longrightarrow$	7
4	34		
		$\longrightarrow$	6
5	40		
		$\longrightarrow$	5
6	45		
		$\longrightarrow$	4
7	49		
		$\longrightarrow$	3
8	52		
		$\longrightarrow$	2
9	54		
		$\longrightarrow$	1
10	55		
		$\longrightarrow$	0
11	55		
		$\longrightarrow$	-1
12	54		

nal value from fishing exceeds the marginal opportunity cost—here a constant $65—but begins to decrease once that inequality is reversed. That implies an economically optimal number of boats is four, where the value of the fishery (column 8) is $80.

Notice, however, that the average profit per boat (column 9) is $20, which means that inputs used to fish are earning $20 more than they could earn elsewhere. Because four boats fishing on the lake earn more than similar inputs in other industries, entry will occur if there is open access to the lake. If a fifth boat embarks it will lower the total net gains from $80 to $75. But that impact is of no concern to the entrepreneur running the fifth boat, who will catch eight fish, worth $80 on the mar-

TABLE II.2
Net Value of Fishery

(1) Boats	(2) Fish caught	(3) Marginal fish	(4) Total opportunity cost [@$65/boat]	(5) Total value and revenue [@$10/fish]	(6) Marginal value and revenue	(7) Average value and revenue	(8) Net value of fishery [(5)-(4)]	(9) Profit per boat [net value/boat]
0	0		$0	$0		—	$0	—
		10			$100			
1	10		65	100		$100	35	$ 35
		9			90			
2	19		130	190		95	60	30
		8			80			
3	27		195	270		90	75	25
		7			70			
4	34		260	340		85	80	20
		6			60			
5	40		325	400		80	75	15
		5			50			
6	45		390	450		75	60	10
		4			40			
7	49		455	490		70	35	5
		3			30			
8	52		520	520		65	0	0

ket, $15 more than the $65 opportunity cost of the boat's inputs. A sixth and seventh entrepreneur will also enter; they lower the total value of the fishery but still stand to earn more than their costs. Only when eight boats go onto the lake are profits brought to zero, leaving no incentive for additional boats to set out.

The problem can be shown more concisely in figure II.1. As the number of boats on the lake on any given day increases, the marginal value declines (column 6 of table II.2). Because the marginal opportunity cost is assumed constant at $65, the optimal number of boats is four, where marginal value equals marginal opportunity cost. At that point, the net value of the entire fishery is maximized, though the profits of the boats that are not on the lake are reduced. But then there is an incentive for more than four boats to fish because average revenues exceed marginal revenues.[4]

As Eggertsson discusses, open access creates problems because entry continues even when the marginal opportunity cost of fishing exceeds the marginal value of fish caught. The incentive to enter persists as long as average revenues exceed the average costs, whereas maximizing the value of the resource net of the costs of exploiting it requires that entry halt as the marginal value threatens to fall short of the marginal opportunity costs. The marginal equality occurs when four boats are on the lake, but average revenue covers average cost for twice that many. The difference arises because new entrants ignore the impact of their own fishing on the profits earned by the other boats on the lake. With eight boats on the lake because entry cannot be controlled, too many fish (52 rather than 34) are being caught, threatening long-run damage to the fishery, possibly even the extinction of the fish population:

> This is why fishermen are not wealthy, despite the fact that the fishery resources of the sea are the richest and most indestructible available to man. By and large, the only fisherman who becomes rich is one who makes a lucky catch or one who participates in a fishery that is put under a form of social control that turns the open resource into property rights. (Gordon 1954, 132)

Property rights offer a solution to the overfishing problem. Various ownership arrangements are possible, as Eggertsson emphasizes. Workable property regimes "usually consist of complex bundles of rights and duties, divided in various ways among different categories of actors" (chapter 3, this volume). If for simplicity one puts aside the costs of excluding those without rights, the private owner(s) would deny entry to more than four boats. The ability to exclude some boats is necessary to overcome the open access problem. "Once the insiders have exclusive rights, an efficient solution may involve a single firm and hierarchical relations or some communal arrangements," Eggertsson concludes.

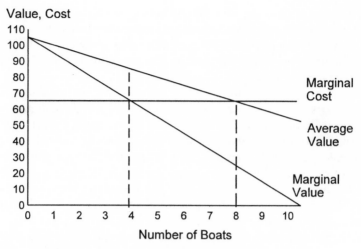

Figure II.1 Optimal Number of Boats in a Fishery

Property Rights and Monopoly

Superficially, there is some similarity between maximizing a resource's net value by curtailing its use and a monopoly's curtailing output below a competitive level. If monopoly restrictions are injurious to the economy, why is restricting resource use by converting open access to private property not similarly injurious? The answer emerges from the foregoing discussion. While monopolization ordinarily results in a restriction of output below the optimal level, open access results in an expansion of output beyond the optimal level.

That can be seen with the aid of figure II.2, which shows outputs (e.g., fish) along the horizontal axis, rather than the inputs (e.g., boats) shown in figure II.1. With decreasing returns the average cost of fish is increasing, as can be inferred from table II.2.[5] But by sheer arithmetic, average cost can only increase if it is exceeded by marginal cost. Thus marginal cost must be above average cost, as shown in figure II.2. The marginal cost curve is the supply curve in a competitive industry that uses privately owned resources. To be clear, the marginal cost curve is the industry supply curve if resources are privately owned, but the average cost curve is the supply curve when resources are in open access. Intermediately, if some resources are in open access and some privately owned, the industry supply curve falls between the marginal and average cost curves.

In a competitive market, a unit of output will be sold for the value that the marginal buyer places on it, so price equals the marginal value of the output. Because supply equals demand (marginal value) in a com-

Value, Cost

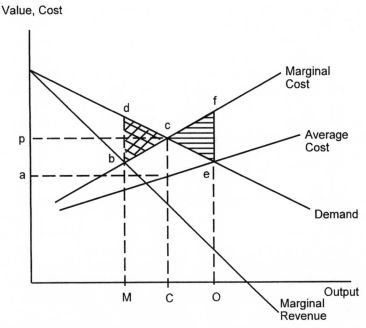

Figure II.2 Deadweight Loss under Monopoly and Open Access

petitive industry, industry output is *C* when the resource base is private. Every unit of output is worth more than the opportunity cost of the inputs produced, but no unit is produced where that opportunity cost would have exceeded the value of the unit. If the competitive industry becomes monopolized, however, the monopoly will not select an output where demand equals marginal cost, but will choose the output where marginal cost equals marginal revenue, resulting in an output of *M*. That leads to a deadweight loss shown by the cross-hatched area *bcd* on figure II.2.

Imagine that the industry remains competitive but its private resource, becomes open access. The firms fail to equate marginal opportunity cost to marginal value, but they miss the mark by increasing output rather than decreasing it as the monopolist did. That is because, as shown earlier in this introduction, the industry's supply curve ceases to be the marginal cost curve and becomes the average cost curve when private resources become open access. Each firm neglects the external costs that its actions impose on other firms, thus the individual perceptions of cost are biased downward. Firms are induced to produce the units of output between *C* and *O* for which opportunity costs exceed the value of the output, leading to the deadweight loss shown by the striped area *cef*. In brief, the inputs used to produce the units between C and O could have produced something different that would have had more value.

In summary, monopoly and open access each deviate from value maximizing output by failing to set marginal opportunity cost equal to marginal value, but they deviate in opposite directions: monopolies produce too little output; competitive firms using an open access resource produce too much. Consequently, each situation leads to a deadweight loss. Depending on the slopes of the various curves, the deadweight loss from monopolization could exceed a deadweight loss in the same industry resulting from a conversion of private resources to open access. Or, as illustrated in figure II.2, moving to open access could be a more injurious change.

But if the optimal output is C, the demand curve implies that the price will be p though average costs will be a, which is a graphical reflection of the profit per boat that was shown in column 9 of table II.2. When the resource is private, that profit accrues to its owner; if a private resource becomes open access the profit is dissipated by the entry of an excessive number of producers. Importantly, open access does not transfer that economic gain from the former owner to the entrants, it destroys it:

> [T]he rational herdsman concludes that the only sensible course for him to pursue is to add another animal to his herd. And another, and another . . . but this is the conclusion reached by each and every herdsman. Each man is locked into a system that compels him to increase his herd without limit — in a world that is limited. Ruin is the destination toward which all men rush, each pursuing his own best interest in a society that believes in a freedom of the commons. Freedom in a commons brings ruin to all. (Hardin 1968, 1244)

REGULATING ACCESS

The theoretical points discussed in chapter 3 all have testable empirical implications. As De Alessi summarizes in chapter 4, empirical studies of different property rights systems have gathered empirical evidence consistent with the property rights paradigm.

The most obvious problem with open access is overexploitation of resources. De Alessi notes several examples, such as the reduction of beaver and bison populations while those species were unowned. Whether the resource suffers extinction depends on the rate at which the species is exploited relative to the rate at which it renews itself,[6] but from an economic perspective the species can be overexploited even if it does not go extinct.

The economic model also predicts that open access will often result not just in overexploitation but in premature exploitation. The only way to benefit personally from an open access resource is to take physical possession first. One who waits until the resource has reached maturity may find it taken by someone else because the criterion for obtaining ownership under open access is first-come first-served. To return to the fishing example, a wealth-maximizing owner would throw smaller fish back to grow and reproduce. But an angler has less incentive to do that if there are many users exploiting an open access resource, because that person is unlikely to retrieve the released fish later or to capture many of its offspring. De Alessi notes that studies of open access oyster beds are consistent with that hypothesis.

Many of the problems arising from open access might be mitigated if some of the sticks in the property rights bundle are owned by the government, either directly or indirectly through government regulation. Bureaucrats usually have an incentive to preserve the resource base on which their jobs depend and wield the power of the state to do so. Evidence indicates that bureaucratic control becomes more attractive as open access resources become scarcer. But, De Alessi continues, bureaucratic command-and-control regulation sometimes proves unnecessarily costly. For example, government reduces overfishing of the oyster beds by mandating more costly gear (e.g., boats, equipment) than those in the industry want or would otherwise use. Though the waste from over-harvesting oysters is reduced, a substantial part of the benefit is wasted in a different way.

Those effects can be seen in figure II.3, which builds on figure II.1. As before, the optimal number of boats, given marginal opportunity costs of $65 per boat, is four—well below the eight that would fish if the lake were in open access. One way to keep the number of boats at four is to mandate equipment standards that increase the costs by $20 per boat, thus reducing each boat's profit by an equivalent amount. As can be confirmed by reviewing table II.2, the profit per boat would then fall to zero once four boats had embarked, and that would eliminate over-fishing. Since average revenue equals $85 when there are only four boats on the lake, and that equals the regulated marginal cost of $85 ($65 + $20), there is no profit incentive for a fifth boat to embark.

The problem is solved at considerable cost, thus raising the question of whether the extra cost induced by government regulation (the rectangle *bmfr* in figure II.3) is worth the gain created by stopping overfishing (the triangle *bad*). That depends on the revenue and cost conditions in a particular situation. For example, if overfishing can be reduced with a small increase in costs, then regulation is more likely to improve allocation. In the end, whether regulation is superior to open access depends on relative slopes of the curves depicted in figure II.3.

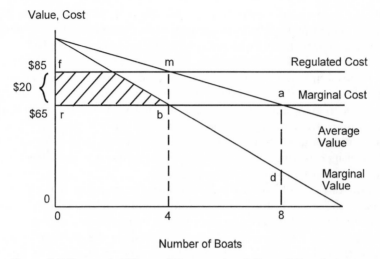

Figure II.3 Economic Effects of Command-and-Control Regulation

Government ownership intended to solve a growing problem of open access can make it more difficult for complete private (communal or individual) ownership ultimately to emerge. Having their employment and influence hinge on regulating it, government bureaucrats rarely give up property without a fight. The bureaucrats will find ready allies in other interest groups (such as the suppliers of oyster fishing gear) who receive tangential benefits from the regulation. De Alessi's theme thus foreshadows McChesney's discussion in chapter 9. While solving some problems, government creates others.

Moving beyond overfishing and premature fishing, which are static phenomena, De Alessi discusses the more dynamic aspects of open access regimes' first-come first-served rules. Individuals have less incentive to make investments in open access resources that would increase the value of the asset over time. Suppose one could increase a lake's yield by stocking it with young fish for later harvesting. Or suppose yields could be increased by altering the lake bottom or the kinds and amounts of food available to the fish. If the value of the increased yield exceeds such an investment's cost, private owners have an incentive to proceed, because they will reap the benefits. But if one sows in an open access resource, someone else often reaps. As Demsetz quotes Aristotle later in this book: "What is common to many is taken least care of, for all men have greater regard for what is their own than for what they possess in common with others." As De Alessi demonstrates, empirical support for this and related propositions is overwhelming.

ENDNOTES

The editors are most indebted to David Haddock for his considerable contributions to this introduction.

1. The notion that scarcity determines price seems straightforward, even obvious. But for centuries it stumped thinkers, who puzzled over a "diamond-water" paradox. Water is necessary for life, but in most places it costs next to nothing. Diamonds are baubles, yet command a much greater price. The solution to the paradox hinges on water being relatively plentiful while diamonds are rare. So in addition to the essential uses for water (like drinking) less important ones (such as lawn watering) can be met. In many places water is so abundant that even trivial uses (water balloons) are readily satisfied. Thus, water's marginal value and, so, its price are relatively low. Like game as compared to the bottle, the *total* value of water is without doubt greater than that of diamonds. But only a relatively few high-valued uses for diamonds (such as engagement rings) can be met before all of the stones are committed. The marginal value of diamonds and, thus, their price are relatively high in consequence.

In many places today so many bottles are discarded that uses of any value can be satisfied, and ordinary bottles command no positive price. But for the movie's bushmen there was but a single bottle and, as far as they knew, no prospect of obtaining another. Even highly valuable uses had to go unmet, so to the movie's bushmen the bottle was a precious thing that was sought by all the clan members.

2. The Gordon–Hardin tragedy, though fundamental, can nonetheless be overstated. Privatizing previously open access resources imposes costs (Demsetz 1967). Gross productivity is often reduced if a resource is in open access, that is, the lesser evil whenever the cost of closing access would exceed the value of the resulting dissipation. In that instance open access reduces the resource's gross productivity but increases its productivity net of the cost of closing access (Haddock and Kiesling 2001).

3. Pauly and Redisch (1973) use a model of closed versus open access resources to compare "closed staff" hospitals, which limit privileges to particular doctors, with "open staff" hospitals, which are open to any licensed physician.

4. To see why overfishing results, consider the situation as the fifth boat arrives. By going onto the lake it lowers the average profits of the first four boats from $20 to $15, or from $80 to $60 in aggregate, as shown in table II.2. The first four boats lose $20 in total as a result of the entry of the fifth, and that exceeds the $15 profit that the fifth boat earns. But that is a matter of indifference to the newcomer, who earns $15 more in fishing than would have been forthcoming from an off-lake pursuit.

5. For instance, compare the situation of two boats on the lake with that of four. Column 4 shows the cost of two boats to be $130 while column 2 shows that the boats land 19 fish. The cost doubles when four boats embark, but due to decreasing returns the catch is not doubled, increasing only by 15 fish to 34. Thus the average cost of fish increases from $6.84 for an output of 19 fish to $7.65 for 34 fish. Similarly, the cost is doubled again when eight boats embark,

but the catch does not double, increasing only by 18 from 34 to 52, resulting in a further increase in the average cost of fish to $10. Any line in table II.2 yields the same conclusion: the average cost of fish increases as does the number of fish caught.

6. The interplay between overexploitation and species extinction has been studied extensively. See, for example, Clark (1973), and Smith (1968).

CHAPTER THREE

OPEN ACCESS VERSUS COMMON PROPERTY

Thráinn Eggertsson

Social science does not have a general theory of economic systems, but the economics of property rights, which matured in the last third of the twentieth century, is a small but important step toward such a theory. A general theory would explain how economic performance depends not just on resource endowments, but on factors such as knowledge, social rules, property rights, organization, and political considerations.[1] This chapter explores two fundamental aspects of economic systems: (1) the condition of open access to resources (absence of exclusive rights), which is a general reference point for analyzing property rights, and (2) common (or communal) property arrangements.

On a scale that measures individualization of ownership, open access lies at one end and individual property at the opposite end. On such a scale, common property is the first step on the long and complex path from open access to individual exclusive ownership. When physical or social forces undermine common property regimes, these regimes may revert to open access, as I explain here. For this and other reasons, people often incorrectly associate common property with open access.

For economic analysis, only true economic rights, not nominal legal rights, are relevant, as Barzel discussed in the previous chapter. The relative efficiency of alternative property rights regimes is situation-specific, which implies that, in some situations, even open access is more efficient than any form of exclusive rights. The full set of property rights in any situation may also entail different rights to different aspects of resource use, meaning that productive activities (production and exchange) usually are governed by a complex mixture of exclusive rights and even open access arrangements at some margins (Barzel 1997).

In this chapter, I discuss the conditions that would lead a social group either to tolerate open access or to establish common property arrangements, on the assumption that the group's sole aim is to maximize joint wealth. Joint wealth maximization in groups is a complex affair in which each individual strives to maximize personal wealth; collective action problems may prevent group members from realizing joint maximization. I ignore issues such as free riding, political struggles over distribution, incomplete knowledge, and noneconomic motives. Even without these complexities, however, armchair theorizing about the wealth-augmenting properties of systems of property rights is not easy.[2]

The chapter begins with a simple framework for analyzing property rights generally, discussing the perennial confusion in the literature between open access and common property arrangements. It then explains the economic consequences of open access, exemplified by exploitation of open access resources such as fisheries and analyzes why economic actors are willing to bear the costs of establishing exclusive rights through private or common ownership.[3]

ANALYTIC FRAMEWORK

Property rights regimes specify user rights for certain actors and comparable duties or obligations for other actors. These rights and duties have many dimensions. Consider the variety of user rights to natural resources. Schlager and Ostrom (1992) identify five types of rights: (1) authorized access to an area to enjoy nonsubtractive benefits (sailing or enjoying the view); (2) rights to withdraw resource units; (3) rights to manage and improve the asset; (4) rights to exclude others from entering and withdrawing resources; and (5) rights to sell or lease the asset. This classification is useful in defining and contrasting open access and common property regimes.

Under a pure or ideal state of open access, everybody is authorized to enter and withdraw resource units, but no person or group has exclusive rights otherwise to manage or sell the asset. In contrast, the members of a common property regime not only have rights of entry and withdrawal, but also full rights of management and exclusion of nonmembers. Pure common property regimes, however, do not give the commoners full rights of alienation or fully transferable titles to their assets, and these limits on the rights of alienation distinguish common property rights from other types of exclusive rights.[4] Joint ownership with (more or less) unrestricted alienability, which is the basis of the corporation and many other popular property rights arrangements in modern societies, thus, is not common property according to this definition.

In the case of common property, efficiency justifications for restricting alienability focus on perpetuating social groups and the structure of local industries (Holderness 2000). Linking user rights in a valuable resource to membership in a particular social group helps to solidify and perpetuate the group and provides a mechanism for resolving disputes. Similarly, limiting user rights in a resource to active participants in a local industry and restricting permissible types of uses maintains and perpetuates the fundamental character of the industry. Whether there are economic benefits in freezing the structure of social groups and the organization of local industries depends on the context. In a dynamic and changing world, restrictions on title transfer prevent or delay reallocation of resources to more productive uses. In a stationary economy, where trial-and-error experiments over a long period have led to superior forms of organization, it may be efficient to curtail further experimentation by limiting alienability of certain assets.

The efficiency of property rights arrangements is situation-specific. As explained further in part III of this volume, property rights are costly to institute and operate (enforce), and the costs depend on relative prices, available technologies, physical characteristics of the assets, types of uses, and the general social setting (the institutional environment). Different circumstances, therefore, call for different structures of property rights. Because property rights arrangements are costly to initiate, we can think of them as investments. Wealth maximization requires that social groups invest in those structures with highest positive yield.

Property rights involve two categories of costs: exclusion costs and internal governance costs. Exclusion costs are the setup or organizational costs of initially establishing rights and the subsequent cost of defending them against outsiders. Internal governance costs are the costs of governing the behavior of independent insiders who share property. When the state or comparable bodies (e.g., tribal councils) provide property rights, they incur costs that must be covered by taxation or other means.[5] Less can be said about costs when property rights rest on social norms, partly because the origins and maintenance of norms are not well understood and because the costs often are highly dispersed. Those who enjoy property rights also bear costs of defending their rights, but their burden is inversely related to how well the state and society define and defend the rights. User costs often involve enforcement measures such as fences, locks, and security guards.[6]

The treatment of common property in the literature is engulfed in confusion. The confusion may be due to Garret Hardin's (1968) famous "The Tragedy of the Commons," which discusses open access and its consequences.[7] Hardin's paper has created something of a tragedy in itself by triggering hundreds of empirical studies showing that, in various parts of the world, well-functioning common property regimes do not create open access outcomes. In retrospect, the confusion over the nature of common property probably was caused substantially by a mix-up of proper names and theoretical categories. In the field, resources that are governed by open access arrangements often are locally known as "the commons" (or have the word "commons" in their name) because previously they were exclusive common property. The confusion is facilitated by the proximity of open access and common property on the privatization scale. Relatively small changes in the economic environment can push a common property regime into open access or vice versa.

Let us consider more carefully how the structure of rules and enforcement mechanisms differ between open access and common property. If no one holds rights to exclude others from the using the asset, its use is open to all. Because the earth's scarce resources with the exception of the high seas or the outer atmosphere are controlled by nation states, however, access to resources, is never open to all. When we talk about open access, what we usually mean is that access is open to all members of a particular community or jurisdiction, but not to all outsiders, including people from other countries. Sometimes access is open also to outsiders, but then they often are excluded by transportation costs. People who withdraw units from open access resources almost always employ tools and other inputs that are exclusively owned, and the so-called rule of capture immediately establishes ownership of resource units once they are withdrawn. Fishers, for instance, own the fish they catch in an open access fishery. The utilization of open access resources, therefore, involves a complex bundle of rights, but entry is free and the users have neither the rights nor much incentive to manage the resource and invest in improving it.

Common property regimes are complex structures that involve rules and enforcement mechanisms, often located at several societal levels, that regulate exclusion and (internal) governance. When an asset is under a well-defined common property regime, an easily identifiable group of insiders controls the use and management of the resource and holds exclusive user rights, which outsiders do not enjoy. The rights of insiders often are formally recognized by the state, although in traditional societies, rights of isolated groups sometimes are based on local customary law and social norms. Ostrom (1997) observes that newly independent states in the Third World, because they were not always fully aware of these regimes or for other reasons, sometimes nationalized the assets without providing effective enforcement. In many cases, nationalization transformed common property regimes into open access regimes.

ECONOMIC CONSEQUENCES OF OPEN ACCESS

Open access problems arise when independent actors (people or firms with independent goals) have both the incentive and the ability to withdraw, at will and on a large scale, resource units from an asset that they access together. When a resource is in high demand, open access has adverse consequences that include economic and sometimes biological overuse of the resource. Although the consequences tend to be complex and subtle, we can summarize the effects under two headings, the supply effects and the demand effects (Barzel 1997). Joint wealth is not maximized on the supply side because of insufficient supply of resource units caused by inadequate provision, maintenance, and investment in improvement. Wealth is not maximized on the demand side because of excessive (inefficient) withdrawal of resource units.

We begin by examining adverse effects on the supply side. Rational actors who hold exclusive rights to some resource have an incentive to invest in maintaining or improving the asset, provided that they expect the marginal benefits to exceed the marginal costs of maintenance and improvement in quality. Under open access, rational actors have little or no incentive to make such investments. The net returns are likely to be negative because the investors cannot exclude other users from collecting some or all of the benefits. Under open access, therefore, users prefer to withdraw resources in their unimproved or natural form. Open access agricultural land is used for grazing rather than for planting fruit trees; those who seek shelter in open access housing units usually ignore maintenance until they somehow establish exclusive rights. In sum, open access is associated with depletion and disinvestment rather than with accumulation and economic growth.

On the demand side, undesirable results of open access include perverse timing and excessive withdrawal of resource units. When a valuable resource is in open access, actors have an incentive to enter a race to be first to appropriate resource units while they are abundant. Berries on open access land are picked before they are fully ripe, fishers in open access fisheries install large engines in their boats to win races to the fishing grounds. In effect, the now-or-never motive drives actors to deplete nonrenewable resources without due attention to optimal time preferences and patterns of demand. Renewable natural resources, such as fish stocks, can support various levels of sustainable yield (various permanent rates of withdrawal) but open access users do not systematically select the level of sustainable yield that maximizes joint wealth. In fact, if their needs are large relative to the resource stock and if their technology permits it, open access users have an incentive to deplete a renewable natural resource and lower its economically usable yield to zero (Gordon 1954; Scott 1955).[8]

Under open access, so-called external effects are important. External effects arise when some activities of actor A impose costs on or bring benefits to other actors, but A ignores these effects in her decisions because she neither is compensated for the incremental benefits nor charged for the incremental costs.[9] The effects are external to her decisions. The theory also postulates that, in their decisions, people watch marginal effects and tend to make efficient decisions (maximize joint wealth), provided they are responsible for all costs and benefits that follow from their actions. But with open access, people are not fully accountable for their actions and therefore the outcomes are inefficient and reflect average values rather than marginal values.[10]

Think of a driver who wants to go from X to Y as fast as possible and has the choice of narrow and slow secondary roads and potentially fast travel on a freeway. The secondary roads are uncrowded, but the freeway is crowded. The driver's only concern is how much time she will save by choosing the freeway. Access to the freeway is open, and being a rational maximizer, the driver ignores the fact that her entry on the freeway will slightly slow down other travelers. The driver gains six minutes by using the freeway rather than secondary roads, but slows down one hundred other freeway drivers, each by six seconds. Her personal opportunity cost of imposing delays on fellow travelers is zero, but the total opportunity cost is the ten minutes (one hundred drivers at six seconds each) of total delay she causes for the other drivers. The ten minutes are external effects because they do not enter into the driver's calculations. In the aggregate, the driver's decision to use the freeway creates a net social loss of the value of four minutes.

The same reasoning explains a fisherman's decision to take his boat and gear into already crowded fishing grounds. It is possible, when the grounds are crowded, that a new boat may catch enough fish to make small profits, but also reduce the profits of all the other boats by an even larger amount and generate a net loss for the fishers as a whole. The new entrant, however, does not care about others' losses, only about his gains.

When a community discovers a natural resource such as a fishery, the new resource offers the promise of a rent (income) that would be a net addition to the joint wealth of the community. If the community wants to maximize the value of this rent, new boats should enter the fishery as long as they make a positive contribution to the net income of the whole fleet. When an additional boat does not add to aggregate net income, entry must stop. In other words, the rent is maximized when productive effort in fishing continues until a marginal increase in effort increases output value for the whole fleet by the same amount as it increases total cost. With open access, individual fishers, however, only consider their private costs and benefits—just like the driver of the previous example. New fishers enter as long as they expect private profits, and entry only stops when new entrants expect zero private gains. If all the fishers have equal skills, their equipment is identical, and they make the same effort, entry will continue until the average cost for each fisher (average cost per unit of output) is equal to output price (price per unit). At that point, all the fishers earn zero profits and open access has eaten up the entire potential rent (extra income) from the fishery.

If excessive withdrawal of resource units (overfishing) dissipates all the rent, the discovery of fertile fishing grounds will add nothing to the long-term wealth of a community. To appreciate this point, think of a community where labor and other productive inputs are fully occupied. A valuable natural resource is discovered and productive inputs (including labor) leave various current activities to exploit the new resource. If entry continues until total cost is equal to total output value (which implies that unit price is equal to average cost per unit), the output of the country is the same as before, only its industrial structure having changed.[11] Wealth maximization, however, involves finding a level of effort that maximizes the difference between total revenue and total cost in the new activity. If the community had followed the marginal rule of adding bundles of inputs only as long as net revenue (revenue minus costs) continued to increase, wealth would have been maximized. The joint income of the community would then increase by an amount equal to the maximum potential rent from the new resource.

How can dissipation of the rent be avoided? One potential solution involves contracting among the fishers to limit excessive withdrawal. With open access, however, contracting is likely to face insurmountable problems because of pressures from a steady inflow of new actors. The more successful the insiders are in protecting the rent, the more attractive (profitable) it is for outsiders to enter, and outsiders are not bound by the contract. When a resource is scarce and the number of potential entrants is large, exclusive rights usually are a necessary condition for avoiding excessive use.[12] Once the insiders have exclusive rights, an efficient solution may involve a single firm and hierarchical relations or some communal arrangement.

Yet another solution has a private owner or the state control the resource and use prices to regulate access. The upper limit for the total of such admission charges equals the entire rent from the resource, which would give the fishers only normal returns on their investments. When the license to enter is free, the license holders collect all the rent.

Most states take measures to prevent open access to their major resources, but fisheries outside national jurisdictions have suffered the ill effects of open access.[13] The introduction in the early 1970s of a 200-mile economic zone in the ocean for coastal states did not immediately end open access fisheries because most fishing nations, after excluding foreigners, did not establish effective exclusion and internal governance regimes for domestic fishers. In recent years, individual transferable quotas have raised hopes for greater efficiency in coastal fisheries of countries such as Iceland and New Zealand which have pioneered these arrangements. Initially, transferable quotas were assigned to vessels on the basis of their fishing history in the years immediately prior to the introduction of the new system.

Usually the government distributes the fishing quotas for free. While giving away the rights solves the economic problems created by open access, the giveaway may have political ramifications. In communities where ocean fisheries are a major industry, this amounts to an immense transfer of wealth that approximately equals the capitalized value of the expected rent in the fisheries.[14] One can speculate whether these transfers reflect implicit bribes politically necessary to acquire compliance of powerful industrial interests with the new system. However, the eventual high value of transferable quotas was not immediately obvious when the system was introduced in times of poor fishing caused by the previous open access problems.

Individual transferable quotas are a good example of how the property regimes that govern particular activities usually consist of complex bundles of rights and duties, divided in various ways among different categories of actors. Under the transferable quota system used in Iceland, there are clearly defined insiders who have rights of entry, rights of withdrawal of resource units, and rights to their catch.[15] Stock management (including decisions about the total catch in each period) lies with agencies of the state, and only the state has the right to withdraw quotas, allocate new quotas, and punish license holders who abuse their rights. The state also is in charge of necessary marine biological research, and it protects insiders against domestic and foreign transgressors.

Unlike classic common property regimes, the transferable quota system generally does not involve insiders in managing the regime, which puts the fishing industry in a different position than most other industries. In her exhaustive study of common property regimes, Ostrom (1990) associates efficiency of the regimes with active user involvement in management. Regimes of individual transferable quotas apparently have been successful in alleviating severe open access problems, but casual evidence (often from disgruntled fishers) suggests that the regimes are still plagued by wasteful behavior at various margins, including attempts to exceed quotas and violate rules for protecting juvenile fish and breeding grounds.[16] Presumably tendencies to free ride on the system would be reduced if the insiders involved themselves in managing their affairs.

The fact that access is not perfectly exclusive does not mean the institution is necessarily inefficient (Barzel 1997). Open access is efficient when there are no net benefits from establishing effective exclusive rights, and such conditions often emerge at the margins of complex property rights structures.[17] Consider the structure of property rights that governs the operation of a restaurant. As Barzel (1997) emphasizes, it often is efficient for the owner of a restaurant not to enforce control at certain margins. Within limits, the time guests spend at their table is not priced, nor is the salt, sugar, and pepper they use. Similarly, many movie theaters sell all their seats at one price. With one price for all seats, people engage in races (use valuable time) to claim a good location in a theater, but we cannot refer to such behavior as inefficient if alternative seating arrangements (numbered seats) would involve greater additional costs (monitoring and enforcement) than benefits.

Exclusion and Common Property

Exclusive property rights enable specific individuals to use scarce resources and exclude others from using them. Exclusion is a costly activity that involves both start-up and maintenance costs. These costs are divided in various proportions between the state (taxpayers) and those who directly enjoy the property rights. It is fair to say that no one arrangement for exclusion will minimize costs in all settings. The state, with its violence potential and organizations of enforcement, enjoys immense economies of scale in providing (and in usurping) property rights (see McChesney, this volume). A credible commitment by the state to defend exclusive property rights will strongly deter potential violators of these rights. When credible state power backs their rights, individual owners often need only take basic precautions: monitor their assets and report violations to the authorities. Potential violators see the large role of the state and elementary precautions taken by owners as reducing expected gains from seizing property, which makes infringements rare.

In other settings, private rather than state action has relative advantage in providing strong property rights at low costs. Society provides inexpensive exclusion through social norms and decentralized enforcement of norms that often occurs as a byproduct of other activities, as discussed in parts III and IV of this volume. Enforcement through social norms is cheap because it does not rely on specialized organizations and officials, and it can be effective because the enforcers are close to potential violators rather than residing, for instance, in a central bureaucracy.[18]

Studying the enforcement of property rights presents a formidable problem in sorting out the relative importance of social norms and formal rules backed by the state. The two types of enforcement mechanisms may interact in complex ways to influence the expectations of potential violators of property rights. In some instances, the state's role as the defender of last resort makes enforcement via social norms possi-

ble and, in other instances, supportive social norms make the enforcement of laws and public regulations possible. These are unsettled issues,
and how they are resolved will affect how we think about the transition
of the former Soviet-type economies from central management to markets.

When members of a group expect to gain by enclosing a resource to
protect the rent, the group often faces serious internal bargaining and
collective action problems over how to allocate the gains (the rent) and
the burdens of operating the regime. Efficient solutions to these bargaining and collective action problems are relatively manageable in
groups that share interests and values and have long-term stakes in a
cooperative solution. The opposite is true when members of user groups
have widely different interests. Failure of collective action in local user
groups, however, is not the only explanation of inefficient common pool
regimes. In fact, local users have a relatively high success rate in establishing efficient property rights compared to higher levels of government
(Ostrom 1990). Apart from providing secure institutional environments
and coordinating overlapping activities of local authorities, regional and
national governments do not seem to have relative advantage in design-
ing efficient common property regimes. Higher levels of government
often pursue goals other than maximizing the value of common pool
resources at the local level. Decisions by governments often reflect outcomes (compromises) of complex factional politics, personal goals of
remote administrators, conflicts of interest between distant levels of
government, and the needs and interests of government bureaus.

At the outset, I introduced an efficiency-based privatization spectrum
with open access at one end and individual exclusive property at the
other end. On this scale, common property is a close neighbor of open
access. It is natural to ask what types of assets or resources we would
expect to find at this far end of the spectrum if regimes of property
rights were efficient? First, consider open access. Except when unexpected events intervene, economic logic suggests that rational actors will
not use their wealth to create assets only to leave them in open access.
In stable times, therefore, we do not expect to find humanmade assets
(capital goods, produced consumer goods, or financial instruments) in
the public domain.[19]

God-given natural resources, however, are potential candidates for
open access. Open access typically involves natural resources (such as
fish), but it is noteworthy that natural resources also are the most frequent asset-type under common property regimes.[20] We can ask therefore: what circumstances sometimes place natural resources in the open
access category, sometimes under common property regimes, and sometimes at the individual property end of the privatization scale?

The answer concerns the potential value of a resource relative to the
cost of exclusion. When natural resources are scarce but still of limited

value, potential benefits of exclusion may not cover the costs, so open access is the most effective regime. As natural resources become scarcer and somewhat more valuable, the simplest form of enclosure becomes worthwhile. The simplest form of enclosure often implies that a group of local users excludes their more distant neighbors. For instance, it is usually cheaper to use labor and fencing materials to enclose a large field in its entirety than to divide the land into many private plots (Field 1989). Divisibility and mobility of natural resources also raise costs and complicate attempts to divide the resources into relatively small, individual plots. The atmosphere, underground oil reserves, and schools of fish come to mind. In addition to physical factors, the cost of enclosure depends on relative prices and technologies of measurement, and changes in these factors can make it economically rational to subdivide an asset into private plots.

Common property regimes lie between open access and full private rights. Common property is efficient when it is too costly (relative to the benefits) to divide a natural resource stock among individual owners, and when there are net gains from assigning individual shares in the flow of services from the asset to the members of a user group. A natural resource sometimes is a marginal case, lying on the border between open access and common property. Relatively small changes in value of a common property resource, or in the costs of excluding outsiders, can move the resource between the open access and common property categories.

The summer mountain pastures of (historical) Iceland were naturally enclosed by mountains, rivers, lava fields, and sands (Eggertsson 1992). Nature and often geographic distance excluded outsiders from the huge common mountain pastures of each region, but costs of fencing and monitoring made it inefficient to divide the area into individual private plots. Private plots would have been impractical for another reason. Changes in temperature and precipitation, sandstorms, and even volcanic eruptions made the quality of grazing in a particular location of a commons vary from one period to another. Private plots would have required costly markets in grazing rights among the individual owners of such plots.

In Iceland, the home fields of each farm were individual private properties that were relatively small and mostly used for haymaking and winter grazing. There was economic logic in relying on exclusive individual property for home fields and common property for the mountain pastures. Icelandic farms were not grouped in villages but strung out, and control of trespassing was essentially an inexpensive byproduct of daily routines. The mountain pastures were vast areas where livestock, especially sheep, roamed unattended during the summer months with no real danger from natural predators. Internal governance in the mountain pastures was simple. The main task involved controlling how many animals each farm was allowed to transfer to the mountain pastures in the spring. Driving animals into the pastures in the spring and rounding them up in the fall were done collectively, which minimized opportunities for free riding.

INTERNAL GOVERNANCE AND COMMON PROPERTY

Internal governance of the commons often is far more complicated than the Icelandic case suggests, and common property regimes will fail unless they solve both the exclusion and internal governance problems. When two or more independent actors share a resource or its yield, some governance arrangements are required to prevent excessive use and to ensure work on maintenance and improvement. The internal governance problem is similar to the open access problem.

In fact, the breakdown of governance on a commons can create pure open access outcomes without transgressions from outsiders. Let us consider the internal governance problem in some detail. When N actors share a resource, actions by actor A can benefit or impose costs on the other $N - 1$ members. If A, for instance, invests in a project benefitting all the members of a commons, he will bear all the costs of the action and receive only $1/N$ of the benefits. The same reasoning applies when A contemplates whether to avoid actions that impose costs on the community. In other words, the internal governance problem has all the features of the open access problem, except one.

The commoners can exclude outsiders and control the size of N. Control of N provides an opportunity to create a system of internal governance that specifies rights and duties, and regulates the behavior of the insiders (the commoners). The problems of coordinating and controlling the activities of commoners are analogous to the problems of regulating the behavior of individual members of a cartel, such as OPEC, which profits by raising prices and restricting output. The cartel is only successful if it can curb the incentives of individual members to sell more than their assigned share of the output at the high price. From a welfare point of view, however, there is an important difference between a cartel and a common property regime. The breakdown of a cartel brings greater output and lower prices to consumers, and the gain to consumers is greater than the lost profits of the cartel members. But the breakdown of internal governance on a commons leads to excessive use, incomplete maintenance, dissipation of joint wealth, and even destruction of natural resources.

The problem of internal governance has several aspects.[21] The insiders must, through some form of bargaining, agree on a hierarchy of rules: rules that control daily operations, rules for settling disputes, and (constitutional) rules that lay down processes for changing the structure of the regime. Ways must be found to enforce these rules at a reasonable cost, and long-term economic success requires that the commoners develop the capacity to adjust the rules to external changes and even to abolish the commons and take up a new regime when circumstances demand.

Many scholars (Ostrom 1990, 1998; McKean 1992; National Research Council 1986; Tang 1992) have analyzed governance systems as affected by factors such as the social and economic characteristics of individuals, existing forms of political organizations at various levels, the economic environment, and the physical features of resources. These studies emphasize that agreement on establishing and enforcing governance rules is relatively difficult when the actors differ greatly in their productive abilities.[22] To return to fisheries, a group of fishers will find it harder to convert their fishing grounds from open access to common property if their skills and equipment differ substantially from one another. All rent will be dissipated in an open access fishery when the productivity of fishers is identical. But with skill and equipment differences, even with open access, the most productive fishers will earn some rent and only the least productive fishers will earn no rent. Substantial differences in productivity make agreement on a governance regime more difficult because the most productive fishers will refuse to accept rules that equalize outcomes. And even when the less productive fishers are willing, in principle, to agree to rules maintaining previous ranks in outcomes, there may be uncertainty about what the ranking is (Johnson and Libecap 1982; Libecap 1989a).

In general, the details of effective internal governance rules obviously depend on the physical characteristics of the resource they regulate. It matters, for instance, whether the resource is water for irrigation, an oil field, or a fishery; whether the terrain is level or mountainous; and whether droughts or floods are common. Effective governance systems must solve a host of problems. What, for example, is the best way to punish users who violate the rules? Ostrom (1990) emphasizes that sanctions should be graduated, which means that light penalties are administered for first offences because first offences often are due to lack of understanding of a regime rather than a will to violate the rules.

In sum, improvements in governance can have similar impact on productivity as have improvements in technology.

CONCLUSION

Open access regimes reflect the unwillingness or inability of the government, society, or current users to introduce and enforce an effective system of control that determines the total number of users and regulates the behavior of insiders. Two functions that all systems of property rights share, exclusion and governance, are missing from open access regimes. When exclusion and governance are absent, economic agents lack the incentive to economize in the use of resources, maintain their quality, and invest in their improvement.

In marginal cases, such behavior is economically efficient, namely when the costs of effective exclusion and governance are high relative to the value of resource units. When it pays to invest in exclusion and governance, the most efficient property rights arrangement is not predetermined. The costs of exclusion and governance are situation-specific and, in some cases, common property is the most efficient arrangement. Economic activities usually are governed by a complex mixture of property rights and, at some margins, open access often prevails.

Various factors can move a common property regime either toward more privatization or push it into open access. Technological change sometimes lowers and sometimes raises the cost of governance. New methods of measurement and enforcement can affect the cost of exclusion in various ways. Casual empiricism suggests that the greatest challenge to common property regimes is changes in technology and relative prices that increase the gains to the insiders who violate their governance rules. In addition to cheating by insiders, transgressions by outsiders may also increase when the output of a commons becomes more valuable.[23] Initially these forces may introduce elements of open access. But after a while, increasing problems with governance could move the regime in the direction of individual property. Field (1989), who modeled how an increase in demand or in population affects the survival of common property regimes by changing the costs of exclusion and governance, finds that the outcome is indeterminate. Some forces push the system toward open access, and other forces toward more individual property rights.

ENDNOTES

The chapter was written while I was a Senior Olin Fellow at Columbia University Law School.

1. "Although our theoretical ideas about capitalism have improved as mainstream economics developed, they never matured into a theory of capitalism. And we have virtually no theory of socialism. Theories of socialeconomic organization surely reside in the economics of property rights, for the fundamental economic difference between social systems is in the treatment they accord property rights, but property rights received little attention from neoclassical economists. Only during the last quarter century has a more analytical view toward property rights emerged from the work of economists" (Demsetz 1998, 144). See also Ostrom (1986).

2. Empirical studies of property rights must allow for the fact that a property rights regime only functions properly when all relevant actors have adjusted the regime to their circumstances, adjusted their behavior to the regime, and formed stable expectations about the behavior of other actors. My discussion is not only highly stylized but static and oriented toward equilibrium.

3. The condition of complete open access, where all human and physical assets are open to raids and confiscation, is approximated by war and is not consistent with investment and productive activity.

4. In real life, property rights are not as clear-cut as these theoretical categories suggest. Rights to common grazing fields, for instance, often are associated with particular privately owned farms and, when the rights to the farmland are sold, rights to the common grazing fields are bundled with them (Eggertsson 1992).

5. These costs arise from deliberations, negotiations and rulemaking, dispute resolution, monitoring, detection, judicial proceedings, and punishment.

6. When we say that at time t, an actor holds certain property rights, we are referring only to the rights that society or the state have conferred on her. The actor, however, may invest in a campaign to acquire additional property rights or to prevent unwanted changes in the structure of her rights. Individuals acquire economic property rights in three ways: (1) the state or society assigns rights to particular individuals without explicit charges; (2) individuals obtain rights through costly campaigns of persuasion and political exchange; and finally, (3) they acquire their rights through contracting and market exchange and receive them as private gifts and transfers (e.g., by inheritance).

7. Ostrom (1997) reviews the confusion and discusses both the legal and economic debates over private versus common property. She traces proper distinction between open access and common property to "a now classic article [by] Ciriacy-Wantrup and Bishop (1975) [who] clearly demarked the difference between property regimes that are open access, where no one has the legal right to exclude anyone from using a resource, from common property, where the members of a clearly demarked group have a legal right to exclude nonmembers of that group from using a resource" (Ostrom 1997, 3).

8. The race to be the first is particularly destructive and costly when the actors only can claim the resource units as they withdraw and not the whole asset (stock). When actors can claim the asset itself (the stock rather than shares in the flow), the economic consequences are less drastic or even favorable in the long run. The principle of first possession (discussed in chapter 8 by Dean Lueck) is perhaps the most common method in history for establishing exclusive private property rights over new resources, for instance, in new territories. Yet the use of the rule of first possession for establishing property rights can lead to costly races because, in the limit, people are ready to spend as much on a race as they expect to gain from it (which depends on the present value of the resource they are competing for). Note also that competitors honor ownership that is based on first possession usually because the rule is backed by mightiest possession — by the power of the state. When private actors compete for an unspecified or poorly defined asset, such as an invention, races (e.g., patent races) are inevitable (Barzel 1968). The state, however, can allocate directly more concrete assets, such as new land, through auctions. For somewhat differing views of the

efficiency and desirability of the rule of first possession as a method for establishing property rights over assets, see Lueck (1995), Haddock (1986), Epstein (1986), and Anderson and Hill (1990).

9. As a rule, exclusive rights do not make the effects (such as pollution) disappear, although their intensity or volume may change when people allow for the effects in their decisions (Coase 1960; Demsetz 1964). In the jargon of economics, complete exclusive rights will internalize external effects.

10. Eggertsson (1990, chapter 4), provides a more detailed discussion of the open access problem along with references.

11. In economics, cost is defined by the value of inputs and goods in their best alternative uses. Total cost in our fisheries example is equal to output foregone in the industries where the fishing inputs previously were employed.

12. A group of isolated users may be able to limit excessive withdrawal through contracting if there is no threat of new entry. Isolation and no access to external markets often has taken the pressure off users in traditional societies and made it relatively easy for them to solve the governance problem.

13. See Libecap (1989a) for examples in the United States of serious open access problems or incomplete property rights at important margins.

14. Of course, only the initial recipients of transferable quotas receive windfall gains. Others must buy quotas in the market and pay the full rental price for access to the fisheries.

15. I rely here on personal knowledge of the Icelandic system. Also see Arnason (1993).

16. The state has limited capacity to monitor behavior of fishers on the open seas and official estimates of regulatory violations essentially are guesswork. A government committee in Iceland estimated in 1993 that discards in the demersal (groundfish) fishery ranged from 1 to 6 percent of the catch, depending on gear and vessel type (Arnason 1993, 217).

17. Open access also is efficient for entire resource systems when they are relatively abundant and the marginal value of resource units is so low that it does not justify the costs of establishing property rights.

18. Cooter (1996) argues that norms often tend to be more efficient than laws, which suggests that legislation has a useful role in reinforcing social norms once they have evolved. Also see Ellickson (1991). Posner (1996) makes the case that the efficiency of norms is not obvious. Norms, like laws, can be inefficient.

19. Wars, rebellions, unexpected technological change, and mistakes sometimes leave humanmade assets in open access.

20. The modern concern with environmental damage very much involves open access or weak property rights. The most vivid descriptions of both open access problems and common property successes involve natural resources such as ocean fisheries, forests, pastures, and underground oil reserves (Libecap 1989a). Government regulations, when not enforced properly, create open access situations. These cases sometimes involve humanmade assets but tend to represent unexpected regulatory failures. Sometimes informal property rights modify these open access conditions, which is what seems to have happened to some extent in the former Soviet Union in response to ineffective formal property rights and control through central management.

21. Ostrom (1998) has exhaustively studied the structure of governance in common property regimes throughout the world and provides an excellent summary of the research.

22. Common property regimes usually restrain the ability of the members to transfer their shares to outsiders. Lueck (1994) offers an efficiency explanation of this restriction and suggests that it is intended to maintain homogeneity in the user group.

23. Increased world market demand for the product will increase the temptation of insiders to withdraw excessive amounts of resource units, which undermines the sharing arrangements on the commons and pushes the system toward individual units. Increased world market demand for the product also might increase pressures from trespassers and the cost of keeping them out, which complicates the problem of exclusion. If we assume that exclusion is most costly and complex under individual private property, the effects of increased trespassing are to weaken or even reverse movements toward individual private property (Field 1989).

CHAPTER FOUR

GAINS FROM PRIVATE PROPERTY

The Empirical Evidence

Louis De Alessi

In a world of scarcity and change, individuals must compete for the right to use resources. Accordingly, the fundamental economic problem within any society is to evolve a set of institutions to control competition, that is, to organize cooperation; the archetypal alternatives are central versus individual planning. Institutions may arise spontaneously or by design, and may be formal (statutory and common laws) or informal (custom).

Institutions provide a mechanism for assigning to particular individuals the authority to choose how specific resources will be employed, given a class of permissible uses (Alchian 1965b). In particular, institutions specify the rights that individuals may hold to the use and transferability of resources (including themselves) and the services they yield. The resulting system of property rights determines, via actual or imputed prices, how the benefits and harms flowing from a decision are allocated between the decision maker and other individuals. Thus, it determines the expectations that individuals can form in their dealings with others.[1]

This chapter examines how alternative property rights affect choices. It reviews some of the empirical evidence concerning the economic consequences of controlling competition for the use of land, animals, and some other resources through open access, private (including communal) ownership, government regulation of open access and exchange, and government ownership. Individual private property rights generally provide the benchmark. As the previous chapter by Thráinn Eggertsson showed, open access may well be optimal in certain settings. Both theory and evidence, however, indicate that private property rights, when economically feasible, yield substantial gains relative to other regimes.

A caveat about value judgments and the meaning of "gains" may be helpful. All efficiency and welfare criteria, Pareto optimality included, embody normative values. In particular, there is no objective social scale for measuring, aggregating, and comparing the welfare gains and losses of the same or different groups of individuals under alternative economic regimes.[2] A voluntary exchange, however, reveals that all parties to the transaction expect to be better off according to their own personal measures of value. Thus, changes in constraints that allow individuals to trade and become better off as each sees it are an unequivocal indication of gain and are free of distributional bias (Buchanan 1988); the main value judgment involved is that each individual is the best judge of her or his own welfare.

OPEN ACCESS

In addressing the economic consequences of common ownership, it is necessary to distinguish between open access and communal property rights (Eggertsson, this volume). Under open access, everyone in the community (village, nation, world) has the right to use a resource and capture its fruits on a first-come first-served basis; individuals lack exclusive, transferable rights to the use of the resource. Under communal ownership, a form of private property, members of a community jointly own a resource and choose the rules controlling its use.

Open access is the initial state of the world. Anyone can enter and there are no constraints on the harvest or the gear used. Open access does not present a problem as long as the supply of a resource is so great relative to the demand that there is no (net) gain from conserving or improving it; those who enter, if any, can disregard the behavior of others.

When an open access resource becomes scarce, individuals lack the incentive to conserve it because they cannot capture the full gains from doing so. Relative to private ownership, all the following consequences ensue (De Alessi 1980):[3] There is increased entry to capture rents. The resource is harvested earlier and more intensively; as a corollary, the quantity of output varies more widely over time, such as a season. The outputs chosen have shorter gestation periods; in the case of land, for example, individuals graze privately owned animals or sow cereals, which mature within months, rather than plant fruit trees, which take several years to begin producing. Less is invested in maintaining and improving the resource and more in the privately owned inputs used jointly in production, such as boats and nets. Over time, outputs and incomes are lower.

The exhaustion of open access resources, often described as the tragedy of the commons (Hardin 1968), has raised some well-justified concerns.[4] Unfortunately, the phenomenon is not new. For example, Paleoindian hunters hastened the extinction of megafauna and several smaller species in the Pleistocene period. Similarly, early Polynesian colonizers of Hawaii and New Zealand pursued many animal species to extinction (Smith 1975; Krech 1999).[5]

Land

A pioneer study by Bottomley (1963) examined the economic consequences of open access in the Libyan province of Tripolitania where, in the early 1960s, 97 percent of all utilized land was open access; at least some of this land was physically as fertile as much of the land held in private. Bottomley found that Arab tribesmen used open access land for lower-valued uses; these included growing occasional crops of barley, whenever and wherever rain seemed adequate, and grazing privately owned sheep and goats. Owners of private land, instead, raised higher-valued crops, such as almonds, that had a longer gestation period. They also invested more in irrigation and other capital improvements. The maximum annual gross returns per hectare were about 2 Libyan pounds on open access land and 11 to 163 Libyan pounds on privately owned land.

If the amount of privately held land is small, its price typically is high. Higher land prices encourage more intensive cultivation characterized by high capital-to-labor ratios that yield a relatively low marginal productivity of capital and decreased employment opportunities. As predicted, Bottomley found that the productivity of labor on open access land was lower, and that of capital higher, than on privately owned land.

Whales

Private property rights in harvested, open access resources often are inexpensive to enforce. Sheep convert grass into wool and meat, and fishermen store the catch in their boats' holds. Informal agreements to manage an open access resource prior to its harvest, however, are more difficult to reach and enforce among heterogeneous users (some people are more skillful or better equipped than others). This is especially true when competition for a resource is strong (Johnson and Libecap 1982).[6]

Nonetheless, Ellickson (1989) showed that rules for resolving some open access problems can arise in a world of anarchy. During the period from 1750 to 1870, whales were very valuable and belonged to those who harvested them. Who did harvest them, however, was not always clear, giving rise to disputes. Although whaling ships were from many nations, their captains typically came from a few seaports in New England; they frequently knew each other, and socialized both at sea and ashore. Thus, they had incentive (maximize wealth) to develop rules for resolving disputes and a mechanism (social ostracism) to enforce the rules in a world of anarchy.

At least three norms emerged, each suited to a different marine environment. The first was a rule of "fast-fish loose-fish." Off Greenland, where the prey was the right whale, claimants owned a whale as long as it was fastened to their craft; loose whales, dead or alive, were up for grabs. Right whales were harpooned from sturdy boats and were slow, docile, and not likely to break a line, capsize a boat, or sound deep enough to induce release. Thus, the fast-fish rule rewarded the first harpooner. A right whale, however, could sink after death and had to be cut loose, resurfacing days later when those who had harpooned it were long gone. Thus, the loose-fish rule allowed a finder to use the whale.

A second rule, "iron-holds-the-whale," evolved for hunting sperm whales. This rule assigned ownership to those who first affixed a harpoon as long as they remained in hot pursuit. Compared to right whales, sperm whales swim faster, sound deeper, fight more vigorously, and school. The rule favored the practice of attaching a drogue to a harpoon to help tire the whale and mark its location; it also encouraged harpooning more than one whale in a school.

The third rule was "split ownership." In the Galapagos, where sperm whales school and some currents prevail, a whaler who fettered a sperm whale with a drogue shared the carcass fifty-fifty with the finder. This system encouraged the first ship that came upon a large school to harpoon and fetter as many whales as it could even though currents might disperse some of the catch. In New England, where fast-swimming finback whales were killed from afar with bomb lances, causing them to sink immediately to the bottom and wash up ashore days later, whalers paid a salvage fee to those who found the beached whale.

Private rights in freely roaming whales were too costly to enforce and did not evolve. Whales were decimated. Regulation by international agencies has reversed the decline, but the rules reflect political rather than economic considerations. For example, there is no attempt to adopt new institutions, including private ownership, in the light of new technologies that allow branding and tracking individual whales (M. De Alessi 1998, 2000).

Beavers

Demsetz (1967) illustrated the shift from open access to communal ownership when the value of a resource increases as well as the shift back to open access when the costs of enforcing exclusivity become too high. Before European colonization, beavers in Canada were an open access resource. Sparse indigenous populations and primitive hunting methods apparently did not threaten the survival of the species.

The introduction of commercial fur trading by Europeans, however, increased the value of beavers to the indigeneous peoples and led to increased hunting. The tribes responded by evolving communal property rights in beavers and auxiliary rules to control their use. Because beavers are sedentary, a tribe could mark the trees near a beaver's lodge to establish its property rights and manage the resource as it saw fit. In time, however, the tribes were unable to prevent increased poaching by white trappers and the system regressed to open access; such an event is not uncommon (Field 1989). Intensive hunting by both whites and Indians quickly wiped out beavers as a commercial resource.[7]

COMMUNAL OWNERSHIP

Private communal ownership with auxiliary rules to control use is a typical transition from open access (North and Thomas 1977; Eggertsson, this volume). As in the case of beavers, it is a practical solution when a resource is sufficiently valuable to justify the costs of organizing the group but not the costs of defining, establishing, enforcing, and exchanging individual private property rights.[8] Such arrangements have worked well throughout the world in managing many resources, including mountain forests and meadows, water for irrigation, and fisheries (Ostrom 1990; Johannes 1992; Leal 1998; M. De Alessi 1998).

Land

The solution observed in Törbel, a village in the Swiss Alps, is particularly useful in exploring the choice of property rights (Ostrom 1990). Törbel is nestled in terrain characterized by steep slopes, different microclimates determined by altitude and exposure to sunlight, and little precipitation. For centuries, villagers have held some land individually and used it to grow grains, hay, vegetables, fruit trees, and other crops. They also have held some land communally in five different categories: alpine grazing meadows, forests, "waste" lands, irrigation systems, and paths. Citizens' associations set the rules for the use and transfer of these holdings, including their subdivision and assignment to individual owners should that alternative become more valuable.

The villagers hold much land individually. Why not all? The forests, in addition to providing wood, also protect the village from avalanches and help maintain the aquifer while the meadows at different altitudes provide pasture at different periods of summer. Apparently, given the physical conditions, the value of land in alternative uses, and existing technology, transaction costs among many individual owners were sufficiently high to make communal ownership preferable.[9]

As circumstances change, owners of communal property do choose other arrangements. In New England, early settlers typically held some land individually and other land in a variety of communal arrangements. When the settlements flourished and land became more valuable, most of the communal land was converted to individual ownership (Field 1984). In Japan, owners of some forests managed as communal holdings have opted to sell to individual owners in response to increased land values (M. McKean 1986).

In the American West, the introduction of barbed wire encouraged the development of private property rights by lowering the cost of enclosing land and enforcing exclusivity (Anderson and Hill 1975, this volume). Indeed, there is evidence that the evolution of American institutions has reflected the costs and benefits of defining and enforcing various kinds of property rights (North 1990). This point is well illustrated by the development of mineral property rights in the American West (Libecap 1978; Umbeck 1977a).

Fisheries

Interesting evidence concerning communal ownership comes from the behavior of tribes along the Northwest coast of North America (Johnsen 1999). Prior to European contact in the late eighteenth century, these tribes had developed a range of property rights in salmon fisheries reflecting enforcement costs. Thus, the mouths of rivers too wide for effective policing by an individual or tribe remained open access. Upstream tributaries and smaller streams were controlled by a house or clan under communal arrangements that closely resembled a corporation, with exclusive control for the management of a stream delegated to a single leader who shared the catch with members of the group but retained residual claim to the catch. The smallest streams often were individually owned.

Johnsen (1999) finds evidence for the hypothesis that private ownership evolved to secure the gains from increased productivity as the Indians acquired and applied knowledge about salmon, including heritability and population dynamics. More clearly defined private property rights encouraged tribal leaders to invest more in acquiring stream-specific knowledge that would allow them to husband the salmon more profitably by selecting for larger-than-average fish size, larger population size, reduced variability, relative timing of run, and stream loyalty. Johnsen (1999) also notes that native tribes built extensive networks of stone traps, suggesting the separate, but not mutually exclusive, hypothesis that private property rights evolved to secure and encourage investment in more permanent traps.[10]

More modern examples of communal fishery ownership abound. In Japan, fishery cooperative associations often provide communal ownership of coastal marine resources (M. De Alessi 1999, 8). These organizations control use of the resources by their members and can exclude outsiders, including polluters and developers.

Elephants

Elephant populations, typically restricted to national parks, have been decreasing in some parts of Africa but increasing in others, including Zimbabwe (Sanera and Shaw 1996, 134–35). A major problem has been poaching, which often is abetted by villagers whose crops can be destroyed overnight by elephant herds who wander outside the park boundaries. In Zimbabwe, villagers have been given some communal property rights in local elephant herds. When an elephant is killed legally, villagers receive a share of the meat and of the income from the sale of the hide and ivory; they also receive a share of hunting fees. As a result, villagers now actively protect elephants from poachers and take other measures to maintain the herds, which have increased rapidly.

Shrimp

If an open access resource is sedentary or roams over a relatively small area, voluntary organizations sometimes can control use. For example, the Gulf Coast Shrimpers and Oystermens Association was established in the 1930s to maintain shrimping along the Mississippi coast (Johnson and Libecap 1982). The group pressured wholesalers to exclude those fishers who did not join the association or did not comply with its rules.

The association discouraged the harvest of smaller shrimp in several ways. It fixed the minimum price per pound of larger shrimp at more than twice the price of smaller shrimp and equal to or less than the market price in adjoining states. It also required captains fishing for smaller shrimp to carry a purchase contract from a buyer at the association price and induced workers at packing houses to refuse to peel shrimp smaller than the minimum size.

These and similar cooperative arrangements in other U.S. fisheries conserved the resource and increased fishers' income. The federal government, however, successfully prosecuted them under the Sherman Antitrust Act and restored open access. The predictable results ensued: depletion of the resource and lower incomes (Johnson and Libecap 1982).

Indeed, open access problems often arise because governments abrogate successful communal arrangements. For example, in many developing countries the nationalization of communally owned resources has resulted in open access regimes with all the usual consequences (Ostrom 1997). Such events are not new. When the Spanish Crown conquered the Philippines, it abrogated indigenous rules to control the reefs and established open access. Today, 90 percent of the reefs are either dead or dying, often the result of fishing with dynamite and cyanide (M. De Alessi 1997). Similarly, the U.S. government destroyed well-established rights among Indians for ownership of land and personal belongings (McChesney 1990).

GOVERNMENT REGULATION OF OPEN ACCESS

Government regulation means that some of the property rights in a resource are held by the state and managed by state employees. Because the welfare of regulators is not tied to the economic consequences of their decisions, except through bribes and the political process or direct effect on utility, they have less incentive to take the economic consequences into account. Government employees enjoy more discretionary authority, including increased opportunity to pursue their own goals, than their counterparts in private organizations. The cost-reward structure embedded in the regulatory institution then helps determine the level and kind of regulatory activity (Eckert 1973; Libecap 1981b).

Over some range, both regulators and regulated have common interests. Politicians and government bureaucrats have incentive to cater to pressure groups and expand their own activities, while those regulated have incentive to seek state action to limit entry and control competition at taxpayers' expense (Borcherding 1977; McChesney 1997). Once the rules are in place, however, regulatees have incentive to circumvent them. For example, restricting the length of fishing boats results in wider beams, limiting the number of nets leads to larger nets, and setting short fishing seasons or requiring boats to be in the harbor from sunset to sunrise leads to faster boats with larger holds and more freezer capacity (M. De Alessi 1998, 32). The regulation-induced investment in privately owned inputs is substantial; for example, a 1970 study of the northern U.S. lobster industry found that more than half of the capital (and labor) used was in response to regulation (Bell 1972, 156).

Government regulation often is introduced when competition for an open access resource is driving it toward exhaustion and individual or communal private property arrangements either are not economic or are blocked by government. Relative to open access, government regulation can save resources from commercial extinction, attenuate conflict, and keep incomes from falling as rapidly as they would otherwise. But relative to private property, it results in all the usual consequences, including lower quality and quantity of output, increased conflict as individuals compete for rents, higher production costs, and lower incomes.

Oysters

States in the U.S. have jurisdiction over coastal zones where oysters grow. State employees typically identify what they consider to be natural oyster beds, define them as open access, and specify the rules for harvesting (De Alessi 1975). Other areas suitable for growing oysters may be leased to private interests for their exclusive use; at least in Virginia, such leases are transferable.

Individuals who harvest the government-regulated oyster beds lack the incentive to maintain or improve them. In Maryland, the state government performs these functions by hiring watermen during the off-season to carry oyster shells to the beds, seed them, and so on. It also controls such things as the fishing season, minimum size of oysters, maximum daily catch, and harvesting techniques, which it limits to tonging and dredging. It further limits dredging to boats powered by sail except on certain days (Thursday at one time, Monday and Tuesday more recently), when the sailboats can be pushed by small motor boats normally carried on deck. Enforcement includes use of helicopters and boats to patrol the oyster beds and inspectors to check landings for size and quantity (De Alessi 1975; M. De Alessi 2000). Nevertheless, private oyster beds are healthier and better maintained and yield higher-quality oysters (Agnello and Donnelley 1975a, 1975b).

Earlier analysis suggests that the average productivity of labor is lower on government-regulated oyster grounds. Agnello and Donnelley (1975b) first evaluated this hypothesis using annual data from 1950 to 1969 for each of sixteen Atlantic and Gulf coastal states. In this series of tests, they regressed the average physical product of labor (total weight of oyster meat harvested divided by total labor force in the oyster industry in each state) against six combinations of independent variables reflecting type of ownership, amount of capital, opportunity wage, and incidence of oyster MSX disease. All test results showed that labor productivity was higher on privately owned oyster grounds. They then tested the same hypothesis over the 1945–1969 period using time-series data for Maryland and Virginia. Because these states are contiguous and similar in many relevant characteristics, the comparison implicitly controls for unaccounted variables that might affect behavior. The results again showed that private property is associated with higher labor productivity. Agnello and Donnelley estimated that a shift to private ownership would have increased the average income of watermen by about 50 percent (1975b, 533).

Agnello and Donnelley (1975a) provide independent support for other implications. Using Virginia and Maryland data from 1945 to 1970, they found that the quantity of oysters harvested earlier in the season was substantially larger under government-regulated open access. Earlier harvesting, given a stable demand, implies that early-season prices are lower and late-season prices higher than otherwise.[11] These results were observed in all sixteen Atlantic and Gulf coastal states as well as in a pair-wise comparison of two sets of contiguous states (Maryland and Virginia, Louisiana and Mississippi) with similar characteristics. Lower prices were also observed in a third test, in which the twenty-year average of ex vessel oyster prices for each of the sixteen coastal states was regressed on the proportion of each state's harvest coming from government-regulated open access grounds. If average output prices and average labor productivity are lower, then average income also is lower. This implication was supported by a comparison of revenue per laborer for the two pairs of similar, contiguous states as well as by the ordinary least-square regression of revenue per worker on the proportion of each state's harvest obtained from government-regulated open access grounds.

Under government regulation, those who control the rights to harvest a resource do not capture the gains from more effective management. Accordingly, they have incentive to adopt administrative processes and rules that serve bureaucratic and political purposes. For example, consider rules that constrain the harvest to cost-increasing gear, such as sailboats to dredge public oyster beds. The rule would be supported by some watermen because it maintains the value of their investment in sailboats, which are oyster-dredging-specific, and inhibits competition from more competent or better equipped watermen. It would also be supported by some bureaucrats within the agency and by outside interests, such as tourist-based enterprises, who benefit from the rule.

Alligators

Commercial hunting of alligators in Florida offers another example of politically-inspired regulatory restrictions. Each year, the Florida Fish and Wildlife Conservation Commission holds a lottery for alligator hunting permits (Farrington 1999). In 1999, the agency allocated 729 permits among 10,006 applicants at $250 each for Florida residents and $1,000 each for nonresidents. Permit holders could hunt alligators during September at thirty-two sites and kill up to five alligators each.[12] Hunters are prohibited from using guns. They must use close-range weapons such as harpoons, crossbows, gaffs, snatch hooks, and bang sticks, which fire a shotgun shell when banged against a solid object. Meanwhile, alligators have adapted to the hunt since it was begun in 1988 and have become harder to kill. The restrictions on gear have increased the cost of harvesting alligators, including the risk of injury to hunters, thereby reducing the value of the permit. Indeed, some hunters claim that their participation is no longer profitable as a commercial operation and depends on the thrill of the hunt.

If the commission were solely concerned with conserving alligators, it could increase the state's revenue by selling transferable permits to the highest bidders and allowing hunters to use suitable gear. Better, it could auction permanent, transferable rights to a percentage of an annually set catch and place no restriction on gear. Better yet, it could auction permanent, transferable rights to hunt alligators in specific sites and let the holders manage the harvest, a system used in some fisheries. Still better, it could sell the land, including the alligators, and let the owners manage the resource.

Halibut

Individual transferable quotas (ITQs) have been adopted successfully in many situations where a fishery was threatened with extinction (Scott 1996). Under the typical program, a regulatory agency grants commercial fishers transferable rights to harvest a specific percentage of an annually-set catch. The agency grants ITQs for a limited period (typically five to ten years) and retains the right to admit new entrants, change allocations when they come up for renewal, and control seasons, gear, and other matters. ITQs allow lower-cost fishers to specialize in the harvest, reduce overall investment in boats and gear, spread the catch over a longer period, reduce pressure on the fishery, and yield higher income. Although ITQs represent an improvement over open access, their establishment is complicated by the heterogeneity problem (e.g., fishers, gear) and political considerations. Moreover, regulatory agencies continue to exercise rights that, if transferred to private owners, would result in still higher quality and quantity of output, better conservation, and higher incomes.

When the Alaskan halibut fishery began to decline, regulators shortened the nine-month season. Fishers responded by improving boats and gear to catch halibut faster. This iterative process continued until the fishing season lasted two days (M. De Alessi 1998, 32). Fishers continued to harvest roughly the same amount of fish but now raced to the grounds, often in bad weather, with increased loss of life and gear. Moreover, they handled fish more roughly and froze most of them immediately, decreasing their quality and value. Eventually the International Pacific Halibut Commission (a joint U.S.-Canada agency) adopted transferable individual fishing quotas (IFQ).[13] Among other changes, it also lengthened the fishing season. Although the IFQs performed as expected, the commission's continued control of season, catch, gear, and so on precludes further gains.

British Columbia also introduced ITQs to salvage its halibut industry. Among other results, the number of vessels decreased by a third (from 435 to less than 300), which is as large a cut as the law allowed (Scott 1996, 56); regulation still favors overinvestment. As some indication of the role of heterogeneity when political forces are at work, before the introduction of ITQs the top 30 percent of the active vessels caught 80 percent of the fish. Afterward, the top 30 percent caught less than 80 percent, reflecting the bias against fishers with higher historical catches in the formula for allocating ITQs (Scott 1996, 56). Again, the rules prevent additional gains.

New Zealand Fisheries

Threatened with the disappearance of some of its fisheries, in 1983 New Zealand passed a Fisheries Act that led to the introduction of ITQs (Arnason 1996). For the paua (abalone) fishery, government officials assigned each fisher a tradable percentage of the annually set catch (M. De Alessi 1998).[14] When the program succeeded, regulators responded to political pressure and granted access to outsiders. The result was a drop in the value of ITQs and a consequent reduction in the incentive to conserve the fishery. Since then, the ITQs have been strengthened, but uncertainty about the regulators' future behavior reduces their value as well as the incentive to maintain the resource, including investment in the habitat.

Currently, all fishery management in New Zealand is based on ITQs, which are permanent, perfectly divisible, and fully transferable (Arnason 1996, 132ff). The consensus is that the system has led to better physical management of the fish stock, reduced investment in jointly-used inputs, and increased profitability, all of which are reflected in higher prices of ITQs (Arnason 1996, 135).

The shift toward ITQs is consistent with the observation that institutions established to control wildlife broadly reflect the cost and benefits of alternative property arrangements and respond to changed circumstances in ways consistent with wealth maximization (Lueck 1989; 1991). Changes in government control, however, typically reflect political compromises including bureaucratic reluctance to relinquish power. Relative to comparable changes in the private sector, they occur more slowly and less completely in response to larger shocks (De Alessi 1980). For example, the outright assignment of a fishery to private interests, say the fishers holding ITQs, would yield a more stable solution and greater gains.

Endangered Species

In many cases, government agencies seek to regulate open access resources by expropriating (taking without compensation) private property rights in related resources (Yandle 1995). This strategy, even disregarding issues of fairness, often is counterproductive. For example, the U.S. Endangered Species Act of 1973 restricts the use of land inhabited by an endangered species but does not require either payment from those individuals who benefit or compensation to those individuals who are harmed (Lueck and Yoder 1997). The failure to ensure reciprocity of costs by making those who benefited (e.g., environmental activists) bear the costs provides them with the incentive to demand more rights for conservation purposes, while the failure to compensate those harmed provides them with the incentive to resist and make the habitat less attractive to actual and potentially endangered species.

The Endangered Species Act is an excellent example of rent seeking. If a group believes that a particular habitat ought to be preserved for the use of an endangered species, the group could lease or buy the habitat — and some do. As a coercive alternative, the group could lobby the state to lease or buy the habitat at taxpayers' expense, or pass a law requiring present owners to preserve it at their own expense. Which option the group chooses depends in part upon the system of property rights, including the propensity of the executive, legislative, and judicial branches to reassign (take) private property rights without compensation.

Imposing limits on individual rights to the use, income, and transferability of resources inhibits their flow to higher-valued uses and, by making the rights less secure, reduces the incentive to maintain and improve a resource. To the extent that these constraints reflect political considerations and/or ignorance of how markets work, the evidence discussed below indicates that they result in reduced investment, smaller output, and lower incomes.

GOVERNMENT REGULATION OF EXCHANGE

Rights to the use or income of some resources may be exclusive but not transferable. Voluntary renting and leasing are prevalent usufruct arrangements that facilitate the bundling of resource rights and their flow to higher-valued uses.[15] In some communal systems, use of certain rights may be assigned to specific individuals but, by communal agreement, may not be transferable to others or convertible into individual owner-ship. Governments may also constrain or prohibit the transferability of some rights. If usufruct arrangements are coerced, rights do not flow to higher-valued uses and their owners are unable to capitalize the future consequences of their decisions into current transfer prices. Among other implications, output is smaller, investment to maintain and de-velop the resource is smaller and shorter-lived, and incomes are lower.

Land — Mexico

Under Mexico's Agrarian Reform Program, twenty or more native-born peasants could form an association (*ejido*) and request outright grant of affectable land within a twenty-mile radius of the village in which they lived (De Vany 1977); affectable land was privately owned land in ex-cess of 200 hectares of unirrigated cropland or 100 hectares of irrigated land. If the request was granted, typically an ejido committee distrib-uted the land among the members of the group (*ejidatarios*) who ac-quired the right to use the land but could not legally sell it, lease it, encumber it, or otherwise alienate rights to it. These restrictions se-verely limited the ability and incentive to borrow and invest. The ejida-tarios had to work the land as full-time employment and could lose it if they did not work it for two consecutive years.

The evidence shows that ejidatarios, relative to private owners of comparable land, made smaller investments in irrigation and other capi-tal improvements, used more labor, and were more likely to grow crops with a shorter gestation period that yielded a smaller income. In partic-ular, the average and marginal products of labor in the ejido were lower, and those of capital were higher, than in the private sector. These find-ings are similar to those for open access discussed earlier (Bottomley 1963; Agnello and Donnelley 1975a, 1975b).

A separate study (De Vany and Sanchez 1979) explained why the ejido led to increased family size. Larger families give a more secure right to the land because they are politically more difficult to displace and because children can work the land to maintain usufruct rights when a parent is ill or seeks employment elsewhere. Moreover, because the ejido restricts the ability to borrow and the incentive to invest, it is more labor-intensive, making children attractive as a relatively inexpen-sive source of labor. Test results show that the ejido system is associated with a higher incidence of marriages, a higher birth rate, a larger num-ber of children ages one through four, and larger families. Thus, the ejido system encourages population growth as well as less productive uses of land, labor, and capital.

Land — U.S. Indian Reservations

Land tenure rules appear to be a major cause of low per capita income on the Navajo reservation. Libecap and Johnson (1981) examined the practice within the Navajo reservation of assigning usufruct rights in grazing land to tribal members on the basis of prior appropriation and continued use, with boundaries established by informal agreement among adjacent herders. A holder may fence land only with the unanimous consent of all neighbors and may sublease it only to family members. As usufruct rights shift from original holders or cover smaller areas, boundaries become more ill-defined. Moreover, enforcement of boundaries is weak; for example, some trespass cases have lingered in the courts for over ten years.

Under this arrangement, land is grazed more intensively than if rights were better defined, more exclusive, and more easily transferable. Thus, even though grazing permits and other rules were used to prevent overgrazing, the number of animal units on the Navajo reservation was about twice the estimated carrying capacity of the range. Moreover, cross-section data for fifteen districts indicated that the intensity of grazing varied inversely with the size of the herd. This was due to the increased vagueness of land boundaries as the size of the usufruct area decreased, and to the reluctance of the tribe to enforce grazing regulation on smaller herders.

Fencing should occur more frequently as the size of the customary use area increases (fencing and transaction costs per acre fenced are smaller) and the value of the land rises (benefits are greater). The evidence supports this hypothesis: The average permit size, a proxy for land area, for fenced land was greater than the average permit size for the entire reservation in forty-two of fifty-five cases examined. Moreover, range land with higher rainfall, a proxy for more productive and, therefore, more valuable land, was fenced more frequently.

Libecap and Johnson (1980, 1981) also examined the grazing patterns for nineteen Southwestern tribes. The tribes had different structures of usufruct rights, some using informal systems of prior appropriation that depended on overstocking to define and enforce claims. Libecap and Johnson found that these informal systems encouraged overgrazing and range deterioration relative to formal permit systems.

On a larger scale, Anderson and Lueck (1992) used a sample of thirty-nine Indian reservations to observe the agricultural productivity of three major land tenure arrangements: fee simple, individual trust, and tribal trust.[16] Under fee simple, the land is privately owned by individuals (some Indians, some not) who are free to use it, lease it, or sell it. Under individual trust, the land is held by individual Indians but their rights to alienate it, lease it, and encumber it are subject to trust constraints administered by the Bureau of Indian Affairs (BIA). For example, BIA must approve the terms of each lease, a process that can take up to six months. The trust also limits use of land as loan collateral to the assignment of income, thereby ruling out a claim against the deed, raising the cost of capital, and reducing the ability to invest in capital improvements. Moreover, government-imposed inheritance rules fractionalize land. Under the third ownership arrangement, tribal trust, the land is managed by the tribe subject to trust constraints administered by BIA. Thus, it is subject to political and bureaucratic maneuvering at both the tribal and BIA levels.

Test results show that, relative to fee simple land, the value of agricultural output per acre is 30 to 40 percent lower on individual-trust land and 85 to 90 percent lower on tribal-trust land. As Anderson and Lueck (1992) point out, similar considerations presumably apply to coal, oil, minerals, timber, and other resources also held under trust arrangements.

Labor

Batchelder and Sanchez (n.d.) examined the Spanish Crown's use of the *encomienda* during the colonization of the Americas in the sixteenth century. Among other things, encomiendas assigned their holders (*encomienderos*) the right to exact labor services from the Indians under their jurisdiction; the Indians were not slaves in that they could not be sold, mortgaged, or borrowed. Further, encomiendas could not be transferred and could be relocated only with consent of the Crown. During the initial period of conquest, encomiendas were temporary. Thereafter, they varied from three years in the Caribbean to perpetuity (or so the holders believed) in Peru. The average length was two lives, that of the encomiendero plus that of one descendant. Encomienderos were not responsible for the state of their encomiendas at the time they surrendered them. Encomiendas that became vacant were reassigned by the local Crown representative.

Under these conditions, encomienderos had incentive to convert usufruct rights in Indian labor into privately owned rights in other resources by working Indians harder and spending less on their maintenance (especially as they approached the end of their indenture) than if they had been slaves. This indeed appears to have been the case: the various Indian populations decreased rapidly, apparently much faster than if slavery had been adopted.[17] Moreover, other things being the same, a shorter encomienda grant period provided the incentive to use up the Indian population at a faster rate. Although Batchelder and Sanchez do not address this hypothesis, their data indicate that the native population in the Caribbean, the region with the shortest-lived encomiendas, fared worst: effectively it was wiped out. In other regions, enough Indians survived until the Spanish Crown alleviated conditions.

The Spanish Crown followed the same procedure in the course of each conquest, initially granting encomiendas and then gradually softening their impact by restricting the encomienderos' rights to the use of Indian populations. Batchelder and Sanchez suggest that the Spanish Crown, which received one-fifth of all the wealth accumulated, used the encomienda not only to reward the conquistadores but also to convert the human capital in the newly conquered colonies into other forms of wealth that it could control and defend more cheaply.

GOVERNMENT OWNERSHIP

Government employees with authority to manage government-owned resources, like government regulators, have incentive to manage them in response to political pressures, bribes, and their personal preferences. Theory and a large, growing body of empirical evidence indicate that government officials typically adopt and implement policies designed to increase their own welfare, especially by enhancing their power and wealth (R. McKean 1964; De Alessi 1980; McChesney 1997).[18] The handling of western lands by U.S. government officials provides an excellent example.

Land

The U.S. federal government owns vast tracts of land administered by various agencies.[19] The Interior Department's Bureau of Land Management (BLM) controls 23 percent of the total area of the eleven far western states (including nearly 70 percent of Nevada and over 40 percent of Utah). The BLM and its predecessor, the General Land Office (GLO), provide textbook illustrations of bureaucratic and private rent seeking (Libecap 1981b).

Beginning in the 1780s, the U.S. Congress passed legislation providing for the sale of all western land to private owners and established the GLO to do it. By the 1860s, legislation reflected the GLO employees' growing efforts to advance their own power and incomes. The GLO rejected arguments that the 160-acre allotments provided by the Homestead Act of 1862 were too small for grazing and denied ranchers' prior appropriation claims to land in excess of 160 acres. The agency successfully derailed attempts in Congress to sell range land in large tracts suitable for grazing and to recognize the informal holdings of ranchers.

The fences that ranchers had built on federal land were torn down, reestablishing an open access regime.

The GLO thwarted the intent of Congress to dispose of all western land and prevented the allocation of land to its most productive uses. The resulting system of open access or insecure tenure encouraged overgrazing and soil deterioration from wind and water erosion. The system also encouraged limited investment in fences, wells, and other improvements, lower livestock quality, and higher animal mortality rates. Outputs and incomes were smaller.

The behavior of GLO employees reflected the incentives established by the agency's enabling legislation. Among other things, GLO's budget was partly determined by total claims filed while the salaries of its officials at land offices were supplemented (up to a limit of $3,000 per year) by fees and commissions for handling claims (Libecap 1981b, 9, 10). Thus, budgets, salaries, and tenure in office favored small allotments.

In 1934, the Taylor Grazing Act changed the emphasis of federal policy from selling land to administering it (Libecap 1981b, 3). The Interior Department, having obtained jurisdiction over the range, established the Grazing Service and, after 1946, the BLM to control the land and grant grazing permits to cattle ranchers. The BLM, like any other government agency, has incentive to expand its budget, staff, and power by expanding its administrative role. Thus, it has incentive to control stocking levels, pasture use, harvest rates, permit transfers, and so on. It also has incentive to enact rules to achieve its own objectives, pursuing goals like maximum sustained yields, and to accommodate political pressures.

Political pressures come from both environmentalists and ranchers. Cattle ranchers obtain grazing permits at below-market prices. These permits, however, are insecure, subject to bureaucratic rules that prevent ranchers from capturing the full gains available under private ownership. Accordingly, ranchers have incentive to overgraze and underinvest. Environmental groups pursue their own goals and priorities.

Overall, BLM practices enhance its survival and the welfare of its employees, but they inhibit the allocation of the land it manages to more productive uses. At the bureau's discretion, land use may be limited to grazing rather than more valuable activities, stocking levels may not reflect local conditions, and grazing fees may redistribute wealth from taxpayers to ranchers and other special interest groups.

Arctic Explorations

The contrast between government and private arctic explorations further illustrates the effect of weakening the tie between the welfare of individuals and the consequences of their decisions. Karpoff (2001) examined thirty-five government and fifty-six private expeditions of geographic discovery undertaken between 1818 and 1909 to Greenland, the North Pole, and Canada. He found that most major discoveries were made by private expeditions and most tragedies were suffered by government expeditions. Government-funded arctic treks also performed poorly by other measures. On average, 9 percent of their crew members died relative to 6 percent for private expeditions. When they employed ships, government expeditions on average used 1.6 ships and lost a third whereas private expeditions used 1.2 ships and lost one-fifth. When expeditions lasted longer than one year, 47 percent of government crew members were disabled by scurvy relative to 13 percent for private expeditions.

Karpoff's tests indicate that these results are due to differences in the way explorations were organized rather than to other variables, such as exploratory objectives, country of origin, number of previous expeditions on which the leader served, or the decade in which the expeditions took place. The key difference was that persons initiating and implementing government expeditions led them only 27 percent of the time relative to 78 percent for private expeditions. Predictably, organizers of government expeditions were less responsive to new information about clothing, diet, shelter, modes of arctic travel, organizational structure, and optimal group size.

CONCLUSION

Private property rights provide workable rules for solving a society's increasingly complex economic problems (Epstein 1995). The evidence in this chapter suggests that individual or communal private property rights promote investment in maintaining and improving resources, development of new institutions and technologies, and faster, fuller response to changes in circumstances. Outputs and incomes are larger than under alternative arrangements.

Relative to open access, government regulation can establish more secure property rights, increasing the incentive to maintain or improve a resource. For example, transferable fishing quotas in New Zealand (M. De Alessi 1998; Arnason 1996) and Pacific Northwest fisheries (M. De Alessi 1998; Scott 1996) gave fishermen more secure rights to a portion of the catch, encouraging investment in the fishery and disinvestment in regulation-induced private capital used jointly in production. Fishers' incomes increased.

Regulatory constraints and uncertainty about regulators' behavior, however, limit the gains. Although there is little doubt that regulation prevented oysters in the Chesapeake from being depleted under open access, shifting from a regulatory to a private ownership regime would increase the bundle of property rights held by fishers and make those rights more secure, increasing incomes by as much as 50 percent (Agnello and Donnelley 1975a, 1975b).

Communal ownership provides property rights that are more secure than those under government regulation because owners make joint decisions suitable to their own circumstances without the additional layer of bureaucracy. Communal ownership of land (Ostrom 1990; Field 1984) and beavers (Demsetz 1967) provided a clear improvement over open access and, as in the case of shrimp (Johnson and Libecap 1982) and land (Ostrom 1990, 1997), over government regulation.

Individual ownership offers the most secure property rights and ties the welfare of decision makers most closely to the economic consequences of their choices. Relative to government-controlled open access, for example, private ownership of land yields higher investment in irrigation and other capital improvements and encourages the cultivation of more profitable crops with a longer gestation period (Bottomley 1963; Anderson and Hill 1975). Similarly, individual ownership of oyster beds (Agnello and Donnelley 1975a, 1975b; De Alessi 1975) yields more investment in maintaining and improving the resource.

Relative to government-enforced usufruct rights, individual ownership of land yields higher investments in various capital improvements (including irrigation and fencing), soil maintenance (less intensive grazing), and longer-lived crops (De Vany 1977; Libecap and Johnson 1980, 1981). In the case of labor, government-granted encomiendas occasioned the decimation of native people as encomienderos sought to convert usufruct rights in native labor into privately owned rights in other resources (Batchelder and Sanchez, n.d.).

Insecure private property rights inhibit conservation. They reduce the ability to invest in capital improvements by increasing the cost of borrowing (property whose title is insecure does not make good collateral). They also reduce the incentive to invest (including the postponement of harvest) by limiting the right to capture the resulting gains. Evidence from U.S. Indian reservations (Anderson and Lueck 1992) and Thailand (Feder and Onchan 1987) supports the implication that insecure title to land, including restrictions on transferability, reduces agricultural productivity by limiting farmers' ability and incentive to borrow.[20]

Increased uncertainty regarding the enforcement of private property rights reduces their security with predictable consequences. When Canadian Indians proved unable to exclude white trappers from their communal hunting grounds, they joined the hunt and helped wipe out beavers as a commercial resource (Demsetz 1967). When the New Zealand government responded to the success of the ITQs by yielding to political pressure and admitting outsiders, investment in the fisheries fell, the fisheries deteriorated, and the values of ITQs dropped (M. De Alessi 1998).

In short, there is much empirical evidence that movement from open access through either communal or some form of government-regulated ownership to full private ownership is potentially beneficial. Where and when such movements occur, measurable economic benefits are found along many margins. Moreover, recent technological innovations have substantially lowered the costs of defining, establishing, enforcing, and exchanging private property rights in many open access resources, including some animal species that migrate over broad areas. Thus, the issue seems to be when and how to move from other forms of ownership to private property.

ENDNOTES

The present chapter reflects earlier work by the author (1980, 1988, 1998a, 1998b).

1. For an introduction to the property rights literature, see Alchian (1961, 1965b, 1967), Demsetz (1964, 1966, 1967), De Alessi (1969, 1980, 1983), Furubotn and Pejovich (1972), Williamson (1985), Joskow (1988), Barzel (1989), Eggertsson (1990), Rutherford (1994), Furubotn and Richter (1997), and McChesney (1997).

2. Comparisons using economic efficiency as a benchmark rest on the particular (often implicit) welfare criteria chosen by the analyst and the unwarranted assumption that values can be measured objectively by an outside observer (De Alessi 1992).

3. Gordon (1954) and Scott (1955) provided the first rigorous analysis of an open access regime.

4. If the market rate of interest exceeds the private rate of return from conserving a resource, private owners may also choose to deplete the resource (Clark 1973).

5. Within 100 years of landing in New Zealand, Polynesians eliminated all eleven species of moa (ostrich-like flightless birds) by hunting as well as by destroying the habitat (Holdaway and Jacomb 2000).

6. Similarly, heterogeneous leases and lack of information about their values inhibit voluntary unitization of oil fields lying under land owned by different individuals who lease drilling rights to different oil companies (Libecap, this volume).

7. The perception of Indians as ideal environmentalists is a myth (Baden, Stroup, and Thurman 1981; Krech 1999). Indians behaved like any other group subject to the same constraints.

8. Uncertainty favors some communal arrangements as a way to share risk.

9. Eggertsson (this volume) describes comparable arrangements in Iceland.

10. Potlatching (reciprocal giving) served to deflect potential attackers, resolve ownership disputes, and change leadership (Johnsen 1999).

11. As expected, private owners postpone harvest to later in the season when prices are higher.

12. The alligator hunting season is in September, when females nest while males roam and are more likely to be killed. In 1999, hides sold for $16/foot and meat for $6–$8/pound (Farrington 1999).

13. Eggertsson (this volume) describes comparable arrangements in Iceland.

14. Faced with a comparable situation (falling fish stocks, overinvestment in gear), in 1986 New Zealand introduced ten-year ITQs for all commercial fin fish species (M. De Alessi 1998, 41). Arnason (1996) offers a detailed discussion of the use and success of ITQs in Australia, Greenland, Iceland, Netherlands, New Zealand, and Norway.

15. Leasing is limited by the cost of protecting large specific investments by one party from opportunistic behavior by the other parties to the contract.

16. Some federal land is used for monuments and administrative purposes, but the amount is small and can be ignored for present purposes (Anderson and Lueck 1992, 429).

17. The Indians obviously would have been better off if they had been able to retain their liberty.

18. Such behavior is independent of the ideology of the political party in power (Meltzer 1991). Haddock (1997b) argues that the major reason the U.S. government has been better than most is federalism; he attributes the latter's erosion to rent seeking and the public-interest fallacy.

19. Federal landholdings include 83 percent of Nevada, 64 percent of Utah, 62 percent of Idaho, 52 percent of Oregon, 49 percent of Wyoming, 47 percent of Arizona, and 45 percent of California (Lueck and Yoder 1997).

20. Besley (1995, 1998) further explores the effect of property rights on investment.

PART III

INTRODUCTION

In explaining the advantages of private property as scarcity increases, the first chapters of this book focus on the overall benefits and costs of having property rights specified. They did not examine the processes by which rational, maximizing individuals actually define and enforce rights to property. But property does not just happen. Rather, different opportunities for gain, relative to the cost of obtaining the gains, determine how and when individuals undertake to define and enforce rights. The next two parts of this volume discuss how property comes to be. As the various chapters detail, there is no one optimal recipe for the evolution of property rights, any more than there is a single property rights regime superior for all societies in all places (Eggertsson, this volume).

In a series of articles and books, Terry Anderson and P. J. Hill have investigated carefully the process by which rights evolve, work that they summarize and extend in chapter 5. The key to evolution of property rights in the situations they study (land, water, and other resources in the West) is the emergence of entrepreneurs who perceive personal gain in taking assets out of open access. (The term "entrepreneur" would also apply to those who reorganize already-existing private rights to make them more productive, as Barzel discusses in chapter 2 concerning entrepreneurial organization of firms.) In other words, Adam Smith's "invisible hand" guides the wealth-increasing emergence of property. In doing well for themselves, property rights entrepreneurs also enhance the total value of society's goods.

By introducing the entrepreneur to the model of property rights evolution, Anderson and Hill must address a series of issues about how the entrepreneurial role in the property rights process works. Thus, they appropriately draw on modern Austrian-school scholarship (e.g., Kirzner 1973, 1985) about entrepreneurship. The entrepreneur gains by appreciating first the existence of profit opportunities, in particular perceiving changes in relative resource values as underlying conditions change. One such condition of great importance is the growth of technology, which alters the cost of defining and enforcing rights. Technology also speeds the discovery and dissemination of information, which is key for the entrepreneur's ability to perceive the benefits of defining and enforcing property rights.

Understanding the entrepreneurial role in the property rights process requires examination of collective-action problems. While a single entrepreneur may suffice for discovery of a profitable opportunity, establishment of new, enforceable rights typically requires cooperation with others. Not only may scale economies exist for defining rights, but one person will often find it difficult to claim and defend rights to all resources worth privatizing. Consequently, as Anderson and Hill explain, private associations were common in the evolution of private property in the American West. Voluntary association came to resemble government in some situations.

Although the role of property rights is sometimes most easily grasped when rights are analyzed in a historical context, the applications of property rights economics are general. Thus, contemporary applications of the lessons Anderson and Hill draw in their focus on America's nineteenth-century West are not hard to find. Consider one current issue, telemarketing. Why do so many people who regard telemarketing as an invasion of privacy nonetheless put up with it? Because, like cattle owners early in the history of the West, they have no cost-effective way to exclude unwanted invasions. Installation of a telephone has made the home an open access resource, one whose borders can be crossed easily by anyone who dials the home telephone number. Homeowners could of course disconnect the phone, but that would be inappropriately costly; many desired calls then could not be received.

The technological solution to western ranchers' trespass problem was the development of barbed wire. It furnished an inexpensive way to keep unwanted trespassers out, while allowing ranchers to admit cattle and personnel that were welcome. An analogous means of excluding unwanted telephone calls has not been technologically available heretofore. And even if it were, collective action would probably be necessary. Some collective entity would have to force telemarketers to identify themselves, such that technological devices to exclude telemarketers could distinguish between unwanted and wanted calls. Until both problems of technology and collective action can be resolved, houses with telephones remain an open access commons for telemarketers, with the predictable consequences.

CONTRACTING FOR PROPERTY RIGHTS

Collective action issues introduce the fundamental concepts of contract and force in the evolution of property rights, as discussed in the remaining two chapters of part III. In chapter 6, Gary Libecap explores the advantages and limits of contracting among competing entrepreneurial claimants. As rational maximizers of their own welfare, contestants are not so much interested in social gain from optimal rights structures as they are in what they will gain personally. Because no one can have as much of a resource as he desires, how to distribute property rights becomes critical to solving the open access problem.

With a simple but powerful economic model, Libecap establishes the conditions when contracts among competing claimants can be concluded and maintained. The key variables capture the benefits and the costs of defining property rights, usefully dividing these two larger categories into their components. The physical nature of the resource bargained over, the size of achievable gains from privatizing, and the transaction costs of achieving agreement are determinants of whether contractual solutions are possible. Each of these factors can be broken down further. Transaction costs themselves, for example, depend on the number and heterogeneity of the bargaining parties, the information each has, and the ultimate distribution of wealth the contract produces.

In several historical and contemporary situations, Libecap shows the model's power in predicting whether contracting for property rights will work. The resource in question may be land in the Brazilian Amazon or oil in the United States and Canada, but differences in the factors Libecap identifies explain observed differences in the spectrum of property rights that result. The different examples also establish an important caveat, Libecap concludes. While the case for property rights rests on the allocative gains available from taking assets out of open access, it is the distributional consequences to the property rights entrepreneur, not social welfare, that drives the contractual process. Smith's invisible hand may produce results superior to leaving resources in open access, but not optimal in any social-welfare sense. And in some instances, Libecap cautions, contestants' preoccupation with distributional issues may prevent establishment of private rights altogether.

MIGHT AND RIGHTS

An alternative to contracting for private property, David Haddock notes in chapter 7, is a rule of might makes rights. The transaction costs of bargaining to a contract are, by definition, avoided. When the strongest claimant takes and holds by force, bargaining costs are replaced by the costs of threatening and perhaps using force.[1] Not only might the cost of establishing and holding rights by force be lower (or more effective at a given level of cost), but the subsequent tensions between allocation and distribution noted by Libecap will not arise. The successful (mightiest) entrepreneur has an incentive to maximize the total value of the resource, since he receives all the gains.

Haddock's points about establishing rights through violence apply in other historical settings (e.g., McChesney [1986], discussed in chapter

9); lessons learned from history apply currently as well. White (1987, 1) describes the fierce competition in Bangkok among those who collect dead bodies in the streets, where police and many others will not collect bodies "for fear of ghosts." Collectors are paid a commission per body (some of them by charitable organizations or foundations with millions of dollars in assets). The analogy is admittedly macabre, but analytically, bodies are another open access resource, a type of fishery, to use the example employed in part II. Ownership (and so the right to be paid) typically is resolved by violence, as body collectors use knives and iron bars in struggles with rivals trying to recover the same resource. Might makes rights in modern Thailand, just as it did in the situations Haddock describes a century earlier.

Haddock's chapter underscores two important points about the use of force in establishing and enforcing property rights. First, because force is costly to use, the mere threat of force often allows the mightiest claimant to establish and maintain rights. Hence, even in a world of might makes rights, violence is not necessarily common. This helps explain why sovereign nations, for example American tribes and the U.S. government did not always battle over territory, but often bargained via treaties. Second, might makes rights does not imply that the mightiest will take all. As Haddock explains, as the mightier party takes more of a resource (say land), the marginal value of that land diminishes. On the other side, for the weaker party left with less and less land, the marginal value increases. Continuing the marginal analysis, as the mightier devotes more resources to flexing his muscle, the opportunity cost of those resources increases. And for the weaker with less land, the marginal cost of defending against a taking falls. These combined impacts in the might makes rights world drive the distribution of property rights toward an equilibrium short of one side having all. The experience of Indian-European relations fits this conclusion. Initially, it was more likely that Indians would give up their land without a fight or without much bargaining. However, as Europeans acquired more land, resistance from Indians increased.

As with the other chapters in part III, Haddock establishes these points — some of them counterintuitive — by positing a simple static model and applying the model to a specific historical situation. He then extends the basic model by introducing more dynamic factors (e.g., capital growth over time and multiplicity of parties claiming a resource) to permit analysis of even more cases. Haddock closes by observing how the might-makes-rights model applies to government, often the mightiest claimant. His chapter concluding part III furnishes a bridge into part IV, in which the role of government in the property rights process is considered in further detail.

ENDNOTE

1. Establishment of rights by force entails the opportunity cost of foregone production, as Haddock notes. Time and resources spent fighting detract from the production of new wealth. This is true also of contracting for property rights: the time and resources spent negotiating reduce wealth production.

CHAPTER FIVE

THE EVOLUTION OF PROPERTY RIGHTS

Terry L. Anderson and Peter J. Hill

In general, students of microeconomics study the allocation of inputs and outputs taking the institutional framework as exogenous. In this context, economists can make good predictions about how well various allocation mechanisms will work. In particular, with property rights well defined and enforced, markets tend to promote gains from trade and encourage efficient resource allocation. As De Alessi points out in chapter 4, there is abundant evidence that well-defined and enforced property rights encourage efficient resource use. On the other hand, with property rights not well specified and access open to all, as Eggertsson explains, resource values are dissipated as people compete to capture the economic rents associated with productive assets.

Accepting the exogeneity of property rights simplifies the analysis of economic activity, but it ignores the question of how property rights evolve. Clearly, the way in which property rights are assigned, enforced, and transferred affects the allocation of resources and, hence, the amount and distribution of output. Who controls what resources? Who receives the benefits and bears the costs of various actions? How clearly are property rights specified? How are they exchanged, and how are these exchanges enforced? The answers to these questions influence the consequences of market processes at any given time.

Harold Demsetz (1967) helped launch economists on a path "Toward a Theory of Property Rights" that explains how property rights evolve and also makes them endogenous to economic models. As he hypothesized, "property rights arise when it becomes economic for those affected by externalities to internalize benefits and costs" (334). Svetozar Pejovich (1972, 310, 316) elaborated on this point saying that "the creation and specification of property rights over scarce resource is endogenously determined" by such factors as "technological innovations and the opening of new markets, changes in relative factor scarcities, and the behavior of the state."

Other economists, especially economic historians, followed Demsetz's lead by trying to make property rights endogenous to their models. Douglass C. North's pioneering work with Robert Thomas (1973) on *The Rise of the Western World* and his similar work with Lance Davis

(1971) on *Institutional Change and American Economic Growth* were among the first extensive surveys of how property rights contribute to economic growth.

In the context of the American West, we expanded on Demsetz's reasoning and asked how property rights to land, livestock, and water evolved (Anderson and Hill 1975). We pointed out that the decision to undertake definition and enforcement activity depends on the marginal benefits and marginal costs of that activity. On the benefit side, for example, adding another strand of barbed wire to a fence may increase the likelihood of capturing the value of ownership. But eventually the marginal value of, say the sixth or the tenth strand, declines. And on the cost side, the opportunity cost of inputs used in property rights activity ultimately rises. Hence, like any economic endeavor, it is worth investing in property rights activity only as long as the marginal benefits exceed the marginal costs. We explore here the factors that affect the level of these benefits and costs.

This static analysis posits that property rights evolve in response to marginal benefits and marginal costs, but it ignores the dynamic role that property rights entrepreneurs play in changing ownership institutions. The process of institutional change is driven by individuals who recognize that they can gain personally by changing the rules governing who has access to resources, who captures returns therefrom, and who bears the costs of use. Joseph Schumpeter saw entrepreneurs as creating value by introducing new goods and new methods of production, by opening new markets, by discovering new sources of supply, and by reorganizing the production process (Schumpeter 1934, 66). The property rights approach adds another category of entrepreneurial action, that of devising new property rights arrangements.

Because the nineteenth-century American West had such a different set of resource constraints and required new technologies to exploit those resources, the region and era offered many opportunities for property rights entrepreneurs. In the remainder of this chapter, we expand on the theory of property rights in the context of the western frontier. We consider the alternative paths available to entrepreneurs who could create property rights or redistribute existing rights from one individual or group to another. Which path was chosen made a big difference as to whether resources were allocated more efficiently or whether resources were consumed in a rent-seeking process. Though we consider the evolution of property rights in the context of the American West, the implications of this theory are relevant for a host of other times, regions, and activities, as we discuss in the conclusion.

PROPERTY RIGHTS ENTREPRENEURSHIP

The fundamental fact of scarcity means that people will compete with one another for use of an asset. In the absence of scarcity, everyone can have all they want of a resource without precluding others from having all they want. As more people claim a resource, however, scarcity sets in so that one person's use precludes another's. When the first radio stations broadcast, frequencies were not scarce, but as more stations entered, use of one frequency could interfere with another. When the first satellites were launched, orbital paths were not scarce, but with more now circling the earth, paths can cross. In other words, when people enter any new frontier, abundance prevails, but sufficient entry creates scarcity, and scarcity creates economic rents.

With open access, scarcity rents are up for grabs, and people will compete to capture them. The tragedy of the commons occurs if this competition results in dissipation of the rents. For example, under open access, radio broadcasts will interfere with one another; satellites will collide; fishing stocks will be depleted; and grass will be overgrazed.

Thought not necessarily referred to as an open access resource problem, incomplete contracts that allow opportunistic behavior on the part of the contracting parties are also examples of rents being left up for grabs. That is to say, when contractual terms cannot be easily measured and monitored, the parties will compete for the rents or gains from trade inherent in the exchange. For example, suppose that party A contracts to pay wages to party B in exchange for B's labor services. If party B can shirk on his side of the contract by devoting less effort to the team project than party A expected, party B will be better off at the expense of party A. Some of the rents associated with the contract will be left up for grabs because the terms of the contract cannot be costlessly measured and monitored and, therefore, the parties will have an incentive to dissipate those rents through shirking or other opportunistic behavior.[1]

Preventing rent-dissipating competition among potential users of scarce resources when rights are not defined requires rules to limit access, rules we call property rights. These rules specify who has access to, use of, and claim on the value of an asset. By allowing some people access to valuable resources and excluding others, rents are preserved and captured by those with access.

Such restrictions on access, at first glance, might appear to be like a monopolist restricting output, but the two are quite different. In the case of the monopolist, rents are generated by restricting output for which the marginal value to the consumer exceeds the marginal cost of production. This creates an inefficiency that the monopolist is willing to

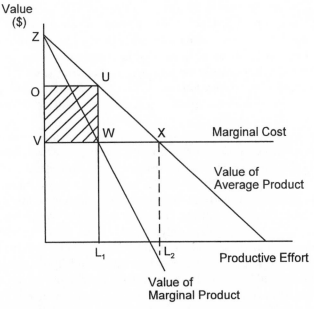

Figure 5.1 Rent Dissipation in the Common Pool (Source: Anderson and Hill (1983), 440)

tolerate because he can raise the price and redistribute to himself some of the net value accruing to the consumer (called consumer surplus).

In the case of restricting access to a resource, efficiency (rather than inefficiency) is stimulated. To understand the potential efficiency gains from restricting entry, consider figure 5.1 where productive effort with respect to a resource, say a piece of land, is measured on the horizontal axis and the value of that effort is measured on the vertical axis.[2] A single individual facing no competition from other entrants to the commons would compare the value of his additional effort (value of marginal product $=$ VMP) with the marginal cost (MC) of his time and would employ effort up to L_1 where $VMP = MC$. At this level of effort, the difference between the total value of the output, shown by the area under VMP, and the total cost, shown by the area under MC, are maximized, making the rents equal to VZW.[3] In contrast to the monopoly case where returns to the monopolist are obtained by restricting output and producing less than the optimal output, restricting access to a resource and applying the optimal labor effort to the land creates new value from using the land efficiently.

If there is open access to the land, however, the rents, VZW, will attract other entrants willing to apply additional effort in order to capture a share of the rents. Obviously, additional effort drives down the value of the marginal product, but new entrants will ignore their impact on previous laborers, worrying only about the average return to effort (*VAP*).[4] Entry will occur because *VAP* is greater than *MC*, and in the limit no rents will remain.[5] Furthermore, in the process, inefficiency will result because of an overcommitment of effort where the value of output created by additional effort is less than the marginal cost of that effort.

The potential for dissipation that occurs with open access creates an incentive to invest in devising rules that govern access to, use of, and claims on the value of an asset. These rules may be general, applying to a wide range of people. For example, ownership of land means that all others in the society without permission of the owner are precluded from using the attributes of the land over which the owner has control. Or the rules may be specific, applying only to one other individual or a small group of individuals. For example, two individuals may engage in a contract governing use of privately owned land by the two individuals.[6] The general property right excludes all others in the society from the attributes in question, while the specific contract determines when and how the two parties to the contract can use the attributes. To the extent that general and specific property rights are well defined, enforced, and transferable, owners who capture the rents will have an incentive to seek efficient uses, and the inefficiency associated with open access will be replaced with gains from trade.

Like any other good, property rights must be produced by entrepreneurs who recognize the potential gains from defining and enforcing them and are willing to devote resources to their formation. Herein lies the evolution of property rights. Property rights entrepreneurs recognize values unforeseen by others and capture those values by engaging in definition, enforcement, and exchange activities that allow them to capture rents associated with ownership.

These entrepreneurial gains can result from at least three sources, specific contracting, general contracting, and redistribution each of which requires changing the rules governing who has access to the asset and its value.

Contracting for Specific Property Rights

To the extent that some margins of asset use are imperfectly defined and enforced, there are potential gains for the property rights entrepreneur who can devise contractual arrangements that better measure and monitor asset use and the distribution of gains therefrom. Suppose that an entrepreneur observes a share crop arrangement between a landowner and tenant wherein the tenant is shirking on the share contract by with-holding some labor effort. The property rights entrepreneur has at least three choices. He can buy the land from the landowner and farm it himself; he can buy the land and devise a better contract with the ten-ant; or he can become a tenant himself and offer the landowner a con-tact that better measures and monitors labor inputs and, thus, increases total output. If he purchases the land, he becomes what Alchian and Demsetz (1972) call the residual claimant, meaning that he has a claim on any increase in value that results from better management of the land. Obviously if he farms his land himself, he has no incentive to shirk.

If the entrepreneur decides to contract with others either as a land-owner or tenant, as a property rights entrepreneur he must measure and monitor the contribution of other input owners. To the extent that all margins of input contributions are imperfectly measured and monitored, some of the rents will be up for grabs with the potential for input owners to engage in what Klein, Crawford, and Alchian (1978) call post-contractual opportunism. Owners of specialized assets can attempt to withhold services from the entrepreneur in an effort to capture a greater share of the rents he has recognized. For example, an owner of a machine crucial to producing a product could act opportunistically by claiming the machine is broken and thus disrupting the production pro-cess unless he is offered additional compensation for speedy repair. To avoid this post-contractual opportunism, the entrepreneur must either purchase the specialized input outright or be able to monitor its contri-bution so as to identify opportunistic behavior by the owner.

In developing firms that substitute centralized decisions for market contracts, entrepreneurs are reorganizing ownership claims to assets and in the process creating new, specific property rights between the contracting parties. Oliver Williamson (1985) refers to this reorganiza-tion as the problem of finding "efficient boundaries." In this search, the entrepreneur must balance the rising transaction costs from organizing inputs under one residual claimant with the declining marginal benefits from eliminating market exchanges characterized by incomplete con-tracts (see Cheung 1983). In effect, the search for efficient boundaries is a search for the optimal scale of production and the optimal contractual form as described by Barzel (this volume).[7]

Defining and Enforcing General Property Rights

Contracting for specific property rights requires that rights to a portion of the attributes of the property exist in the first place, in which case the entrepreneur's task is to get control of the existing attributes so that he can capture value from new ones. For some resources, there may be no existing rights recognized by law or the other players, so that the entrepreneur can gain by defining and enforcing property rights to an entirely new set of attributes. In other words, contracting for property rights requires that there be reasonably well-defined and enforced property rights. When there are not, the property rights entrepreneur gains from creating them and capturing their value. By defining and enforcing property rights, the entrepreneur can eliminate the dissipation of value associated with the tragedy of the commons. Referring again to figure 5.1, property rights entrepreneurs who can successfully restrict entry will capture the difference between the maximum value of the rents, VZW, and the value of resources that must be spent in the definition and enforcement process.

For the entrepreneur who recognizes the potential gain from restricting access, it is worthwhile to define and enforce general property rights against a wide range of other potential users. In this case, the property rights entrepreneur must be able to enforce his property right against others either by calling on their self-restraint or by threatening the use of force. Self-restraint can be sufficient in relatively small, homogeneous groups where customs and culture govern behavior. Where self-restraint is insufficient, the property rights entrepreneur must threaten force, either on his own or through collective action with others, against would-be entrants to the property in question. At this stage the distinction between specific property rights enforced by voluntary collective action (e.g., a club) and general property rights enforced by involuntary collective action (a government) becomes blurred. Both restrict access, but government is a contract writ large wherein the government is taken to have a legal monopoly on coercion (Buchanan 1975). This legal monopoly that can restrict access to the commons opens up another avenue for institutional entrepreneurs.

Redistributing Property Rights

The entrepreneurial search for rents does not mean that property rights entrepreneurship will always create net gains. As Baumol (1990, 894) points out:

> [T]here are a variety of roles among which the entrepreneur's efforts can be reallocated, and some of those roles do not follow the constructive and innovative script that is conventionally attributed to that person. Indeed, at times, the entrepreneur may even lead a parasitical existence that is actually damaging to the economy. How the entrepreneur acts at a given time and place

depends heavily on the rules of the game—the reward structure in the economy—that happen to prevail.

In other words, the pursuit of profits by entrepreneurs is not always a positive-sum game; by channeling their efforts into redistributing existing property rights or acting opportunistically in contractual agreements, they can play negative-sum games. Collective action to define and enforce property rights depends upon coercion to exclude, but coercion has the potential to be used for very different ends—it can be used to take (see Epstein, this volume; Fischel, this volume). If it is used to make property rights less secure, profitable exchanges become less likely, and resources are prevented from moving to higher valued uses.

Property rights entrepreneurship aimed at redistributing existing property rights and the rents associated therewith is negative sum because it consumes resources on the one side in trying to take the rights and on the other in trying to defend them. Whether the redistribution is effected through private actions (theft) or through governmental action, the result is the same; resources are consumed in the process but no new wealth is created.

One winner in this rent-seeking process is the politician who can sell his ability to change the rules of the game and thereby extract some of the rents for himself (see McChesney 1997). For example, a politician can threaten to take away private rents through regulation or taxation. The threat need not be carried out as long the owner can be induced to purchase forbearance so that his ownership claims are not taken by the political entrepreneur. As with rent seeking, rent extraction is a negative-sum game in which politicians compete with each other for the power to threaten.

DETERMINANTS OF EVOLVING PROPERTY RIGHTS

Like all other entrepreneurship, property rights entrepreneurship is switched on by the perception of heretofore unseen profit opportunities (see Kirzner 1973). For such perceptions to be useful, the entrepreneur must establish control over the factors of production or resources that he thinks will be more valuable in other uses. Thus the entrepreneur is first and foremost a contractual innovator who must respond to exogenous changes and find ways to capture the rents associated with the new perception.

Acting on entrepreneurial perceptions regarding property rights means that the entrepreneur sees the marginal benefits and marginal costs of definition and enforcement activity differently from others. What the entrepreneur perceives will depend on several exogenous constraints.

Assuming that property rights entrepreneurs are driven by the quest for economic rents associated with different sets of property rights, we ask: What are the exogenous factors that change the potential rents available to entrepreneurs?

Changing Relative Prices

Changes in the value of a resource obviously influence willingness to invest in definition and enforcement activity. As long as an incremental unit of land in the West was worth little, property rights entrepreneurs would not put effort into restricting entry. As land values rose, however, the return on restricting entry increased and so did definition and enforcement activities. Initially, settlers simply announced their claims through newspapers and signs. Over time their efforts became more organized as they formed associations or clubs which were specific contractual arrangements with other settlers on the frontier to resolve internal conflicts over property rights.[8]

Changing prices worked in the direction of reduced definition and enforcement activity with the decline in the value of horses toward the end of World War I. As horse power was replaced with tractor power on farms and ranches, people reduced their investment in definition and enforcement activity by turning their unbranded horses loose on the public domain.

Rising values for recreational opportunities stimulated by rising incomes induced property rights entrepreneurs to find innovative ways to capture rents from environmental amenities as early as the nineteenth century. Specific contracting for privately owned land created dude ranches for easterners wanting to experience the wild West (see Anderson and Leal 1997). General contracting in the form of legislation created what is now Yellowstone National Park (see Anderson and Hill 1994), allowing railroads to capture rents from the amenities by carrying passengers to the park and providing services within it. The Northern Pacific Railroad in particular lobbied Congress to establish the park because the various homestead acts would have destroyed the very amenities that the railroad wanted to preserve for its passengers. That was because the homestead acts required farming, logging, or mining to establish private property rights to land. As one Northern Pacific official put it:

> We do not want to see the Falls of the Yellowstone driving the looms of a cotton factory, or the great geysers boiling pork for some gigantic packing-house, but in all the native majesty and grandeur in which they appear today,

without, as yet, a single trace of that adornment which is desecration, that improvement which is equivalent to ruin, or that utilization which means utter destruction. (quoted in Runte 1990, 23)

Moreover, the various homestead acts limited the size of holdings (initially to 160 acres, but ultimately to 640 acres) to a size that was far less than necessary to maintain the aggregate value of Yellowstone's amenities.

Thus the officials of the Northern Pacific who recognized the amenity value of the Yellowstone region had to find an alternative mechanism for defining and enforcing a right to the amenity attributes of the area. That mechanism was to establish a national park for which the railroad had a monopoly in passenger delivery, internal transportation, lodging, and meal service. The railroad financed early expeditions to the park and made sure that reports to Congress included the suggestion that the area be set aside as a government preserve. The railroad hired Nathaniel P. Langford to lobby for the legislation, and paid to have a collection of William Jackson's photographs placed on the desk of every member of Congress and to have Thomas Moran's watercolors distributed to especially influential senators and representatives (Bartlett 1974, 208).[9] The lobbying efforts were successful; the Forty-Second Congress passed legislation establishing the park in February 1872, and on March 1, 1872, President Ulysses S. Grant signed it into law. The lobbying efforts of the Northern Pacific and other railroads with an interest in the region were not driven by "altruism or environmental concern; rather the lines promoted tourism in their quest for greater profits" (Runte 1979, 91).

To capture the value of abundant grass on the northern Great Plains, entrepreneurs had to develop specific contractual arrangements for moving cattle from Texas. The person who could assure Texas cattle owners of his ability to move the animals north and market them once they had been fattened on abundant grass would be able to turn a handsome profit. But this required contracting with many cattle owners and with the cow hands needed on the long cattle drives. Economies of scale dictated that the optimal size herd for a cattle drive was approximately 2,500 head (Wellman [1939] 1967, 111). Because this herd size was larger than the herd on a typical cattle ranch, cattle had to be pooled from several owners. If the rancher were to hire the services of a drover, he would have to measure and monitor the drover's performance between the Texas ranch, the rich grasslands, and railhead where they were eventually shipped to market.

Once on the trail, the potential for post-contractual opportunism was great. The rancher could not easily distinguish legitimate losses due to sickness or rustlers from theft by the drover. To overcome this problem, drovers became residual claimants, purchasing the cattle in Texas and selling them on their own account after they had been fattened.

Labor contracts for the cow hands also offered potential for post-contractual opportunism and, thus, an opportunity for entrepreneurs who could solve the problem. Once on the trail and far from alternative labor sources, cowboys could act opportunistically by threatening to leave part the drive unless they received more compensation. To avoid this potential opportunistic behavior, trail bosses contracted with their crew for the entire duration of the journey. Wages were not paid until the drive was completed and the herd was delivered to its final destination. Both the firm driving cattle north and the specialized labor agreement represented contractual innovations by institutional entrepreneurs in response to new profit opportunities.

The increased value of inputs and outputs as the West developed made using coercive power to gain control over resources more profitable. Early irrigation projects were privately financed, but western farmers saw substantial gain from having others pay some of the costs of development. The *Reclamation Act of 1902* brought the national government into the dam building and water delivery business and encouraged massive rent seeking by those who could capture subsidized water. Although the original legislation stipulated fees sufficient to repay the costs of irrigation projects, interest charges were omitted from the law. That resulted in enormous interest subsidies to those water users who obtained an allotment. Some subsidies ran as high as 95 percent of original cost (Wahl 1989, Table 2.1). Also, agricultural interests successfully and repeatedly lobbied Congress to defer payments (Wahl 1989, 28–33).

A similar story of rent seeking associated with rising resource values can be told in the case of Indian tribes and their land. Numerous reservations were created in the West and Indians began making the transition to sedentary agriculture on these allocations. They were creating rights based on those that had existed in their nomadic culture and, despite the cultural and technological adjustments necessary, were moving to relatively efficient property rights (Anderson 1995). As the reservation lands became more valuable, however, outsiders began to covet their value. The *General Allotment Act of 1887* (the Dawes Act) facilitated this by dividing the reservation into 160-acre parcels, establishing a system of bureaucratic control for much of the land that was to be held in trusteeship, and opening so-called surplus reservation land (what was left after the 160-acre parcels were allotted to Indians) to homesteading. In this case, the coercive power of government was used to obstruct the evolution of Indian property rights and to transfer existing rights to homesteaders.

The Technology of Property Rights Formation

Technology affects the formation of property rights in two ways; first, directly through the technology of definition and enforcement, and second, indirectly through the technology of production. The former is illustrated by the invention of barbed wire which lowered the cost of defining and enforcing private rights to land and livestock. On the Great Plains, the absence of trees and the large expanses required to maintain livestock meant that enclosure was expensive. Initially cattlemen used human fences in the form of cowboys living in line camps, patrolling the boundaries between customary ranges, keeping the cattle on their respective sides of the boundary, and guarding against rustling. The invention of barbed wire in the 1860s with over 360 patents issued, however, lowered the cost of definition and enforcement by substituting fencing capital for labor. As a result of this substitution, over 80 million pounds of barbed wire were sold by 1880 (Webb 1931, 309), enough to fence 500,000 miles with four strands of wire.

The indirect effect of production technology is seen with roundups on the open ranges of the western frontier. Before barbed wire, cattle had to be rounded up twice each year, once in the spring for branding calves and again in the fall for marketing. To avoid costly duplication of roundup efforts on the open range, cattlemen formed associations that determined who would be involved and set dates for roundups. Once formed, cattlemen's associations became effective organizations for specific contracting to settle disputed claims among members and for general contracting to exclude outsiders. After a cattlemen's association declared a region fully stocked, it would not let newcomers participate in the common roundup. By limiting access to the roundup, cattlemen were able to control cattle numbers and to prevent overgrazing:

> If an interloper tried to crowd his stock onto someone else's range, local ranchers could refuse to allow him the privileges of belonging to the roundup district. In 1885, for instance, John H. Conrad, a Fort Benton area rancher, moved 6,000 cattle on the rangeland east of the Musselshell River which was claimed by the Niobrara Cattle Company. A fall meeting of the Miles City stockmen condemned Conrad for this violation of range law and warned him that they would not handle his stock or cooperate with him in any way. He got the message and withdrew his herd. (Malone and Roeder 1976, 123–24)

Production technology can also reduce the extent of definition and enforcement for private rights, as illustrated by what Robert Higgs (1982) called "technologically induced legal regress" in the Washington state salmon fishery. Prior to the arrival of Europeans, Pacific Northwest Indians had well established claims to smaller streams and to strategic fishing locations such as shoals and cascades on large rivers (e.g., the Columbia River) through which salmon were naturally channeled. Predictably, these ownership claims encouraged owners to sustain fish populations by letting the larger salmon pass upstream to enhance the gene pool (see Johnsen 1999). When the Europeans arrived, however, they ignored the Indian claims and progressively moved nets to the mouths of the rivers, taking all the spawning fish. The resulting tragedy of the commons ultimately forced the state of Washington to ban commercial fishing on the rivers, forcing fishers to chase salmon in open ocean waters.

The Nature of Collective Action

In addition to the individual's benefits and costs of defining and enforcing property rights, entrepreneurial efforts are influenced by the benefits and costs of collective action (see Haddock 1997a). By banding together, individuals can take advantage of scale economies in defending property rights and can encompass more potential spillover effects. Hence cattlemen's associations were more effective than individuals acting alone on the western frontier, and producer's associations are more effective at lobbying today in Washington, D.C. On the cost side of the equation, however, transaction costs will rise with the size of the collective. It will be more difficult to organize a larger group, to exclude free riders, and to monitor agents acting on behalf of the collective. This combination means that larger collective regimes will be better able to exclude potential claimants from open access resources, but will face higher costs of collective action. Successful entrepreneurial action to create or redistribute property rights therefore requires a search for the optimal size and type of collective action (see Olson 1965, Williamson 1985).

EXTENT OF SPILLOVERS

The optimal size of the collective unit used to restrict entry to the commons will vary with the geographic size of the commons. In turn, this size will vary depending on the nature of the resource and the production function. The optimal collective organization for restricting entry to a small fishing lake will be smaller than the collective for restricting entry to the ocean within 200 miles of the shore which will be smaller yet than the collective for restricting entry to the entire open ocean. A small mining camp could effectively limit entry to ore bodies that were relatively confined though not necessarily well known, but an Indian tribe was insufficient to restrict entry to the buffalo herds that migrated across large territories.[10] Similarly, as noted earlier, a cattlemen's association consisting of a dozen or so members could control access to an unfenced grazing territory by not allowing nonmembers to participate in collective roundups. But the same association had to rely on territorial or state governments to enforce brand registration because cattle were traded across larger territories than they grazed. Therefore, *ceteris paribus*, the larger the geographic territory over which potential spillovers occur, the larger the optimal size of the collective unit.

Likewise, if rent dissipation occurs because of competing claims between only two individuals, a specific contract that better measures and monitors the activities of those individuals is an appropriate institutional response. If more individuals are involved, the entrepreneur must include all of these competing claimants in his new contract, thus raising the costs of measuring and monitoring contractual terms. In this context, we can think of the optimal size of the firm as noted by Coase (1937), Cheung (1983), and Barzel (this volume).

DIFFERENTIAL ADVANTAGE IN THE USE OF FORCE

The main economic reason for collective action is to define and enforce the boundaries of a territory from which outsiders are excluded. Preventing entry requires that members of the collective threaten or even exert force against trespassers and that they do the same against one another to prevent free riding in the production of force. Obviously, a larger collective encompasses more people and therefore has fewer outsiders to worry about, but it also runs into diminishing returns in the production of force.

Another determining factor in the optimal size of the collective is the extent to which there are scale economies in the production of force. If every individual were equal in his ability to exclude others from his domain and if there were no scale economies in the production of force, there would less need to band together to define and enforce territorial rights. As John Umbeck (1981) has pointed out, this was the case in the California mining camps where the six-gun minimized scale economies and equalized the ability of individuals to threaten or use force.

When either scale economies in the use of force exist or the geographic area of the spillover is big, large-scale collectives are likely to evolve. Such large-scale collectives can create differentials in the power of coercion, thus leading to efforts to capture the collective for purposes of redistribution. A case in point was the rise of standing armies which

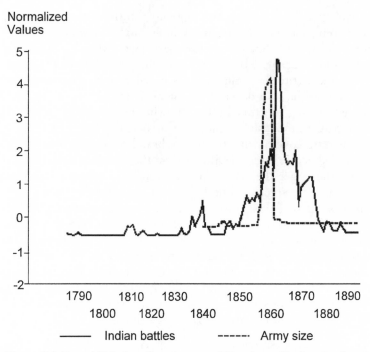

Figure 5.2 Size of U.S. Standing Army and Number of Indian Battles (Reprinted by permission of Westview Press, a member of Perseus Books, L.L.C.. L. Barrington, *The Other Side of the Frontier*, 1999, 220)

increased the potential gains from using force to redistribute valuable assets (see Anderson and McChesney 1994). Early in U.S. history, local militia were the collective force unit. With the Civil War, the creation of a standing army altered the calculus of negotiating versus fighting by lowering the cost to individuals of calling on force to take land from Indians and by creating a special interest group with an incentive to engage in warfare. Not surprisingly, as figure 5.2 shows, the rise of the standing army was positively correlated to the number of battles.

AGENCY COSTS

As the benefits increase with the size of the collective unit, either because the larger unit can encompass a larger geographic territory and include more spillover effects or because it can capture scale economies in the use of force, those benefits are offset by higher agency costs. Agency costs arise because a governance structure requires agents to act for the collective members. In this principal-agent relationship, it is always costly to ensure that agents act on behalf of the principals and do not use the coercive power of the collective to redistribute property rights and capture rents for themselves.[11] If principals (citizens) cannot effectively constrain their agents (politicians and bureaucrats), then those agents can act as political entrepreneurs for their own benefit and alter institutions to capture or redistribute rents. In some cases, those rents come from gaining control over resources, but in others the threat of removing part of the bundle of property rights through taxation or regulation forces the owner to pay to prevent the extraction (McChesney 1997).

By the very nature of principal-agent relationships, agents are not residual claimants to the rents they help create.[12] In the collective process, the main purpose of the principal-agent relationship is to hire enforcement agents who restrict access to the commons, thereby generating rents for the collective. The problem then becomes one of monitoring the agent.

One reason monitoring costs increase with the size of the collective is that each member captures a smaller share of any rents that are created in a large collective and, therefore, has less incentive to monitor the agent. It becomes preferable to act as a free rider on monitoring by others. In a smaller group, however, each member captures a larger share of the rents not dissipated and, therefore, has more incentive to monitor agents and discourage rent dissipation. With the degree of residual claimancy inversely related to group size, *ceteris paribus*, we can expect less efficient institutions and more rent seeking as group size increases.

It follows that, if the rules governing the formation of property rights are designed by agents with little claim to the rents created, agents will have less incentive to search for efficient rules. The larger the group involved, the less the return to any one individual and the more likely that the rents from privatization will be dissipated by the process. To the extent that property rights evolve within smaller groups, individuals involved in the definition and enforcement process have more incentive to guard against rent dissipation. On the other hand, if property institutions emanate from larger collective groups, there is a greater likelihood that rent dissipation will occur.

Efforts to establish property rights to land on the American frontier in the nineteenth century offer an excellent example of these alternatives. Ignoring the costs of establishing property rights and considering only production costs and revenues, the time path of rents from a specific resource such as a section of land is depicted by the S-shaped curve in figure 5.3. Initially rents from a piece of land will be negative because the land is so far from market that the value of output falls short of

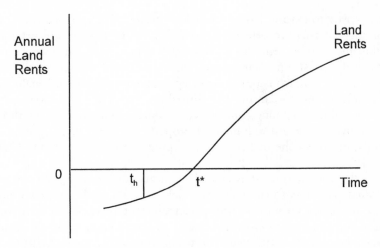

Figure 5.3 Time Path of Land Rents (Source: Anderson and Hill (1990), 180)

costs. However, if the market moves closer to the land (or if transportation costs decline), rents will rise and can ultimately become positive.[13] With private property rights well defined and enforced, the optimal time to bring land into production is when the annual rents turn positive, shown as t^* in figure 5.3.

If property rights are up for grabs, however, there will be tendency for competing potential owners to race to the property and settle prematurely, meaning at a time when the land rents are negative. In this case, rational calculus will induce rent dissipation with settlement occurring when the discounted value of negative rents is just equal to the discounted value of positive rents, shown in figure 5.3 at t_h. Note that the area of rents between t_h and t^* almost always will be smaller than the area of positive rents after t^* because the negative rents occur sooner than the positive ones and, therefore, are discounted less.

For the first seventy-five years of U.S. land policy, the national government minimized dissipation in the process of establishing property rights. With involvement from local settlers and with a small national government, agents had an incentive to minimize rent dissipation in the process of establishing property rights. Initially they attempted to sell land at competitive auctions as a way of raising money for the treasury (Anderson and Hill 1990; Anderson 1987). In these auctions buyers were willing to pay a positive price as soon as the discounted value of the auction price (usually a minimum set by government) was equal to the discounted value of expected positive land rents.[14] In this case the land was not put into production until the rents turned positive at t^*.

In fact, the auction system still had a tendency to attract squatters who settled before the auction and either were able to have their first possession rights officially recognized under the Preemption Act or to prevent others from competing in the auction. To prevent competition, squatters agreed to have "one individual in each township to bid off the whole of the land that they or any of their body may wish to buy, and the balance of their company to be armed with their rifles and muskets before the land office door, and shoot, instantly, any man that may bid for any land that they want" (quoted in Hibbard 1939, 199).[15] To the extent that the squatters had heterogeneous perceptions that correctly anticipated the future value of the land, they would have captured some of the rents. Moreover, they may have provided a service to the national government by helping maintain the U.S. claim to the land against Indians and other governments (see Allen 1991).

To help enforce their claims and reduce rent dissipation, squatters formed voluntary land claims associations (see Anderson and Hill 1983). These associations were formed before land was officially offered for sale and were created to register land claims and to enforce the title of members. One resident of Fort Dodge, Iowa, recalled that the local association advertised "that any one attempting to Settle on any Lands Claimed by any Member of the Club Would be dealt With by the Club and his life Would not be Safe in the Community" (quoted in Swierenga 1968, 17). The clubs chose their own rules for registering, adjudicating, and enforcing claims. Because members were residual claimants to rents not dissipated in the definition and enforcement process, the methods they chose required far less expenditure of resources than the subsequent homestead acts. They did not require occupancy of the land to establish and maintain claims and, when they did require investments to show that the land was occupied, those investments were in keeping with productive investments that would have been made anyway. In Johnson County, Iowa, for example, association members were not required to invest resources until they found it to be profitable. In other counties, the clubs required a minimal amount of labor effort every month to prove ownership (Bogue 1963, 51).

With time the national government's policy shifted away from land sales and preemption by squatters to homesteading under which settlers could only establish ownership by occupying the land and making various investments such as building cabins, digging irrigation ditches, or planting trees. All of these became part of the dissipation process. In the context of figure 5.3, because settlers could not claim the land without producing from it, they brought land into production long before t^*. In the race for property rights won by settling and producing, homesteaders were willing to go to the frontier as soon as the discounted value of the negative rents was equal to the discounted value of the positive rents at t_h. Since this decision was made under great uncertainty, it is not surprising that life on the frontier was arduous, and some optimistically misestimated t_h. Failure rates were high in many places, as evidenced by the fact that 80 percent of all original entries were relinquished in the Benchland District north of central Montana's Musselshell River (Fletcher 1960, 146). Another estimate from Montana indicates that of the 70,000 to 80,000 people who homesteaded in the state between 1909 and 1918, "by 1922 about 60,000 or 80 percent had starved out or given up" (Fulton 1982, 66).

The extent to which rents were dissipated in the process of privatizing the public domain in the nineteenth century reflects the importance of both the group and geographic size of the collective unit. As the group size increased with population growth, each citizen had a smaller stake in the outcome of the privatization process. For a given aggregate return from land sales, the pro rata share for citizens was declining, giving each person less reason to monitor whether land sale revenues were maximized.

There are two reasons that rent dissipation will be greater as group and geographic size increases. As the geographic size of the collective unit becomes larger, it will be more costly to prevent squatting. In the case of U.S. expansion to the west, initially squatters were removed by military force, but as the frontier expanded, preventing and expelling squatters was virtually impossible. Second, the larger the geographic size, the greater the cost of exit and, hence, the greater the potential coercive power. This is known as the Tiebout effect (1956). Competition limits the monopoly power of regimes because people and resources can more easily migrate between regimes if coercive power is used inappropriately; in other words, they can vote with their feet. The larger the regime, however, the greater the monopoly power and the greater the potential for agents to inaccurately reflect citizen preferences.

Other factors besides group size, geographic size, and competition from other regimes can help mitigate agency costs. First, group homogeneity can lower the costs of monitoring agents. In relatively stable societies with numerous repeat dealings, it may be cheaper to rely on evolved norms and moral constraints rather than formal laws enforced by official government agencies. The more culturally homogeneous a group, the more norms and customs can resolve conflicts. Such social and cultural norms develop over time as efficiency-enhancing norms replace efficiency-reducing ones, and as those who disagree with norms move to other groups where the norms better suit their preferences.[16] Through common language, understandings, and objectives cultural homogeneity lowers the transaction costs of specifying property rights and negotiating over their use.[17]

Robert Ellickson (1989) provides convincing evidence that norms devised by homogeneous local whaling communities in the eighteenth and nineteenth centuries tended to minimize the community members' transaction costs and deadweight costs associated with the potential tragedy of the commons. If cooperation were not possible, Ellickson hypothesizes that dissipation rather than wealth maximization would be the norm. For example, "[I]f ship A had a wounded or dead whale on a line, ship B would be entitled to attach a stronger line and pull the whale away" (Ellickson 1989, 87). But such norms would have been absurd in a community of residual claimants. Instead the "fast-fish loose-fish" rule applied in the Greenland fishery where right whales were slower and less aggressive. This rule established that "a claimant owned a whale, dead or alive, as long as the whale was fastened by line or otherwise to the claimant's boat or ship" (Ellickson 1989, 89). Alternatively, where larger, more vigorous sperm whales were the primary prey, the "iron-holds-the-whale" rule applied giving ownership to the first boat to place a harpoon in the whale and remain in pursuit of it. Ellickson (1989, 95) concludes that "members of close-knit groups define their low level property rights so as to maximize their joint objective wealth."

Maintenance of cultural homogeneity requires excluding outsiders from collective action and helps explain limits on transferability of property rights. Usufruct rights can be rationalized in this context. These rights give the holder the right to use a resource and to capture the returns from it, but do not allow transferability to members outside the collective. In a society that depends upon shared values and repeated interactions as the mechanism for enforcement, it would be damaging to allow a member of that society to transfer rights at will. Such a transfer could allow new people to become members of the group without appropriate social conditioning and could break down social consensus regarding the just distribution of rights.[18]

Water law in the West provides an example. As water rights evolved from remote mining camps and irrigation projects, the rules often followed custom and seldom had much formal codification. And even when states did begin to codify rights, local water users created informal structures to determine allocation. For example, if a junior water rights appropriator does not have sufficient water in a drought year, informal mechanisms among irrigators can reallocate water without formal contracting. Moreover, when formal legal disputes do occur, standing is limited to those who actually hold water rights on the stream in question. By not allowing the transfer of rights outside traditional uses such as irrigation, laws may thwart allocation to higher-valued uses such as maintaining environmental amenities, but they help maintain the cultural homogeneity that can reduce transaction costs.

When norms and customs are insufficient, formal rules offer a way to constrain agents. These rules include constitutions, statutes, common law, and so on. Such rules serve to constrain the coercive power of the political agents so that rents will not be dissipated through redistribution of property rights. The takings clause in the U.S. Constitution is an obvious example (see Epstein, this volume; Fischel, this volume). If such rules are binding, the options of property rights entrepreneurs are confined to reorganizing or defining property rights; if they are not, negative-sum redistributive action can result.

And the Beat Goes On

The examples used in this chapter were drawn mainly from the American frontier, but the evolution of property rights continues as property rights entrepreneurs discover new frontiers. After private rights were claimed to most of the West, millions of acres of land were placed in the federal estate. Saying that the land is owned by the government, however, begs the important property rights questions: Who has access to the lands? What can the people with access rights do? Who captures the rents from the land? Until these questions are answered, the rents remain up for grabs in a political process that allocates them (see Nelson 1995). Initially livestock owners and miners obtained control of these lands through legislation such as the *Mining Act of 1872* or the *Taylor Grazing Act of 1934*. More recently, however, environmental and recreational interests have lobbied for and gotten increased constraints on these commodity activities and reserved more lands for wilderness uses (see Nelson 1995).

The evolution of property rights is not a historical artifact, but an ongoing process. An excellent example of property rights evolution today is occurring with respect to wildlife. As Lueck (1989) points out, the wide-ranging nature of wildlife combined with diffuse landownership patterns can make the establishment of property rights prohibitively costly. However, as the value of wildlife increases, it becomes worthwhile for landowners to incur additional transaction costs to limit access and define property rights to the wildlife. Hence, in Africa, private and communal landowners are contracting with hunters and safari companies to capture the value of wildlife and its habitat (see Anderson 1998). In the American West, landowners and hunters are working to change state laws to allow landowners to charge access fees and thereby obtain addition revenue from the wildlife asset (see Leal and Grewell 1999).

Similar evolutionary pressures are changing property rights to water. As the prior appropriation doctrine evolved in the mining camps and irrigation districts of the West, diversion was required to perfect and maintain a water right, thus use-it-or-lose-it. Under this constraint, individuals could not maintain their claim if the water was left to flow downstream; if left in the stream, it became susceptible to appropriation by downstream users. However, in recent times, as the demand for instream flows to dilute pollution and provide aesthetic and recreational values has increased, environmental groups have been pushing for changes in western water laws to allow willing buyer-willing seller exchanges to meet these demands (see Anderson and Snyder 1997; Landry 1998).

Just as barbed wire transformed property rights on the frontier, technological changes are impacting the definition and enforcement of property rights today (see Anderson and Hill 2001). Satellites can track whales and other wild animals that have been equipped with transmitters (Christiansen and Gothberg 2001). Fisheries can be monitored by satellites to be sure that only those with rights to the fishery are there and to measure and monitor catch (Huppert and Knapp 2001). Pollution plumes in the air and water can be tracked with satellites, tracers can be introduced into smoke stacks to determine sources of pollution, and contaminant source analysis generally can be used to strengthen property rights to clean air, water, and land (Michalak 2001). Remote cameras can be connected to the web for continuous monitoring of assets, and lasers can instantaneously detect trespassers. In short, technology changes the costs of definition and enforcement, and entrepreneurs are reacting accordingly.

In a world with zero transaction costs, the evolution of property rights would not merit attention because they would develop instantaneously, and in a static world no new property rights would be necessary. In a dynamic world with positive transaction costs, however, understanding the evolutionary process whereby property rights are defined and enforced is important as understanding how they are reallocated to improve efficiency. Because property rights determine who captures rents from assets, entrepreneurs will respond to changing relative prices and new technologies by investing in altering property rights. This investment may reduce the rent dissipation associated with open access, or it may redistribute existing rents through the political process. Our knowledge of the evolution of property rights makes it clear that an institutional environment that encourages the former and discourages the latter leads to economic growth. Our knowledge of how societies create this institutional environment, however, is still in its development stages.

ENDNOTES

1. For a thorough discussion of opportunistic behavior see Furubotn and Richter (1997, 121–77).

2. This analysis was first presented in Anderson and Hill (1983).

3. It can be proven that the area VZW is identical to $VOUW$. See Anderson and Hill (1983).

4. For an excellent discussion of how this process proceeds, see Cheung (1970).

5. At L_2 the value of the total output (the area under VMP) will just equal the total cost (the area under MC). Put another way, inefficiency, shown by the area WXY, results from too much labor effort being applied to the parcel of land; for units between L_1 and L_2, VMP is less than MC.

6. Furubotn and Richter (1997) distinguish between absolute and relative property rights. Their category of absolute property corresponds to what we term general contracting, and their category of relative property rights corresponds to what we term specific contracting.

7. This balancing is part of what Demsetz discusses in chapter 11. The entrepreneur must balance potential external costs and benefits from his actions with the costs of contracting to eliminate those external costs and benefits.

8. These efforts at specific contracting for property rights blur with general contracting (and hence government) to the extent that the clubs threatened force against potential entrants, thus generally protecting the rights claimed by club members. For a more complete discussion of land claims associations, see Anderson and Hill (1983).

9. Both Jackson and Moran accompanied early expeditions to the area in their roles as photographer and landscape artist, respectively, with the Northern Pacific paying Moran's expenses.

10. For a discussion of the potential impact of the tragedy of the commons caused by the interface between tribal and buffalo territories, see Martin and Szuter (1999). Also see Lueck (1989) for a discussion of how the optimal size of production units affects transaction costs.

11. The principal-agent problem increases in a firm as the contract encompasses more input owners. It is in this context that the original principal-agent concept was formulated (Jensen and Meckling 1976).

12. See Alchian and Demsetz (1972) for a discussion of the difficulty of monitoring agents when they are not residual claimants.

13. The exact shape of the rent curve depends on a variety of factors such as the productivity of the land relative to other lands and to other inputs, the demand for products from the land, and length of time that the land will have productive value. Indeed, the rent curve could turn downward and return to a negative value.

14. The exact time when this will occur will depend on the discount rate and

the expected value of future rents. The time will also be reflected by any price floor the government puts on land as it did throughout most of the nineteenth century. For a complete discussion of the economic reasoning behind this analysis, see Anderson and Hill (1990).

15. For a further discussion of the problems with selling the public domain and of the switch to homesteading, see Friedman (2000, 119–22).

16. For a more complete discussion of the role of norms in defining and enforcing property rights, see Ellickson (1991).

17. See Anderson (1995) for a discussion of the impact of differences on Indian-white relations in the nineteenth century.

18. See Libecap (1989a, 20–21) for additional discussion of the distributional consequences of group homogeneity.

CHAPTER SIX

CONTRACTING FOR PROPERTY RIGHTS

Gary D. Libecap

One of the major debts that economists, legal scholars, and other social scientists owe Ronald Coase is that his work drew attention to the institutional structure of production (Coase 1937, 1960; Barzel, this volume; Yandle, this volume). Through the late 1970s at least, the dominant neoclassical paradigm in economics focused on the behavior of firms in different market settings based on the assumption that the underlying institutions were well defined and operational. If they were not, marketlike forces would generate pressures for institutional change; in other words, the market continually disciplined institutions so they could not stray far from what would be considered optimal. Hence, institutions were neglected, deemed undeserving of serious scholarly concern. The wide exposure of Coase's work, his Nobel prize for economics in 1991, Douglass North's similar award in 1993, and the provocative questions raised by other scholars changed all that.[1]

Two new research streams followed. One was an evaluation of economic outcomes under different property rights regimes; the other was investigation into transactions costs and why property rights came in so many varieties, often straying from what would appear to be optimal.

The first line of this research offered plausible explanations as to why societies with similar resource endowments could have wildly differing economic performance records, despite decades of economic advice and massive infusions of foreign financial aid in the post–World War II period. The central thesis was that the particular structure of property rights in an economy influenced the allocation and utilization of economic resources in specific and predictable ways. Weakly defined or poorly enforced property rights could explain why some economies chronically underperformed. Accordingly, a property rights solution appeared as a policy recommendation for developing and transitional economies.[2]

On a more micro level, attention to property rights gave insights as to why some intractable resource problems, such as depletion of common-pool (open access) fisheries, seemed to defy managerial solution. In this area, too, devising new regulations, such as individual transferable quotas (ITQs) seemed to be a more effective approach to the problem (Gordon

1954; Johnson and Libecap 1982; Libecap 1989a, 73–92; Arnason 1993; Gauvin, Ward, and Burgess 1994; Johnson 1995, 1999; Eggertsson, this volume; De Alessi, this volume). After an initial flurry of optimism, frustration set in as things did not work out as smoothly as anticipated. Property rights regimes could not always be easily transferred from one society to another as part of economic development policies, and often were resisted or attenuated by local practices. Slow, incomplete, and controversial privatization efforts contributed to a stagnation of the economies of Russia, the Ukraine, and other transitional economies. In fisheries, ITQ policies were not embraced readily by the fishers they were supposed to assist, and either met with resistance or could not be implemented until the fishery was so depleted that there were few other options.

These events shifted some attention to the second line of property rights research, investigation into how property rights develop, and why efficient regimes are not always observed (in fact, the ideal types are rarely observed). Analyses have required investigation into the details of the bargaining or contracting process among the parties establishing or modifying property rights and into the transactions costs they encounter. In these investigations, the number and heterogeneity of the parties involved, the information that they hold, and the physical nature and value of the asset over which they are bargaining are identified as critical factors in agreement on and enforcement of property rights.

Distributional issues are not normally considered by economists. How the proposed rights arrangement blends with existing distributional norms affects its popular support and legitimacy. Additionally, individual net gains determine the position of the negotiating parties in property rights discussions. Even when there might be aggregate or collective economic benefits to a secure and well-defined property rights structure, if some parties perceive that they are better off under the status quo, they resist the new arrangement. As a result, to secure a consensus, modifications in the proposed property rights regime often have to be devised, such as side payments (transfers) or restrictions on rights to be granted others.

These modifications, however, change the nature of the proposed new regime and its ability to promote new investment and trade. Demands for compensation in bargaining reflect both legitimate concerns about the impact of a new property rights regime and rent seeking or extortion (the hold-up strategy). As a result of research into these bargaining conditions, property rights have come to be viewed as more complex institutions than has been previously appreciated. Transactions costs and other bargaining problems can thwart negotiations and constrain possible arrangements and, correspondingly, the potential economic options. Coase (1960, 39) warned: "The reason that some activities are not the subject of contracts is exactly the same reason why some contracts are commonly unsatisfactory—it would cost too much to put the matter right."

In this chapter, I summarize the basic attributes of private property rights, how they affect incentives for economic behavior, and how they impact aggregate economic welfare and wealth distribution. I also describe why effective property rights regimes often are so difficult to assemble, despite their economic and social advantages. The bargaining problems associated with institutional change, especially within the political arena, are detailed. Empirical examples of contracting for property rights are provided from case studies on the Amazon frontier and North American oil fields. Some broader implications of the bargaining costs associated with defining or modifying property rights are developed in the chapter conclusion.

PROPERTY RIGHTS AND INSTITUTIONAL CHANGE

All societies and settings require some sort of property rights arrangement to control access and use of valuable resources if the losses of the common pool (open access) are to be avoided. Otherwise, the value of the resource will be wasted in competition for control, unproductive defensive and predatory activities, emphasis on short-term uses when long-term may be more rewarding, associated neglect of long-term investment, limited market development for transfer of assets to higher-valued uses, third-party effects (externalities), and so forth. These losses underlie what Garrett Hardin termed the "tragedy of the commons" over thirty years ago.[3] Preventing these losses motivates individual agents to bargain privately (in small settings) or politically (in larger settings) to define a property rights structure and to modify it as conditions warrant.

Property rights refer to the sanctioned behavioral relations among economic agents in the use of valuable resources. They range from defining access and use of natural resources to defining the nature of market exchange and to work relationships within firms. They can assign ownership to private individuals, groups, or the state. Regardless of the nature of the allocation, property rights must be clearly specified and enforced to be effective, and the degree of specificity depends upon the value of the asset covered (Libecap 1978, 1979). For relatively low-valued assets or in cases where the number of parties is small and where there is a history of interaction, informal norms and local customs are sufficient for defining and enforcing property rights. For high-valued assets where the number of competitors is large and where new entry is common (so that the parties are heterogeneous and have little or no history of interaction), more formal governance structures, such as legally defined private property rights, become necessary. In this latter case, the power of the state usually is necessary to supplement informal constraints on access and use.

Because of their impact on incentives for resource use, investment, and trade, property rights institutions underlie performance and income distribution in all economies. In general, the ownership of an asset consists of three elements: (1) the right to use the asset (*usus*), (2) the right to appropriate the returns from the asset (*usus fructus*), and (3) the right to change its form, substance, and location (*abusus*). This last element, which amounts to the right to bear the consequences from changes in the value of an asset, is perhaps the fundamental component of the right of ownership. It implies that the owner has the legal freedom to transfer all or some rights in the asset to others at a mutually agreed-upon price. The flexible right of transfer induces an owner to operate with an infinite planning horizon and, thus, to be concerned with the efficient allocation of resources over time.

In the limit, if property rights are so well defined that private and social net benefits are equalized in economic decisions, benefits and costs will be entirely borne by the owner. Resource use decisions made under these circumstances will maximize total wealth, given the existing income distribution and market demand composition. An alternative, although complete, property rights assignment will have a correspondingly different income distribution, demand structure, and production mix. Nevertheless, the output chosen will maximize aggregate wealth, given the new rights distribution. In a general efficiency sense, the issue is the completeness of the definition of property rights and not the specific allocation. When rights are not well defined or when they are attenuated by a group or the state, there are negative implications for economic performance. Restrictions on property rights may range from the significant to the trivial. The attenuation of property rights in an asset affects the owner's expectations about asset uses, the value of the asset to the owner and to others, and, consequently, the terms of trade. Whatever specific form it takes, attenuation of property rights implies a shrinkage of economic options for the asset owner and a corresponding reduction of the asset's value. If widespread in a society, attenuation of property rights can result in reduced economic performance, lower wealth, and fewer economic opportunities for its members.

Because property rights define the behavioral norms for the assignment and use of resources, it is possible to predict how differences in property rights affect economic activity. The comparative statics of assessing the impact of property rights institutions on economic performance are complicated because causality runs in the opposite direction. Competitive forces may erode institutions that no longer support economic growth. Population expansion and other changing market conditions exert pressure for dynamic adjustment in the existing rights structure through the refinement of rights and privileges or their transfer to others to facilitate responses to new economic opportunities. Predictions regarding the way in which property rights respond over time to changing economic opportunities, must consider transactions costs and equity factors. If transactions costs are low, then the initial assignment of rights may not matter because it can be modified routinely as necessary. This condition, however, does not describe most market situations. Rights often cannot be easily or quickly modified as economic factors change. The existing rights structure can have a durable and perhaps negative effect on production and distribution. Transactions costs include the costs of bargaining, information, measurement, supervision, enforcement, and political action, and they help to determine how property institutions respond to changing economic conditions.

In general, there can be no assurance that institutional change in property rights will always be structured so as to bring about rational resource use and rapid economic growth (Libecap 1989a). What actually happens depends upon bargaining or contracting in the process of creating or modifying property regimes. Changes in property rights arrangements affect distribution as well as production. Specifically, any redefinition of decision-making authority over resource use brings about shifts in the distribution of wealth and political power. What can be expected, then, is that the attitudes toward institutional change taken by the individuals involved in the rights-allocation process will be decided by the net gains they anticipate from a restructuring plan. Given this explanation, it is easy to understand why disagreements can occur, and why bargaining can result in compromise and the establishment of rights structures that diverge from the pattern required for a fully efficient, competitive system.

The problem of producing property rights reduces to one of creating effective agreement (in a group setting or in the political arena) on any proposed institutional reorganization:

[T]he heart of the contracting problem is devising politically acceptable allocation mechanisms to assign the gains from institutional change, while maintaining its production advantages. By compensating those potentially harmed in the proposed definition of rights and by increasing the shares of influential parties, a political consensus for institutional change can emerge. Those share concessions, however, necessarily alter the nature of the property rights under consideration and the size of the aggregate gains that are possible. If influential parties cannot be sufficiently compensated through share adjustments in the political process to obtain their support, otherwise beneficial institutional change may not occur, with potential economic advances foregone. Even though society as a whole is made worse off, the distributional implications lead influential parties to oppose institutional change. (Libecap 1989b, 7–8)

Accordingly, the process of private institutional change is complex and can become derailed by high transactions costs. The bargaining underlying the creation or modification of institutions involves debate over the aggregate benefits of the new arrangement and the distribution of those benefits among the interested parties. Negotiations can break down if there are disagreements about either the net benefits of institutional change or their allocation. Conflicts that block cooperative solutions can arise from, among other things, information asymmetries among the parties, bounded rationality, and an inability to devise side payments to compensate those who believe they will be harmed by institutional change. These problems increase with the size and heterogeneity of the bargaining group. As a result, institutional changes that would be anticipated in a transaction cost-free environment may not take place or they may emerge only in abbreviated form.

CONTRACTING FOR PROPERTY RIGHTS

The existence of aggregate gains from new institutions that reduce transactions costs is not sufficient to ensure that such arrangements will emerge. The distribution of those gains is often of key interest to the negotiating parties, and the distributional conflicts may block or seriously modify the types of institutions that ultimately result. Problems of cooperation have been the focus of game theory where free riding and prisoners' dilemmas provide incentives for individuals not to cooperate regardless of the actions of the other parties. On the other hand, Ostrom (1990) provides empirical examples of how these contracting problems have been overcome in certain instances in the provision of public goods. Generally, the empirical cases of successful cooperation involve fairly stable, small communities where information is available on each individual's contribution, and where the parties have frequent contact with one another. In such communities, the existence of social norms facilitates cooperation. But the adequacy of those social norms and their durability in the face of relative price increases and entry by nonmembers remain questionable. In examining conditions for cooperation, Harsanyi (1968, 321) argues that "*social norms* should not be used as the basic explanatory variable in analyzing social behavior, but rather should themselves be explained in terms of people's individual objectives and interests."

In general, agreement on a new, socially beneficial institutional structure depends upon (1) the size of the aggregate gains to be shared, (2) the number and heterogeneity of the bargaining parties involved, (3) extent of limited and asymmetric information, (4) distribution issues, and (5) the physical nature of the resource. Each of the bargaining parties is motivated to support beneficial institutional change by the size of their expected share in the gains that the new arrangement will bring. Haggling over any of these factors can block agreement and impede institutional change (Wiggins and Libecap 1985; Libecap 1989a, 1989b).

The larger the expected aggregate gains from cooperation, the more likely some agreement will take place. All parties anticipate being made better off, and distributional conflicts become less critical. Indeed, in some cases, the total benefits of a new or modified property rights regime will not be controversial—the wealth losses associated with common-pool competition are apparent to all. This is often the case after some depletion has occurred due to competitive common-pool extraction. The consequences of uncontrolled access and uses are made clear, demonstrating the need for a new property rights arrangement. If the alternative of no agreement is so dismal, then negotiations may proceed quickly. This condition explains why institutional change frequently occurs late in the history of the exploitation of a resource after common-pool losses have become so large that distributional concerns are relatively unimportant.

By that time, much wealth may have been lost and the resource may not recover. Empirically, for example, acceptance of regulatory measures to restrict fishing effort typically comes only when the fishery is so seriously depleted that there is little recourse. At that time draconian measures may be necessary, and any rebound of the stock may take a long time (Johnson and Libecap 1982). In other cases, the benefits of agreement on a property structure are so obvious that the parties can devise an informal arrangement quickly. This condition characterizes many of the mining camps in American economic development where local miners' rules governed prospecting and mining, allowing miners to focus on the search for and extraction of precious metals and to avoid wasteful competition and uncertainty of control (Libecap 1978, 1979; McChesney, this volume). This condition also describes the ability of initial settlers on the Brazilian Amazon frontier to define informal rights during the early stages of settlement.

The number and heterogeneity of the bargaining parties make initial agreement and subsequent adherence difficult. This is a standard outcome in cartels and other collective action settings (Schmalensee 1987).

The greater the number of competing interests with a stake in the new definition of property rights, the more claims that must be addressed in negotiations to build a consensus on institutional change. The problem is compounded if the parties have different expectations, costs, wealth, size, or other important attributes. Under these conditions, it is more difficult to reach agreement on a definition and distribution of property rights that satisfies all parties. For example, some parties may decide they are better off under the status quo than under a new definition of property rights, even though there is a consensus that the group as a whole would be better off under the proposed arrangement. Side payments are a way of compensating those who resist potential change, but deciding the amount to be paid, the nature and timing of the payment, and the identities of the parties to fund and to receive the transfer may be contentious.

Information problems can complicate an accord on side payments under consideration intended to draw in recalcitrant parties. Agreement on a transfer requires agreement on the amount to be paid, which in turn requires agreement on the value of current holdings and of any losses that some parties expect as a result of the new definition of property rights. The valuation of individual wealth under current and proposed property rights can be a serious problem when there are information asymmetries among the parties regarding the value of individual holdings. These disputes will occur aside from any strategic bargaining efforts if private estimates of the value of current property rights and of potential losses from the new system cannot be conveyed easily or credibly to the other bargaining parties. In this case, an accord on share adjustments or other compensation either may not be reached or achieved only with great difficulty, delaying institutional changes to address common-pool (open access) losses. In addition to honest disagreements on the values of individual claims, the information problems encountered in devising side payments will be intensified if the parties engage in deception or opportunistic behavior. Deception can be used to increase the compensation given as part of an agreement on a new property rights arrangement. It occurs through willful distortions of the information released by various interests to inflate the value of current property rights and the losses institutional change might impose. Widespread deception reduces any trust that might otherwise promote the more rapid consideration of individual claims in side payment negotiations.

Agreement on a new rights structure will also be affected by the distribution of wealth that it authorizes. All things equal, skewed rights arrangements lead to pressure for redistribution through further negotiations, a lack of enforcement of existing ownership, theft, and violence (Alston, Libecap, and Mueller 1999a, 1999b, 2000). If the wealth allocation under the existing property rights regime is so highly concentrated that few have a stake in it, then it will likely be unstable. Under these circumstances, the property rights system will not be an effective response to open access losses. Enforcement costs will be high, and those costs will drain wealth and resources from productive endeavors.

Indeed, if the property system is perceived to be closed, that is, if nonowners have few practical means of becoming owners (either through legal restrictions or through the size of the capital accumulation necessary to acquire assets), then owners and nonowners will have different incentives to maintain the property system. Some parties may prefer an incomplete specification of property rights because such an arrangement allows for greater redistribution. The tension between wealth creation through secure property rights and redistribution to redress a skewed distribution of wealth presents problems for effective institutional change. By contrast, if entry is relatively open, that is, if there are recognized opportunities for social and economic mobility, pressures for redistribution may be mitigated. With economic mobility, the wealth assignment over time will be seen as more flexible and more parties can anticipate improvements in well-being. If that is not the case, however, and the proposed system of property rights is seen as having specific beneficiaries, then a broad group consensus for change may not occur.

Finally, the physical nature of the resource affects private agreement on institutional change for defining or modifying property rights. The nature of the asset can make it difficult to calculate share values for negotiations. It may raise the costs of marking and enforcing property rights. Relatively nonobservable, migrating resources are particularly difficult in the assignment of property rights, as experiences with fish, water (especially aquifers), and oil demonstrate. Stationary, observable resources with a history of stable prices are more readily defined, valued, and traded in property rights negotiations.

Contracting for Property Rights on the Amazon Frontier

Economic frontiers provide a special opportunity to examine the emergence of rights structures—when they occur, the characteristics of the individuals involved, and when modification of property rights becomes necessary. In that sense, they are laboratories for examining the contracting issues described in the previous two sections. Frontiers are defined with respect to distance from a market center, with land rents declining as remoteness increases. The economic frontier is the point where the net present value of claiming land just covers the opportunity costs of the claimant (Anderson and Hill 1990). Beyond the frontier, there are neither property rights nor markets. At the frontier, the conditions for market behavior begin to emerge, and the closer one moves toward the market center, the higher are land values and the more likely that formal property rights will exist. By analyzing the settlement of a frontier, it is possible to identify the factors underlying the demand for and supply of property rights, both informal arrangements and formal title; to ascertain the economic characteristics of the first settlers on the frontier; to examine what the claimants do to obtain property rights; and to determine what conditions facilitate agreement and which ones force further contracting.

The frontier examined here is in the Brazilian Amazon.[4] Some 5 million square kilometers of land comprise the Brazilian Amazon and, as government land, most of it has been open to private settlement and claiming in a manner similar to the North American frontier of the nineteenth century. Vast tracts of territory have been opened through construction of road systems, such as the Belém-Brasília and Trans-Amazon highways. As the frontier has moved across the region, individuals have settled, claimed government land, negotiated informal property agreements with their neighbors, and, later, sought title as formal recognition of their property rights. In some cases, conflict has resulted with land invasions by squatters on land that is already privately owned.

Frontiers have the potential to improve the economic and social welfare of settlers, but whether or how they do so depends upon the property rights regime and how flexible that regime is to fluid economic conditions that emerge. If property rights are clearly assigned and enforced, individuals can exploit frontier resources in ways that maximize their wealth and that reduce environmental problems. Frontiers also have the potential to be the site of conflicts over property rights and associated wasteful practices because, by definition, they are a place where formal legal and government institutions are largely absent. The provision of government infrastructure and services, such as land titles and enforcement mechanisms (judiciary and police force), is socially costly and is provided over time as land values rise. But just how smooth the process will be and how complete are the property rights that are assigned will depend upon local agreements, political conditions, and the nature of the land and other natural resources over which rights are to be defined.

With secure rights to land and the existence of land markets, price signals will direct land to those who will place it in its highest-valued use at any point in time (Demsetz 1967). This may involve consolidation of frontier plots and their subsequent transfer from initial settlers to those who arrive later with more farming experience and access to capital. The more broadly understood and accepted the property right, the more extensive will be the market for frontier land. This condition enhances the wealth of frontier settlers because it extends the number of potential buyers who are willing to pay more for the land than are other people on the frontier. Land often is the major (and only) asset held by early migrants, and their ability to claim and sell land and then move on to settle, claim, and sell yet again is a critical element in social and economic advancement. Through this process, eventually individuals acquire enough wealth to stay on site, develop it, and become permanent farmers. This process suggests a life cycle dimension to frontier settlement whereby relatively young individuals with little education, wealth, or options move to the frontier as entrepreneurial or risk-taking land speculators. The plots initially cleared by frontier settlers necessarily are small, often well under 50 hectares (about 125 acres). These early farmers have limited access to labor markets and, often, minimal farming experience, and forest clearing and soil preparation are extremely difficult. Moreover, at the margin of the frontier, there are no markets for agricultural output, so that initial settlers engage in rudimentary, subsistence agriculture. As transportation costs decline and population densities rise, local markets for farm products develop, and with sufficient improvements in roads and other forms of transportation, opportunities arise for specialization and the export of production to even more remote markets. Such production likely involves some minimal economies of scale as well as experience in farming and in commercial sales that many of the initial settlers on the frontier lack. By transferring land from original settlers to more experienced arrivals market sales prove beneficial to both parties.

Another advantage of recognized and enforced property rights on the frontier is that they allow settlers to focus scarce labor and other inputs on clearing, farming, and other productive activities, rather than on defending their land claims. Subsistence farmers with limited resources can afford few distractions. Any circumstances that divert labor from agricultural pursuits to defensive ones, such as clearing swaths of land (that otherwise would be left in forest) to demarcate holdings and to allow for routine patrolling, reduce production and potential wealth. Indeed, defensive efforts could be so taxing that they would make frontier farming untenable. In the aggregate, violent conflict over land dissipates resource rents, and the associated uncertainty of control reduces land exchanges, investment, and land values. (See Haddock in the next chapter for a discussion of the role of violence in property rights definition, enforcement, and reallocation.) Violent conflict occurs in many parts of the Amazon.

In addition to the above-mentioned advantages, secure property rights promote land-specific investment. They allow for longer-term planning horizons because landowners have the assurance that their preferences will be implemented and that they will capture the returns from their investment activity. There will be little or no dissipation of the increased resource rents from investment due to competition for control. Absent a recognized property rights structure, however, short time horizons dominate, and resource exploitation is more rapid and excessive than is socially optimal. Under such circumstances, the private net returns fall below social net returns from production. The private incentives created by open access are the source of many of the environmental and wasteful resource-use problems encountered on frontiers today, including the depletion of valuable rain forest stands, the overgrazing of natural pastures, and the rapid exhaustion of soil nutrients. Recognized title promotes investment by providing collateral, allowing landowners access to capital markets. The poor are those most likely to settle the frontier, and if they receive title to the land they clear, it serves as collateral, facilitating more substantial capital-intensive investments in irrigation, pasture improvements, planting of permanent crops (such as orchards), and timber management.[5]

Early settlers on frontiers can rely on informal property arrangements, locally understood and respected. Where transportation costs are high, land values and expected returns from farming are low. Individuals with low opportunity costs are the first on the scene. Among early settlers, informal land allocation and use practices dominate (Anderson and Hill 1983). Land values are too low to justify formal documentation of individual land claims or to justify costly conflict among claimants. With abundant, cheap land, conflicting claims are avoided by the voluntary movement of one of the contending claimants to another area. Rudimentary methods of denoting individual holdings are sufficient to divide land, and informal, temporary conflict resolution mechanisms are sufficient to address occasional disputes. Moreover, low resource values on the frontier typically mean that the resident population will be small and homogeneous with respect to education, wealth, age, gender, and expectations for land allocation and use. Small numbers of homogeneous individuals provide conditions for successful collective action. Individuals understand, appreciate, and support local, informal land institutions. Since land claims are uncontested, local land markets can develop among frontier residents, whereby exchanges occur without title. Through these exchanges, some consolidation of holdings occurs, and some settlers move on to new frontiers.

Alston, Libecap, and Schneider's (1995) analyze property rights among 249 small farm settlers in the northeastern Amazon state of Pará. Settlers on the most remote sites were younger, less educated, with less urban experience, and had less wealth. In this regard, they were relatively homogeneous, differing from older, wealthier farmers with more education and larger farms closer to markets. In the areas furthest from market centers, property rights were informal—farmers did not have formal title to their lands, but there was little demand for title. Among the small claimants, there were few conflicts. Land exchanges were regional among local buyers who were familiar with local property arrangements. Land turnover among the first settlers was frequent, with the first farmers often settling and clearing property, selling it (even without formal title) to another settler, and then moving on. In this manner, young settlers appeared to acquire capital over time that enabled them later to take up more permanent settlement. On the frontier, property boundaries were observed by the settlers and trespass uncommon. Small holders with fewer than 200 hectares (500 acres) occupied their lands and could detect intrusion. Farm boundaries were clearly marked by planting trees, often cashews. Their lands also were in production, that is, cleared of forest and placed in pasture and crops. Clearing made monitoring easier. Additionally, in Brazil property rights to farms in "beneficial use" are respected by both custom and law. Larger farms of 5,000 hectares (12,500 acres) or more with forested lands not in production were more likely to have their property rights ignored with land invasions and redistribution to squatters (Alston, Libecap, and Mueller 2000).

For farms closer to markets, with lower transportation costs, land values were higher and the potential for disputes was greater. Informal property rights institutions and conflict resolution mechanisms no longer were sufficient to allow claimants to appropriate potential land rents. With easier access, settlement density was greater, locational rents higher, and competition for the land more intense. With greater competition, private enforcement costs rose. Moreover, increased migration to the frontier brought more, heterogeneous individuals to the scene. These new claimants often did not understand or recognize local land property regimes. Efforts to negotiate new local property arrangements among existing and new claimants under remote and fluid frontier conditions would have been plagued by high transaction costs of negotiation, especially when there was limited information about the value of the assets being claimed or traded (as would be the case for frontier land in the absence of much price data), free riding, and monitoring problems (dense forests which hide boundaries and conceal infringement or trespass).[6]

These issues suggest that early frontier property rights will be limited in scope and based on local, informal arrangements. They will be difficult to maintain as additional migrants appear, having different experiences and expectations regarding the allocation and use of frontier lands. Violation of local rules, trespassing on prior land claims, and absence of permanent conflict-resolution institutions, such as courts and police, ultimately will lead to dissatisfaction with existing local arrangements. If they break down, competition for control ensues diverting resources from production to defensive and predatory activities. As a result, settlers will begin to feel the uncertainty of tenure. This uncertainty will dampen any investment plans and encourage more rapid land use activities. Now that land is more scarce, those wishing to make long-term investments to raise productivity or take advantage of new commercial opportunities, such as planting permanent crops, investing in untried field crops, or improving pastures, will require more formal and secure tenure assurances.

Secure tenure, as represented by formal, enforceable title, will provide collateral for accessing capital markets for such investments and facilitate land sales to those with higher opportunity costs and greater education, wealth, and farming experience. These are the people most likely to be aware of new investment opportunities and to have experience in implementing them. By promoting investment and the transfer of land as necessary, titling will maximize land rents. If secure property rights are not provided, land transfers will not take place as readily, and individuals will focus on short-term, existing farm activities, foregoing investment, limiting sales opportunities, and channeling productive resources to defending their claims or seizing those of others.

As transportation costs fall due to road construction and as the frontier shifts further into unsettled lands, having title offers greater returns, justifying the costs of traveling to local land offices, requesting surveys, and completing the legal documents for title. According to those surveyed (Alston, Libecap, and Schneider 1995), numerous trips to land offices were necessary to secure land agency responses. Title gives legal standing to the landowner with survey descriptions, recorded boundary markers, and date of recording to establish precedent for the claim. Previous owners are listed. This record can be valuable if there are disputes over land transfers. With title, the police power of the state can enforce private property rights to land. The courts can issue eviction notices against trespassers or arbitrate boundary disputes, and law enforcement officials can implement court orders.

To illustrate the value of having title, Alston, Libecap, and Schneider (1996) examine the interaction of the effects of title, land value, and investment for 206 small holders in the state of Pará. We found that title was a powerful determinant of investment among these settlers. With investment measured as the percent of farm land in pasture and permanent crops, having title significantly stimulated investment, increasing it by 21 to 48 percentage points, depending on the site. Investment, in turn, was the most important determinant of land value. Survey responses indicated title increased land value by 20 to 50 percent.

The Amazon frontier case illustrates the ability of individuals to negotiate effective informal property rights arrangements under conditions where there is a small number of relatively homogeneous bargainers. As those conditions change, there is demand for an institutional shift toward the more formal property rights provided by title. How smoothly this process takes place, however, involves political factors and the response of politicians and bureaucrats to the demand for title. The situation in the Amazon frontier also illustrates the problems encountered in establishing and maintaining property rights when the parties are heterogeneous.

Further, the Amazon case demonstrates the resource costs of insecure property rights. In the region, there are both small and large farms. As noted, among small holders there is no record of important conflict over property. But between small land claimants (squatters) and large landowners there are serious disputes. Under Brazilian constitutional law, land must be kept in beneficial use, which in the Amazon means deforested and placed into pasture or crops. Some large farms of 3,000 hectares (7,500 acres) or more have significant amounts of forested land, and these properties are vulnerable to invasion and occupation by squatters.

Once land is occupied and placed into cultivation, under land reform laws, squatters can call for the redistribution of the land from the current official owner. Landownership in Brazil is highly skewed, and Brazilian governments respond to the demands of the landless (Alston, Libecap, and Mueller 1999b, 37). The government may seize farms and redistribute them to squatters. Brazilian courts, however, attempt to protect title, and usually rule in favor of the landowner. The uncertainty over control leads to violence, a reduction in land values, reduced investment, and paradoxically, greater deforestation. To show beneficial use, landowners harvest the rain forest more rapidly than they otherwise would and squatters, to prove their intention to stay on the land and to place it into cultivation, also cut the forest. In resolving the dispute, the government typically provides compensation to either the landowner or the squatters based in part on how much land the parties have placed in to cultivation (deforested) (Alston, Libecap, and Mueller 2000). There are international concerns about maintaining the stock of rain forest, and this objective is not helped by uncertain and confused property rights.

Contracting for Oil Field Unitization

A summary of some of the issues encountered in unitizing oil and gas reservoirs illustrates the transaction costs that can arise in contracting for property rights. Transaction costs stem from information problems, equity concerns, and the physical nature of the hydrocarbon formation. The complexities of old field shares bedevil efforts to define or modify property rights despite large aggregate gains from agreement.

The production of crude oil and natural gas potentially involves serious common-pool losses.[7] These losses arise as numerous firms compete for migratory oil and gas lodged in subsurface reservoirs. Under the common law rule of capture practiced in the United States, private property rights to the hydrocarbons are assigned only upon extraction. Production rights are granted to firms through leases from those who own the mineral rights, often surface landowners. Each of the producing firms has an incentive to maximize the economic value of its leases, rather than that of the reservoir as a whole. Firms competitively drill and drain, including the oil of their neighbors, to increase their private returns, even though these actions reduce the aggregate value of the reservoir.

In effect, the reservoir is a fishery. Oil reservoir value or rents are dissipated as capital costs are driven up with excessive investment in wells, pipelines, surface storage, and other equipment. Rents are also dissipated as production costs rise with too-rapid extraction. Rapid production of oil results in the early venting of natural gas or water, which otherwise help drive the oil to the surface. As natural gas and water are voided from the reservoir, costly pressure maintenance or secondary recovery actions must be implemented. These processes involve additional pumps and injection wells. Total oil recovery falls as pressures decline because oil becomes trapped in surrounding formations, retrievable only at very high extraction costs. Finally, rents are dissipated as production patterns diverge from those that would maximize the economic value of the reservoir over time.

The most complete solution to the open access problem in oil and gas reservoirs is unitization. With unitization, a single firm is designated as the unit operator to develop the reservoir as a whole. The unit operator often is the firm with the largest amount of leased area. Each firm that otherwise would be producing, as well as the unit operator, receives a portion of the net returns of production according to a negotiated, preset allocation formula. In effect, all firms become shareholders in the ownership of the complete reservoir, rather than owners of individual leases. Indeed, under unitization, the lease loses its production significance. Wells and other equipment can be placed to maximize recovery and to minimize costs, and production can be controlled to maintain subsurface pressures and to increase overall recovery. With a single unit operator and the other leaseholders acting as residual profit claimants, there are incentives to jointly develop the reservoir in a manner that maximizes its economic value over time. With unitized development and operation of reservoirs, no difference exists between the amount of oil and gas privately supplied and the socially optimal amount. When producers expect unitization to occur, exploration is encouraged because greater recovery rates and reduced costs are anticipated. Bonuses and royalties to landowners are higher because the present value of the oil and gas resources is greater with unitization.

Gains can be huge, both from savings in capital costs and from increases in overall production that can be from two to five times unregulated output.[8] With so much at stake, oil firms are motivated to reach agreement to form complete units. Despite this motivation, complete unitization is more limited than one would expect. Joe Bain commented (1947, 29): "It is difficult to understand why in the United States, even admitting all obstacles of law and tradition, not more than a dozen pools are 100 percent unitized (out of some 3,000) and only 185 have even partial unitization." Similarly, Libecap and Wiggins (1985) reported that as late as 1975, only 38 percent of Oklahoma production and 20 percent of Texas production came from reservoir-wide units.

Achieving consensus on a unit contract is difficult, with agreements often completed only after years of negotiation, when many of the efficiency losses already have occurred. Even when unitization agreements are reached, not all are complete, leaving the potential for competition among owners that dissipates rents.[9] In an examination of seven units in Texas, Wiggins and Libecap (1985) and Libecap (1989a) showed that negotiations took from four to nine years. Moreover, in five of the seven cases, the area in the final unit was less than that involved in early negotiations. As some firms became frustrated, they dropped out to form subunits. Subunits led to a partitioning of the reservoir and the drilling of additional wells. Generally, they did not minimize common-pool losses. For example, after unsuccessful efforts to completely unitize the 71,000-acre Slaughter field in West Texas, ultimately twenty-eight subunits were established, ranging from 80 to 4,918 acres. To prevent migration of oil across subunit boundaries, 427 offsetting water injection wells were sunk along each subunit boundary, adding capital costs of $156 million.

Other costs of incomplete unitizing are shown on Prudhoe Bay, North America's largest oil and gas field, first unitized in 1977. Two unit operators, separate net revenue sharing formulas for oil and gas, and associated competition among the oil and gas owners resulted in protracted and costly conflicts among the parties.[10] This arrangement did not effectively address the common-pool problem. In 1996, concerns about wasteful production practices led the Alaska Oil and Gas Conservation Commission to initiate hearings on a mandatory restructuring of the Prudhoe Bay Unit.

Even though unitization of a reservoir increases the aggregate returns to be divided, this fact alone is not enough to bring rapid agreement on unitization plans. Negotiations must settle several issues. The parties must negotiate a sharing rule or participation formula for the allocation of costs and revenues from production. Because production often lasts twenty years or more, the rules must be durable and responsive to uncertainty over future market and geological conditions. Units require preset agreements and no renegotiation. All entry or exit of parties must follow specified parameters if property rights are to be stable. There may be different sharing rules for different phases of unit production, such as primary and secondary production, and the rules should apply to all firms on the reservoir. This is termed a single participating area, and there should not be separate participating areas for oil and gas. Otherwise, different incentives for oil and gas production will emerge, as happened on Prudhoe Bay. To align all of the interests in maximizing the economic value of the reservoir, development, capital, and operating cost shares must be equal to revenue shares. In that case, each party will be a residual claimant to the profits from effective operation of the entire unit. Under these circumstances, the parties would not want to hold up needed investment or delay new production practices (such as drilling injection wells) in order to opportunistically force a renegotiation of the contract. Such actions would reduce unit profits and invite similar strategic behavior by other parties, eroding the basis for long-term cooperation to maximize the value of the unit. The profit-sharing formula provides for self-enforcing cooperative behavior among the working interests and expands the "self-enforcing range" of the contract.[11] Although reaching agreement on the sharing formula involves long and costly negotiations, once established, the formula reduces *ex post* enforcement costs.

If there is a wedge between the cost and production shares assigned to any party, then the consensus will fail and conflicts will emerge. For example, if the sharing formula does not uniformly allocate each type of cost in the same proportion as production, certain owners will advocate actions that would skew development in the direction of those expenditures (such as injection wells) in which they carry a relatively light load — even if it is inconsistent with maximizing the overall value of the unit. Dissension, violation of the unit agreement, and rent dissipation are likely results.

To resolve such disputes, some parties (typically those with the largest leases and the most to lose) may devise side payments that restore consensus and allow development to proceed. Although side payments may balance interests at one particular point in time and persuade all parties to support a common course of development, they do not assure incentive compatibility over the remaining life of the unit. New disputes and conflicts will emerge (and the need for additional side payments will arise) if cost and production shares are not made equal. Interests can easily fall out of balance as soon as circumstances (expected prices, costs, or production possibilities) change, which they inevitably do. Further, efficiency losses inflicted on the unit from disagreement, and non-optimal production practices may be irreversible due to resulting changes in reservoir dynamics.

Accordingly, *ex post* efforts to align interests via side payments are not apt to be as effective as the *ex ante* proportionate assignment of costs and production to each party. Importantly, aligning incentives through a profit-sharing formula reduces the information necessary for implementing a unit agreement. The contract can be left relatively simple because new information will be incorporated and plans adapted by consensus over the life of the unit in a manner that maximizes its value and the returns to the parties. For example, new information about the configuration, extent, and communication of reservoirs is revealed through production. This knowledge may require extension or contraction of the unit with the corresponding addition or dropping of interests from the unit. When parties are added or deleted, the relative position of the incumbent interests is maintained as outlined in the initial profit-sharing formula. Renegotiation of the formula is not required. Similarly, the allocation formula is robust against unexpected changes in oil prices, costs, or recovery methods. The incentives of the working interest owners remain aligned (without side payments or recontracting) even as these features of the project are unpredictably altered.

A single unit operator must be selected to develop the field. Multiple unit operators lead to conflicting objectives and hinder the coordinated production practices necessary to maximize the value of the reservoir. Supervision of the unit operator by the other interests must be determined, with voting based on share ownership. If an incentive-compatible sharing rule is adopted, each party will favor a production plan that maximizes the economic value of the unit. Thus, execution can safely be left in the charge of a single unit operator without requiring detailed definition of performance provisions or enforcement guidelines at the initiation of the contract. Any firm with a lease interest in the reservoir and the technical competence to develop it would provide incentive-compatible management. Beyond this, reliance on a single unit operator reduces the transaction and coordination costs that would arise if there were multiple unit operators, further enhancing the overall net value of the reservoir.

Determining which firms should be included in the unit and selecting the unit operator can be contentious, but reaching agreement on the basic sharing or participation formula is the most difficult. Shares are based on estimates of each firm's contribution to the unit. Those firms with leases that have a natural structural advantage will want to retain the value of this advantage in the unitization formula. Such firms are unlikely to agree to a unitization agreement that does not give them at least as much oil or gas as they would have received by not unitizing. Even if the increase in ultimate recovery from unitization is so great that these parties will receive more from unit operations than from individual development, firms with a natural structural advantage have a stronger bargaining position in negotiations than less-favored tract owners. They can hold out for the most favorable allocation formula, secure in the knowledge that the regional migration of oil will continue toward their tracts during any delay in negotiations. Indeed, holding out may increase the value of a structurally advantageous location. If the firms form a subunit without the participation of the owners of better-located tracts, the pressure maintenance operations of the unit may increase the amount of oil migration toward the unsigned tracts. The holdouts then benefit from the unit without incurring costs of the pressure maintenance activity.

Other significant problems involve incomplete and asymmetric information about current lease values and the effects of unit-wide production, such as secondary and enhanced recovery, which are risky technologically and economically. These actions change the time pattern of oil and gas production, perhaps lowering short-term payments to some royalty and working interests, while increasing payments over the long-term. Production patterns, however, are estimated only imperfectly so that there may be disagreement as to the present value of leases and proposed unit shares. Some parties may refuse to join the unit because they have different information and assess the risks and rewards differently than do the proponents of the unit.

Estimates of preunitization lease values determine unit shares, and each firm wants the most favorable valuation possible. The level of information available to the contracting parties for determining lease values depends upon the stage of production at which contracting occurs. In exploration, little is known regarding the location of hydrocarbons and commercial extraction possibilities. At that time, all leases are relatively homogeneous, and unitization agreements can be comparatively easy to reach, using simple allocation formulas, often based on surface acreage. Since no party knows whether the formula is to its particular advantage or disadvantage, negotiators can focus on the aggregate gains from unitization. Information problems and distributional concerns, however, arise with development, as oil and gas reserves are proved and expanded. With the initial discovery well and the drilling of subsequent wells, lease heterogeneities emerge. Because reservoirs are not uniform, the information released from a well is descriptive of only the immediate vicinity. Hence, through drilling their individual leases, firms gain knowledge of their portion of the reservoir. The full extent of the deposit and the productive potential of other areas of the reservoir are revealed only through the drilling activities of other firms.

There are usually disagreements among the unitizing parties over the nature of lease information produced and over the setting of lease values. Some of the information is public, objectively measured, and noncontroversial, such as the number of wells on the lease, its surface acreage, and the record of current and past production. Other data are private, more subjective, and more likely to be disputed, such as the amount of oil below lease lines, remaining reserves, net oil migration, and bottom hole pressure. As a result of disagreements over subsurface parameters, unit negotiations often must focus on a small set of objectively measurable variables, such as cumulative output or wells per acre.

These objective measures, however, may be poor indicators of lease value. Differences in the data available for estimating lease values and unit shares in negotiations inhibit agreement between the lease owner and other firms on the formation of a unit, even when there are large aggregate gains from such action. These conflicts over lease values and unit shares continue until late in the life of a reservoir. With the accumulation of information released through development and production, public and private lease value estimates converge as primary production (production based on natural subsurface pressure) approaches zero. At that point, a consensus on shares and the formation of the unit is possible. This suggests that unit agreements are more likely to be reached late in the life of the reservoir after most of the open access losses have been inflicted.

In unit negotiations, each of the bargaining parties compares the expected value of its returns under the status quo or nonunitized production with the expected value of returns with unitization, based on its offered share in the unit. The status quo returns are net of the firm's share of common-pool losses, if the unit is not formed at that time. If the firm's private information indicates that the organizing committee's estimates of its lease values, based on public information, are too low, the firm may delay joining the unit. The decision will be based, in part, on whether the firm expects future production data to confirm its private value estimates and justify an upward revision in its unit share. The firm will also be concerned as to whether this gain in unit share offsets its portion of reservoir damage from delaying the unit. In addition to delay due to conflicts based on information asymmetries, the firm may decide to delay joining if it can obtain concessions from other parties by holding out. In the meantime, nonunitized production shares are determined by relative lease production capabilities, subject to constraints imposed by regulatory authorities. Most states, as well as the federal government, have some type of compulsory unitization rule to limit the ability of a minority of holdouts to block a unit. Due to political opposition by small firms that receive regulatory-related benefits, Texas, the second-largest oil producing state, does not have a compulsory unitization law.[12]

Even when unit agreements can be reached, the contracts may not fully align incentives to maximize the value of the reservoir over time. Libecap and Smith's (1999) empirical investigation makes use of the largest data set of unitization contracts compiled to date — sixty unit contracts in the United States and Canada.[13] In their survey, they find that units with relatively simple and homogeneous geologic structures (no clustering of oil and gas in separate parts of the reservoir) and only one production phase (no secondary recovery) have effective unit contracts and no history of wasteful contention among the parties. These units have sharing or property rules that assign costs and revenues equally to each party and, hence, align incentives for optimal unit-wide production. These conditions describe 78 percent (47 of 60) of the units, underscoring the importance all parties place on reaching effective agreement to maximize the value of the reservoir over the life of the contract.

Twenty-two percent of the units, however, do not have the requisite sharing rules. These are more complex units with multiple production phases or separate concentrations of oil and gas (gas cap). Because of complicated geological conditions and uncertainty over lease values, negotiating conditions are more complicated for these units. Such conditions affect the ability of the parties to reach agreement on an incentive-compatible property sharing formula. Especially in formations where oil and gas are in separate pockets (gas caps), incomplete agreements exist, and conflicts and rent dissipation follow, as illustrated by the Prudhoe Bay Unit. In these cases, negotiating over unit shares amounts to the trading of disparate assets among the parties. Because the reservoir has distinct physical properties that are not uniformly distributed, the respective leases generally reflect assets that differ in kind, as well as quantity.

Some lease owners may have mostly gas beneath their leases while others have mostly oil. To completely unitize the reservoir, the two sides have to adopt (at least implicitly) agreed terms of trade by which an interest in gas is exchanged for a compensating interest in oil. Similarly, certain parties may hold leases that provide natural sites for production wells during primary production (for example, high on the formation), while others may hold leases that are better candidates for water or gas injection during secondary production (for example, low on the formation). It is necessary for the parties to adopt terms of trade based on the lease locations and the potential for enhanced recovery efforts to supplement the natural reservoir drive.

Through repeated negotiations, the parties typically are capable of translating differences in quantity of resources into ownership shares in the unit. However, differences in kind are more problematic. The basis for placing relative values on the oil and gas assets often is not obvious to the bargaining parties. Gas ownership presents a particular problem. The valuation of gas in the reservoir depends on whether it is assumed to be marketed, as opposed to being reinjected in support of enhanced oil recovery efforts. Due to limited transportability in some cases, the existence of an external market for the gas may be doubtful, especially in remote locations.

To the extent that the imputed value of gas is speculative, the parties find it difficult to adopt definite terms of trade of oil for gas and are unable to agree on particular distribution of equity in the unit as a whole. Gas values are more volatile than oil values, and they do not always track one another, making valuation and exchange of gas and oil properties difficult. In response to these conditions, the parties may elect to partition the unit in a way that isolates differences among tracts and permits them to be negotiated separately. The simplest example of this occurs when a reservoir is spatially partitioned into separate gas cap and oil rim participating areas (PAs), based on the preponderance of oil or gas in various parts of the reservoir. Individual sharing formulas are then negotiated for each PA. Under these arrangements, each party is assigned a distinct share in the operations of the participating area, but *not* the unit as a whole. The party whose lease overlies a relatively large share of the oil, for example, is assigned a relatively large share of equity in the oil rim PA, and perhaps little or none of the equity in the gas cap PA.

Alternatively, a reservoir may be partitioned across time, as when production efforts are divided into primary and secondary recovery phases, with each working interest owner accepting distinct interests in reservoir operations during each of the two phases. Both types of partition (dual PA and multiphase recovery) are common in the industry because they reduce the costs of reaching initial agreement on the unit. But they may weaken the ability of the unit to align incentives and, hence, maximize the economic value of the reservoir. When the reservoir is partitioned along any dimension, a boundary is created that may incite competition for resources and for value. The existence of such partitions may render the unit incomplete, creating conflicts of interest that must be managed by the lease owners to avoid inefficient, competitive development.

CONCLUDING REMARKS

Property rights are essential social institutions for combating the potential wealth losses associated with open access. That is, when there is no clear definition of ownership over valuable assets, then parties will wastefully compete for them and underinvest in them. In the most extreme case, the value of the asset will be fully dissipated through competition for control and through lost opportunities for investment and exchange (Anderson and Hill 1983; Lueck, this volume). More commonly, such extreme cases will be avoided, but the potential wealth from effectively exploiting the resource will not be reached, and some unsatisfactory, underperforming state will prevail. To remedy this situation, individuals have incentives to negotiate privately or through government to develop more complete property rules. The desire to mitigate the losses of open access and to secure the associated gains is not always sufficient to bring beneficial institutional change. Even when some agreement on property rules is possible, its form may deviate sharply from what would seem to be the most desirable arrangement.

The details of the bargaining or contracting process explain why. The parties are motivated by rational self-interest in distribution—their share of the aggregate social returns from agreement. If the anticipated shares make the parties better off relative to the status quo, then agreement is likely. If not, the parties are motivated to continue under the current regime, even if there are aggregate social losses from so doing. The larger the total benefits of devising new or modifying old property rights, the more probable is agreement.

The more homogeneous the parties, the more likely they will be able to construct and agree upon an assignment of property rights (shares). Where the parties differ in important dimensions, such as production cost or access to information about the value of the asset, then agreement on property sharing rules will be more difficult. If the numbers are large, the transactions costs of reaching agreement will be increased. These points help explain the persistence of seemingly ineffective property rights arrangements across societies and across time. The parties may agree that something must be done, but they cannot agree on how to proceed most effectively.

The Amazon frontier and oil field unitization illustrate a number of the issues raised here. Given the importance of property rights institutions for efficient resource use, more attention must be paid to their development, and where they are effective, they must be protected. There is always tension between the productive benefits of secure property rights and the distributional results of a property allocation. Distributional concerns drive the negotiations for developing and modifying property rights. Understanding these concerns and how they impact contracting for property rights are necessary in explaining why a society has the kinds of property rights that it does and the obstacles that are faced in attempts to modify them. High levels of economic welfare cannot be taken for granted. As property rights are abridged in response to distributional concerns, the range of economic opportunities available to the owner is narrowed. The resulting shift in expected returns can lead to different (and less valuable) resource uses with profound economic welfare consequences for the entire society.

ENDNOTES

1. Oliver Williamson, Harold Demsetz, and Yoram Barzel provided more legitimacy for analyses of the roles played by institutional arrangements in economic decisions and performance (Demsetz 1964, 1966, 1967; De Alessi 1980; Davis and North 1971; Barzel 1989; Anderson and Hill 1975; Eggertsson 1990; Furubotn and Richter 1997; North 1981, 1989, 1990; Williamson 1975, 1979, 1985, 1996; Libecap, 1986, 1989a).

2. For work on property rights in developing economies, see Feder and Feeny (1991); Feder and Onchan (1987); Alston, Libecap, and Schneider (1996); and Alston, Libecap, and Mueller (1999b). For transitional economies, see Bull and Ingham (1998) and Brady (1999).

3. For discussion of the commons problem, see Gordon (1954); Hardin (1968); Cheung (1970); Johnson and Libecap (1982); Libecap (1989a, 10–28; 1998a, 1998b); Ostrom (1990); and Lueck (1995). See also Eggertsson, this volume; Anderson and Hill, this volume; and Lueck this volume.

4. This discussion is based on Alston, Libecap, and Schneider (1995, 1996); and Alston, Libecap, and Mueller (1999a, 1999b, 2000).

5. The important roles of title and collateral in economic development are shown by Feder and Onchan (1987) and Feder and Feeny (1991) for small farmers in Thailand. De Soto (2000) makes this same point for the urban poor in developing countries.

6. See Olson (1965) for a description of the problems of negotiation among heterogeneous parties.

7. For general discussion of the common-pool problem using fisheries to illustrate the issues, see Gordon (1954) and Cheung (1970). For application to oil see, Libecap (1998a, 1998b) and Libecap and Smith (1999).

8. Libecap and Wiggins (1984) cite industry trade journals for predictions that unitization would raise oil recovery by 130 million barrels from the Fairway field in Texas.

9. Wiggins and Libecap (1985) and Smith (1987) examine some of the bargaining issues faced by unit negotiators.

10. The problem may be resolved with the purchase of ARCO, one of the unit operators, by British Petroleum, the other unit operator.

11. As described by Klein and Murphy (1997, 417), "the self-enforcing range measures the extent to which market conditions can change, thereby altering the gains to one or the other party from nonperformance, without precipitating nonperformance."

12. For discussion of state regulations, see Libecap and Wiggins (1985) and Libecap (1989a). Libecap and Smith (2001) outline why firms might legitimately oppose compulsory unitization regulations.

13. The empirical investigation used sixty unit operating agreements from oil and gas reservoirs in Alaska, Illinois, Louisiana, Oklahoma, New Mexico, Texas, Wyoming, and Alberta, Canada.

CHAPTER SEVEN

FORCE, THREAT, NEGOTIATION

The Private Enforcement of Rights

David D. Haddock

The first chapters of this volume have elucidated how "open access" resources that are available to everyone for every purpose will be poorly utilized. Discussion of those benefits of exclusion left unspecified the process by which individuals are able to prevent encroachment on their investments. That has been the topic of the two preceding chapters. This chapter examines yet another pair of interrelated mechanisms used to define and protect private rights: force and threats.

When the potential to control the use of and returns from some asset becomes valuable to competing individuals, will one of them be able to hold it against the others? If so, how? The instinctive answer invokes higher authority: The government is imagined to award ownership of all valuable resources, often registering title formally. Tax-financed courts are expected to adjudicate title disputes. Public authorities — the police and the military — are assumed to enforce title and court directives against violators.

As West underlines in chapter 1, that viewpoint actually reverses cause and effect — the existence of property is a precondition to government formation, not the result of it. Unless someone already can control returns from at least some resources (property), there will be no value that can be taxed. Property owners may innovate government (possibly to register, adjudicate, enforce, and facilitate exchange of their pre-existing property rights, including pernicious ones such as rights in slaves), but government cannot be the primordial origin of property. Having been formed, a government may recognize and help defend property, though it may as readily attempt to confiscate the more vulnerable assets (Acemoglu, Johnson, and Robinson 2001).

The point becomes obvious on reflection. With no pretext of taxes, government definition or enforcement, many animal species hold territories, rights to food caches, even simple tools.[1] Animals — as individuals, extended families, or at-will associations — define and enforce rights via credible threats against would-be violators.[2] Similar historical and theoretical instances that involve humans are presented later in this chapter. Humans sometimes create governments, but often resolve property issues themselves by violence and threats of violence.

Property can be defined and held for private use without a government, and even against the wishes of a government, providing one's own power on the margin exceeds that of one's competitors. Might makes rights even if it is private might, as John Umbeck (1977b; 1981) discovered while studying the history of the California gold fields.[3]

It is widely recognized that both fighting and threatening divert resources from investment in new assets and consumption and toward acts intended only to achieve or thwart redistribution of existing assets and thus, seems wasteful. This chapter notes, however, that bargaining for a transfer also consumes resources in a way that is not directly productive. Thus, bargaining differs quantitatively rather than qualitatively from fighting. Could fights occasionally be a cheaper way to transfer assets from lower-valued to higher-valued uses? A historical illustration of such a possibility is drawn from the California-Nevada border during the mid-nineteenth century, a time when ranchers were beginning to invade the traditional but sparsely populated range of the nomadic Paiute peoples. Cultural differences between the Paiute and the ranchers made negotiation and even comprehensible threats difficult during the first few years of interaction, with the result that the groups initially fought sporadically during a period of mutual discovery of the relative value to the two groups of the land.

Starting from the Paiute-rancher example, this chapter derives a series of increasingly general models to illustrate if, when, and how an initially bellicose pattern can resolve itself into stability where the acquisitiveness of the powerful is contained. An oft-neglected though crucial insight is that even the powerful are subject to an opportunity cost if they use their time to threaten or fight neighbors — time spent struggling over assets is time that cannot be spent utilizing them (Umbeck 1981). As initial encroachments increase the assets that the powerful hold — but can use only poorly while involved in further encroachment — that opportunity cost increases (as it decreases for those whose assets have been taken). With diminishing marginal productivity, the value to the powerful of additional units of a resource diminishes (even as it increases for the opponents whose holdings have decreased). Thus, successful initial encroachment can increase the opportunity cost of further encroachment but decrease its benefits. In consequence, an equilibrium may be reached in which a number of competing parties with diverse fighting abilities can maintain similarly diverse holdings of assets.

As further elaboration of the model shows, the situation becomes more complicated if the parties are able to divide capital investments between production (e. g., producing plows) and fighting (e. g., producing guns [Hirshleifer 1995]). But the general result remains—a number of parties with diverse fighting abilities may be able to hold a position. The result would be a familiar one in other economic arenas, such as industrial organization. Consider for example that General Motors and Ford seem to be powerful firms, but Honda and Saab retain sectors of the automobile market—smaller ones to be sure—despite the unwillingness of governments to recognize company entitlements to market share.

A final complication arises when hostility for the sake of hostility is introduced. Sociobiologists and the parents of adolescent boys recognize that individuals sometimes willingly incur fighting and threatening costs not to acquire resources from others but merely to inflict injury and humiliation on them. A common motivation arises when a greater injury leaves its recipient less attractive to the opposite gender when compared to a less injured opponent. A society in which many individuals would willingly suffer smaller injuries for the sake of inflicting larger ones will be impoverished if its members cannot institute mutual controls over such impulses.

Cultural controls sometimes suffice to prevent a small-injury-for-large-injury equilibrium, though they often do not. Our understanding of culture formation remains poor. If a society creates a government—the mightiest of the mighty—to fill that void, the government itself must be closely controlled or it will become the problem rather than the solution. Observation teaches that controlling government is a difficult, murky task. Whether or not we understand the means by which they have done it, modern first-world nations have been exceptional by historical standards in the degree of control over government that their citizens have achieved. The book's final chapters examine government behavior and its control.

Might makes rights is not a claim of a normative superiority. In fact, it is undesirable when contrasted with an ideal world, as it induces diversion of resources from useful production to struggles over ownership.[4] But, just as one would not deny the Holocaust merely because it was abhorrent, one cannot deny might makes rights merely because it seems to waste resources. Might makes rights is deficient as theory only if its predictions accord with the world more poorly than those of competing theories, not because we wish it were wrong.

A SIMPLE MODEL OF FORCE

The chapters by Anderson and Hill and by Libecap show how private property can emerge from an interconnected set of contracts, even when governments are remote. Lying behind (perhaps well behind) any contract is an implicit threat of unwanted consequences to a party that violates the contractual terms. Human relations do not begin and end with contracts; at the outset, threats or force sometimes emerge, not agreement.

Overt fighting imposes significant physical losses on disputants, ordinarily on all of them. That damage is only a part of the total loss from fighting. Fighting distracts parties from productive activities. As Libecap (chapter 6) notes, contesting ownership is a substitute for actually employing the assets. Fighting can be an all-consuming activity while it continues, making productive use of the assets during that time ineffectual if not impossible.

Competitors ordinarily rely on threats — potential rather than manifested violence — to support rights, and usually negotiate when a transfer is credibly threatened.[5] Credible threats require preparation and notification, which take time and other resources that cannot be devoted to production. The cost of threatening violence is usually lower than the cost of combat, so rights are ordinarily enforced more cheaply when societies become less bellicose. All else equal, the overall cost of enforcing rights is then less. Those societies will more thoroughly employ private rights, will use resources more productively, and will be wealthier.

Private Might Makes Private Rights

Because humans are primates, clues (not conclusions) regarding human behavior can often be observed in other primates. Based on DNA analysis, our closest relative species is the chimpanzee. Although chimpanzees live in semi-permanent groups, they have no government. Instead, they rely on might (frequently aggregated through alliance) to enforce their rights (Goodall 1971). That reliance is commonly manifested in threats (for which our kin possess an extensive and subtle vocabulary), but rarely results in the violence that can lead to mutual injuries. Even minor injuries can prove fatal where predators lurk.

As with chimps, human fights impose costs on combatants — each party expends resources solely to destroy some resources of the other — which has led some observers to argue that mutually incompatible expectations are necessary before violence over rights will occur.[6] Though it may be a convenient simplifying assumption, the fight-as-mistake perspective misleads one to envision combatants as expecting definite outcomes rather than a range of plausible possibilities. An actor basing decisions on any given probability distribution inevitably is mistaken *ex post* in that many foreseen possibilities fail to materialize, but is simultaneously correct in that the realized outcome is within the *ex ante* distribution. In consequence, the fight-as-mistake lens obscures parallels between negotiations, threats, and fights. However claims to resources are reorganized, costs will be incurred to narrow the probability distributions. One might similarly characterize negotiations or threats as arising from mistakes; if information were perfect, the parties would incur no costs in those activities.

Because bilateral information exchange will prove costly however it is transmitted, a party will judge whether negotiating, threating, or fighting is cheaper. In a few instances, learning-by-fighting may be the predictable choice. It is no accident that allied belligerents (and negotiators) sometimes assure each other, "we are going to teach them a lesson." They should add, "And they are going to teach us one." Subtler models (Anderson and McChesney 1994; Hirshleifer 1995; Coelho 1985) take such complexity into account.

To summarize, fighting over assets consumes resources, as do alternatives to fights. Resources are consumed whenever and however ownership rights are defined or reorganized. Threatening an opponent to induce uncompensated abandonment of a claim without a fight or negotiating a peaceful exchange of one bit of property for another (though in the shadow of implicit threats) also consumes resources. Resource consumption during negotiation looms so large that economists have given it a special name: transaction costs (Coase 1937). Actual fights could occur when the participants expect that form of communication to convey essential information more cheaply than threats or negotiation (Anderson and McChesney 1994).[7]

The Owens Valley Dispute

History is replete with fights that erupt as combatants from alien backgrounds struggle to narrow probability distributions over relative preferences and fighting abilities. Fighting is often replaced by threats or negotiation as information is gathered and mutual understanding of cultures and languages improves. One such instance occurred in the western United States as the Civil War began.

New gold- and silver-bearing lodes were discovered along the California-Nevada border northeast of Mono Lake. Since that territory was isolated, profits awaited those bringing food, tools, and other materials to the miners. Ranchers began driving cattle northward through the Owens River Valley, to the mines thirty miles beyond the headwaters.[8] Even the shortest drives covered several hundred miles, in the process traversing passes through the Sierra Nevada, the highest U.S. range south of Alaska.

The Paiute Indians had long subsisted on vegetation and game in the Owens Valley and beyond, including the area around the new mining district. Miners occupied little territory, disturbed few native plants, and extracted minerals that no Paiute used. As with many indigenous American tribes, Paiute custom recognized private land rights, but only as long as a party was actively using the claim (Anderson 1995, 32–40; Getches, Wilkinson, and Williams 1998, 167). Miners were violating no rights asserted by the Paiute, so little dispute occurred initially between miners and Indians.

Unlike the miners, however, the herds moving up the Owens Valley grazed plants that the Paiute and their game ate, but the irritation was apparently insufficient to motivate fights, threats, or negotiations. Each drive was in transit, and to keep individual animals from straying, drovers narrowly confined the herd. That self-interest limited the incompatibility of resource use between cattleman and Paiute.

The Paiute were nomads who maintained no permanent abode along their annual circuit among food sources. One could easily have mistaken an encountered Paiute as someone passing through, like the drovers. Consequently, to the ranchers, the Owens Valley seemed unclaimed. To reduce the distance between pasture and mine, particularly the dangerous and arduous miles across the Sierra, some ranchers relocated permanent herds to new spreads in the Owens Valley, resulting in a heavier grazing burden. Though the ranchers had seen an unoccupied valley, the extreme land-intensive lifestyle of the Paiute meant that, from their perspective, they had been crowded even as the first cattle arrived. The nomads had been poor and often hungry before, and that did not improve with the arrival of permanent cattle herds.[9]

Like hunter-gatherers everywhere, the Paiute harvested few calories per land unit compared to what ranchers could extract. Consequently, a narrow strip of land through the valley was of higher value to the ranchers than to the Paiute, as measured in calories. The cost to the Paiute of successfully preventing cattle drives through the valley would have been high. Excluding the drovers would have required patrol and defense of large areas by a sparse, wandering population with little political coordination, and with an urgent need to be wherever a harvest could be had at that moment, rarely where the cattle were passing. In contrast, those driving the herds up the valley occupied a limited (albeit moving) geographical area and had a chain of command that facilitated coordination.[10]

In sum, the initial land occupations by the ranchers were of high value to them and easy to take, but of low value to the Paiute, who would have found the ranchers difficult to exclude. When the drovers entered the valley, the Paiute undoubtedly grumbled amongst themselves, but took no action.

That would change as ranchers took up permanent occupancy. As the

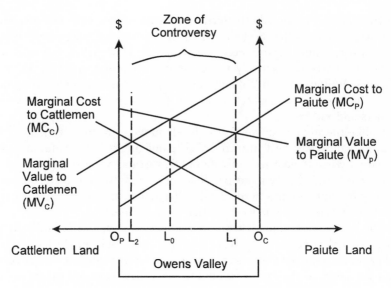

Figure 7.1 Model of the Owens Valley Dispute (Adapted from Anderson and McChesney (1994))

ranches spread the value of a single land unit to the Paiute would have increased because less land remained over which they could freely hunt and gather. More seriously, since cattle need water as well as forage, the ranchers selectively preempted riparian areas in that semi-arid region, forcing the Paiute toward the Sierra foothills to the west, Death Valley, and the Nevada desert to the east. The Paiute's accustomed plants and prey that dwelled only along or in the river became unavailable.[11]

The Owens Valley history just outlined can be elucidated by a graph from Anderson and McChesney (1994), as adapted in figure 7.1. The horizontal axis between O_p and O_c represents the disputed land rights in the Owens River floodplain. Measure Paiute land toward the right from the origin labeled O_p. Land in cattlemen hands can be measured toward the left from the origin labeled O_c, since at any moment each land unit was within the control of either the cattlemen — drovers first, then ranchers — or the Paiute.

The figure's vertical axis indicates the valuations the two groups placed on the land. As discussed earlier, when the Paiute had access to the entire valley, the value of one additional land unit to them was relatively low, as shown by MV_p directly above O_c. But as they conceded land to the cattlemen — as their holdings contracted toward O_p — the value of a land unit increased for the Paiute. The value of each food unit increased as Paiute hunger did, so they searched for food more assiduously when

internal rule of capture, but in many cases membership is restricted to relatively homogeneous individuals (Eggertsson, this volume; Lueck 1994), and this homogeneity is maintained by limiting membership transfers. This common feature is consistent with the different paths of rent dissipation that emerge depending on how first possession rules are applied.

THE LAW OF FIRST POSSESSION

The foregoing analysis shows there are two potential paths of dissipation associated with first possession — racing and overexploitation. In light of these two paths an analysis of the law of first possession reveals an economic logic. Where claimant heterogeneity is present, legal rules mitigate dissipation from racing. Dissipation associated with open access exploitation is mitigated by limiting access and restricting the transfer of access rights.[17]

This section examines eight applications of legal first possession rules which illustrate how the law mitigates dissipation.[18] In these legal applications, judicial opinions and statutes may use such terms as "first in time, first in right," "priority in time," or the "rule of capture." The first two phrases refer to cases in which stocks can be claimed, while the last phrase uniformly refers to cases (e.g., wildlife and oil and gas) in which the flow can be claimed. Regardless of the precise legal terminology, each refers to establishing ownership through possession before anyone else. Each application summarizes the fundamental legal rules related to first possession and links them to the economics of first possession. Most importantly, the discussions illustrate how the possession rules limit racing by defining legitimate possession in ways that invoke heterogeneity. The rules are generally consistent with the model of racing under heterogeneity. In many cases, heterogeneity in claiming is almost self-evident (e.g., first to invent owns the patent) and is difficult to prove otherwise. There is no suggestion that racing is completely eliminated, nor are there estimates of the actual dissipation.[19]

Unowned and Unclaimed Chattels

The law of finds, which has both common law and statutory authority, includes lost property (involuntary parting), abandoned property (voluntary parting), salvaged property (property retrieved from the ocean), and treasure-trove.[20] Essentially, the "finder can acquire title against all the world" by demonstrating the intent to acquire the property and demonstrating possession or a high degree of control.[21] Under property law, the finder generally gets either all or none of the find, but salvage rules under maritime law allow for a division of the spoils (sunken ships and their cargo) between the finder and the former owner.[22] The salver has priority rights over all other claimants besides the original owner. In the sunken treasure case of *Columbus-America Discovery Group, Inc. v. Atlantic Mutual Ins. Co.* in 1992, the court allowed the establishment of rights through the use of remote video cameras which produced live images—coining the term "telepossession"—and did not require physical possession. The court held that the first finder could legitimately use cameras to show its capability of retrieving the treasure. Granting ownership prior to the bulk of the production process prevented costly exploration. Indeed, the court enjoined other salvers who had followed the original salver and began their own duplicative efforts to bring the treasure to the surface. Granting ownership by telepossession is an example of defining possession in a way that exploits the heterogeneity among the claimants and mitigats racing to obtain the treasure.

Intellectual Property

The protection of intellectual property—copyrights, patents, and trademarks—has it roots in common law and the U.S. Constitution.[23] Dukeminier and Krier (2002) call this first possession rule "acquisition by creation." The rules for establishing possession of intellectual property assets address the potential for wasteful races by granting ownership early, when claimant heterogeneity is still large. Exclusive and transferable patent rights are acquired under a "first to invent" policy.[24] Patentable ideas do not require commercial success, only evidence that a skilled person is "enabled" (by the patent description) to use the idea, regardless of its likely value.

Like patents, copyrights are exclusive and transferable; they are established automatically when a work is created. Although copyright protection had required notice and registration, these formalities have been removed. As a result, current copyright protection is simple to obtain. Because a work must be original to receive copyright protection, first possession is the rule for rights acquisition.

Trademark law, like patent and copyright law, grants exclusive and transferable rights to marks that distinguish a merchant's product from those of others. Similarly, trademarks are acquired by adoption and use. The mark must be original and distinct from the marks of others and, in case of conflicts, "first to use" determines priority. Grady and Alexander (1992) examine numerous cases and show that court decisions regarding patentable subject matter and the scope of patents implicitly consider various margins for dissipation.[25]

The Radio Spectrum

The regulation and use of the radio spectrum have generated significant attention from economists (Coase 1959, Hazlett 1990, Herzel 1951, McMillan 1994). Less attention, however, has been given to the early days of radio broadcasting when broadcast rights were granted on a "priority-in-use" rule by the Commerce Department, which had licensing authority under the 1912 *Radio Act*. These rights were exclusive and transferable, and were traded in an active market. When the Commerce Department officially abandoned the first possession rule in 1926, the spectrum devolved from private property to open access, resulting in a period of chaos fraught with "wave jumping," frequency "pirates," and other symptoms of overexploitation.[26] The ensuing race created incentives to reestablish spectrum ownership, and the state courts were quickly awash with interference cases. In *Tribune Co. v. Oak Leaves Broadcasting System* (1926), the court assigned property rights to radio broadcasting on the priority-in-use basis used by the Commerce Department a few years earlier. Other courts appeared likely to follow the example of *Oak Leaves*, but by February 1927, the federal government had claimed ownership of the spectrum under the *Radio Act*.

The radio spectrum is a good illustration of first possession rules establishing ownership in a previously undiscovered resource. Each frequency band can be thought of an asset which generates a flow of service over time. Auctions during the 1920s would have been unworkable during the initial era of radio use. Beginning in 1994, however, the Federal Communications Commission auctioned off spectrum previously used by the military for use in personal communications services (PCS) such as pocket telephones, portable fax machines, and wireless computer networks. Notably, the auction does not establish property rights, only reallocates existing rights.

Land

Throughout history land has been reduced to ownership via first possession, often called initial occupation.[27] First possession of land has determined initial ownership under the English Common Law (*terra nullius*), traditional sub-Saharan African law, and Islamic law. Within the United States, the establishment of private rights to extensive U.S. territory relied on both first possession rules and land sales. In the 1823 case of *Johnson v. M'Intosh*, Chief Justice John Marshall traced the original title of the entire United States to first possession ("discovery" of *terra nullius*) by the Europeans.[28]

After the American Revolution, the states ceded their unsettled western lands to the federal government for the purpose of disposal to the citizenry. Although early disposal policies emphasized sales, first possession, a common practice from the beginning of the Republic, became the dominant policy. The *Preemption Act of 1830*, as well as other preemption laws, legitimized the claims of squatters. The growth of squatting and its formal recognition by the preemption acts indicate that the cost of enforcing rights to land by nonusers was increasing as the frontier rapidly expanded beyond established settlements. The *Homestead Act of 1862* went further, establishing a formal system of land claims based on first possession. Under preemption and squatting, there were rules that limited the size of claims and defined the terms under which legitimate possession could be obtained. Squatters formed local associations known as claim clubs that established rules for governing claim sizes and for settling disputes between competing claimants; federal homesteading policies limited the acreage that could be claimed and typically required some active form of use (e.g., cultivation, timber harvest) before the claim matured into legal title.[29]

In many cases, groups have owned land and have allocated its use through an internal rule of capture. In feudal England, for example, both custom and common law doctrine often defined rights—which inhered to groups—to certain attributes of what was otherwise private land. The commons of pasture (grass), estover (wood), diggings (coals and stones), turbary (sod), and piscary (fish), for example, allowed township citizens access to these characteristics of the land while the cultivated crops remained private. Under the law of "commons" the rule of capture was limited by establishing common property rights. English villagers had equal access to the common resources and transfers of these rights were not allowed.[30] Although equal sharing can appear to be a rule of capture, the exclusion of outsiders generates rents for members of the group. The routine prohibition of selling one's membership enhances homogeneity among users by restricting each member's rights to use only for household consumption. Members of the group were subject to other rules on use of the commons, such as number and type of livestock, seasons of use, and types of technology used.

Similar common property arrangements have been found throughout the world, including in the United States (McKay and Acheson 1987). During the Colonial period, there was extensive use of commons for grazing, wood gathering, and even fruit collection. In the northern states common pastures seem to have been replaced by private holdings in the late 1800s but, in the South, grazing commons (under open range or "fence-out" laws) persisted until the late 1970s. In 1922, Justice Holmes (*McKee v. Gratz*) noted the widespread American tradition of allowing local citizens common hunting access on undeveloped private lands. Today, this type of common property is rare in the formal law, although the lobster territories in Maine are an informal case.

Water

Water law in the United States illustrates the stock-flow distinction and the implications of first possession rules that can potentially generate dissipation from racing (stock) and open access (flow). The prior appropriation doctrine is a rule that leads to private rights in water stocks, but has the potential to encourage racing, while the riparian doctrine is a rule that only allows claims on current flows, but has the potential for open access overuse. The details of both regimes and related areas of water law conform to the economic logic developed in this chapter.

In nineteen western states, case law and statutes have codified a system of customary law that originally developed among miners in the 1800s.[31] During this period, those claiming the lands of the West for mineral exploitation required water at locations distant from riparian land, but the common law doctrine of the time excluded the use of water by those who did not own riparian land. As a result, miners developed a new customary system of water rights called prior appropriation, which separated rights to water from rights to land. Many state court decisions supported these customs. *Coffin v. Left Hand Ditch Co.* (1882), in particular, is a leading case wherein the Colorado Supreme Court formally established the prior appropriation doctrine and explicitly rejected the older common law doctrine of riparian rights. The doctrine of prior appropriation severs water rights from the land by granting permanent ownership of a portion of surface water body on a priority-in-use basis. More importantly, prior appropriation establishes rights to the stock of water and allows these rights to be transferred.

Possession under prior appropriation requires the diversion of water with the intent of beneficial use, typically for such out-of-stream uses as irrigation or mining. Establishing bona fide appropriation does not require the completion of water projects or specific use. In the earliest years, claimants only had to notify others of their intent to divert and use water (e.g., by posting notice on trees). Ultimately, the claimant had to implement the rights claimed or the claim was abandoned. In modern administrative systems, state water authorities often date appropriation from the time of permit application, so no actual diversion is initially required. By allowing claims to be made early in the process of water use, heterogeneity among potential claimants is large and, thus, dissipation from racing is reduced. For example, if possession required actual diversion to a mine or a field, one would have observed the simultaneous construction of canals and diversion dams. In fact, diversion need not always be physical to establish beneficial use. Livestock watering, natural irrigation, and, recently, instream uses have been recognized as legitimate uses.[32]

The traditional legal doctrine governing water in the United States is the riparian doctrine, and in contrast to the appropriation doctrine, it limits the rule of capture by creating common property rights in the water stock among riparian landowners. In *Tyler v. Wilkinson* (1827), Justice Story settled a dispute by stating that, among riparians, a stream was owned "in perfect equality of right." Riparian rights are governed by the common law and, in their modern form, grant correlative and reasonable use rights to water for landowners whose property borders a body of water. Riparian water rights are tied to the riparian land; they require that water be used only on that land and they may not be sold apart from the land.[33] The law essentially defines the group (riparians) that equally shares access to the water resource, but as common property analysis shows, an internal rule of capture remains. Following the standard open access model (Cheung 1970; De Alessi, this volume; Eggertsson, this volume), rent dissipation from overuse increases with the number of riparian landowners. Statutory restrictions on new uses have emerged in many riparian jurisdictions, presumably to limit excessive water exploitation among a large group of users.

Groundwater law has similarities to riparian water law.[34] In ruling on a conflict between two parties drilling in the same aquifer, an English court developed the "absolute ownership" rule on groundwater (*Acton v. Blundell* 1843). By this rule, the landowner has absolute rights to pump underground water without liability to any other groundwater users. This rule is identical to the rule of capture doctrine in oil and gas law. The plaintiff in *Acton v. Blundell* had been pumping water for twenty years longer than the defendant and claimed, by right of first possession, perpetual ownership of the quantity of water he had been using. The defendant claimed, also by first possession, ownership of any water he could bring to the surface from his well. The debate in this case exactly mimics the stock-flow distinction made earlier. American law generally adopted this English rule, but, as the analysis suggests, the absolute ownership doctrine has led to overexploitation problems in areas where the number of users has grown large relative to groundwater supplies. Like riparian doctrine, access to the stock of water is only limited by landownership, so with increased subdivision, the use of the resource begins to approach an open access outcome. In some cases, private landowners have effectively unitized aquifers by forming groundwater districts. In many other jurisdictions, the development of reasonable use and correlative rights doctrines have limited the rule of capture by making groundwater users liable for at least some of the effects on neighboring wells. Both of these rules are like riparian rights to surface water because they create an equal sharing rule for those landowners whose holdings overlie the groundwater basin. As with surface water, western states have tended to go one step further by establishing a prior appropriation doctrine that, following the argument by the plaintiff in *Acton v. Blundell*, grants a perpetual right to withdraw a specific quantity of groundwater.

Wild Animals

The rule of capture (first possession only of an asset flow) has been the fundamental property doctrine for wildlife since the beginning of the English common law.[35] In one of the most famous American property law cases, *Pierson v. Post* (1805), the court considered the possession, and hence, ownership of a wild fox, and ruled that the first possessor gains ownership of the wild fox. Further, the court ruled that possession required physical capture and not simply "hot pursuit." The manifestly high cost of establishing possession of live animal populations meant that they were not subject to ownership until individual animals were killed (the usual case) or otherwise physically captured. The potential for open access dissipation, in turn, created incentives for the modification of legal institutions.

By the nineteenth century, the common law had effectively established ownership rights in wild game for English landowners, essentially creating private ownership of populations (stocks). In the United States, where private ownership of game populations was prohibitively expensive because of both small, scattered private landholdings and wide-ranging species, states were granted extensive regulatory control over access and use of wildlife. Game laws in the United States have tended to limit access to wildlife stocks by restricting the time and method of taking and by restricting the market for wildlife product markets. Because ownership of the stock of wildlife population is prohibitive, limiting access and restricting the transfer of access rights reduces open access overuse. In Great Britain, where ownership of wildlife stock is well established, markets in wildlife thrive.

The legal history of ocean fisheries is comparable to the history of wild game. Like wild game, the dominant rule has been the rule of capture. Even here the rule could vary, as in nineteenth-century Atlantic whaling (Ellickson 1989). The "fast-fish loose-fish" rule required that a whaler's boat be attached to the mammal before a legitimate ownership interest was established. In the case of the aggressive sperm whale, however, the "iron holds the whale" rule granted ownership to a whaler whose harpoon first was affixed to the whale so long as the whaler remained in fresh pursuit. The precise way in which possession is defined determines the costs of possession and the extent of racing. In the whaling cases, the rules seem to define possession so that waste from fruitless whaling effort is minimized.

The potential for rent dissipation under a rule of capture applied to fishing was often great enough to lead to the formation of rights to live fish stocks. In particular, because of the economies of group enforcement, common property rights to fisheries have been widespread in North America and around the world. In other cases, new technologies (e.g., large-capacity fishing vessels) led to the erosion of informal common property fisheries. Also, until the *Fishery Conservation and Management Act of 1976* (FCMA) gave the United States the authority to limit foreign fishing within two hundred miles of the coast, there was no mechanism to establish a formal system of rights to ocean stocks. Historically, the eight Regional Fishery Management Councils established by FCMA have regulated total catch or fishing effort; because these rules do not limit access to the stocks, dissipation from overfishing still is severe in many fisheries.

In the past decade, the regional councils have altered their policies by establishing individual transferable quota (ITQ) systems in several fisheries (e.g., Atlantic wreckfish, Pacific halibut, sablefish). An ITQ system limits total annual catch and allocates a permanent, transferable share of the catch through quotas. By establishing limits to periodic claims on flows, ITQs indirectly establish rights to the fish stocks. ITQ policies have also been implemented in Australia, Canada, Iceland, and New Zealand, and may well be the preferred policy for future fisheries management. Once an ITQ system is chosen to govern a specific fishery, the initial allocation of quota must be determined. As a rule, existing fishers have been given quota rights based on historical catch records. In essence, this is a first possession rule. It is possible that there may be racing for these quotas but in many cases these regulations are determined decades after the initial use of the resource, so the potential value of the quota right is not known. The magnitude of the dissipation from racing will depend on the heterogeneity among claimants. Some fish stocks have been discovered by a single firm, so racing was limited. This is especially true for the Atlantic wreckfish and the orange roughy in New Zealand. Both of these fish stocks were discovered during the 1980s and the overwhelming share of ITQs was formally allocated to those fishers who first discovered and exploited those stocks.

Hard Rock Minerals

In both England and the United States, the common law doctrine of *ad coelum* grants landowners the exclusive right to subsurface minerals.[36] The mineral rights are severable and transferable, like other attributes of real property. As usual, exceptions to this rule could be found. In England, the Crown retained rights to all gold and silver or royal mines and in some areas — notably the tin regions in Cornwall and Devon — a custom developed whereby those first discovering a vein of ore gained legal title to that vein wherever it led them. In the United States similar customs developed on unsettled public lands, most notably in the gold fields of California during the middle of the nineteenth century. These customs were introduced into America by Cornish miners who had initially settled in the Midwest and by Mexican miners who moved to California after the discovery of gold. A complex body of custom and law quickly emerged to govern the size of ore claims and settle disputes over conflicting claims.

The *General Mining Law of 1872* (still in force, though amended) codified these customary rights, allowing people to establish bona fide claims to tracts of public land for the extraction of minerals. To get a patent to mineral land, the miner must find a valuable deposit, locate the claim, do assessment work, and apply for a patent. While prospecting and before discovery, the miner's claim is legally protected. Mining law gives full transferable title to the mineral-bearing land to the first person who discovers a deposit. Claimants need not show that the deposit is commercially important, only that surface mineralization is present. Granting patentable title early in the process is likely to limit excessive racing investment because it assigns ownership when claimant heterogeneity is relatively high.

The distinction between placer and lode claims illustrates how the definition of possession can influence the assignment of rights. Placer claims apply to diffuse concentrations of ore (specks of gold scattered in a stream bed); lode claims apply to contiguous, concentrated claims (veins of ore). Ownership of placer claims is tied to surface tracts of land by the first possessor; ownership of lode claims is tied to the vein, irrespective of overlying surface claims.[37] Veins of ore, almost by definition, are well-defined natural resource stocks over which rights can be assigned cheaply. To define rights to ore for diffused mineral concentrations associated with placer mining, however, would be more costly than to define those rights in terms of surface acreage.

OIL AND GAS

As with hard rock minerals, the doctrine of *ad coelum* gives landowners the right to drill for oil and gas, yet oil and gas law has more in common with wildlife law than the law of hard rock minerals. The difficulty of locating the boundaries of a reservoir and the fluidity of oil and gas beneath the surface of numerous landowners makes it prohibitively costly for surface owners to establish rights to a petroleum reservoir (stock) as against those of neighboring drillers. These factors led to the rule of capture. The legal principle of the rule of capture, if not the term, emerged first in the 1889 case of *Westmoreland Natural Gas Company v. DeWitt* in which the Supreme Court of Pennsylvania clearly stated that ownership of land is not sufficient to have ownership of the underlying gas. In *Westmoreland*, the court made the analogy between wild animals and oil and gas. Under this rule of capture, rights to the petroleum reservoir remain ill defined, but rights to the flows are clear once they have been brought to the surface.

COMPLEXITIES FOR FIRST POSSESSION RULES

Because assets are usually comprised of bundles of valuable attributes, first possession rules may have effects that are not illuminated by the previous analysis. Land, for example, is valuable not only for surface uses, ranging from farms to industrial parks, but possibly for minerals, oil, water, and wildlife. An economically ideal or first-best system of ownership would define rights to each of these attributes rather than to the surface boundaries. Because ownership is costly, property rights to some attributes will be more clearly defined than rights to other attributes (Barzel 1997). Thus, a first possession rule that leads to a system of ownership for one attribute can leave rights unspecified to another attribute. Establishing rights to land for farming under first possession, for instance, has resulted in the rule of capture and accompanying open access overexploitation of wildlife and groundwater.

The process of establishing possession might also damage adjacent environmental assets, as when the diversion of water under prior appropriation damages instream resources. Environmentalists have often criticized first possession rules, especially appropriative water law and the 1872 mining law, on these grounds.[38] They argue that valuable environmental assets are either damaged by first possession claims to land for traditional uses or that these claims make it costly to establish rights for other land uses. Indeed, the application of first possession to environmental goods, such as scenic views or wildlife habitat, is not well developed in the law. For example, claiming water for instream flows has long been prohibited under prior appropriation. And there has been no mechanism for claiming large parcels of land for scenic areas. The formation of Yellowstone National Park by Congress in 1872 followed ill-fated attempts by entrepreneurs to establish ownership to a vast area of geysers and hot springs (Anderson and Hill 1996). When the initial ownership of large tracts is prohibited, the only method of solving the ownership problem for the attached resource is to use private contracting to consolidate landholdings. The costs of consolidation can be substantial, especially when the ownership of the parcels is scattered among many small owners with diverse interests.

Rules for maintaining ownership after first possession are linked to enforcement, abandonment, and adverse possession. In general, the law tends not to require a claimant to continually exert the effort required for an initial claim, but he cannot remain an owner without incurring some continued possession costs (Holmes 1881).[39] In the words of Holmes: "Everyone agrees that it is not necessary to have always present power over the thing, otherwise one could only possess what was under his hand" (236).[40] An owner must actively and continuously enforce his ownership claim, regardless of whether he obtained ownership by first possession or by subsequent method such as purchase, inheritance, or bankruptcy. The law has two responses to a party lax in exerting effort at continued possession. If an owner intentionally ignores his property, it can become abandoned and subject to possession by another person. In certain cases, (e.g., minerals, trademarks, water) specific rules, often lumped together as use-it-or-lose-it, have developed to determine precisely when the right has been abandoned. If an owner is inattentive enough to allow another party to establish continued use of the property, the adverse users can ultimately gain ownership under the doctrine of adverse possession. The general rule of not requiring the same effort for continuing possession as for establishing possession recognizes economies of enforcement by collective institutions and a protection of specific investments by the original claimant.

Adverse possession is related to continued possession costs. This doctrine establishes title in property to the current user or possessor without the consent of or compensation to the original legal owner.[41] To gain title, the adverse possessor must "openly and notoriously" maintain exclusive possession for a statutorily specified term that ranges from five to thirty years in the United States. The precept of adverse possession is embedded in the common law and can be traced to an English statute enacted in 1275. Contemporary American law is a mixture of statutory and case law in which statutes define required time periods and other specific conditions, while court decisions define notorious possession and other, less specific requirements.

Adverse possession is really a first possession doctrine. The adverse possessor has relative title, by virtue of prior possession, or has "rights against the rest of the world from the moment that he claims possession" (Epstein 1986, 675, note 33). Excluding the original owner, the adverse possessor acquires relative title through first possession. Moreover, in a successful adverse possession action, the original owner's title is deemed to be invalid. The law essentially treats the property as abandoned by the original owner. Consequently, first possession becomes an accurate description of the process by which ownership is established.

Historical adverse possession cases have dealt with such issues as abandoned farmland, cabins in the woods, and old mining sites, but more modern cases deal with title to real estate in situations where property boundaries are either unknown or misunderstood. Consider the case of a homeowner who builds an addition that is actually on the neighbor's legal property. Under adverse possession the homeowner gains title of the property in question by virtue of his possession through building the addition. In the historical cases, heterogeneity probably served to mitigate dissipation from first possession. In the modern real estate boundary cases, heterogeneity is at its extreme. Because there is only one potential claimant, the neighbor, there can be no dissipation. More important, the creation of rights generates new wealth.

To summarize how first possession and continued possession are related, consider the following nineteenth-century case:

> [T]he plaintiff employed two men to gather into heaps, on the evening of April 6th, 1869, some manure that lay scattered along the side of a public highway, for several rods, in the borough of Stamford, intending to remove the same to his own land the next evening. The men began to scrape the manure into heaps at six o'clock in the evening, and after gathering eighteen heaps, or about six cart-loads, left the same at eight o'clock in the evening in the street. The heaps consisted chiefly of manure made by horses hitched to the railing of the public park in, and belonging to, the borough of Stamford, and was all gathered between the center of the highway and the park; the rest of the heaps consisting of dirt, straw and the ordinary scrapings of highways. The defendant on the next morning, seeing the heaps, endeavored without success to ascertain who had made them, and inquired of the warden of the borough if he had given permission to any one to remove them, ascertained from him that he had not. He thereupon, before noon on that day, removed the heaps, and also the rest of the manure scattered along the side of the highway adjacent to the park, to his own land. (*Haslem v. Lockwood* 1871)

Who owns the heaps of dung? How is possession gained or lost? There are several possible answers to the questions of possession and ownership of the heaps. Likely candidates for ownership included Haslem, the farmer who first piled the heaps, Lockwood, the man who hauled them away the next day, the owners of the horses who deposited the dung, and the citizens of Stamford borough who owned the road. The court decided for the plaintiff, Haslem, and in doing so, clearly articulated the relationship between ownership and possession. The court ruled first that the manure was property abandoned by the horse owners in a public ditch (whose citizens had also abandoned any claims). The court then ruled that Haslem established ownership via first possession by piling the dung into heaps. Finally, the court ruled that the plaintiff, Haslem, having already established ownership, did not have to exert round-the-clock vigilance to maintain possession and was therefore justified in returning home to fetch his carts.

FIRST POSSESSION BEYOND THE LAW

In addition to legal rules, first possession rules evolve in other arenas such as custom, regulation, and science. In this section, these applications are examined in the context of the models of racing and overexploitation.[42]

Custom

The use of customary first possession rules in businesses, families, and social settings is universal. In business, first possession is used to establish rights to customer service and to claim merchandise for later purchase. Thus, people claim service by standing in line, putting coats over chairs, depositing earnest money, making reservations, and putting holds on goods.[43] In families, first possession is used to allocate household goods such as books, chairs, and tools. In schools, children claim first dibs on books, seats, and tasks. First possession is well known in labor contracts where it manifests itself as seniority privileges for layoffs, overtime, and other perquisites. At ski resorts, fresh powder is allocated among paying customers by first possession.

How do these well-known practices relate to the economic framework and the law discussed in this chapter? Nearly all of these cases have a clear asset owner (e.g., café tables, ski hill), so first possession does not grant the victorious claimant perpetual ownership. Instead, the claimant gets a temporary right under the rule of capture. The basic model predicts that open access dissipation can result. The persistence of these rules suggests that dissipation is minimal compared to alternatives. For example, most of these business practices seem to be for claims on assets whose demand changes frequently and whose prices are costly to change. Within families, first possession can be viewed as an internal rule of capture associated with common property ownership of family resources and is simply a cheap way to allocate temporary use of an asset. In many cases, the assets are durable (e.g., chairs, parking spaces) so that rule of capture causes little dissipation. As the analysis implies, in these cases the temporary rights of the claimants are not transferable. Even in these cases of short-term claims on an asset, there may also be racing within the shorter period. The distinction between racing for complete ownership, however, is with how the resource will be used. In these cases, resource overuse is still predicted because no current user benefits from future use of the resource.

Regulatory Rights

The recent trend in environmental regulation toward using transferable emissions permits requires initial allocations of the permits. As with fishery ITQs, current polluters are usually grandfathered into the permit system based on historical emissions, as in the case of the sulfur dioxide trading program under the *Clean Air Act* amendments of 1990. Some economists have considered this a "free distribution" (Stavins 1995) or give-away, but it is more appropriately viewed as an allocation based on first possession. In these cases, first possession may protect the specific investments made by the original users of the assets and avoid the administrative and rent-seeking costs of auctions. Like fishing quotas, racing is possible and depends on the heterogeneity among claimants. In cases where historic use long precedes the quota system, racing may be of little importance.

Science

For centuries, the dominant rule for ownership of new ideas in science has been priority.[44] Property rights in science, such as intellectual property, are awarded via first possession. The return from scientific discoveries is different than the return on patents, copyrights, and trademarks that can generate revenue from periodic leasing or sale of the idea or a derivative product. The discoverer and owner of new science is rewarded by eponymy (attaching the scientist's name to the new idea), prizes, and publications, and, indirectly, through enhancement of the discoverer's reputation. Eponymy is common as with Darwin's theory of evolution, Einstein's theory of relativity, Haley's comet, Pythagoras' Theorem, and, in economics, Coase's Theorem and Nash's Equilibrium. Prizes are also common; there are Nobel Prizes in several disciplines and numerous other scientific awards, most of which have large monetary components. Universities and other research centers pay large salaries to pioneering scholars.

These rewards are in contrast to intellectual property, where owners are able to lease and sell their asset. What is the reason for this distinction? The answer seems to lie in the distinction between knowledge and information. Knowledge is the purest or least applied version of an idea, such as calculus, the properties of a normal distribution, or the theory of relativity. Science is the production of knowledge. Information is codified knowledge, such as a statistical software package. The law of intellectual property has permitted ownership of information, but has not permitted ownership of knowledge.[45] Instead, what has emerged in the customary and formal institutions of science is an ownership system, like intellectual property, based on first possession. Accordingly, rewards are not explicitly tied to the use of the idea but rather rewards come in lump-sum packages. Because ideas are public goods, pricing at zero marginal cost is ideal as long as the owner can be compensated in some other manner, as through eponyms and prizes. For more applied ideas, per-unit pricing is possible through royalties and leasing.

In science, first possession and the attendant rewards create a system of rights that reward productive activity and clearly involve heterogeneity among potential claimants. A scientific idea can be viewed as an unowned asset, so the question of dissipation through racing must be addressed. As the model implies, the key is the amount of heterogeneity among potential claimants (discoverers). In many cases, scientists are working alone and on isolated projects, so that racing is minimal and dissipation is not likely to be a problem. There are clearly cases, however, where races for discovery take place. One of the most famous is the search for the structure of DNA won in the early 1950s by Watson and Crick.[46] In some cases, there are multiple discoverers as in the calculus developed by Newton and Leibnitz. Although Newton went to great lengths to show he was first, he seems to have been unconvincing. We call it "calculus" not "Newton's mathematics." While there is potential for racing in science, those studying scientific institutions suggest this is not an overwhelming problem and is offset by the incentive it gives researchers for not shirking (Stephan 1996). In addition, under the standard system of compensation, if a scientist cannot completely capture the full value of the asset he will make the claim (i.e., the discovery) later than would be the case with a race leading to complete ownership.

Conclusion

An understanding of how property rights evolve requires an understanding of first possession, the dominant method by which rights are established both in custom and in law. Two of the greatest common law jurists — William Blackstone in England and Oliver Wendell Holmes in the United States — defended the rule of first possession without hesitation. Yet neither took pains to develop a theory of first possession. Blackstone noted ([1766] 1979, Book II, Chapter 1, 2):

> There is nothing which so generally strikes the imagination, and engages the affections of mankind, as the right of property; or that sole and despotic dominion which one man claims and exercises over the external things of the

world, in total exclusion of the right of any other individual in the universe. And yet there are very few, that will give themselves the trouble to consider the original and foundation of this right.

In Holmes' words, the law "abhors the absence of proprietary or possessory rights as a kind of vacuum" (1881, 237). He intuitively saw the potential for waste under open access.

Economics illuminates the incentives under first possession and predicts a structure for these rules. Inspection of first possession rules reveals a structure that implicitly recognizes potential dissipation and systematically works to reduce or avoid it. The structure is straightforward. First possession can lead to races to claim assets, but these are mitigated if possession requirements exploit heterogeneity among potential claimants. The law of land, minerals, prior appropriation, and, especially, intellectual property are consistent with this proposition. First possession can lead to the rule of capture under open access when claims can only be made to flows from the asset. Here the potential for dissipation arises from overuse of the asset, but the experience of oil and gas, riparian water, and wildlife law indicates that limitations on access have mitigated dissipation, without creating ownership in the resource stocks themselves. In other settings such as custom, regulation, and science, they seem to work because they are simpler than auctions and administrative regimes. In short, people have tenaciously adopted and retained rules of first possession because they work to establish property rights necessary for wealth creation.[47]

ENDNOTES

1. See Berger (1985), Epstein (1979), Rose (1985). Rules of first possession are intimately related to the "justice of acquisition," a major topic in philosophical and political discussions of distributive justice (Nozick 1974). In John Locke's ([1690] 1963) labor theory of property, each man has a natural right to himself and can gain ownership of natural resources such as land or game by "mixing" his labor with the resource. Thus, a man acquires ownership to a plot of virgin land by tilling and cultivating it. Many scholars have noted the limits of Locke's theory (e.g., Epstein 1979, Nozick 1974, Rose 1985), particularly for his vague specification of labor and the extent of the resulting property claim, for the "Lockean proviso" that a labor-based property claim must have "enough and as good left in common for others," and for the ambiguity surrounding his use of the term "things held in common." Still, Locke's theory of property remains a powerful defense of individual rights, more or less consistent with real-world application of the rule of first possession.

2. This analysis relies heavily on Lueck (1995, 1998).

3. This result was first shown in the context of the race for innovation by Barzel (1968).

4. The distinction between claims to and ownership of resource stocks and flows was recognized long ago by Blackstone ([1766] 1979, Book II, Chapter 1). More recent distinctions have been made too. For example, Hirschleifer and Riley (1983, 260) note the difference between "rights to fish" (a right to a current flow from the fish stock) and "rights in fish" (a right to the fish stock itself). Haddock (1986) similarly notes a distinction between assets that are "fixed" (where first possession leads to perpetual ownership of a resource) and assets that are "migratory" (where first possession leads to only short-term claim). Among natural resource economists, this distinction is well known and made between stocks of minerals, oil, fish, trees, and output flows of mined ore, barrels of oil, caught fish, and harvested timber.

5. Even within these broad categories the precise meaning of possession can be important. In the famous case of *Pierson v. Post* (1805), the court was divided over whether possession of a wild fox was determined by "hot pursuit" (by dogs) or by physical capture. See Dharmapala and Pitchford (2002) for a detailed analysis of this case.

6. To make this analysis simple, this case considers only a single period. One could, however, consider each period to be a discrete season and allow for racing within this time period, too.

7. See Cheung (1970) and Gordon (1954) for explicit derivations. See Eggertsson (this volume) and Libecap (this volume) for further discussions. Open access results in suboptimal investment because there is no owner to capture the returns from investment (Bohn and Deacon 2000). Heller (1998) has termed this situation the "anticommons."

8. Continued costs of possession can be thought of as increasing the costs of enforcing rights, thus delaying the optimal time to establish possession.

9. Wright (1983) shows that the race equilibrium (Barzel 1968) is exactly analogous to Gordon's average-product rule for exploiting an open access resource. Barzel's (1974) analysis of rationing by waiting with homogeneous customers is another example of full dissipation.

10. Barzel (1974) shows that with heterogeneous customers, rent dissipation is limited in rationing by waiting. This argument is also developed in Barzel (1994) and Suen (1989).

11. The analysis remains the same with rental value differentials, different expectations about the rate of growth of the flow value, or different interest rates. See Lueck (1995, 1998).

12. Fudenberg et al. (1983) and Harris and Vickers (1985) develop this analysis.

13. These issues also arise in Anderson and Hill (this volume), Epstein (1979, this volume), and McChesney (this volume).

14. McMillan (1994) discussed these issues in the context of the broadcast spectrum, as do Anderson and Hill (1990) and Allen (1991) in the context of homesteading.

15. The owners' tax bill to support the legal systems must be included as a cost in calculating the net present value of the asset.

16. Epstein (1985b) and Rose-Ackerman (1985) examine these issues.

17. Cheung's (1970) model shows that the dissipation from "nonexclusive resources" is not complete unless there are an infinite number of users. This

implies that rents are retained by limiting access, even though the rule of capture still operates.

18. The analysis here suggests broad confirmation of the economic models. It should be noted, however, that the literature shows considerable disagreement among law and economics scholars on the merits of first possession rules (Merrill 1986). For instance, in studies of homesteading (Anderson and Hill 1990), oil and gas (Libecap and Wiggins 1984), and water (Williams 1983) first possession has been criticized as causing wasteful races. In contrast, studies of the broadcast spectrum (Hazlett 1990), homesteading (Allen 1991), and patents and mining (Kitch 1977) argue that racing dissipation was minimal.

19. Such estimates would require detailed data on claimants and their costs for specific cases.

20. The key sources for this section are Schoenbaum (1987).

21. In *Armory v. Delamirie* (1722), the classic English case, a chimney sweep is awarded title to a jewel found on the job.

22. Property law governs land and its associated assets such as water, minerals, and wildlife. Maritime law is a separate body of law that governs the use of and behavior on the open ocean. For example, in property law, a finder's claim will depend on whether the find is considered to be part of the land or not. See Lueck (1995, 413) for more details on property versus maritime law.

23. Key references are Blackstone ([1766] 1979), Chisem and Jacobs (1992), and Grady and Alexander (1992). After Barzel (1968), a literature on innovation and patent races quickly emerged (e.g., Dasgupta and Stiglitz 1980, Loury 1979, and Mortensen 1982) and is summarized by Reinganum (1989).

24. European countries typically use a "first to file" system which requires a patentee to file a plan with a government recording agency. This likely increases the possibility of racing, but mitigates later conflicts of interfering rights. Lerner (1997) finds evidence consistent with racing in the U.S. disk drive industry.

25. The limited duration of the right (seventeen years for patents and one hundred years for copyrights) mitigates dissipation even when a race occurs. The incentive to race is reduced to the extent that ideas are public goods. Friedman (2000) makes a distinction between patents and copyrights. He argues that patentable ideas are more likely to be subject to racing because multiple parties are apt to perceive the target in advance, whereas copyrighted materials are not. Therefore, a patent's relatively short life is designed to mitigate racing. Haddock (1986) presents some evidence of patent racing.

26. Hazlett (1990) discusses this period.

27. On land and related issues see Allen (1991), Anderson and Hill (1983, 1990), Blackstone ([1776] 1979), Kanazawa (1996), Lawson (1975), McKay and Acheson (1987), Ostrom (1990), and Rose (1986).

28. Rose (1986) notes that first possession, not discovery, better describes the case, since in many cases tribes never possessed clear title in the eyes of Anglo-American law. Here too the issue of which claims are legitimate is important. Competing claims can lead to violence (see Haddock, this volume).

29. See Anderson and Hill (1983, 1990, this volume) and McChesney (this volume) for more on U.S. land policy. There is little empirical evidence of the extent of racing among homesteaders. The five Oklahoma land rushes would

seem to be the most obvious case of racing for land, although restrictions on access to "Indian Territory" clearly delayed the timing of settlement by Europeans.

30. Garrett Hardin's famous example of the English commons misrepresents these land regimes as open access.

31. See Anderson and Snyder (1997), Scott and Coustalin (1995), Epstein (1985b), Rose (1990), Tarlock, Corbridge, and Getches (1993), Trelease and Gould (1986). Ostrom (1990) discusses cases of private groundwater districts. Ramseyer (1989) examines Japanese water law and finds striking similarity with American legal evolution.

32. Most instream uses have not been assigned via first possession, although some, such as water for power generation, have been (Anderson and Johnson 1986).

33. It is possible that racing to claim land and the attached riparian rights might occur under first possession. Again, claimant heterogeneity would determine the magnitude of the dissipation.

34. It is similar to oil and gas law.

35. See Lueck (1989) on wildlife, and Durrenberger and Palsson (1987), Edwards (1994), McEvoy (1986) McKay and Acheson (1987), and Runolfsson (1997) on fisheries.

36. On the common law see Barringer and Adams (1900) and Lindley (1903). See Gerard (1998) and Leshy (1987) on the 1872 *Mining Law*. On oil and gas see Hardwicke (1935), Kramer and Martin (1989), Libecap and Wiggins (1984), and Lueck and Schenewerk (1996).

37. In *Del Monte Mining & Milling Co. v. Last Chance Mining & Milling Co.* (1898), the Supreme Court articulated the "follow the vein" rule for lode claims. Oil was governed by placer claims. Gerard (1998) noted that placer claims could generate wasteful overdrilling so, ultimately, oil was removed from the mining laws jurisdiction. An unresolved puzzle is why lode claims for entire petroleum reservoirs were not allowed.

38. Wilkinson (1992) has a good summary of these arguments.

39. Ownership, says Blackstone ([1766] 1979, Book II, Chapter 1), remains with the original taker, "till such time as he does some other act which shows an intention to abandon it." Property rights can also be relinquished by gift or sale.

40. Stanford University, in order to maintain its private claim on streets generally open for public use, closes them for one day each year. This is an example of the relatively low costs of maintaining possession.

41. The doctrine has little rationale in the absence of transaction costs and is viewed typically as a method of clarifying title that has become clouded over time. See Dukeminier and Krier (2002, 122), Netter, Hersch, and Manson (1986), and Miceli and Sirmans (1995).

42. Biologists (e.g., John Maynard Smith 1982) have noted the use of first possession rules among predators in claiming kills.

43. For an entertaining discussion of first possession of street parking, see Eig (2001, A1).

44. Stephan (1996) summarizes this history and relies heavily on the work of the sociologist Robert Merton.

45. The distinction here is fine and not always easy to see. For example, in

some cases it is possible to patent medical procedures, not only tools and phar-maceuticals. Copyright law allows "fair use" (e.g., making one copy of a recipe) without compensating the owner.

46. The details of the race, sometimes amusing and other times pathetic, are described in Watson (1968).

47. In the process, a society that agrees to honor first possession rules avoids the costs of allocating resources through violence (Haddock, this volume).

CHAPTER NINE

GOVERNMENT AS DEFINER OF PROPERTY RIGHTS

Tragedy Exiting the Commons?

Fred S. McChesney

> For once I can say
> This is mine, you can't take it.
> —Stevie Wonder[1]

The previous chapters have developed several fundamental propositions. First, most obviously, property rights matter. They matter within
particular institutions (including firms, as Barzel explains in chapter 2),
and they matter in a more macro sense within societies generally. There
may be cases in which communal property (or less than fully private
ownership) is desirable, as Thráinn Eggertsson discusses in this volume.
But in most situations, the full definition of private property rights increases the total welfare of specific economic units (such as firms) and,
thus, the welfare of society generally.

Second, both in theory and in practice, private contractual arrangements are capable of capturing the gains from defining property rights.
The very gains from defining property rights create incentives for private actors to attempt to do so. Numerous examples provided in prior
chapters attest to the success of private citizens in defining rights
privately.

Third, private definition of property rights is subject to several real-
world limitations. This has meant that, in some situations, private definition of property rights either has not been achieved optimally or, to
put the point differently, the extent of wealth-increasing privatization
has been less than complete. Limitations on the private definition of
rights are discussed in greater detail in the first section of this chapter.
As will be seen, each limitation on private definition of rights furnishes
a plausible rationale for a central authority, government, to assume the
burden of defining property rights. The remainder of the chapter explores (1) the theoretical ability of government to improve on systems

of private definition of property rights, and (2) evidence on whether government, in fact, can be counted on to define rights optimally.

When it substitutes for private systems of defining rights in order to solve the tragedy of the commons, government often creates problems. Three problems are the focus here. First, government may choose inefficient means to privatize, dissipating the gains from defining private rights. Second, government often reneges on its promises to define rights, retaining them for itself. Finally, if retention of rights for itself is advantageous to government actors, one would expect that government would sometimes seek to destroy private solutions to defining property rights, so as to increase demand for its own services in managing those resources instead. When these problems arise, they create a tragedy in exiting the commons.

The potential tragedy in exiting the commons is only one part of the general interplay between private property rights and government. In discussing the role of government as definer of property rights, this chapter does not consider in any detail issues arising after rights are defined, such as public (governmental) enforcement of existing property rights. (For a recent survey of literature, although one that does not draw on the property rights literature, see Polinsky and Shavell 2000.) Subsequent chapters of this book develop important aspects of the government's role once rights have been developed. That role ranges from a regulator of property rights (as the chapters by Yandle, Demsetz, and Fischel discuss in this volume) to government as an outright taker of existing rights (as analyzed in chapter 12 by Epstein). For the moment, the focus is government as a definer of rights.

Government's Role in Defining Property Rights

Costly Private Definition of Rights

As Anderson and Hill note in chapter 5, the extent to which private rights will be defined is a function of the benefits and costs to individual, rationally maximizing actors. In the Anderson–Hill model, those actors are private citizens. The gains they can appropriate are taken to be exogenous, dictated by the demand for various goods (e.g., horses, range land) in the market. As those demands fluctuate, so do the benefits of privatizing, and so will the efforts to define or maintain private rights.

The costs of defining rights may be exogenous. With the introduction of barbed wire, for example, the cost of privatizing range land declined and private definition of rights expanded. Eggertsson (this volume) notes how natural features like mountains assist in defining private rights and excluding outsiders. But many of the costs of defining private rights are not exogenous. At least four types of endogenous costs can be identified.

First, there are decision costs associated with defining rights. Getting together and determining how rights will be defined and to whom they will be distributed is far from costless, as indicated by the Anderson–Hill discussion of transaction costs to assemble and make decisions in cattlemen's associations. As Johnson and Libecap (1982) point out, these costs may vary according to the degree of group homogeneity among those claiming the particular good or resource. More hetero-geneous populations will find it more difficult to agree on how to define rights and particularly on who will receive what shares of the privatized good. The cattlemen in the West were sufficiently homogeneous that they could agree on the definition of rights and the shares to be received by each rancher. Likewise, in the gold mining camps described by Um-beck (1977a, 1981), miners carrying the same types of pistol—"the great equalizer"—found it possible to define and divide property rights to land among themselves. But the shrimpers in Johnson and Libecap's Texas shrimp industry could not overcome the relatively high costs of collectively agreeing on property-definition issues.

A second sort of transaction cost attaches to private definition of rights, the cost of defending them. Definition of rights for some neces-sarily entails denial of rights to others. The new private system will have to be defended—a costly process—against those who have not been included in the initial allocation of private rights. If not all potential users of the commons are included among those to whom private rights are accorded, persons excluded have no incentive to respect the alloca-tion agreed to. Private definition of rights must countenance the need to exclude, over space and time, because over time new claimants will emerge (e.g., Field 1989).

Making decisions about rights and defending those decisions can be achieved contractually. For example, group A and group B might agree that members of group A will have exclusive access to a resource with-out encroachment from group B, while members of group B get exclu-sive access to another area or another resource without encroachment from group A. The incentives to do so include lowering the costs of exclusion for both groups, and the possibility of later gains from trade between the two groups. Military treaties followed by trade agreements among nations illustrate this process.

Another set of costs arises outside the contract context: the costs of violence, discussed by David Haddock in chapter 7. When the alloca-tion of rights leaves some persons worse off than before (or excludes them altogether), those deprived can resort to violence to take more than is available under the private rights arrangement. Violence is a subset of the more general costs of defining and defending property rights. But it is identified separately here because it has been of particular concern to many observers, as Haddock summarizes.

Finally, there are the costs of racing for property rights, as discussed in chapter 8 by Dean Lueck (see also Barzel 1968; Dennen 1977). Because privatizing property creates rents (or quasi-rents), private individuals will expend resources to be the first to appropriate them. These costs may include violence in a world where might makes rights, but the costs are not limited to that sort of deadweight loss. Merely peaceful competition to be the first to privatize will dissipate the rents available. "Even if violence is suppressed, costly competition will occur in more subtle ways whenever first possession yields economic rents. . . . [T]he cost of these other forms of competition will match the cost of the competitive threat of violence that has been replaced" (Haddock 1986, 776). Premature racing for property rights is yet another a transaction cost that reduces overall the gains from private definition of property rights.

The Government Alternative

The basic model of private ordering summarized in earlier chapters has been referred to as the "naive theory" of property rights. "The naive theory looks at the emergence or nonemergence of exclusive rights in terms of the costs and benefits of exclusion and the cost of internal governance when individuals share property rights" (Eggertsson 1990, 249). Focusing on the costs to private individuals of defining rights in effect ignores the possibility that other institutions might do the job more efficiently. An alternative to individuals' costly definition of private rights is government definition of rights. Manifestly, many rights are government-created. The absence of government from the model of defining rights produces the alleged naivete.[2]

To describe the fundamental model as naive is in one sense accurate. Many articles in the Anderson–Hill tradition do focus on the role of private actors to resolve for themselves the problem of the commons. But the accusation of naivete is unjust in another sense. With slight expansion, the basic model permits integrating the possibility of a beneficial governmental role in defining property rights.

LOWER TRANSACTION COSTS THROUGH GOVERNMENT

In the expanded property rights model, the role of government arises directly from the costs of defining rights privately. The benefits of private rights are still treated as exogenous, depending on the demand for goods and resources. The value-creating potential for government arises from possibly lower costs of government compared to private definition of rights.

The potential for lower-cost definition of rights stems from the nature of government. Government is distinguished from purely private sources of defining rights by its legitimate (generally acknowledged) possession of a monopoly on the use of force. As Friedman (1973, 152–54) writes:

> Government is an agency of legitimized coercion. The special characteristic that distinguishes government from other agencies of coercion (such as ordinary criminal gangs) is that most people accept government coercion as normal and proper. The same act that is regarded as coercive when done by a private individual seems legitimate if done by an agent of the government. . . . For instance, governments build roads. So, occasionally, do private individuals. But the private individuals must first buy the land at a price satisfactory to the seller. The government can, and does, set a price at which the owner is forced to sell.[3]

Events in Northern Ireland illustrate the point. Attempts to establish a government recognized by both Catholics and Protestants have repeatedly collapsed when one group or the other has refused to disarm. With both Catholic and Protestant groups armed, no side has a monopoly on the use of force, nor can the British government enforce its edicts. Lacking the effective ability to coerce, it is a government *de jure*, but not *de facto*. Instead, different factions profess fealty to different armed groups, which themselves have the might to coerce their members.

Government will coerce legitimately by coercing only to the extent its citizens have agreed to be coerced. When definition and defense of property rights are deemed desirable, citizens may agree to be coerced, as long as others are similarly coerced. (Monopoly on the use of force also creates the potential for government to solve problems that arise once private property rights exist, a point discussed in the chapters by Yandle, Demsetz, Epstein, and Fischel.) The ability to coerce means that government offers a potentially lower-cost solution to defining property rights.

The gains from doing so are demonstrated in figure 9.1, which adapts the fundamental Anderson–Hill "naive" model of property rights definition. The marginal benefits schedule (MB) is taken as given. The costs of private definition of property rights (MC_P) exceed those of government definition of rights (MC_G). The gains from having property rights defined expand from ABC (if done privately) to ADE (if done governmentally). The net gains from having government rather than private citizens define rights is measured by the cross-hatched area, $CBDE$. More privatization occurs ($Q_G > Q_P$), at a lower per-unit cost.

How in fact can government solve the tragedy of the commons more

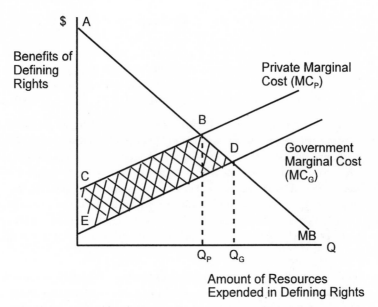

Figure 9.1 Anderson–Hill Model of Property Rights Definition

cheaply than private action? Consider the costs discussed earlier. Decision-making costs are a function of the number of those whose agreement is required for any decision, all other things equal, as well as the voting rules in effect among the group. If unanimity is the rule, bilateral contracts covering all n members of the society will require $[n(n - 1)/2]$ separate agreements, with transaction costs increasing geometrically as group size increases. This is shown in figure 9.2.

Even in a small group, perhaps 250 citizens, over 30,000 contracts are necessary to attain group agreement. The costs of private internal decision making and collective governance might be reduced by having only a few (possibly elected) members of the group meet to decide the relevant issues of how and to whom to accord the rights. Suppose the group is divided into five subgroups of fifty people each, with each group having one elected representative; the five representatives will then vote legislation binding on all two hundred and fifty members of the group. The potential costs and benefits are clear. First, only ten contracts among the five elected representatives would be required. And the rest of the group would be free to engage in more wealth-increasing activities. While just a handful of cattlemen met to resolve property definition issues, the majority of the cattlemen could continue their more productive work on the range.

Those few who make the decisions must be able to enforce them. But

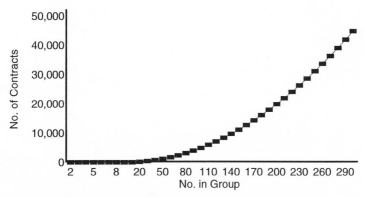

Figure 9.2 Effect of Group Size on Transaction Costs

by definition, government monopolizers of the use of force have the might to enforce their decisions. Likewise, its ability to coerce means government can offer a lower-cost means of excluding others. In particular, its monopoly on the use of force means, at least in principle, that rights can be defined and enforced without violence. The costs of using force to define and enforce rights decline when only one side is armed.[4] Overall, to the extent defining rights governmentally is cheaper than private definition, the extent of private property rights and societal wealth increase.

LOWER RACING COSTS

Along with its ability to control violence over private definition, the entity with a monopoly on the use of force can obviate the problem of premature racing for property rights. "A benevolent legal authority that was powerful enough to police its assignments of entitlements, and one that also knew everything that ultimately would have positive value, could today assign title to each asset and later avoid the resource drain that comes from individuals trying to establish title" (Haddock 1986, 777; Dennen 1977).

This point can be illustrated by another adaptation of the basic Anderson–Hill model, shown in figure 9.3.[5] Assume a resource commonly owned at a point at time t, such that, if there were no costs to defining and enforcing private rights, there would be gains to having the resource privately owned. The benefits from efforts to create property rights today (time t) are shown as MB_t. But the costs of creating enforceable property rights (the costs of decision, exclusion, violence prevention, and so forth) are sufficiently high at time t that it is economically undesirable to incur them: $MB_t < MC_t$ for any given level of effort

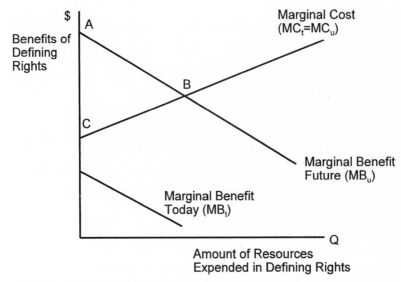

Figure 9.3 Anderson–Hill Model of Property Rights Definition (adapted)

to create rights. Over time, however, for whatever reason (e.g., population growth that increasingly depletes the commons), the benefits of private rights increase. In some later period u, the benefits of creating private property are expected for the first time to exceed the costs over some range: $MB_u > MC_u$. Gains ABC are available, but only starting in the future (period u).

The racing problem arises because private parties will find it attractive to incur costs in the earlier period (t) to be the private party who will get the benefits. Specifically, at time t, they will incur costs up to $ABC/(1 + r)^u$, where r is the relevant rate of interest, to get the benefits available at time u.[6] If the benefits are available in periods beyond u as well, the cumulative benefits from all periods will cause parties to incur even greater costs in period t to get the benefits expected over time, starting in u. (Continued benefits over time, starting in u, would predictably be available if privatization's benefits come from a continually growing population.)

How exactly the costs will be incurred depends on the institutional specifics. If might makes rights, for example, a person could hire gunmen to exclude other takers today in order to begin reaping the rewards tomorrow. Or a person might squat on the land to prove first possession (see Lueck, this volume). These activities represent true deadweight losses because resources expended in racing have opportunity costs.

A potential alternative is to have government use its monopoly on force, take the commonly owned resource before racing begins, and allocate private property rights. Government could claim the rights in period t, create property rights, and sell those rights to the highest bidder.[7] Alternatively, it could claim the rights, hold the resource until period u, when exploiting the resource becomes economically desirable, and then sell it at that later period. Because payment for the land in period t is a virtually costless monetary exchange, there is no social welfare difference between a sale now and a sale later, *ceteris paribus*.[8]

The argument for government is a Coasean one (Coase 1937). As the costs of using government fall relative to the costs of private definition of rights, demand for the government alternative rises. With the benefits of private property rights taken as given, the issue is whether the transaction costs of obtaining those benefits are lower when government defines the rights. Viewed from this perspective, governments evolve endogenously in response to problems of private transaction costs in defining and enforcing property rights.

It is important to note that government definition of private property entails one potential complication. To obtain the net benefits of government allocation of property rights, one must first accord ownership of the land to government for subsequent private allocation. (Even if the government does not hold a piece of paper attesting to title in the ordinary sense of the word but does have the ability to realign ownership interests in the resource, it effectively has title.) Government can only allocate property rights to the extent that it has ownership rights itself. This point may seem obvious, but its significance is sometimes missed. Ceding to government the role of defining property rights is giving the sole possessor of force the ability to allocate property interests, and thus represents a belief that government can and will do the right thing. If government does not do the right thing, an unarmed citizenry will have to deal with a state holding a legal monopoly on force as well as the property rights at issue.

The Case of Nevada Mines

Libecap (1978) shows how government can solve problems of defining rights when private definition is relatively costly. He analyzes the emergence of government as definer of rights in late nineteenth-century Nevada. Nevada was initially settled as a mining territory, famed especially for its Comstock Lode. By 1889, "the Comstock Lode alone had produced over 12 percent of all the gold and silver ever mined in the United States" (Libecap 1978, 339). At its peak the Comstock Lode produced double the mineral output of the entire state of California. Unlike California, where ore could be mined relatively cheaply because the minerals were close to the surface, Nevada's mineral deposits lay in veins deep below the surface.

As was true in California (Umbeck 1977a), much of the mineral-rich land in Nevada was not privately owned. Nominally, it was federal government land, but the government neither mined it nor excluded private individuals wanting to mine it. The land was effectively an open access commons, and so subject to the welfare-diminishing problems that typify open access.

Miners on the commons discovered only bit by bit that the land was mineral-rich. Initially, with Nevada land thought to have only moderate mineral-producing value, there were only a few miners (100 in a forty-square-mile area). With little scarcity, there was little benefit to defining property rights. But as information increased about the land's value, the perceived benefits of defining private rights increased. In particular, the discovery of the Comstock Lode in 1859 revealed that the land was far more valuable than had been suspected, and from 1859 to 1861, the miner population rose from 100 to 20,000.

At first, the Nevada miners were successful, as were miners in California, in defining rights among themselves. The solution was establishment of privately governed mining camps.[9] "In general the mining camp regulations described the recording requirements for locating a claim, the size of individual allotments, the procedures for marking claim boundaries, and the work requirements necessary for maintaining ownership. By following the rules of the mining district, claimants were granted locally recognized possessory rights to mineral ground" (Libecap 1978, 343).

As the extent of wealth under the soil was gradually appreciated, however, the mining camps could not define and enforce property rights efficiently. Richer veins of ore were located well underground. They ran parallel to the surface under the land of different miners, creating boundary disputes. Worse, main veins had offshoots whose ownership was difficult to establish:

> Mining camp rules clearly defined subsurface claim boundaries between mines along the same vein, and they were not subject to much dispute. Those rules, however, were less definite regarding boundaries between mines on *different* veins. This lack of precision for side boundaries was due to the practice of granting extralateral rights which allowed miners to follow their section of a vein wherever it traveled beneath the earth. Those rights . . . made it possible for a mine to run under a claim of another as long as the two mines were accessing separate veins. Because of their indefinite side boundaries, rich Comstock mines were open to competition from "vampire" claims which tapped the same ore deposit while asserting that it was in a separate vein. (Libecap 1978, 345–46)

In principle, the private mining courts could have handled these problems. But the problems were so prevalent and the factual determinations necessary to untangle them were so costly that specialization in resolving property conflicts became desirable. Miners' comparative advantage was in mining, not resolving property disputes. Moreover, any equilibrium attained in the process of defining rights privately was constantly upset by new ore discoveries and arrivals of new miners. So, in 1861, the Nevada Territorial Government was created, along with a system of territorial courts and specialized judges, precisely to resolve the innumerable property disputes.

Even this solution was short-lived. Resolving claims case by case (for example, determining which veins were offshoots of the main vein and which were separate) was costly to determine for even specialized territorial judges. The territorial judicial system was "overwhelmed by the massive case load" (Libecap 1978, 346). Miners' litigation costs amounted to 11 percent of their total costs. And the backlog of cases kept growing. Worse, the very basis of the private rights being disputed — the federal government's willingness to let private actors define rights to government land on what was otherwise open access — was being undermined by external events. The national government, hungry for revenue during the Civil War, debated selling the western mineral lands it owned but had never governed very strictly. Land sales would have upset the system of rights being locally defined and enforced.

That possibility receded once Nevada became a state in 1864, giving the state jurisdiction over its own lands. Rapidly, the newly created state courts and state legislature resolved the question of subsurface boundaries:

> By 1868 Comstock mining rights were well established. . . . While during the six-year period 1863–1868, the [Nevada Supreme Court] had thirty-two mineral rights cases (60 percent of the total considered through 1895), there were only seven cases in the following six years; after 1880 Supreme Court rulings on Comstock mining rights almost ceased. . . . Mineral rights law became highly defined through the enactment of 178 statutes and Supreme Court verdicts by 1895 — the situation stood in sharp contrast to the general, unwritten rules that had existed in 1858. (Libecap 1978, 347)

Libecap provides a detailed numerical account of government's progressively stabilizing force in defining property rights, the issue of greatest concern in the territory (and later the state) of Nevada during this time. He demonstrates empirically that the quantity of government activity supplied, both in judicial decisions and legislative enactments, was a function of the demand for definition and clarification of property rights. As property was defined and disputes abated, the cumulative total of government activity slowed. Regression analysis to test the hypothesis that the value of mining output was a significant determinant of the pace of government action to define property rights reveals that mining output did in fact drive government activity up until 1878, by which time uncertainty over property rights had largely disappeared. Libecap (1978, 361) concludes that, overall, Nevada mining law evolved as a result of an adjustment to replace relatively costly private definition of property rights: "The pattern of legal change in Nevada from the mining camp through the state government was largely determined by efficiency needs—the need to reduce ownership uncertainty as competition for mine income grew."[10]

Other instances of apparently value-enhancing government definition of rights, as compared to private definition, could be analyzed. Following colonization of the New World, the English government controlled the development of America by making large land grants to particular individuals, who in turn managed the devolution of smaller plots to newcomers (Boorstin 1958). Centuries later, likewise, the U.S. government sold off land to railroads as it became a valuable resource, rather than open the land to racing:

> [The] government bartered a great deal of Western land to railroad companies in exchange for new rail construction. The new trackage would not have been profitable without the land grants, and much of the land was worthless without a source of transportation. Due to the new construction, both the railroad companies and the government were able to sell off land that otherwise would have lain idle for some time. (Haddock 1986, 791 n. 27)

The avoidance of racing costs by the American sovereign in this case is all the more striking, given the race for rights in America among competing European powers throughout the previous two or three centuries. The fact that no sovereign could claim title undisputed by another power meant there was no single entity with a monopoly on the use of force in the colonies, so racing and violence (e.g., the French and Indian War) were used to resolve competing claims. Once there was but a single sovereign (first England, then the nascent United States), governmental alternatives superior to private definition of rights were possible.

The Costs of Government Definition of Property Rights

In defining property rights, as in any other economic domain, there are no free lunches. Although government can reduce the costs of defining rights, it cannot eliminate them. Resort to government entails costs of decision making and collective governance, just as private solutions do. The issue is one of relative, not absolute, costs. Can government resolve issues of collective decision making, governance, violence, and racing for property rights more cheaply than purely private processes to define property rights? Or can cattlemen allocate and enforce property rights more cheaply than a government? Can state courts and legislators resolve disputes over mining land at a lower cost than private mining camps?

These are empirical questions. The answers predictably will depend on the specific situation, meaning that no one solution will be optimal in all settings. On the theoretical level, resort to government processes requires consideration of a new set of issues.

Information Costs

Having government define rights creates a risk that information about the relevant benefits and costs of privatizing (including those of alternative ways to privatize) will not be known to the government actors responsible for private rights definition.[11] Concerning government definition of rights as avoiding the problem of racing for rights, Haddock (1986, 777) notes that racing costs could be avoided if the government sovereign "knew everything that ultimately would have positive value" and thus "could today assign title to each asset and later avoid the resource drain that comes from individuals trying to establish title." Only in nirvana, however, will the sovereign have such knowledge. Knowledge is naturally costly for private definers of rights to obtain, too, but private actors will keep the fruits of their knowledge, whereas the relevant government actors often will not.[12] Overall, the incentive to procure the requisite knowledge is likely to be greater for private individuals.

The fact that information is costly and that, often, government will have less incentive to invest in obtaining information about who values resources most highly means that government will sometimes define rights in those who make less valuable use of them. In a laboratory world of zero transaction costs, it would not matter to whom the rights were granted; subsequent transactions would ensure that the highest-valuing users came into possession of the newly privatized resource. But in the real Coasean world of positive transaction costs, it does matter to whom the initial rights are accorded. Subsequent transactions to move resources to higher-valued uses are costly, and may not offer benefits to potential contractors sufficient to offset the costs of transacting.

Rent Seeking Costs

Another source of potential welfare loss, rent seeking, may be more important. Even if it were costless to define initial rights to resources and subsequently reallocate them to higher-valued uses, potential possessors are not indifferent as to who gets the rights initially. Having the initial rights for oneself not only confers a valuable resource, but the rights bestow the ability to realize additional exchange value when higher-valuing users appear. Therefore, the familiar Tullock (1967, 1993) costs of rent seeking will predictably attend any political process in which resources are privatized. Tullock develops his points in terms of tariffs and other rent-creating economic regulation, but they apply just as forcefully in the context of government definition of private property rights.

Agency Costs

In order to concentrate on producing private wealth (e.g., mining), private individuals turn to government as specialized agents to act on their behalf in defining rights. But in any principal-agent situation, agents will be tempted to advance their own welfare rather than that of their principals. Because government actors are not rewarded in accordance with achieving optimality in defining rights, considerations other than welfare maximization predictably will drive their decisions over privatizing rights. Government agents not only have less incentive to get information about the optimal configuration of rights, but less incentive to use what information they have to define and enforce rights optimally. Private actors who cede rights to define property rights to a government may find that government actors are more interested in their own welfare than in that of the citizens who appointed (elected) them. Government agents' increasing of their own welfare can occur in several ways.

DEFINING RIGHTS INEFFICIENTLY

Advancing their own welfare often means that government actors will favor the interests of a particular pressure group that is willing to provide the things that politicians seek. Some of these things may be pecuniary (campaign contributions, bribes), but votes also matter. Because government is by definition a political institution, politicians' personal incentives will entail response to electoral pressures. Anderson and Hill (1990) explain the shift away from efficient Hamiltonian sales of land toward inefficient land rushes caused by the growing number of less wealthy voters. The idea that public lands be sold "dominated the first fifty years of land policy as large tracts of land were sold to individuals and companies who acted as brokers for smaller owners" (Anderson and Hill 1990, 185), meaning that the American government at first continued England's relatively efficient land policy in developing its New World colonies.

But as nineteenth-century western populations grew, so did pressure for obtaining title by possession (squatting) rather than purchase. Squatters often could not buy land, but they had lower opportunity costs in rushing for land and in occupying land in order to own it. Therefore, they were more inclined to incur the costs necessary for ownership. To politicians, more votes could be had in appealing to this group:

> The retirement of the national debt in 1835 and growing population in the western states added pressure to allow squatters the first opportunity to buy newly open lands. In 1830, this pressure culminated in the first of a series of preemption acts that granted this privilege.
>
> Pre-emption was only the first step toward attempting to make the land available at a zero price; politicians rallied around the free-land position and eventually passed the Homestead Act of 1862. With this legislation and subsequent laws passed in 1873, 1877, 1878, 1909, and 1916, land was to be given to anyone willing to endure the hardships of frontier life. Generally these acts required residing on the land, usually for five years; developing irrigation systems; constructing buildings; planting trees; and plowing a specified portion of the claim. The passage of these acts essentially signaled the end of disposal by sale. (Anderson and Hill 1990, 185)

In short, disposition of government-owned land shifted for political reasons from sale (transfer payments that did not consume real resources) to occupation (requiring real costs for irrigation, plowing, and so forth).

Land races were another form of inefficiency observed in government definition of western lands. Racing has occurred for two reasons. First, as discussed by Dean Lueck in chapter 8, the traditional legal rule for converting commonly owned resources into private property has been the right of first possession. Faced with the issue of how to define rights, "the common and civil law (both of which accept the desirability of private ownership) have responded with the proposition that taking possession of unowned things is the only possible way to acquire ownership of them" (Epstein 1979, 1222). Classic common law cases such as *Pierson v. Post* (1805) and *Ghen v. Rich* (1881), involving wild animals and whales, established that resources not privately owned become private property by being taken (or "reduced to possession"). Ellickson (1991) notes that common law rules of first possession in fact involved judicial enforcement of first-possession norms that had already evolved privately. Because first possession involves taking too much too soon, overwhaling was a result of whalers' first-possession rules (Ellickson 1991, 205–6), just as too many oysters are harvested too soon when they grow in open access areas (De Alessi, this volume).

First-possession rules create an incentive for racing, the costs of which could be controlled by temporary government ownership of the resources. As already noted, government ownership followed by outright sale of resources is an alternative way to define and allocate rights. It is noteworthy, though, how often government removes resources from the commons and then stages its own races, rather than sell off the resources as would be preferable. Perhaps the most remarkable instance of racing for resources in the United States occurred in the late nineteenth century, typified by the Oklahoma Land Rush of 1889. The land rush is often decried because it started with the taking of Indian land, "an act that still shocks America's conscience" (Day 1989, 192). But as Anderson and Hill (1990) point out, even when government did not take land from Indians but allocated land it already owned, land races were a frequent feature of the government's divestiture of the public domain, particularly after 1860. (For a good summary of this episode, see Friedman 2000, 119–23.)

In other words, the solution to racing that in principle government offers — sale of lands as they become valuable — has not always been the policy government actually follows. Although Alexander Hamilton's position that public lands be sold prevailed for several decades, disposal of the public domain ended with a series of statutes in the latter half of the nineteenth century that encouraged racing. Most of government land disposal required actual residence on the land for some period of time, and often (as in Oklahoma) required that certain improvements be made to the land during the period of residence. More important, government conveyances into private hands were done on a first-come, first-served basis, meaning that whoever got to the land first and made the necessary improvements would ultimately obtain title. The combination of premature racing and required improvements meant that much, if not all, the surplus of defining private property rights was dissipated. "Efforts to give away the public domain created a commons into which squatters and homesteaders rushed to compete for the rents. In the process, pioneers paid for the land in terms of forgone wealth, privations, and hardships, demonstrating that 'there ain't no such thing as free land'" (Anderson and Hill 1990, 195).

The basic point is worth emphasizing. To solve the problem of open access, the government used its monopoly on force to keep private claimants off the land — for a time. This is a necessary condition to avoid the costs of racing that would otherwise arise without government. Ultimately, it proved desirable to define private rights to land rather than continue ownership in the hands of government, which was doing little to realize the value inherent in the land. But having taken the land out of open access, the government created a new government-managed commons in which first possession again dictated ownership. The real resource losses, including the costs of premature racing, were considerable. The costs were unnecessary as well, since its ownership of the land permitted government to undertake the value-maximizing solution to privatizing rights. Given that the argument in favor of government definition of property rights is lower transaction costs, the outcome from events like land rushes is difficult to justify.[13] There was, in short, a tragedy in exiting the commons.

POLITICAL PRESSURE NOT TO DEFINE RIGHTS AT ALL

The cost of government allocating western lands underscores a point made earlier. When private citizens (for example, in Nevada or Oklahoma) allow the government to allocate private property rights, they are effectively conceding government ownership of the resource in question. Doing so represents a gamble that rights will be defined efficiently. That gamble was won in Nevada, but lost in Oklahoma and other areas where land rushes were used to define rights. In the latter, political pressures dictated an inefficient process by which rights were allocated.

Once government effectively owns a resource to be privatized, a more dire possibility presents itself. Supposedly temporary government ownership for purposes of effecting definition of private rights creates the possibility that government actors will opportunistically retain the rights for themselves. After all, they have the monopoly on the legitimate use of force. They also have a monopoly on legislation, and on supervision of the bureaucracy charged with implementing legislation. Even if the initial statute by which government takes possession requires the government to privatize, the law can be changed, or simply ignored.

In chapter 4, Louis De Alessi explains how government ownership is sometimes good news and sometimes bad. The good news is that government frequently increases welfare by taking resources out of open access (perhaps because it can do so at relatively low cost). But government may retain ownership when privatizing would offer further welfare gains. De Alessi details several situations in which government has solved the tragedy of the commons but then created a new tragedy by refusing to privatize.

Numerous other examples indicate that government may refuse to define private rights, despite the social welfare gains from doing so. Consider the process of government definition of land rights on Indian reservations (McChesney 1990). Once western tribes had been subjugated and confined to federally owned reservations, Congress passed the *General Allotment Act of 1887* to give Indians title to reservation land. As did the *Homestead Act of 1862*, the *General Allotment Act* (also known as the *Dawes Act*) created plots of 160 acres to be allotted to private owners. As Indians reached majority age, they became eligible for allotments.

Definition of private rights came with several provisos, however, two of which proved especially important. First, Indians receiving allotments did not get unrestricted title; they could use but not sell the land for twenty-five years, during which the federal government as so-called trustee remained the owner of the land. Second, land not needed for allotting the specified acreage to individual tribe members was thereafter the property of the tribe itself, which could dispose of the land as it chose. By this latter aspect of the Dawes Act, tribal ownership of lands not needed for allotment effectively substituted tribal governments for the federal government as owners of unallotted reservation lands. Tribes responded by rapidly selling off reservation lands to private holders, many of them non-Indians. The 155 million acres owned by Indians in 1881 fell to 78 million in 1900; almost half the land had been sold. At that point, Congress began to authorize federal government retaking of lands the Dawes Act had ceded to the tribes, subject to the Fifth Amendment requirement of compensation for the takings. Government reneging on treaty commitments to the tribes and the legitimacy of compensated taking were validated by the Supreme Court's *Lone Wolf v. Hitchcock* (1903) decision.

But *Lone Wolf* did not cover the lands already semiprivatized under the Dawes Act, lands previously allotted to private owners who did not yet (before passage of twenty-five years) have complete ownership. Starting in the 1920s, however, the Bureau of Indian Affairs began to slow grants of outright ownership to individual owners of allotments. Then, in the *Indian Reorganization Act of 1934*, Congress statutorily put an end to further allotments and to awards of full ownership of lands already allotted but not held in fee simple.

So, within some forty-five years, the government went from a policy of compulsorily defined private property rights to one that prevented them from being defined. In the process, the law changed to allow government to seize (with non-negotiated compensation) Indian lands that otherwise were available for privatization. In the meantime, many Indians who had achieved full ownership had sold their lands and left the reservation. By reversing its policy favoring private ownership by Indians and tribes, the *Indian Reorganization Act* guaranteed that these trends would not continue. Henceforth, landownership on reservations was frozen into the three-part pattern observed today. Some land is privately owned in fee simple (i.e., alienable because the federal trust provisions expired after twenty-five years); some land is owned privately but inalienable because it is still subject to the trust provisions imposed by the *Dawes Act*; and some land is owned tribally and also inalienable.

Two points about government as definer of property rights on reservations merit emphasis. First, as Anderson and Lueck (1992) have demonstrated empirically, the benefits of private ownership are evident from the pattern of landownership on the reservation. Holding several other factors constant, Anderson and Lueck show that land productivity is maximized when land is owned privately and alienable (i.e., not subject to federal government trust restrictions):

> In particular, our estimates show that the per-acre value of agricultural output is 80–90 percent lower on tribal-trust land than on fee-simple land and 30–40 percent lower on individual-trust land than on fee-simple land. The magnitude of these results should not be surprising in light of the trust constraints on land use. In particular, the inability to use trust land as collateral, the transaction costs resulting from multiple owners of small parcels, and the inability to alienate trust lands all make it difficult to maximize land rents. (Anderson and Lueck 1992, 448)

As Louis De Alessi (this volume) indicates, the Anderson–Lueck findings are what one would expect from similar natural experiments involving other resources (e.g., private versus open access oyster beds).

Second, the entire episode of defining rights — from the *Dawes Act* initiating private ownership to the *Indian Reorganization Act* abolishing definition of new private rights almost fifty years later — shows how government may decide to retain rights for itself, even if private ownership is welfare-enhancing. Why, one might ask, would government do so? In the case of reservations, the answer was bureaucratic budgets. As Libecap (1981a, 153) summarizes:

> Bureaucracies must respond to pressures placed upon them by Congress and voter groups, but they are more than merely passive respondents. Self-interested bureaucrats seek to expand the administrative role, budget, and staffing of their agencies, which in turn enables them to secure higher salaries, longer tenure, greater political and patronage power, and the means for implementing personally desired programs.

Allotments that ripened into alienable title led Indians to sell their land and leave the reservation. The budgets of the Bureau of Indian Affairs (BIA) were a positive function of the number of Indians on the reservation, all other things equal. Initially, allotment had been good for BIA budgets, because of the administrative chores (surveying, recording of title, and so forth) needed to implement it. But as allotments ripened into full title and lands were sold, there were fewer chores for the BIA, fewer Indians to govern, and so lower budgets.[14] The solution for a budget-maximizing bureaucracy was the *Indian Reorganization Act of 1934* — personally written and urged upon Congress by the Commissioner of Indian Affairs.

Similar episodes indicate more generally that entrusting government with the role of defining private rights, a process that begins with government ownership of the resource to be allocated, entails a risk that government will keep the rights for itself. Libecap (1981a) describes the history, similar to that concerning ownership of Indian lands, of the evolution of western grazing land rights at approximately the same time. With the Louisiana Purchase, government owned much of the land in the American Midwest. But in the 1860s, starting with the *Homestead Act*, government began to privatize the land. Initially, the administrative chores associated with the land sales made privatization popular with the government agencies most affected, the Department of the Interior and the Department of Agriculture. But as more land was sold, there was less land to administer, and so congressional budget allocations to the affected departments began to drop. Just as the BIA did when more Indian reservation land was sold, the Departments of Interior and Agriculture in the 1920s began to push for an end to privatizing government land under their jurisdiction. Their campaign succeeded when the *Taylor Grazing Act of 1934* (the same year as the *Indian Reorganization Act*) put an end to government sale of lands. Henceforth, government would manage the land rather than sell it, a shift that increased bureaucratic budgets.

In short, government will predictably refuse to privatize when the costs to the privatizers — government officials — fall short of the benefits to them. Government cannot be expected to act principally in altruistic ways any more than the ordinary person is primarily motivated by the welfare of others rather than himself. As long as defining private rights was beneficial, not just to Indians but to the government agency responsible for governing them, the BIA was pleased to define rights privately. So, too, were the Departments of Interior and Agriculture in the case of western grazing land. But as the personal costs to them of private rights rose, government actors found it more advantageous to retain ownership of the land, thereby guaranteeing a continuing role for the bureaucratic office responsible.

GOVERNMENT DESTRUCTION OF PRIVATE RIGHTS

The fact that restricting private ownership of resources may be beneficial to government actors raises a more dire possibility. If government ownership of rights is valuable to government agents, might not government — the possessor of a monopoly on force — seek to destroy private rights in order to supplant private ownership with government ownership? That is, might government go beyond a passive (if opportunistic) role in refusing to privatize resource ownership, as in the case of Indian and grazing lands, and actively seek to convert private ownership into government ownership?

There is considerable evidence that sometimes the answer is yes.[15] When contending parties for property rights have equal abilities to employ force, force actually is not used (Umbeck 1977a, 1981). Conversely, however, when one party has a preponderance of power, it will use this power against a contending party, at least up to some point (Anderson and McChesney 1994). The current problems that Third World nations face in defending private property against government destruction of rights indicates that giving government a monopoly on the use of force can be a double-edged sword; government alleviates strife among private contenders for rights but uses its monopoly to take rights for itself (De Soto 1989; Acemoglu, Johnson, and Robinson 2001).

Many episodes in American history likewise suggest that government involvement in property rights affairs often results in government taking of property rights. For example, firefighting in this country was initially supplied by individual volunteers through private clubs (McChesney 1986). The clubs were exclusive and prestigious fraternal organizations; Franklin, Washington, Jefferson, Revere, Samuel Adams, Jay, Hancock, and Hamilton were all firemen. The clubs supplied fire services to support their activities, financed by cash bonuses that local governments and insurance firms paid to the first fire company to "get water" on a fire.

However, the bonus system converted each fire into an open access commons. Rival clubs raced to fires to get the bonuses (presumably what cities and insurance firms wanted them to do), but often arrived at the same time. Only one would be paid to fight the fire, creating the need to define the fire as a club's property in order to be paid. Those rights were frequently defined by violence. When rival companies arrived at a fire simultaneously, they often brawled to be the first to get water on the fire. A common tactic was forcibly excluding rivals from sources of water at the scene. Time and resources spent defining rights violently translated into greater fire losses.

As violence grew worse in some cities, the clubs naturally turned to local government (with its monopoly on force and responsibility to maintain order) for assistance in keeping the peace. They also instituted their own reforms to reduce the problem of violence. But in both respects, government proved to be the problem, not the solution:

[T]he lack of cooperation and active interference from police and politicians played a large part in municipal violence. One company in Boston solved the problem of violence over access to sources of water by equipping an engine to carry its own water. The city government outlawed the innovation. In New York efficient fire fighting required co-operation between firemen and the police, as the latter were responsible for detection of fires and maintenance of order at the scene. Police, however, simply refused to turn out for fires, apparently with impunity. . . . New York's chief engineer, Alfred Carson, complained persistently to city hall about the lack of police protection, as did his predecessors, but the politicians were unresponsive. . . . Sometimes the political interference was more direct than mere refusal to enforce the law. Chief Engineer Carson once expelled William (later "Boss") Tweed from the fire department for leading his company in an attack on another. But "Tammany knew a good man in the making and he was quickly restored to his post." (McChesney 1986, 86–87, citation omitted)

Private clubs might have tried to solve the tragedy of the commons, but the clubs faced substantial problems from toleration and even encouragement of violence by city police and politicians.

Why did this happen? The growing problem of violence among private clubs in fact increased the demand for cities themselves to provide firefighting services. In turn, that meant city politicians could control the fire departments, permitting patronage appointments at higher levels and regulations (e.g., residency requirements for firefighters) that increased voter support for politicians in exchange for being paid. Both phenomena were routine as firefighting shifted from private volunteers to paid public employees.

Raising the demand for its services, government adeptly exploited public perceptions that violence and other problems created a crisis requiring government intervention in the form of public ownership. Although the problem actually arose from government's failure to do its own job (not to mention its interference with volunteers' own solutions to the violence problem), a rationally ignorant public will naturally know more about the effects of a problem rather than about its causes. It would be perfectly plausible, even if wrong, to conclude that if the private system engenders violence and inefficiency, a public system must be the answer. Perceptions of crisis in the structure of private ownership predictably will advance the cause of government abrogating those private rights in favor of public ownership.

The firefighting episode is not an isolated example. More recently, one observes in Zimbabwe the same phenomenon of government tolerance for and encouragement of violence. Government indulgence of kidnapping and murder over property rights is ascribed to the electoral advantages of allowing a majority of citizens to dispossess a minority, the very "politics of faction" that Madison warned about in *The Federalist*, No. 10. On the eve of an election that the Zimbabwe government wished to avoid, the supposed crisis allowed the government to postpone the election.

Robert Higgs has explored in detail the link between perceptions of crisis and government self-aggrandizement, or what he calls the Crisis Hypothesis for the growth of government (Higgs 1987, 17). Higgs notes that crises (such as war or business depression) allow government actors plausibly to claim that heightened government powers are needed to cope with the situation (see also Porter 1994). Once rights are ceded to government and the crisis alleviated, however, the private rights are rarely returned to their previous owners. Worse, once government arrogates to itself certain rights to solve a particular crisis, "a legal precedent has been established giving government greater potential for expansion in subsequent *non*crisis periods, particularly those that can be plausibly described as crises" (Higgs 1987, 18).

One could pursue this theme further, discussing the more general literature on the growth of government overall.[16] Canvassing it, however, would shift the focus from the subject of interest here, government as the definer of rights. It suffices to note that Higgs' point about the overall growth of government applies as well to the process of rights definition more specifically. Creation of a belief that a crisis afflicts the system of defining rights privately furnishes an excuse for government to use its monopoly on force to override the private process.

First Possession Reconsidered

The problems discussed here that can make government definition of private rights a tragedy—allocation of rights according to politics rather than wealth maximization and refusal to award private rights at all—adds to the defense of the traditional common law rule of first possession (Lueck, this volume). In first possession, government merely validates and enforces the rights established by private claimants. It was noted above that the first possession rule apparently encourages inefficient racing for resources, with associated welfare losses, as the experience in the American West illustrates. A seemingly superior rule would be one whereby resources were merely sold off.

First possession avoids the necessity of government itself owning the resources. A first possession rule obviates the possibility that government, supposedly holding the rights only temporarily, will then keep them for itself. First possession also means that property rights disputes will ordinarily be adjudicated by relatively disinterested judges, rather than by politicians, likely reducing the extent to which outcomes will be driven by rent seeking.[17]

First possession may not be ideal in theory, but will frequently be better than real-world alternatives. Epstein (1995, 60, 61–62) makes this point in positing first possession as the optimal real-world rule for establishing private rights. "To evaluate this, or indeed any other rule, it is necessary first to ask what other rule you could put in its place. . . . [T]o depart from it requires embracing some regime of centralized authority — some strong system of state allocation — to decide how to parcel everything out to everybody." The relevant question is not the abstract issue of which system can define rights best, but which system will define them better. And a "strong system of state allocation" entails risks that first possession rules avoid.

Lueck (this volume) discusses Hazlett's (1990) history of attempts to define rights to the broadcast airwaves, which illustrates this point and also serves as a useful review of the other points in this chapter. In the early 1900s, new technology made it possible for radio broadcasting to begin. At first, most broadcasting was local and done merely for pleasure. Space on the radio band (the ether) was not scarce. But soon, radio's commercial potential was appreciated, and hundreds of stations flooded the ether, jamming one another's signals. The radio waves were an open access commons, and the predictable tragedy developed.

The federal government responded by asserting control over the entire band, and then allowing private claimants to develop their own property rights. As with mining land in the West earlier, the federal government initially did not attempt to define rights to use the ether, but left the process to private claimants. Private claimants established rights in state courts through a rule of priority in use (a variant of first possession). The first user of a particular radio band width acquired enforceable property rights to that band space in the area where it broadcast. By 1927, the initial chaos that naturally accompanied open access to the ether commons was in the process of resolving itself via first possession rules enforceable in state court.

But in Washington, D.C., many were not happy with this process of first possession backed up by the state courts. The first-possession rule being established in the states cut Washington out of the action. Secretary of Commerce Herbert Hoover had long sought federal government control of the ether, which was finally achieved by passage of legislation in 1927 creating the Federal Radio Commission (the FRC, precursor of today's Federal Communications Commission). The FRC immediately increased scarcity by establishing a narrower broadcast band than was technologically available (smaller, too, than the one used in other countries). Federal licensing of broadcasters then replaced the private system of establishing rights by possession. All of this was done in the name of avoiding the alleged chaos that supposedly would result without centralized government control — despite the fact that the first-possession rule being enforced by state courts had already converted the commons into private property. "Ironically, 'chaos' was a necessary input to achieve this political result. It was clear that the 'breakdown of the law' created the urgency Herbert Hoover had been unsuccessfully using as an argument for new legislation since at least 1922" (Hazlett 1990, 158).

If the 1927 legislation had merely substituted the FRC for state common law in validating the first possession rule, perhaps no great harm would have been done. But the legislation in effect revoked the property rights already defined, establishing instead a system of licenses to be granted (or not granted) by the FRC.[18] Supposed chaos in private definition of rights furnished the excuse to abrogate private rights in favor of attenuated rights and government supervision:

> The fact was that the policy debate was led by men who clearly understood — and articulated — that interference was not the problem, interference was the opportunity. [Government regulation was] a goal that had been sought for years, when the fear was not interference, but the assertion of private rights to spectrum. (Hazlett 1990, 162–63)

CONCLUSION

Treating the process of defining property rights without consideration of government may produce naive models of the process. However, government is easily included in the model. In principle, government has the potential to define rights at lower cost, increasing the extent of private rights definition and, thus, social welfare.

Including government in the property rights model solely as a public-interested reducer of costs risks creating an equally naive model of government definition of private rights. Government may lower the costs of allocating private rights, of excluding other claimants, of controlling violence, and of racing for property rights. But it can only do so because of its monopoly on the use of force, which gives it at least *de facto* and often *de jure* ownership of the resource at issue. It is naive to believe that the government rights-definition monopoly is always used for the public good.

In discussing the tension between private and governmental definition of property rights, this chapter has taken the approach of looking at specific episodes to illustrate the fundamental points. But the same points have been explored in more sweeping terms, looking intertemporally at American history (e.g., Higgs 1987) and cross-sectionally at current property rights problems in foreign countries (e.g., De Soto 1989; Acemoglu, Johnson, and Robinson 2001). The same conclusions emerge:

government can be part of the solution, but it can also be part of the problem (see also Lepage 1985).

In the end, no stronger conclusions can be reached. The case for government definition of rights rests on empirical claims about relative costs. These include the costs of politically driven inefficient rights, and of opportunism when government refuses to define rights at all or even takes them after they have been defined. As Epstein (1995, 62) admits in arguing for a rule of first possession, "the justification for the rule is empirical." But the same holds for arguments in favor of any process, private or governmental, for defining property rights.

ENDNOTES

1. Ronald N. Miller and Orlando Murden, *For Once in My Life* (Jobete Music Co., BMI).

2. The term "government" is used as a portmanteau summary for the various political (including legislative and bureaucratic) processes that go into public (rather than private) decision making. Of course, "government" does not do things. Only people do, a point developed further in this chapter.

3. Working with a similar definition of government, Barzel (2002a) elaborates a detailed theory of the state. Barzel notes in particular that in creating governments, citizens will try to constrain the areas in which government can use its monopoly on force, lest private rights themselves be overridden and dictatorship arise.

4. Having only one side armed increases incentives for the armed side to use force illegitimately to take for oneself, a point discussed in this chapter.

5. For simplicity, the schedules shown in figure 9.3 ignore the impact of discounting over time.

6. The precise magnitude of the predictable costs depends on various game-theoretic assumptions that are of no consequence for the present discussion.

7. Government's ability to run an auction assumes, again, that it is the sovereign monopolist over the use of force, and so does not face competing claims from other governments. Auctioning the rights guarantees that they go to the highest-valuing user. In a Coasean world (i.e., one free of transaction costs), the auction would be unimportant. The government could just assign the rights randomly and allow subsequent transacting among private owners to move the property rights to their highest-valuing users. But the presence of transaction costs is the reason for introducing government into the "naive" model of private rights definition in the first place.

8. The lack of difference between a sale now and a sale later assumes that the money would be put to equally productive uses in private and government hands. See Anderson and Hill (1990) for a detailed discussion.

9. As Libecap writes (1978, 343):

Within five months of the Comstock ore strike, a formal mining camp government, Gold Hill, was established by prospectors at the site of the earliest discoveries. The

Gold Hill District had written rules regarding the establishment and maintenance of private holdings, and the rules were enforced by a permanent claim recorder and an ad hoc miners' court. Three months later a similar government was organized at Virginia City, and the Devil's Gate District followed in early 1860. Ore discoveries in the latter areas were made after those in Gold Hill, suggesting that more formal property rights arrangements were not developed until competition for the land [i.e., scarcity] forced the miners to do so.

10. Libecap (1978, 358–60) considers other possible explanations for government activity during this period in Nevada, but finds them not supported by the evidence.

11. This point applies to the displacement of private activity by government more generally. One problem with government production of so-called public goods is that one loses the information about consumer valuation that private markets generate, information necessary to know how much of the good optimally to produce, for example. See Demsetz (1969).

12. Government incentives depend on the structure of government. A single sovereign can reap higher tax revenues from more productive property. He therefore has a greater incentive to define rights optimally than does a legislator, who must share with other legislators any tax revenues collected (whether used personally, or indirectly to benefit constituents in exchange for votes).

13. Allen (1991) argues that premature racing was worth the cost, since early residence by new settlers freed the government of even greater costs that stationing troops on the frontier would have required.

14. One recalls the story of President Reagan visiting the Bureau of Indian Affairs, where he saw one BIA official weeping at his desk. When Reagan asked the man why he was crying, he exclaimed tearfully, "My Indian just died!"

15. A central theme of Barzel's analysis of the state is that individuals will create a government over them "only *after* they erect a collective action mechanism to reduce [its] ability to confiscate their property" (2002a, 2).

16. Higgs (1987, 3–19) summarizes the principal themes and provides detailed notes and citations to the literature. On the subject of war and the state, Porter (1994) is insightful.

17. Although there is considerable debate over what motivates judges, it is safe to say that, at least to the extent judges are not elected, they are better insulated from political pressures than legislators.

18. As Hazlett (1990, 172) notes, the effect of diluting ownership can be measured, in part, in terms of the costs of compliance with the new regulatory regime. "Market transfers are screened by federal authorities; license renewals are less than costless or riskless; new spectrum use for broadcasting is prohibited by law. The system has transferred net resources to incumbent broadcasters, broadcast regulators (including oversight congressional committees) and advocates of the 'public interest.'"

PART V

INTRODUCTION

The tragedy of the commons (open access) analyzed earlier in this volume with respect to fisheries, oil pools, and other resources also applies to waste disposal. Frequently, the air, water, or land into which effluent is disposed is unowned, open access space. If effluent disposal is open to all, the now-familiar tragedy will develop in predictable ways. Notably, there will be too much disposal, which in turn will create conflict between those who want to use an area for waste disposal and those who want to use it for recreation or other purposes.

EXTERNALITIES VERSUS TRANSACTION COSTS

As Bruce Yandle notes in chapter 10, most economic analysis of pollution has followed the lead of British economist A. C. Pigou, who saw pollution as a cost imposed on the rest of society. If no one owns the atmosphere, the lack of enforceable property rights results in what economists call an externality: those using air for effluent disposal (e.g., carbon monoxide from cars) impose costs on the rest of society without consent or compensation for those who wish to breathe clean air. If polluters do not take into account all costs they impose, the atmospheric commons is overused by the polluters, just as an open access fishery is overfished.

Pigou's solution to the externality problem was a government tax on each unit of pollution. By using its coercive power to tax, government can raise the cost of polluting, and thus lower the amount of pollution. Just like the costly regulations modeled in figure II.3, cost-increasing taxes will reduce use of the open access resource. An optimal tax seemingly would restrict use to the point where all societal costs are taken into account.

Pigou's tax solution is conceptually simple but operationally complex, for at least two reasons. First, there is the problem of knowing what per-unit tax will bring about the optimal amount of pollution. Nobel laureate Friedrich Hayek (1945) emphasizes that calculating social benefits and costs to determine the optimal tax and the optimal amount of pollution requires enormous amounts of information. And even if the information can be had, implementing a truly optimal tax is politically unlikely, given the special interests of affected parties. In particular, if the parties wishing to use the atmosphere for cheap disposal are well organized and the parties wanting clean air are diffuse and unorganized, the likelihood of implementing the desirable tax solution is minimal.

Yandle presents the work of another Nobel laureate, Ronald Coase, who counters Pigou's conceptually simple, but operationally complex, taxation solution. Coase's fundamental contribution (1960) to what he called "the problem of social cost" brings property rights into the externality discussion. Comparing Pigou with Coase, Yandle notes that the externality issue is best approached as a problem in competition for the use of scarce resources. As mentioned in this volume's introductory chapter, scarcity drives property rights. Without scarcity, defining and enforcing property rights are unnecessary. Anyone can enjoy a resource without depriving others of their employment. With scarcity, however, one person's use precludes another's, introducing a potential for positive returns in definition and enforcement of rights.

In this context, Yandle points out that the externality problem is not a matter of one person imposing costs on another, but rather a matter of competition for the use of a scarce resource. As the first step to resolving this competition, property rights must be defined to remove the resource from open access. Thereafter, bargaining (Libecap's "contracting for property rights") can begin. As Coase explained, if transaction costs are relatively low, property rights will be well defined and enforced, and bargaining will result in the opportunity costs of alternative uses being taken into account.

Most of the literature on pollution assumes that transaction costs are prohibitively high, which would make it difficult for Coasean bargains to proceed. But that assumption is typically made without empirical support. Yandle details several examples of how property rights and bargaining actually do solve many of Pigou's externality problems, through combinations of private contract and the law. Under common law, courts have consistently closed access to the commons by assigning property rights. If an upstream polluter dumps garbage into a stream and causes harm to a downstream owner of rights to clean water, courts have typically enforced the rights to clean water and required the polluter to pay damages, cease the polluting activities, or both. In England, for example, where fishing rights on streams are held by individuals and clubs, the Anglers' Co-operative Association (recently renamed the Anglers' Conservation Association, ACA) has been bringing actions against polluters since 1948. It has brought over 2,000 actions against polluters and, remarkably, lost only two (Anderson and Leal 1997, 102–3).

Yandle goes beyond common law cases as a solution to conflicting resource uses to discuss how other market forces can induce firms to take account of the opportunity costs of pollution. If those desiring cleaner air or water or better management of forests are willing to pay for their demands, firms can profit from being good stewards through green certification programs. Just as an independent laboratory can certify the safety of a product and allow the manufacturer to sell the safe product at a higher price, third-party green certification can provide a market incentive for firms to demonstrate they are supplying cleaner air or water or better land management. In a sense, green certification gives the firm a property right to the resources being stewarded, a property right that can be marketed for a profit. In essence, Yandle argues, the evidence shows we should not be too quick to assume that high transaction costs preclude Coasean bargains.

Transaction Costs Are Costs

Harold Demsetz pushes the Yandle point a step further by asking how firms might contract to take Pigouvian externalities into account. He begins with the hypothetical case of a steel mill and a laundry competing for the use of clean air; the steel mill wants to use the air for waste disposal, and the laundry wants to use it for drying clothes. For Pigou, this would be an externality imposed by the steel mill on the laundry, requiring a tax on the mill. For Coase, it would be a matter of competing uses. Assignment of a right to pollute or a right to dry clothes would provide a basis for bargaining as long as the transactions costs are relatively low, so no tax would be required.

Demsetz contemplates a different sort of bargain to solve the problem. If the two affected parties integrated into a single firm, all costs would be internalized, solving the property rights problem. Demsetz asks what generally could constrain firms from integrating, and concludes that it is higher organizational costs. That is, integration may involve gains such as economies of scale, but it also involves transaction (organizational) costs. In the case of a Pigouvian externality between the steel mill and the laundry, there are potential gains from taking into account the opportunity costs of using the atmosphere for waste disposal, but there are added transaction costs of operating the two firms as one.

In a sense, Demsetz claims that Coase did not take his transaction cost argument far enough. By concluding that bargaining could solve the Pigouvian externality problem provided transaction costs were low, Demsetz worries that Coase provided a faulty justification for government intervention. If individuals and firms are not integrating to take into account the opportunity costs of alternative uses of air, water, and land, the costs of integration must exceed the benefits. Transaction costs are like any other input cost—a cost of doing business. If the government can lower those costs (frequently a dubious proposition), perhaps governmental regulations can improve efficiency. But that is an empirical claim, not one that is necessarily true.

Understanding that transaction costs are simply the opportunity cost of resources used in bargaining and organization, the Coase theorem has more to say than is commonly appreciated. Again the lens of property rights analysis presents a new outlook on externality problems.

CHAPTER TEN

PROPERTY RIGHTS OR EXTERNALITIES?

Bruce Yandle

In his fascinating biography of John D. Rockefeller Sr., Ron Chernow (1998) tells how Cleveland refineries in 1867 struggled to meet the demand for kerosene. In the process, much unwanted gasoline was discharged into the Cuyahoga River:

> Before the automobile, nobody knew what to do with the light fraction of crude oil known as gasoline, and many refiners, under cover of dark, let the waste product run into the river. The noxious runoff made the Cuyahoga River so flammable that if steamboat captains shoveled glowing coals overboard, the water erupted in flames. (Chernow 1998, 101)

John D. Rockefeller commented that "hundreds of thousands of barrels of it [gasoline] floated down the creeks and rivers, and the ground was saturated with it" (Chernow 1998, 101). A fire hazard even then, the Cuyahoga River became famous one hundred years later as America's burning river (Meiners, Thomas, and Yandle 2000).

Some 140 years since Cleveland's refinery heydays, state and federal regulations now control Cuyahoga polluters. Friends of the Crooked River, a local volunteer organization, has taken major steps to clear away debris and remove pollution from the stream; they take pride in pointing to picnic grounds and recreational areas that have developed along the crooked Cuyahoga. Through hard work and heavy politicking, the Cuyahoga's friends in 1998 saw their river named one of the first of President Clinton's American Heritage Rivers (Thomas and Yandle 1998). Now, the full firepower of the federal government is directed toward the river's protection and development.

From floating and flaming gasoline to picnicking and fishing, the Cuyahoga story illustrates the relationship between externalities and property rights. Focusing on the pollution problem, this chapter considers three approaches for managing environmental use. Externality analysis is considered first. Pioneered by A. C. Pigou (1920, 1932), externality analysis rests on the notion that the state can and should tax or regulate polluters and others who impose unwanted costs (negative externalities) on parties not involved in the decision to pollute.

Then, with the work of Ronald H. Coase (1960), a second approach to the problem, property rights analysis, is introduced. Where Pigou saw pollution as a cost imposed by polluters on others — a negative externality — Coase saw competition among different parties for the use of an environmental asset lacking fully specified property rights. Unresolved pollution problems may be evidence of a need for the state to enforce environmental property rights that can be traded. With rights defined and enforced, those who wish to modify existing uses of the environment must bargain with the rights owner.

The next section of the chapter looks to broader market forces for solutions that go beyond the discussion of command-and-control (Pigou) and direct bargaining (Coase). As the environment becomes more valuable, a combination of environment-preserving legal rules, warranties, and quality assurance devices arise in competitive markets. Therefore, firms and organizations subject to market forces that engage in costly polluting activities do so at their own peril. Pigou-type externalities can be reduced without Pigouvian remedies and without Coasean bargaining.

THE CUYAHOGA STORY:
EXTERNALITIES OR PROPERTY RIGHTS?

Ron Chernow's description of Cleveland refinery discharge practices is well suited to a modern discussion of externalities. The lecture goes like this: A dirty oil refinery, under cover of night, pours thousands of gallons of gasoline into an urban river. Costs are imposed on barge operators, watercraft, and other river users. Part of the cost of producing refined oil products has been forced on others. Instead of bearing the cost of waste disposal, the refinery has externalized it — shifted the costs to others. There is too much kerosene and not enough clean water. The market has failed to provide the optimal mix of goods and services. Government action is required to internalize the externality.

Or is this a property rights problem? Did the refineries hold implicit rights to use the Cuyahoga as a disposal system? Did other property owners raise no objections? Where was the sheriff? Saying yes to externalities stops the analytical engine and leads inevitably to an externality solution — government action. Saying yes to property rights keeps the analysis going down another path, which may or may not call for costly government action. Only by considering both analytical paths and not being yoked to one or the other can we discover the power of property rights and bargaining to counter externality problems.

Locating One More Refinery on the Cuyahoga

Think back to Chernow's description of Cleveland in the mid-1800s. Suppose a group of investors is considering the construction of another refinery on the Cuyahoga River. At the time, there were no statutes guarding the nation's rivers and streams. (The first meaningful statutes did not arrive until 1972.) There are no meaningful city, county, or state statutes, although Cleveland has established industrial zones for refineries. And if refineries discharge distillates "under cover of dark" to avoid detection, there is little scientific understanding of harms that may be generated by the action. As Goklany (1999, 95–102) reminds us, the absence of perception precludes an institutional transition for safeguarding human health and well-being.

But is it possible that, in spite of the gasoline discharge, there is no need for command-and-control regulation? At the time, there was common law, that body of judge-made law that protected property owners from unwanted harms and losses (Brubaker 1998). And while scientific understanding of pollution harms was crude at best, common sense alone would prompt notice by river boat captains or owners of threatened warehouses, wharves, and other improvements along shorelines when rivers catch fire.

Suppose a modern economist is provided this institutional background and told that the planned refinery will likely discharge unwanted gasoline into the waters of the Cuyahoga. Asked to offer a policy for siting the refinery and to comment on the practical aspects of adopting the policy proposal as a general rule, what framework would the modern economist use?

Most economists would consider two primary theoretical approaches for analyzing the problem.[1] The first approach involves an externality analysis, where the refinery pollutes the river, imposing costs on downstream parties and riverboat captains, costs that do not enter the refinery owners' profit calculations. This is the well-known problem of social cost. An economist taking this approach would be using an analytical framework developed by A. C. Pigou (1920, 1932). Pigou argued that when pollution generates a social cost, government should take action. As he put it, the government should engage in "certain specific acts of interference with normal economic processes" (1932, 172). Pigou proposed a system of taxes, bounties, and regulations for resolving the problem. An economist using this market failure framework would recommend some form of effluent taxes or regulation to control the refinery's discharge.

The second approach considers the refinery and others who consume or enjoy water quality as part of a competitive market where people bargain for the use of rights to scarce property. This analysis does not focus on polluters imposing costs on society, but on competing demands for use of an asset. If rights to Cuyahoga water quality are defined and assigned to owners of land along the river, then those planning to build the refinery must bargain with the rightholders to determine just how much, if any, they will discharge into the river. If the refinery holds the rights, then existing communities or landowners located along the river must bargain with the refinery owner for rights to water quality. Bargaining determines the amount of discharge into the river.

This second approach relies on the work of Nobel laureate Ronald H. Coase (1960), who considered the Pigouvian solution and established a different way of thinking about the problem of social cost. Using his framework, an economist might recommend a meeting of the refinery owners and others who have access to the river to determine who has what rights. If existing river users owned water-quality rights, the refinery would have to buy the rights in order to discharge specified amounts of waste. If the refinery held the right to pollute, existing river users would have to buy water quality from the refinery, paying the refinery to limit its discharges. This approach sees property rights and the market as the solution, while the first approach sees the market as the problem (Barzel 1997).

Theoretical reasoning is one thing, but what about the practical aspects of the two policy options? Pigou's approach requires much information, which is costly to assemble. Still, it might be possible to deal with one refinery being built on one river. It would be impossible to determine the optimal amount of discharge for hundreds of thousands of industrial dischargers located along hundreds of rivers and streams, a difficulty Pigou recognized late in his career.[2]

While the Coasean solution theoretically handles the information problem because the parties involved are the decision makers, it can fail because of transaction costs that emerge if thousands of people along a river are expected to bargain with multiple dischargers. The pure Pigouvian and Coasean alternatives are difficult to apply in the real world. Failure to find a silver bullet suggests two possibilities: (1) the refinery will locate and do nothing to limit its discharge, or (2) the troubled community will call on government to regulate. After all, it is results that matter most. Regulation seems to offer greater certainty than bargaining. Coase gets the Nobel Prize and academic recognition for having developed a powerful approach for analyzing social cost; Pigou seems to have won the policy battle by default.

But we should not be too quick in naming Coase the loser in a contest he did not enter. He was not developing an environmental policy prescription. Quite the contrary; Coase explains how an appropriate interpretation of market forces relying on a rule of law could eliminate the need for specialized statutes for handling "the problem of social cost," which includes environmental issues. In doing so, he calls attention to institutions that evolve, often spontaneously, to reduce the inevitable costs that are generated in communities. Government regulation is one of the many approaches that might be taken. Indeed, Coase might remind us that water quality in the Cuyahoga River today results from a combination of forces that include property rights, statutes, and the result of a rich market process that, while generating prices for scarce resources, helps to form resource-conserving customs and traditions (De Alessi 1998a). The cost and benefits of organizing and running the various institutions dictate which approach, if any, might be utilized. Along these lines, Demsetz (1967) teaches us that the definition and enforcement of property rights is itself a part of the market process.

Staring Externalities in the Eye

The classic negative externality story is often presented in terms of an upstream discharger and a downstream receiver of unwanted wastes as in the Cuyahoga River example. Economists define this as a technological externality: "A technological externality exists when some activity of party A imposes a cost or benefit on party B for which A is not charged or compensated by the price system of a market economy" (Whitcomb 1972, 6). Notice the exclusive focus on prices and the market economy. To make progress in analyzing the way the world works, we must add a note of realism. We must consider law and economics.[3] For water pollution to be recognized under the common law of nuisance, the avenue for legal redress often taken when market prices do not adequately compensate for harms, the costs must be imposed on an owner or occupier of land or on some party who holds the right not to be harmed by the unwanted actions of others. Rights matter. They matter because rights identify opportunity costs. By choosing to hold the asset, the individual rightholder has foregone other opportunities. Rightholders have incentives to conserve the assets they hold and to be alert for wealth-maximizing opportunities. When a rightholder claims to be damaged by pollution or any other spillover effect, the harm claimed must be of sufficient size for an objective observer to identify the losses (Meiners and Yandle 1999). In addition, the aggrieved rightholder must be able to link his harm to the polluter's discharge.

The limits of the law recognize that there are at least two actors involved in meaningful externality or nuisance problems. One is the party who holds a valuable right and bears the opportunity cost in doing so. The other is the actor who imposes costs, without recognizing the opportunity cost and the related rights of the affected party. Either party can initiate an action to resolve the externality problem. The receiving party may settle for damages or sell the rights he holds. Obviously, the polluting party can alter his action or contract with the receiver for the transfer of rights so that cost can be imposed. In either case, the nuisance and externality disappear. Recognition that people, not nature, hold rights that must be protected and that externalities are unwanted invasions of rights held by people is critical to understanding the law and economics of an externality problem.

The term externality is often applied inappropriately to a broader category of events. Without specifying any system of property rights and opportunity cost, the term is commonly used to describe any undesirable outcome that springs from human activity. Under this broad rubric, automobile drivers impose negative externalities from their tailpipe emissions when they drive through almost-deserted ghost towns in the rural south, even though the emissions are too small to be detected and make no biological contacts. Just the assertion of externalities supposedly justifies the imposition of limits on the noise produced by ascending and descending aircraft, which encourages continued encroachment of residential communities on airports. Development activities once praised for providing homes, schools, and health care in suburban areas become labeled urban sprawl when viewed through an unconstrained externality lens; then the solution to the perceived problem becomes regulation. As Boudreaux and Meiners (1998) characterize existence value, if the thought of a Cleveland oil refinery discharging thousands of barrels of petroleum waste into the Cuyahoga River beclouds an otherwise pleasant moment for someone, that would be enough to require that the discharge activity be stopped. So perceived, externalities and related opportunities for government to improve human well-being are ubiquitous.

A better definition distinguishes relevant from irrelevant costs when we examine an externality. Buchanan and Stubblebine (1962) ask if the effects being considered impose enough cost on recipients to cause them or others to discover mutually beneficial ways to reduce the harmful effect. This distinction between relevant externalities, those that impose marginal costs worth removing as revealed by actions being taken by affected parties and irrelevant externalities as opposed to those that do not, identifies two paths that may be taken to resolve externality problems. Relevant externalities can be resolved through the market; irrelevant and relevant externalities can be resolved politically.

When applied to the Cuyahoga River in 1867, the analysis must determine if the landowners along the river had property rights to environmental quality and, if so, did they seek damages or injunctions against the refineries. Alternately, the polluting activities might have yielded a net positive outcome for otherwise aggrieved sufferers from pollution. For example, a net beneficial combination could result from a polluting refinery that increased the value of industrial land and yielded better-paying jobs or from flame-threatened river boat operators who were simultaneously the main carriers of refined petroleum products. These could be compared to situations where refinery owners purchased most of the riparian land that would be affected by the pollution.[4]

It is likely that the early Cuyahoga externalities were initially irrelevant. Rising incomes and growing environmental scarcity would just as likely change this outcome. Indeed, the record shows that later Cleveland residents eventually did attempt to bring common law suits against Cuyahoga polluters (Meiners, Thomas, and Yandle 2000). Unfortunately for the aggrieved landowners, the polluters were shielded from suit by city and state regulations. The citizens' previously held common law rights had been taken by legislation. As a result of political action taken by the state, the polluters may have been imposing relevant, but legal, externalities on parties downstream.

How Pigou Describes the Problem

Pigou (1920, 183–94) offers air pollution as an example of the full cost of production diverging from the firm's supply cost: "Smoke in large cities inflicts a heavy uncharged loss on the community, in injury to buildings, vegetation, expenses for washing clothes and cleaning rooms, expenses for the provision of artificial light, and in many other ways" (Pigou 1920, 184). Pigou's solution for too much pollution calls for government action: "It is, however, possible for the State, if it so chooses, to remove the divergence in any field by 'extraordinary encouragements' or 'extraordinary restraints' upon investment in that field" (1920, 192). In other words, Pigou would recommend imposing a tax on the refinery equal to the additional cost imposed downstream when the refinery discharges waste to the river. Skipping over the difficult matter of "if it so chooses," he indicates that taxes and bounties are the most obvious restraints that might be used, leaving open the possibility of using regulation where government specifies what must be done and how it is to be carried out:

No "invisible hand" can be relied on to produce a good arrangement of the whole from a combination of separate treatments of the parts. It is therefore necessary that an authority of wider reach should intervene to tackle the collective problems of beauty, of air and light, as those other collective problems of gas and water have been tackled. (Pigou 1920, 195)

If, because of high transaction costs, people in local communities fail to act, Pigou (1920, 195) argues that "power [should be] given to the appropriate department of the central Government to order them to take action." An authoritarian, command-and-control regime is as much a part of the Pigouvian prescription as taxes and bounties. Although Pigou recognized that government action is costly, his prescription took on a life of its own and extended a public finance tradition in economics that overlooked the purpose and function of the legal and cultural environment that supports and surrounds all market transactions. In discussing divergences between social and private cost, Pigou never mentions the role played by private law, customs, traditions, and community associations. Property rights are never discussed, and market forces are seen as steering in the wrong direction. He, like so many economists, performed the analysis in an institutional vacuum.

In spite of the justification of government regulation and taxes spawned by his seminal work, Pigou saw little reason to expect politicians to deliver efficient solutions to externality problems.[5] Speaking of efficient outcomes, Pigou (1932, 332) said:

> [W]e cannot expect that any public authority will attain, or will even wholeheartedly seek, that ideal. Such authorities are liable alike to ignorance, to sectional pressure and to personal corruption by private interest. A loud-voice part of their constituents, if organized for votes, may easily outweigh the whole.

While Pigou saw these political difficulties, he could hardly have recognized that government enterprises could become the worst polluters and the least likely to respond to the spur of competition. Moreover, his analysis provided intellectual credibility for government intervention and regulation. With Pigou's strictures in hand, future generations of political favor seekers were armed with a kind of Old Testament interpretation of how to make the world a better place. If enough rules are written and enforced, better things would emerge, especially for well-organized interest groups.

Pigou's inability or failure to account for the functioning of property rights institutions and markets led him to call for collective solutions for controversies that could have been, and were, settled by private law and other, less formal ways. Worse, the collectively determined solutions could legalize externalities that would have been otherwise eliminated and could take property rights without compensation as when the state classified the Cuyahoga as an industrial stream.

The Pigouvian Prescription Applied

Pigou's influence on the politics of externalities seems great. In 1997, there were at least thirty-four environmental taxes imposed across twenty-five countries (Barde 1997). These include taxes on oxides of carbon and nitrogen in Scandinavian countries, bottle charges and CFC taxes across the United States, effluent charges in Germany, the Netherlands, and France, emission and effluent fees operating across Central and South America, emission taxes on industry in California, and various fuel taxes in many states that attempt to adjust for smog production (Brannlund 1995; Egenhofer 1996). There are even environmental taxes on disposable razors. In each case, public authorities can claim to be adjusting for market failures; they are attempting to place a price on environmental use. In some cases, there are arguments that income taxes can be replaced with environmental taxes thereby generating a "double dividend," which is to say a cleaner environment and a more efficient use of labor in the economy (Bovenberg and Goulder 1997; O'Riordan 1997).

Every industrialized country has taken the Pigouvian approach in a larger sense. Property rights-eroding centralized command-and-control regulation is found more often than taxes and bounties (DeLong 1997; Marzulla and Marzulla 1997; Pipes 1999, 248–53). But it is erroneous to credit Pigou with these laws. Long before Pigou, we find Pigouvian solutions at play. Pigou did not invent the regulatory state, but rather provided academic credibility to support the natural tendency of people to seek political power over others.

Intellectual credibility is surely important for those who would empower the state. And when credibility is added to apparent simplicity, the Pigouvian approach is almost unbeatable. Consider the apparent simplicity. To rid the world of unwanted externalities, simply calculate the correct tax and impose it on polluters. As the Pigouvian alternative, identify the quantity of waste to be allowed from particular polluters and impose regulations mandating the amounts.

Upon reflection, the proposed simplicity entails obvious complexity. In addressing the earlier example of distillates being discharged into the Cuyahoga, government authorities must estimate the demand for kerosene and the prices people are willing to pay for different amounts of output or determine the appropriate quantities of kerosene to produce, an accomplishment that even the best nineteenth-century managers would find difficult to achieve. Next, as Macaulay (1972) notes, the politician must have estimated the amount of damage to people downstream. Estimating damage in the absence of market-generated information on the cost of avoiding harm is no simple matter (Head 1974, 186–87). For example, what if a person downstream can take actions to avoid the harm of dirty water by moving to another location at a cost of $5,000, yet the estimate of damage without taking offsetting action is $10,000? It is the $5,000 damage that should be relevant to the policy maker, not the $10,000. But the $10,000 estimate is easier to obtain than the $5,000 estimate. If the tax or quantity adjustment is based on $10,000, the refinery and its customers will pay more than the social cost of producing kerosene. The river will be too clean.

Estimation is more complicated when there are many receivers of waste, each with a different level of harm from the water pollution. Consider the complication that comes when a national government attempts to set an appropriate tax or quantity restriction for each producer that pollutes water, all users of their products, and all downstream water users to take care of multiple externalities across a vast geographic area with many rivers.

A final complexity arises when each tax imposed induces substitutions in input and output markets. A pollution tax or quantity restriction imposed on kerosene makes the product relatively more expensive to consumers and producers. They in turn shift their purchases to substitute products. Demand curves shuffle, and environmental effects rise and fall across markets. In discussing this problem, Whitcomb (1972, 133) warns us:

> Serious error will result if we rush ahead and put taxes on a few pollutants and ignore others. For example, a tax on phosphates in laundry detergents will (quite properly) raise the price of these detergents and cause substitution of other detergents and substitution of paper towels and diapers, and the like, for now-more-expensive-to-wash cloth ones. The disposal of waste paper will increase inefficiently unless a tax has also been placed on paper.

These difficulties are found in efforts by Mexico and Colombia to implement Pigouvian effluent fees to control water pollution (World Bank 1996, 30–33). Mexico's system of pollution charges has been in place since 1991, but little has been accomplished. Due to the complexities of setting fees based on damages or cost of clean-up, the government sets a charge based simply on volume of wastewater discharged, neglecting completely the amount of pollutants in the waste stream. The program's recognized failure is attributed to high monitoring and enforcement costs. Opposition from industry, based on competitiveness arguments, has also taken its toll. On the other hand, Colombia has attempted to take a true Pigouvian approach, at least officially. The Colombian statute requires that pollution taxes be based on estimates of damages somehow related to people, property, and the environment. But the institutional basis for determining appropriate fees and for monitoring and enforcing compliance are lacking. From 1974 to 1994, only $116,000 was collected from a revenue base that, according to the World Bank, should have generated $90 million (World Bank 1996, 31).

Suppose all the technical complications could be resolved and government officials could determine the appropriate per-unit tax or quantity individually tailored and imposed on the harmful waste discharged by all refineries and other producers. Would the problem be solved? There are two answers. At a technical level, the answer is yes. But in a world of human action, the answer is no.

Politicians are concerned when constituents complain about pollution. Concerned citizens want cleaner rivers. They have no way of knowing what the optimal pollution should be, nor do they care. They just want cleaner water. When the politicians impose a tax on polluters or set discharge limitations, the constituents are understandably pleased. But once the appropriate regulation is imposed, some level of pollution continues to make its way into rivers. All along, the friends of the environment have not been charged directly for their enjoyment of the river. When the river becomes cleaner, they continue to receive benefits at no cost to themselves.

People who live along affected rivers come and go, but tax-paying oil refineries have a way of staying put. When the price of something people value is zero, people want a relatively large amount of it. People consume the valued resource until the last unit consumed is approximately equal to the value given up in exchange for the unit. A zero price goes with zero enjoyment of the last unit. With pollution still in the water, though it be the optimal amount approved by Professor Pigou, the mobile population along rivers — and environmentalists in other regions — will likely call for more pollution control, which means a higher tax or some form of regulation.[6] Of course, political action is not costless, so the concerned population may not clamor for complete elimination of pollution, although complete elimination would be desirable from their standpoint. Unless the Pigouvian solution calls for zero discharge, the solution tends to be politically unstable. A reading of the *Federal Water Pollution Control Act of 1972* clearly communicates this point. The statute called for zero pollution in the nation's rivers and streams by 1985. That goal obviously was not and cannot be met. But that goal, which everyone had to know was an impossibility, satisfied the dedicated environmentalists who influenced the writing of the statute.

Here is a commons problem with a one-sided solution. There is demand for water quality, which is scarce but unrationed. One component of demand relates to industrial production. Refineries want to discharge waste into the river to produce kerosene. People along the river who wish to enjoy nature's bounty generate a second, but competing, component of demand. Thus, there is competition for use of the commons. If oil refineries are required to pay a price for using the commons, we can predict that their use will decline. But the competing groups, including political action groups, which pay nothing directly will lobby for more control. They understandably want to expand their use of the commons. The one-sided solution leaves an unstable outcome.

In contrast, when rights are defined and enforced for all users of the environment, those who want greater purity can enter the market and purchase rights (Abelson 2000). Those who seek more production compete in the same market. When only one group pays, the rights system tends to break down again. A commons is a commons so long as a group of users has free access. As Louis De Alessi (1998a) points out, a policy that fails to ensure reciprocity of costs will fail to solve environmental problems. Even worse, as noted by Ridley (1996, 236–37), a one-sided attempt to solve a perceived tragedy of the commons can yield even more serious tragedies; the controls installed by government can erode normal private incentives to conserve resources and create wealth, and transform a desire to produce goods into a desire to produce laws.

Coase and Property Rights

Ronald Coase examined the Pigouvian solution and arrived at a different way of looking at pollution, as well as every other problem of social cost. Assuming a system of well-specified property rights, his analysis concluded that were it not for transaction costs, that is, the costs parties incur in dealing with one another, there would be no relevant externalities to deal with. Yes, there would be pollution, but the amount would be agreed upon voluntarily by producers and receivers of pollution. The environmental outcome would be accepted as the lower cost alternative.

The Coasean story, like the Pigouvian one, can be told in terms of a refinery located on a river that seeks to minimize the cost of producing kerosene. The location of the refinery is not a random occurrence. The river is an important input to the production process, providing water for the refining process and then carriage for waste discharged. So, the refinery operators value the river.

Like all production inputs, use of the river is determined by its cost to the refinery. If river use comes without a bill because it is freely available to all users, the refinery will use more water than if it had to pay for the input. If river use is free, the refinery will tend to discharge waste to the point where the net marginal benefit is zero.

Now suppose people live downstream from the refinery in a remote location. The spot was selected by a developer who constructed a community complete with recreational facilities and a boat dock. As explained by Rinehart and Pompe (1997), developers assign value to riparian land, even though the adjacent stream or ocean is an open access resource. The real estate developer estimates the marginal benefits of the unpolluted river that passes the downstream development, and like all marginal benefits, these diminish as the development expands. Because units of the river can be consumed at no additional cost to the developer, the developer will construct units until the last unit built yields zero benefit from the river's location. Similarly, the homeowners will use the river up to the point where the net marginal benefit is zero.

At the outset, the refinery imposes no cost on the downstream community; the waste discharged to the river is assimilated at it moves downstream. The downstream community is aware that the refinery exists somewhere upstream but is not bothered by the refinery's operation. Everything is fine until the refinery increases its production, which comes when demand for its product increases. Increased production burdens the assimilative capacity of the river. Eventually, with rising demand for kerosene and more daily discharge, water quality begins to deteriorate.

Residents, much to their distress, now see odd colors in the water, notice a peculiar odor, and then see dead fish. Their isolation from the city has been ruined by pollution. Some of the marginal benefits enjoyed previously have been taken away. The refinery enjoys 100 percent discharge of wastes; the homeowners are gradually losing their previous 100 percent of the river's value. Expansion of water quality means reducing discharge by the refinery, and vice versa. Coase reminds us that trade-offs are inevitable. Is kerosene production more valuable than water quality to the community?

Suppose it is election time; a candidate seeking a seat in the House of Representatives hears about the voters who live along the river. The voters have a problem they hope the politician will solve. The politician is asked to talk about her platform, "Where do you stand on the environment?"

In today's context, the politician may say that if she is elected she will sponsor a bill that gives environmental rights to communities like this one, "No polluter should have the right to destroy the environment." The politician receives support from members of the community. True to her word, she sponsors a river protection act that contains the details she promised. The act becomes law, and the refinery cuts its emissions to zero. The refinery incurs a high cost for handling its waste in another way. With zero discharge, the community owners enjoy marginal benefits of zero. The marginal benefit to the refinery of being allowed to discharge a small amount of waste is larger than zero. There are potential gains from trade. If transaction costs are small enough, the refinery operator may be able to entice the community to accept a little waste in the community's river.

Suppose the refinery operator calls a citizen and asks: "Would you allow us to discharge some waste into your river?" The refinery operator adds: "We will pay you for each unit we discharge. Our records of discharge will be monitored by a certified environmental engineer. If we violate the contract, you can take us to court." Because marginal benefits of discharge to the refinery, across some zone of discharge, are larger than the marginal losses sustained by the community, the refinery operator can pay enough to purchase some discharge rights from the community.

Suppose the community agrees to sell the refinery some discharge rights and uses the funds generated to make improvements worth more to them than the slight deterioration of the river. As the two parties transfer rights, the marginal benefits of discharge to the refinery start to equal to the community's losses caused by the discharge. Since the outcome is based on voluntary agreement between the affected parties, both sides must be better off.

Three points emerge from this hypothetical story. First, property rights to the river were assigned to one of the trading parties and the rights were enforced by statute. Second, the statute allowed for exchange between parties, so long as all affected parties agreed to the outcome. Finally, the refinery operator agreed to an enforceable contract based on outcomes assured by a third-party auditor.

Let us alter the first assumption. Let there be another politician running for office who promised: "If you send me to Washington, I will push through a statute that gives rights to use rivers and streams to all firms that produce valuable products for the marketplace." The refinery operators and its employees' union offer their support for the campaign and this politician defeats the candidate who supports environmental rights for the downstream community.

Members of the downstream community install air conditioners and odor reducing devices and build fences to block the view of the dead fish in the river. Recall that the refinery received little benefit for the last units of waste it discharged, and the community suffered considerable harm as the river reached its biological death. As before, when pollution was prohibited, there are potential gains from trade if homeowners can entice the refinery to reduce its discharge.

Let the homeowners call the refinery operator and say: "We despise what you are doing, but the river is yours. Would you consider reducing your waste by a small amount? Just take out the big chunks. We will pay you for each unit of waste removed." As before, the community can outbid the refinery for water quality to a point. The value of cleaner water is likely to be higher than the cost to the refinery of alternative effluent disposal. In fact, gains from contracting extend to the same point that was reached when the community owned the river, and the refinery was doing the bidding.

It is natural to sympathize more with one party than the other. The point, however, is not to argue one side or the other, but to see that each party imposes costs on the other. This is one of Coase's key points. Externalities flow both ways because costs and benefits flow both ways. There is no such thing as a one-sided externality problem.

Most important, assuming zero transaction costs, the outcome is the same, no matter which party holds the rights. The deeper implication of this outcome relates to the value of the two activities. Bidders for more valuable use of the river are able to outbid the less valuable uses. Put differently, the low-cost avoider of the problem makes the largest adjustment. In addition, the system is forward-, not backward-looking. Instead of looking at the current users and finding solutions that fit the needs of existing technologies and plans, the more dynamic approach encourages all users to focus on the future: What is the lowest-cost way to organize my use of the environment? Can I find a new approach that enables me to bid more for the resource? Putting it this way makes another point: Trade based on property rights brings a solution that minimizes society's costs for managing valuable water quality.

The stylized river story, which presents the essence of Coase's bargaining model, yields some interesting insights, but it leaves a concern that in many cases one will not find two well-identified and organized groups such as the refinery and homeowners that can bargain at such low cost. The world is too complicated for this to happen. Does high bargaining cost leave us with no alternative but to return to Pigou? Coase addresses this question in a retrospective of his 1960 article: "It would not seem worthwhile to spend much time investigating the properties of [a world with zero transaction costs]. What my argument does suggest is the need to introduce positive transaction costs explicitly into economic analysis so that we can study the world that exists" (Coase 1988, 15).

Coase was not analyzing a world of zero transaction costs. While he did not emphasize the crucial role played by the cost of transacting, his discussion was based on common law — judge-made law that focuses on contracts, torts, and property. His challenge to Pigou really involved the legal environment, not the economic analysis of pollution. As explained by Elizabeth Brubaker (1998), common law protection of environmental rights has an ancient heritage. At the time of Pigou's analysis, England had long operated under rules of common law where downstream holders of riparian rights could bring suit for damages if their rights were taken. Property rights formed the basis for common law rules. If a refinery discharges wastes into a river that flows by land owned or occupied by other people, the dirty water might infringe on the landowners' common law rights by reducing the value of the land, the quality of fishing, or just making life miserable.[7] The common law causes an open access resource, the river, to be treated like private property. Property rights are an explicit component of common law.

Meiners and Yandle (1998, 1999) emphasize the links among property rights, environmental quality, and the rule of law in their treatment of what they term "common law environmentalism." Far from an abstract theory of how markets might limit the occurrence of negative externalities, the common law story is real; it is supported by case law outcomes involving air pollution, water pollution, and hazardous waste. Like all human institutions, common law remedies were not perfect, and the opinions reached by different judges reviewing similar fact situations could vary substantially. But until shoved aside in the 1970s by the politically more attractive federal statute law, common law processes put polluters on notice: The environmental rights held by owners and occupiers of land had to be recognized. No polluter had the right to impose unwanted costs on the owners of private property. Effective enforcement of common law rights closed the circle and forced opportunity costs on all users of environmental resources.

Unlike the Pigouvian solution, common law remedies are two-sided. If a downstream landowner invests in land, relying on a certain level of water quality, he has paid for environmental rights. The landowner bears an opportunity cost for environmental quality. Then, if a refinery operator desires to degrade water quality by discharging waste, he must first gain the approval of the downstream rightholder, usually by purchasing the environmental rights or the land itself (Davis 1971). Having purchased rights, the refinery owner bears the opportunity cost of the environmental quality he seeks to use. Both transacting parties bear the cost of their environmental preferences. Credible threats of common law suits discipline the market process.

A court could be harsh on a refinery operator who failed to obtain rights to degrade water quality from downstream holders of environmental rights. An early 1920 Rhode Island case, *Kirwin v. Mexican Petroleum Co.*, illustrates the point. The plaintiff, who operated a resort called Kirwin's Beach, sued for damages and an injunction under the law of nuisance. As described by the court, the defendant, Mexican Petroleum, did discharge and suffer to escape from its plants, steamers, barges, etc., into the waters of the Providence River, large quantities of oil and kindred products, which were carried by the winds, currents and tides of the Providence River upon plaintiff's beach, fouling and polluting the beach and waters, and rendering the same wholly unfit for bathing, whereby the value of plaintiff's property and business is destroyed.

Mexican Petroleum claimed that the pollution was a normal part of doing business, that it had exhibited diligence and care in operating its refinery, and had not been negligent. Unpersuaded, the judge held for the Kirwin and said:

A nuisance may be created by the conduct of a business with all the care and caution which is possible, and with appliances in perfect order and most perfectly operated. . . . It is the general rule that negligence is not an element in an action for a nuisance, and need not be alleged. Actions for nuisance, properly speaking, stand irrespective of negligence.

In other words, a property right is a property right. No matter how diligent the damaging party might be in avoiding harm, when a violation occurs, the common law remedy follows.

The logic of the law was spelled out clearly in *Whalen v. Union Bag & Paper Co.* in 1913, a New York case involving a new pulp mill representing a $1 million investment that polluted the waters that passed a downstream farmer's pasture. The farmer asked for $312 in damages and an injunction forcing the mill to stop its pollution. On final appeal, New York's highest court supported the damage award and imposed the requested injunction. The court ruled that

[a]lthough the damage to the plaintiff may be slight as compared with the defendant's expense of abating the condition, that is not a good reason for refusing an injunction. Neither courts of equity nor law can be guided by such a rule, for if followed to its logical conclusion it would deprive the poor litigant of his little property by giving it to those already rich. (208 N.Y. 1 at 5)

Emphasizing the opportunity cost imposed by the law, but not calling it by name, the court reminded the mill operators (and all future New York polluters) that

[t]he fact that the appellant has expended a large sum of money in the construction of its plant, and that it conducts its business in a careful manner and without malice, can make no difference in the rights of the stream. Before locating the plant the owners were bound to know that every riparian proprietor is entitled to have the waters of the stream that washes his land come to it without obstruction. . . . [T]hey were bound also to know the character of

their proposed business, and to take themselves at their own peril whether they should be to conduct their business upon a stream . . . without injury to neighbors. (208 N.Y. 1 at 5)

How the Market Process Responds

Firms that hope to survive in a property rights regime requiring compensation for unwanted costs imposed on downstream rightsholders will take action to minimize the associated costs. Among the options considered and bundled are (1) installation of more effective systems of environmental control, (2) improved environmental monitoring and management, (3) alteration of production processes to reduce environmental exposure, (4) relocation of facilities to avoid environmental contact, and (5) purchase of environmental insurance to indemnify the firm in the event of environmental accidents. Each option is costly, yet firms exposed to environmental risks tend to build an environmental control portfolio that includes some of each activity.

Consider the insurance option. The purchase of environmental insurance brings additional scrutiny and control. For insurance to work, the insurance company must accurately set prices based on future claims. Future claims depend largely on actions taken by the firm to limit accidents. Accident-prone firms generate losses in the short run and cause the price of insurance to rise in the long run. Less is sold. Neither outcome is desirable from the insurance firm's standpoint. Insurance companies therefore specify actions to be taken by their customers, inspect plants, and work to reduce environmental accidents. Those firms that cooperate gain relative to their competitors. They pay lower insurance prices and experience fewer losses. The market process rewards environmental stewardship.

The power of consumer response to information that links a firm to environmental degradation is seen in recent activities undertaken by the Geneva, Switzerland, International Organization for Standardization, which issues voluntary standards for manufacturers. Best known for its ISO-9000 standards that relate to manufacturing quality control, ISO has also developed environmental management standards (ISO-14000) that require a fully integrated management approach aimed at eliminating pollution. To qualify for any ISO standard, a firm must develop costly plans and stand periodic audits to assure that its programs are functioning effectively. Home Depot, a major national seller of building supplies, requires all of its suppliers to be ISO-14000 certified. The firm's action reflects its perception of consumer interests, on the assumption that consumers want more assurance that manufacturers are taking steps to reduce pollution.

With the voluntary ISO environmental management approach gaining ground, we might expect to see a competitive response from EPA. After all, the rise of more effective voluntary standards poses a threat to EPA's well-established monopoly on environmental regulation. EPA is now embracing and attempting to influence the ISO-14000 process, which has become increasingly popular with state regulatory agencies (*State Environmental Monitor* 1997). The EPA has provided grants to eight state environmental regulatory agencies to learn more about the prospects of ISO-14000 and to blend into the program EPA's definitions of pollution prevention and regulatory compliance.

Another example of how market forces generate demands for improved environmental management is seen in the golf course certification program developed by the New York Audubon Society (Watson 1999; Costa 1996, 176). Golf courses use pesticides, herbicides, and fertilizers heavily to provide the near-perfect greens desired by golfers. When combined with the heavy use of irrigation and sprinklers, concentrated chemicals can lead to contamination of surface water and groundwater. Absent other constraints, golf course operators have an incentive to go after the last weed when manicuring their courses. The incremental cost of chemicals is low, and the perceived value of extended lush fairways is high.

Providing better information to golf course operators, the Golf Course Superintendents Association (1996a, 1996b) developed guidelines for chemical use and information on alternative ways to improve greens. In 1990, the Audubon Society of New York began to work with the U.S. Golf Association to improve environmental quality, leading to the Audubon certification program. Golf course operators who see value in having the Audubon seal of approval petition Audubon and document the details of their environmental management program, including information on chemical use, water conservation, and maintenance of wildlife habitat. Audubon Society staff work with golf course managers to improve overall environmental management. A similar effort is under-way for advanced planning and certification of new golf courses. Managers of certified golf courses display the Audubon logo and in some cases provide each golfer with a flyer telling about their environmental practices. The cooperative effort is voluntary and the steps being taken to protect environmental assets are evidence of market forces at work in a positive transaction cost world.

Investors in the stock of polluting firms are also interested in the firm's environmental behavior. Managers who are careless with rivers and other features of the environment may also be careless when producing and delivering products. Profit maximization implies careful use of all resources over time. Investors generally assign negative value to news of lawsuits that affect their portfolios. Negative reactions lead to sell orders, which cause stock prices to fall. When stock prices fall, the managers of affected firms find it more costly to obtain additional capital; investors can punish polluting firms.

Recent work on requirements that U.S. firms provide annual data on the number of pounds of more than six hundred chemicals emitted from their plants illustrates how financial markets react to news about pollution. Konar and Cohen (1997) gathered data on the annual listing of emissions, known as the Toxic Release Inventory, and matched the data to the discharging firms listed on major U.S. stock exchanges. Using financial market analysis to isolate the effects of an event on the movement of specified stock portfolios relative to the market as a whole, the researchers found that firms associated with chemical releases on the annual list experienced systematic losses in share values. Looking at data for a later period, the researchers found that firms that suffered the largest reductions in share value reduced their emissions significantly in the next period. In other words, financial market monitoring matters. Investment in reputational capital, fear of common lawsuits, and investor monitoring give polluting firms three reasons to discipline their behavior.

Eco-labeling of consumer products by independent organizations may be seen as yet another approach to reducing the cost of bargaining for improved environmental quality (Thomas 1999). Now popular outside the United States, eco-labeling programs operate in Austria, Canada, Denmark, Finland, France, Germany, Iceland, Japan, the Netherlands, Norway, Sweden, and several Asian countries. Generally developed and administered by quasi-governmental organizations, eco-labeling programs, which are voluntary, require interested producers of specified consumer products to provide detailed technical information on the environmental impact of the manufacture, consumption, and final waste disposal of their products, in some cases requiring a full life-cycle environmental impact analysis. Firms that satisfy requirements and agree to periodic random audits receive authority to affix a highly recognized label on their products and to use it in their advertisements. Ideally, eco-labeling enables uninformed buyers to make better consumption choices, thereby sending market signals that promote an additional element of market competition.

Eco-labeling may induce producers to take efficient steps toward internalizing the cost of environmental use, but domestic producers seem to have a systematic advantage over their international counterparts in obtaining eco-label authority. Part of the advantage stems from the development of criteria to be used in judging the relative merits of products, which are inherently technical and, therefore, subject to special interest influence. In addition, governmental authorities, such as the European Union, have moved to harmonize and institutionalize the eco-labeling process (European Council Regulation 1992). What began as a quasi-competitive use of market forces to provide consumer information could become a part of a bureaucratic process that chills international competition.

There is one last property rights-based motivation that nudges factory managers in the direction of providing better care for the environment. Factory managers and employees generally live in the vicinity of the factory; some will likely live downstream. If the pollution that spews from a factory contaminates drinking water supplies and in other ways diminishes the value of rights held by employees, the managers and owners will eventually bear some of the cost. The extent to which this concern causes managers to reduce pollution nudges the firm's supply curve closer to the marginal social cost curve.

Protection of brand-name capital, avoidance of common law suits, fear of investor punishment, and efforts to avoid damaging rights held by community members yield a set of forces that can push profit-maximizing management in the direction of environmental protection. When firms take these actions, the associated costs become embodied in the firm's supply curve, internalizing what would otherwise be externalities and mitigating market failure. Responding to these and other market forces is costly, and firms will struggle mightily to minimize costs. A free market form of environmental protection emerges from the competitive struggle (Anderson and Leal 1991).

The May 16, 2000, decision of 3M Company to stop producing Scotchguard™, a fabric protector generating annual sales of $300 million, out of $16 billion in corporate revenues, illustrates how a competitive firm responds to environmental and market forces (Friedlin 2000; Weber 2000). Scotchguard contained perfluorooctane sulfonate (PFOS), a highly persistent chemical detected by academic researchers and by 3M in the blood of 3M workers, executives, and people who had no direct connection with 3M. Later evidence indicated PFOS was present in the tissue of birds worldwide. Unable to identify PFOS-related human health effects through the efforts of corporate-funded research at the University of Minnesota and University of Michigan, 3M found evidence that linked the chemical to tumors when research efforts were extended to include animal testing. The firm informed the U.S. EPA of the findings and struggled with the costly decision to phase out Scotchguard. The jobs of some 1,500 3M workers were put at risk. There is still no evidence that the persistent chemical is harmful to human health.

What explains 3M's decision to abandon Scotchguard? Some might suggest the firm made its move to avoid EPA action and costly common lawsuits. Still others can argue that the action was taken to protect 3M brand-name capital and to reduce risk-offsetting wage premiums that might otherwise be paid to 3M executives and workers. Surely, the national environmental organizations were watching. We cannot know the precise set of reasons that triggered the 3M decision. What we do know is that no Pigouvian action or Coasean bargaining occurred. The institutions of the market appear to have taken their toll on the firm.

Final Thoughts

This chapter was motivated by a fundamental question: How important are externalities? The question was not posed to impugn the theory of externalities, rather to challenge lazy or incomplete thinking. To raise a pollution problem, assert existence of an externality, and then call immediately for government repair of market failure is unconvincing. There are too many market institutions that enable human beings to conserve the environment and create wealth at the same time. Calling for government repair of markets that are not broken destroys or reallocates property rights and leads to expansion of the political commons where opportunity costs are invisible and individuals have incentives to overgraze (see McChesney, this volume). Of course, the same accusation can be made of those who see no place for government action in defining and enforcing property rights and assisting institutional change. A fixation on markets where neatly bundled rights are bought and sold can cause a myriad of less formal market processes to be overlooked.

A constant flow of technological change, new knowledge, and new products raises the specter of unrecognized harms that may be imposed on people with no voice in the production decisions. Just as in Cleveland in 1867, budding externalities were emerging. The challenge in the future may be about the ozone layer, global warming, genetically engineered foods, or preservation of sensitive species habitat. No matter what the problem, there will be a temptation to call out "externality" and cry for command-and-control regulation.

It is easy to trade off freedom and property rights. The intellectual debate between Pigou and Coase has to do with a search for solutions to human problems that enable people to hold on to those institutions that preserve freedom and inspire creativity. By shedding the externality yoke, we may continue to blaze an institutional trail that preserves those values.

Endnotes

1. For example, see Tietenberg (1992, 51–69).
2. F. A. Hayek (1969, 264) describes Pigou's misgivings this way:

Perhaps even more instructive is the case of the late Professor A. C. Pigou, the founder of the theory of welfare economics — who at the end of a long life devoted almost entirely to the task of defining the conditions in which government interference might be used to improve upon the results of the market, had to concede that the practical value of these theoretical considerations was somewhat doubtful because we are rarely in a position to ascertain whether the particular circumstance to which the theory refers exist in fact in any given situation. Not because he knows so much, but because he knows how much he would have to know in order to interfere successfully, and because he knows that he will never know all the relevant circumstances, it would seem that the economist should refrain from recommending isolated acts of interference even in conditions in which the theory tells him that they may be sometimes beneficial.

3. F. A. Hayek (1969, 123) expresses concern about the tendency for economists and other scientists to become overspecialized: "But nobody can become a great economist who is only an economist — and I am even tempted to add that the economist who is only an economist is likely to become a nuisance if not a positive danger."

4. This is the type of solution discussed by Demsetz (this volume).

5. Much of the discussion in this chapter is taken from my previous work (Yandle 1997, 1998, 1999). However, in my earlier work on Pigou, I erroneously described him as being unaware of the political forces that might strategically deal with his proposed solutions (Yandle 1998). John G. Head's (1974, 184–213) work on Pigou and externalities made me aware that Pigou fully recognized the mischief that could be done by legislative bodies.

6. This second round of pressure is referred to as post-equilibrium bargaining (Turvey 1963; Cordes 1981). Opinion surveys regularly indicate that the public thinks more needs to be done about the environment, even where improvements have been so great that there is little evidence of a problem.

7. Common law rules provide owners of land adjacent to a stream the right to beneficial use of an uninterrupted supply of water of undeteriorated quality. If an upstream user has unreasonably reduced water quality, the holders of riparian rights have a cause of action against the polluter.

CHAPTER ELEVEN

OWNERSHIP AND THE EXTERNALITY PROBLEM

Harold Demsetz

> And is not that the best-ordered State in which the greatest number of persons apply the terms 'mine' and 'not mine' in the same way to the same thing?
>
> — Socrates, from Plato's *Republic*

> That which is common to the greatest number has the least care bestowed upon it, . . . Everyone thinks chiefly of his own, hardly at all of the common interest, and only when he is himself concerned as an individual . . . [E]verybody is more inclined to neglect the duty which he expects another to fulfil.
>
> — Aristotle's *Politics*

The debate about the virtues and sins of private ownership has a long history, as the above quotations illustrate. Earlier chapters in this book update the debate. The data to date support Aristotle's view. Economic systems based on the rule of law, private ownership, and free markets have been more effective at generating wealth and encouraging efficient resource use.

The debate served to improve our understanding of the institutions and processes of capitalism and, in particular, of the price system that is so important to the functioning of markets. Mainstream economists who wrote during the classical and neoclassical periods of economics are responsible for much of this improvement. Their view of capitalism has not gone unchallenged. Questions have been raised about the macro-instability of capitalism, about the degree of competition that exists in capitalistic-leaning economies, and about the distribution of wealth that seems to emerge in these economies. Many of these questions deal with what people see as the outcome of capitalism, rather than with the theory that had been produced by mainstream economists.

The central concern of the present essay is with the externality problem. This problem questions the validity of theoretical deductions made by neoclassical economists, particularly those deductions derived from the perfect competition model of capitalist economic organization. The central message of these deductions is that exchange within the framework of the competitive price system, for any given distribution of wealth, allocates resources efficiently. It accomplishes this by making all resource owners face the benefits and costs, evaluated subjectively, that result from the uses to which they put their resources.

The externality problem denied the truth of this. It posed situations, seemingly compatible with the perfect competition model, in which some of the benefits and costs of the use to which a resource is put do not influence the owner's decision as to how to use the resource. The short-hand description for this is that private costs (or benefits), which do influence a resource owner, are not equivalent to the total of social costs (or benefits) associated with the way an owner uses his resources. An example to which I will make frequent reference concerns the use of soft coal by a steelmaker. The soft coal produces soot. The soot descends on a neighboring laundry, making it more difficult for the laundry to clean its customers' clothes, but this cost is not faced by the owner of the steel mill when he decides to use soft coal to fuel the steelmaking process.

Henceforth, to economize on exposition, I shall refer only to costs in my discussion, setting aside an explicit consideration of benefits; a cost associated with the use to which a resource is put, but which does not influence the resource owner's choice of use, is an external cost, or, more briefly, an externality. As can be inferred from this example, the externality problem lies at the core of many problems of concern to environmentalists. Thus, a stock of fish or a petroleum reservoir may be depleted too quickly for social interests to be properly served if fishers or oil well drillers do not take into account the costs that their actions impose on others, including the future users of these resources.

The problem of externalities became important to economics after the publication by A. C. Pigou (1920) of his book on economic welfare, although Pigou had written about externalities earlier than this. Pigou argued that the presence of externalities invalidates deductions made by mainstream neoclassical economists about the ability of a competitive price system to allocate resources efficiently. Pigou's argument marched through economic theory largely unchallenged, becoming a durable part of economic doctrine until 1960.[1] It was in 1960 that R. H. Coase published his now-famous article on social cost, and his thoughts on the externality problem succeeded in persuading economists to question the validity of Pigou's argument.

The central ideas in the present essay are a commentary on the externality problem as this problem has been viewed by Pigou and Coase.

Some of these ideas can be found in subjectivist-contrarian literature (see especially Buchanan [1987b]. The approach I present here argues against the emphasis given by Coase, and now by the profession, to transaction cost. The approach also argues that more emphasis should be given to the conditions of ownership. This important contrast with Coase's reasoning notwithstanding, what I have to say, because I deny the importance attached by Coase to transaction cost, allows us to reject the externality problem in cases in which transaction cost is positive as well as those in which it is zero. In this sense, my argument can be viewed as extending the reach of Coase's essential intuition that Pigou had failed to recognize key elements of the externality problem. The elements I stress differ from Coase's, but they also serve to restrict the set of economic activities described as exhibiting policy-relevant externalities.

The debate being joined here involves an attack on and defense of neoclassical theory, so I preface my argument with a brief revisit to neoclassical theory. My intent in doing this is to expose more clearly that which is only implicit in neoclassical theory, the dependency of its conclusions on private ownership arrangements.

If we suppose that each person is a self-sufficient island unto himself, with no exchange taking place with others, and with no dependency on others, the resource allocation problem becomes that of one person managing the scarce resources he possesses. This problem was not of much interest to neoclassical economists, for they were concerned with social aspects of resource allocation. Social aspects become an important part of the allocation problem in neoclassical theory because the theory implicitly presumes that specialization is more productive than is self-sufficiency. If specialization is more productive, freely acting people have reason to live in a condition of dependency on each other rather than, as Crusoe lived before Friday arrived, in a condition of isolation from others.

It is increased reliance on specialization that is the source of costly interactions that bear the externality label. These costly interactions keep a real capitalist economy from achieving as much specialization of resource ownership as might otherwise maximize the value of these resources. This is so because costly interactions between different productive activities are sometimes best mediated by having these activities owned and controlled by a single owner, and, thus, by bearing the greater management cost that comes with the management of facilities devoted to different purposes.

The degree to which there is specialization of ownership in a capitalist economy is nonetheless great. Specialization of ownership implies exchange between owners of resources, and exchange, at a minimum, requires knowledge about and acceptance of ownership arrangements.

Gains from exchange, and the usefulness of exchange more generally, are compromised if people have no confidence about the ownership of that which is offered to them for that which they purport to supply in return. Supply and demand lose their operational power in neoclassical theory if private ownership is not acknowledged; hence, underlying the neoclassical model of the price system is a base of private ownership entitlements. As indicated in part I, neoclassical economists took this base as an implicit given. In their analysis of the price system, they hardly pause to mention underlying ownership arrangements. They certainly do not discuss the conditions of ownership that enable the price system to do what they claim it does. Nonetheless, if their logic is to be understood, it must be that private ownership arrangements have substance and that this substance is known to and accepted by all.

Private ownership serves two functions. The first is to identify persons who own resources, so that others will know with whom they must deal to influence the uses to which resources are put. The identification function can be had without private ownership. A state bureaucrat may have responsibility for choosing the uses to which a parcel of state land is to be put, and he may be widely identified as the person who bears this responsibility.

The second function of private ownership, more important to this paper, is to create powerful incentives to put resources to high-value uses. The bureaucrat just mentioned may be identified well enough, but his decisions about the use of state-owned resources bring a set of consequences to bear on him that are different from those that would be brought on him were he the private owner of these resources. Private ownership confronts controllers of resources with consequences that are unique and are particularly appropriate to guide resources toward uses that maximize their values. Although incentive systems of various kinds might be employed in an attempt to modify the consequences of decisions made by bureaucrats, these modifications cannot so remake these consequences that they correspond to those associated with private ownership without creating private ownership.

The failure of neoclassical economists to expose clearly the ownership premises on which their model of the price system rested made it easier for socialists to market the economics system they favored. A. P. Lerner, in his influential book *The Economics of Control* (1944), recommended that socialist economies adopt the price system as their primary tool for allocating resources. He argued that the socialist state can employ a price system in much the same way as can a capitalist system, thereby realizing efficient resource allocation while avoiding the wealth distribution consequences of capitalism. His discussion ignored the necessity for bolting the price system firmly to a private ownership foundation in order to motivate those who controlled resources to put them to value-maximizing uses. The incentivizing function of private ownership goes unrecognized. This is equivalent to assuming a socialist nirvana, in which all citizens of the socialist society seek social efficiency when they exercise control of collectively owned resources.

OWNERSHIP STRUCTURE AND THE EXTERNALITY PROBLEM

Because neoclassical theory takes the ownership system for granted, it does not delve into questions about the structure of ownership of the firms it discusses. In particular, it does not analyze the conditions that determine whether facilities that produce different goods are owned by a single person or by different people. This question is important in revealing the essential deficiency in externality theory and in the transaction cost approach to the externality problem. It is a topic that I touched on some time ago (Demsetz 1967, 357) when discussing costly interactions between abutting parcels of land.

Assume the initial distribution of parcels across different ownership interests is random. There will ensue a rearrangement of ownership interests in response to existing cost interactions:

> Owners now negotiate among themselves to internalize any remaining externalities. Two market options are open to the negotiators. The first is simply to try to reach a contractual agreement . . . that directly deals with the external effects at issue. The second option is for some owners to buy out others, thus changing the parcel size owned. Which option is selected will depend on which is cheaper.

When I wrote the above, my thoughts were focused on the positive economics question of how external costs might affect ownership structure. I did not grasp the full significance of ownership rearrangements for the externality problem. It should have been clear to me that the optimal ownership rearrangement not only economizes on transaction cost, but that it essentially undermines the very existence of the externality problem.

If the parcels of land that generate the costly interaction are owned by one person, then the owner is fully "incentivized" to take the interaction cost into account when deciding on the uses to which he puts his land. He will curtail (or indulge) uses on one parcel of his land if these adversely (beneficially) affect the wealth that can be generated from his other parcels. The interaction between these uses does not escape his attention. There is no externality. Moreover, but less obviously, this conclusion carries over to situations in which the ownership of interacting parcels of land is dispersed across different owners. Holding constant the many other considerations that affect ownership structure and focusing only on the costly interaction between the uses to which different parcels of land may be put, separate ownership of parcels of land will arise only if the cost to a single owner of managing multiple parcels exceeds the transaction cost borne by separate owners to influence the uses to which neighboring land is put, via transactions between owners. Separate ownership is used when it allows for a better accommodation of costly interactions than is possible if multiple parcels are managed by a single owner.

It follows from this, since there is no externality if ownership is unified, that there is no externality if separate ownership is the chosen ownership arrangement. To merge or not to merge ownership interests is the question, and the answer is the ownership arrangement that maximizes the value of the land. The cost of reducing the interaction, as well as the gain from doing so, must be taken into account when judging the efficiency of the solution. The interaction between the uses to which different parcels of land are put is not a source of inefficiency because these costs and benefits influence the ownership arrangement that is chosen.

There is nothing special in a land usage example. A steel mill uses soft coal which emits soot-containing smoke from its stack. This soot, when it descends on a neighboring laundry, increases the cost of cleaning cloths. Full account would be taken of the interaction if both steel mill and laundry were owned by the same person, who, of course, would weigh the advantages and disadvantages of substituting hard for soft coal in terms of the tradeoff between fuel cost and laundry operating cost. There is no cost that is unattended to in this ownership arrangement. There is no externality problem. Interaction cost wears the cloak of an externality problem only if the steel mill and the laundry are separately owned. But, as has just been shown, ownership is separate only if this ownership arrangement, through the transactions to which it will give rise, takes this interaction into account more cheaply than does unified ownership.

Ownership structure adjusts to the available opportunities. We may suppose, in the case of the steel mill and the laundry, that the price of hard coal initially is less than that of soft coal. In this case, ownership specialized to a steel mill does not adversely impact ownership specialized to the laundry, for hard coal, with no significant soot output, will be used to fuel the steel mill. However, if the cost of using soft coal falls as new deposits are uncovered and brought to market, then the owner of the steel mill finds it advantageous to substitute soft for hard coal. The resulting costly interaction with the laundry may give rise to negotiations between the owners of these enterprises. These negotiations may be maintained with an ownership structure that keeps the ownership of these two firms separate if this is the least costly way to accommodate the newly emerged costly interaction. Alternatively, if less costly, these negotiations may lead to a merger of the firms that permits a single management to manage the degree to which soft coal is used.

A more general comparison can be made between separation and unification of ownership. Consider two cases of unified ownership.

In case A, no added cost is borne by the owner-manager to manage the interaction between the two activities. He substitutes hard for soft coal to the extent that the increase in fuel cost is less than the savings that result from the laundry's operation. He need not substitute hard for soft coal completely, or even at all. The degree of substitution depends on the arithmetic of the situation. Whatever the mix of fuels that results from correct calculations, it will be an efficient mix. The owner-manager has taken all relevant costs into account. In doing so, he has maximized the sum of the values of the assets he has committed to making steel and cleaning clothes.

In case B, owing to the increased complexity of his operations, the owner-manager bears an added cost to manage the interface between the two activities. He now chooses a mix of hard and soft coal that reflects the same considerations as in case A but, because of the added cost of contemplating the fuel mix problem, he does not seek so fine-tuned a solution. Instead, he settles for a mix of fuels that is about the same as in case A, but that perhaps contains somewhat more or somewhat less hard coal. To be efficient, he must economize on management cost as well as interaction cost, and this calls for acceptance of a fuel mix within a range of fuel mixes that includes all mixes for which the attempt to fine-tune the solution more precisely yields less expected benefit than it yields more expected management cost. Although there is a range of acceptable mixes of fuels, a mix chosen from within this range is efficient. All relevant costs have been considered.[2]

The conclusions regarding efficiency in these two cases lead directly to identical conclusions if the best ownership arrangement is to have separate ownership of the resources used in steelmaking and laundering. Case A is equivalent to a zero transaction cost case in which the efficient solution is for the separate owners of these two firms to tailor a solution involving a unique mix of fuels, one that maximizes the combined values of the two enterprises. Case B is equivalent to a positive transaction cost case, in which greater management cost is incurred to manage two activities instead of one. The efficient solution in this case is for the separate owners of these two firms to accept a mix of fuels within a range of mixes for which greater preciseness is expected to yield gains too small to be worth incurring the additional transaction cost.

In the latter comparison, transactions between separate owners coordinates their operations. These transactions substitute for the managing that would be needed if ownership were unified. It costs something to engage in transactions, but it also costs something to complicate managerial operations in a unified ownership structure. The choice of ownership structure is influenced by a comparison between these costs and by the reduction in interaction costs that can be achieved by bearing either of these two costs. If we suppose, as in the first comparison, that transaction cost and management cost are zero, then full account is taken of even the last "iota" of the effect of interaction cost on profit, irrespective of ownership arrangement. If transaction cost and management cost are positive, then some effects of interaction cost seemingly are "neglected" if profit is maximized. But efficiency requires this neglect, since costs of coordination should be taken into account in deciding just how finely to "tune" the interaction between these activities. To ignore costs of coordination surely is to allocate resources inefficiently.

In this second comparison, reduced fineness of solution is not equivalent to the neglect of interaction cost. A decision not to tune the solution more finely cannot be made rationally without estimating the reduction in interaction cost that would be realized from a more finely tuned solution. A profit-maximizing stopping point in the adjustment to interaction cost implies that there is attention to the expected savings to be secured from a more accurate coordination of the two activities. Interaction cost that is not eliminated is judged to be less than is the cost that must be borne to eliminate it. The interaction cost that remains is taken into account in reaching this judgment. Hence, all relevant costs have been incorporated into the decisions as to whether to have unified or separate ownership structures and whether to more finely tune the adjustment to the interaction cost.

The transaction cost that needs to be borne in order to react appropriately to interaction cost is generally larger if, instead of one laundry, there are many whose operations are affected by the steel firm's choice of fuel. In this case, if ownership were unified, there also would be greater management cost in controlling the more complicated interface between the steel mill's operations and the operations of many laundries. There would be larger costs of coordination. In itself, this does not invalidate the conclusions drawn above. Resources are efficiently allocated. That this is so even if transaction cost is positive suggests the need to reconsider Coase's logic, since Coase concludes that positive transaction cost creates the possibility that resources are misallocated.

COASE AND THE PROBLEM OF SOCIAL COST

Coase showed that resources are not misallocated in neoclassical theory's competition model if transaction cost is zero. Persons affected by the interaction between independently owned productive activities bring all interaction costs into the profit-maximizing calculus through their negotiations with each other. No costs remain outside the decision process. There are no externalities. Coase is correct, since zero transaction cost allows coordination between two independently owned firms to substitute perfectly for unified ownership.

This seems to imply that external cost of a Pigouvian sort does exist if transaction cost is positive. Yet, as argued in the preceding section, this implication is undermined by the rational choice of ownership structure. Unified ownership takes all costs into account, and separate ownership is chosen only if it is superior to unified ownership in its ability to cope with costly interactions. A Pareto-optimal solution does not require that the solution of choice contain no interaction cost.

The perspective gained by focusing on ownership arrangements is illustrated by F. H. Knight in "Fallacies in the Interpretation of Social Cost," an article written in 1924, barely four years after Pigou's *The Economics of Welfare* had appeared. The article is a rejoinder to an argument made by Pigou pertaining to the allocation of traffic on two roads, one of which is superior, narrow, and congested, and the other of which is of lesser quality, broader, and free of congestion. Pigou's claim is that, if left to the unfettered choices of drivers, traffic will be misallocated between these two roads. Too many drivers will use the superior road because they will ignore the additional congestion cost that their use of it imposes on other drivers on this road.

Congestion cost is viewed by Pigou as an external cost, imposed by drivers on other drivers when they choose to use the narrow road. A tax on the use of the narrow road is called for by Pigou. Knight writes in his critique:

> If the roads are assumed to be subject to private appropriation and exploitation . . . [t]he owner of the broad road could not under effective competition charge anything for its use. If an agency of production is not subject to diminishing returns, and cannot be monopolized, there is, in fact, no incentive to its appropriation, and it will remain a free good. But the owner of the narrow road can charge for its use a toll representing its "superiority" over the free road, in accordance with the theory of rent, which is as old as Ricardian economics. An application of the familiar reasoning to this case will show that the toll will exactly equal the ideal tax. . . . This is clearer if we think of the owner of the road hiring the trucks instead of their hiring the use of the

road. The effect is the same either way; it is still the same if some third party hires the use of both. The toll or rent will be so adjusted that *added* product of the last truck which uses the narrow road is just equal to what it could produce on the broad road. No truck will pay a higher charge, and it is not to the interest of the owner of the road to accept a lower fee. And this adjustment is exactly that which maximizes the total product of both roads. (Quotation from 1924 article as reprinted in Knight (1935, 220–21; italics in original)

Knight's reasoning demonstrates the advantage to be had by bringing ownership into the analysis. Knight, unlike Coase, makes no reference to transaction cost. Were he asked to deal with transaction cost, he would have treated it as he would any other cost. Its presence reduces the number of drivers using the road, but the reduction is required if resources, including those used to transact, are to be allocated efficiently.

Knight saw the source of Pigou's problem in the failure of incentives that arises from the absence of private ownership, whereas Coase seems to see the source in positive transaction cost. The distinction between them may be illustrated. The government bureaucrat who does not own the resources that he manages may, hypothetically, be put in a setting in which transaction cost is zero. This implies that he can more cheaply learn about the consequences that spring from the way he manages these resources. All persons affected by his management, whether adversely or beneficially, can bring these consequences to his attention.

Yet, the fact that he does not privately own these resources alters the nature and share of these consequences that he personally bears. It might be claimed that the law that bars these resources from being owned makes it impossible to enter into negotiations with him that would violate the law. Certain agreements are barred. All this is true, but it is the fact that the state is the owner that makes them true and not costs of contacting, discussing, contracting, and enforcing an agreement with the bureaucrat; it is the law behind the ownership arrangement that makes the contract illegal. To put the blame on positive transaction cost confuses the identification of the source of the difficulty.

Coase does not ignore private ownership. His (1959) article made a strong claim for allowing ownership of parts of the frequency spectrum, so that negotiations between owners could reduce the degree of interference between broadcasts. He certainly understands the strong forces that ownership unleashes. Coase (1960) makes private ownership of scarce resources a right of those whose activities conflict and his description of the dealings between these owners leaves no doubt that the incentivizing effects of private ownership are at work. Coase also discusses several cases in which conflicts in the use of resources cause courts to decide between petitioners as to who has the right to act without incurring liability for doing so.

These discussions are used mainly to illustrate that the interaction problem is mistakenly viewed as damage done by one party to another when, more accurately, it results from the desire of both parties to use the same scarce resource in conflicting ways. This is a perceptive view of the problem, and his discussion of these cases is exemplary as a method of showing the symmetry in the externality problem. But it does not itself contribute to the analysis of the problem once ownership is established.[3]

Despite the considerable attention Coase gives to ownership, it is not on this that his analysis is focused in his social cost article. Rather, once private ownership is acknowledged, Coase uses it to show the importance of transaction cost to the solution of the externality problem, demonstrating that resources necessarily are allocated efficiently if transaction cost is zero, but not if transaction cost is positive. His emphasis on transaction cost has misdirected his analysis of the positive transaction cost case. Let us see why.

Coase considers two productive activities. Here, let these be steelmaking and laundering. The steelmaker uses airspace to carry smoke away from his steel mill; the launderer uses airspace to aid in the process of drying washed clothes. The soot contained in smoke makes it more difficult to dry clothes cleanly. Coase first argues the zero transaction cost case. He demonstrates that the choice of which of the owners of these firms has the right to control a resource (airspace) has no effect on the mix of goods that is produced (quantities of steel and washed clothes). If the steelmaker has the right to use soft coal and chooses to do so because it is cheaper than hard coal, the launderer has an incentive to offer payments to the steelmaker to entice him to substitute hard coal for soft. If the launderer has a right to soot-free air, the steelmaker has an incentive to offer payments to the launderer to entice him to allow some soot to enter the air. Coase shows that these negotiations, associated with different assignments of ownership rights, yield the same mix of goods. The mix is that which maximizes the sum of the competitive values of all goods that are involved. It is a Pareto-efficient bundle of goods.

Coase argues that, in contrast to this result, the mix of goods produced if transaction cost is positive depends on the choice of which party has the right to control the intensity of the interaction between the two activities. This is most easily understood in an extreme case of positive transaction cost. Assume that transaction cost is so high as to be prohibitive of all negotiations. If the steelmaker has a legal right to use soft coal, the launderer, because transaction cost is prohibitively high, would not find it worthwhile to offer payments to the steelmaker to persuade him to switch to the use of hard coal. Hence, soot is emitted from the steelmill's smoke stack, laundering is more costly, and less laundering service is purchased. If the launderer has a legal right to soot-free air, the steelmaker, because transaction cost is prohibitively high, would not find it worthwhile to offer payments to the launderer to entice him to accept some amount of soot. Hence, hard coal is used and soot is not emitted from the steelmill's stack; laundering is less costly than if the factory owner has the right to use soft coal, more clothes are laundered, steel production is more costly, and less steel is purchased. Coase concludes, and correctly so, that the mix of goods produced depends on the choice of who has the right to control the degree of interaction if transaction cost is positive. The difference between the bundles of goods produced under these alternative rights assignments is less extreme if transaction cost, instead of being prohibitively high, is small enough to allow some transactions to take place.

We may note in passing that this way of viewing the problem, by focusing on transaction cost instead of ownership, sets aside the possibility of having but one owner for both the steelmill and the laundry. This offers no opportunity to inquire into the economic conditions that justify this ownership structure. Coase's transaction cost perspective, because he is led to deal with a structure of ownership in which each firm is separately owned, forces him to compare the different bundles of goods that result from the different assignments of ownership rights. To decide which assignment of rights is best in the positive transaction cost case, he proposes that these bundles should be ranked by their value.

It is at this juncture that Coase breathes life into the externality problem. He observes that the assignment of rights that is chosen might not be that which yields the most valuable bundle of goods. Trapped by this observation, the best he can do is to call for a careful study of the situation. Although Coase gives keen insights into difficulties that may result from the adoption of Pigou's policies, he cannot rule out the possibility that such study would show them to be appropriate if transaction cost is positive. He writes:

> What I showed . . . was that in a regime of zero transaction costs — an assumption of standard economic theory — negotiations between the parties would lead to those arrangements being made which would maximise wealth, and this irrespective of the initial assignment of rights. . . . However, I tend to regard [this] . . . as a stepping stone on the way to an analysis of an economy with positive transaction costs. . . . Of course, it does not imply, when trans-

action costs are positive, that government actions . . . could not produce a
better result than relying on negotiations between individuals in the market.
(Coase 1994, 10–11)

Pigou, if he could have read and commented on this part of Coase's
social cost paper, after conceding that Coase has a point in the zero
transaction cost case, would have said that a difference between social
and private costs exists if transaction cost is positive. The better assignment of rights might make the difference between social and private
costs smaller than would the poorer assignment, but there nonetheless
remains a difference. Coase, having focused so much on positive transaction cost, might have difficulty replying to Pigou. An answer has already been given here, in the comparison of unified and separate ownership of the resources used to produce the two goods.

This answer does not deal with the issue of which of the two parties
should own a given property right if we insist on separate ownership of
the assets involved in the interaction. Nor should it. The point, overlooked by Coase, is that this question and the answer given to it are not
germane to a judgment about the efficiency with which the *economic*
system works, although it is of great use in notifying courts of the consequences that may flow from the arrangements they endorse. As long
as rights are well defined, there is a full accounting for interaction and
transaction costs. This is all that is needed to refute Pigou's claim that
the neoclassical theory's competitive model errs in its conclusion that
price-taking private owners allocate resources efficiently. True, there is
no accounting for the assignment of rights, but this task lies outside the
price system in the legal system. The legal system is not privately
owned, and its operations are not being analyzed by neoclassical theory.
So we do not know what motivates decisions made within it or on what
basis it assigns ownership rights. It was never part of Pigou's externality
theory to question the workings of the legal system, and Coase has
confused issues by bringing the legal system's problems into his evaluation of Pigou's theory.

If the legal system confers rights of action that result in the production of the less valuable mix of goods, the proper test of the efficiency
of the economic system is whether it facilitates mutually beneficial exchange. It does this through private ownership, by creating incentives
for these parties to engage in negotiations and by leading them to carry
these negotiations forward as long as, subjectively, the gain from reducing interaction cost is larger than the cost of transacting. That a more
valuable bundle of goods would have resulted from a different assignment of rights signifies nothing about the efficiency with which private
ownership copes with the problems that are its own.

There may be better or poorer choices of rights assignment, just as there may be better or poorer distributions of wealth. These choices, one made by the legal system and the other by the political system, may affect the value of goods produced in a society. A variety of concerns lead to the support and criticism of wealth distribution policy, but we do not proclaim inefficiency in the operations of the economic system because a wealth distribution policy has reduced the total value of goods produced. Why should we claim an externality-associated inefficiency in the operations of the economic system because legal policy has reduced the value of the mix of goods produced?

The appearance conveyed by focusing on transaction cost is that, should the steelmaker have the right to use soft coal, this cost prevents the launderer from bringing all the soot-related cost of laundering to bear on the steelmaker's choice of fuel. The appearance is inaccurate. Transactions are undertaken until a point is reached at which the cost of transacting is expected to exceed the reduction in cost that would be obtained by the laundry if an additional transaction were to be made. How do transactors determine the point at which to cease transacting unless they estimate the expected reduction in cost to the laundry? True, transactions are not undertaken for that range of soot abatement in which the gains from exchange are less than the costs of exchange, but ascertaining this range requires attention to, not neglect of, the expected gains to the launderer from a further reduction in soot output. Efficient resource allocation requires that transactions cease if the benefit these would confer on the launderer is less than the increment to transacting cost plus the increment to the steelmaker's fuel cost.

While Pigou would be wrong to claim that positive transaction cost implies the continued presence of an unaccounted-for interaction cost, Coase needlessly weakened his argument by making transaction cost the central consideration in his analysis of the externality problem. Transaction cost and ordinary production cost do not play different roles in the externality problem. To see this, let us conjure a "pure production cost" case. Suppose that transaction cost is zero and that the cost of hard coal exceeds that of soft coal. The steelmaker, let us assume, has the right to use soft coal, and he will do so unless he is compensated sufficiently by the launderer to substitute of hard for soft coal. There comes a point in the negotiations at which the launderer recognizes that the gains from reducing airborne soot are too small to compensate the steelmaker adequately for the added expense of using still more hard coal. The negotiations end, but, in the general case, not all soot is removed from the air. There is no inefficiency, no divergence between social and private cost.

How does the equilibrium in this case differ in principle from that of a "pure transaction cost" case, in which transaction cost is positive and the cost differential between hard and soft coal is arbitrarily close to zero? It does not differ at all. There is no reason to proclaim a special role for transaction cost in the externality problem except for the fact that, if we insist on separate ownership, positive transaction cost creates the problem of choosing between two alternative assignments of ownership rights. And this, as argued above, is a problem for the legal system, not the economic system.

IMPROVING THE OUTCOME

Improvements in the outcome of competitive private resource allocation are conceivable. Those who believe that most people do not know what is in their best interests share a belief in the net gain that can be realized by relinquishing personal freedom in return for well-intentioned guidance by the state. Those who believe that competition is grossly wasteful share a belief in the net gain that can be realized by centralizing production. However much such beliefs bolster support for the substitution of socialism for capitalism, they are irrelevant when it comes to externality doctrine.

Externality doctrine accepts all the major premises of neoclassical competition theory and superimposes on these the notion that private cost does not always equal social cost. Its claim, as a result of this inequality, is that the state can improve matters through taxes and subsidies that bring private cost into equality with social cost. What has been demonstrated to this point in the present essay is that no difference between private and social cost arises within the economic system simply because transaction cost is positive, and that the fault lies outside the economic system in the legal-political sphere if the social value of output is not maximized. Improvement requires better performance from the legal and political systems.

The sources of this improvement are not Pigou's taxes and subsidies, for the competitive market is measuring costs and benefits correctly given the choices made by the legal-political system in regard to the assignment of private rights of ownership and the implicit barring of unified ownership. The sources lie partly in better performance by the political and legal systems in regard to their traditionally important roles in defining and enforcing private rights of ownership, and partly in the substitution of the coercive powers of the state for the voluntary agreements of private ownership arrangements. The use of coercion has not yet been discussed here. I discuss it in the context of what I shall call "high control cost." This term refers to the high cost to private owners of exercising their right to exclusive use of that which they own.

Some readers may define high control cost as a special transaction cost, although this seems to me to abuse the English language and to define any obstacle to efficiency as a transaction cost problem. Even if high control cost is thought of as a special and more restricted category of transaction cost, the important thing is not that transaction cost has reentered the analysis but that this category excludes much that Coase and externality doctrine describe as transaction cost.

High Control Cost

It sometimes is difficult to prevent the use of a resource by persons who have not secured permission for this use from its owner. Control cost may be so high that it undermines the value of the technically possessed right of exclusive use. There are two categories of circumstances that give rise to such a condition. One category allows for the state or legal system to reduce control cost through refinement of the private ownership system. The other category does not allow for this type of improvement.

Let us return to the road congestion problem discussed by Knight. That use of a road is free does not in itself bar private negotiations between would-be users. Drivers who put a high value on time can offer payments to low value-of-time drivers if the latter agree to stay off the road. Assume that all such agreements are honored. It would appear that the road congestion problem can be resolved in this manner even if the road is not privately owned, but this is not so.

These agreements do not overcome a demand revelation problem that is inherent in a *freeway*. Drivers are disinclined to make these agreements because they are able freely to benefit from reduced congestion that is an outcome of agreements made between other drivers. The true demand for reduced congestion is not revealed because of this strategic behavior. The strategic behavior is a consequence of allowed free access to the road.

Private ownership of the road reduces or eliminates this behavior by creating a right to exclude nonpayers from use of the road. It is because Knight assumes that private owners can exclude nonpayers that he is able to show the error in Pigou's claim that private decisions result in an overcongested road. Free access to the road belongs in the first category of circumstances, that in which feasible actions can be taken by the state or courts to reduce the high cost of excluding nonpayers. Free access is "social convention."[4]

The cost of excluding nonpayers may be high in some situations even if the most appropriate assignment of private ownership rights is in place. Compare the provision of home protection against burglaries to home protection against incoming enemy missiles. Private funding of protection works well in dealing with burglaries because the service provider can exclude nonpaying householders from receiving his services. There is no reason to expect under-revealing of the true demand for security in this case. The same financing technique cannot be used to protect homes from incoming enemy missiles because the deterrence that is presumably the result of an anti-missile system and which might be purchased by some, cannot be denied to those who have not paid. Judged pragmatically, deterrence in matters of national defense is necessarily a communal good given the military possibilities of modern warfare. There is no refinement in ownership rights, such as there is in the creation of a private tollway, by which a practical degree of exclusion can be implemented. The under-revelation of demand problem is resistant to improvement sought in this way.

It is important to note two aspects of the free rider problem being discussed. First, it is not a consequence of ordinarily conceived high transaction cost. The cost of negotiating with persons can be zero, and contracts entered into can be honored at no cost, but the prices used in these agreements still can misrepresent true demands. The misrepresentation results from a situation in which strategic behavior is rational. The situation gives rise to the perception of an ability to influence the price paid for a service. A successful free rider has in fact reduced to zero the price that he pays for a service. This aspect of the situation violates the price-taker assumption of neoclassical theory. It comes from the high cost of practicing exclusivity in the use of a good or service, not from ordinarily conceived high transaction cost. If this is an important aspect of a situation, private ownership does not guarantee that resources will be allocated in accordance with *true* private demands. Second, the problem is quite different from that which is customarily associated with an externality. An externality is perceived to exist if some costs (or benefits) are unaccounted for because ordinarily conceived transaction cost bars a full accounting. Costs (or benefits) are, in part, unaccounted for in high control cost cases because these costs (or benefits) are *misrepresented* voluntarily as part of strategic maneuvering.

The state, if it is the source of finance for a missile defense system, is not constrained as are private owners by relying on voluntary payments to provide the anti-missile system. It can coerce citizens to pay or, what is the same, it can commandeer resources from the private sector. The building of the missile system can be a task undertaken by the state or, as is true in large part, it can be built by competing private contractors financed with state funds. The state is not free of difficulties in judging the demand for an anti–missile defense system, especially since it cannot rely on voluntary purchases of the service of such a system. It is forced to use indirect methods. These include scientific consultation, opinion gathering, and political pressure, and these methods may not yield an answer in which much confidence can be placed. But they yield an answer.

The state as allocator of resources faces special problems of its own. Consider again the road congestion problem. The state itself can operate the road as a tollway. Yet we do not observe the state doing this as much as conditions of congestion would seem to warrant. Why not? Drivers who put a high value on time would pay a toll to drive on a road that is not congested, but drivers who attach low value to their time and who, therefore, do not much mind road congestion would rather travel a free access congested road than travel surface streets or pay a toll to use an uncongested road. Drivers who put a low value on time have an incentive to use political pressure to keep the road as a freeway. If political pressure succeeds in keeping access to the road free, the cost of the resulting traffic congestion is borne disproportionately by those who put a high value on time. The political arena itself offers fertile ground for strategic free rider behavior. Pressure such as this succeeds frequently, and it probably constitutes an important source of opposition to the conversion of a public road to a private road.

The presumption that beneficial state intervention is easy in high control cost problems is not a side issue. It is of paramount importance to the perception that there is an externality problem and that state action can eliminate or reduce it. Without this presumption, there would be no distinction between costs. The cost of preventing free riding becomes the same as the cost of, say, iron ore. Both must necessarily be borne to secure particular goods because there no longer is any ground for using the state's abilities to treat them differently. A cost of barring free riding that is so high as to make the production of clean air uneconomic is no different from a cost of iron ore that is so high as to make steel production uneconomic. We are left with a rationalization for state involvement in the production of both goods if the state can reduce the costs of free riding and of steel production as well, and, more generally, with a rationalization for socialism. It is only the presumption that the state can reduce the cost of free riding and can do so beneficially for society, and that it cannot similarly reduce the cost of steel production, that allows these costs to be differentiated in the way they implicitly are by externality theory.[5]

It is neither "soot" nor transaction cost that is the source of the externality problem; it is widespread acceptance of different degrees of competence in the ability of the state to apply coercive power in the service of society. One may hold this belief for a narrower range of situations than that contemplated presently by externality theory, restricting its application to those cases involving serious free rider problems not remediable through changes in private ownership rights. And one may withhold its application in cases distinguished by the fact of high transaction costs.

ENDNOTES

1. See the rejoinder by F. H. Knight (1924), discussed later in this chapter.

2. Note that this solution process differs from one in which the owner-manager starts from one extreme, say 100 percent soft coal, and proceeds to substitute hard for soft coal as long as the incremental decision cost plus incremental fuel cost are less than the expected gain in profit from the laundry. There is no presupposition that it is more sensible to start calculations from 100 percent soft coal than from 0 percent soft coal. What is at issue is how finely to adjust the mix of fuels and the resulting mix because decision cost is positive, and may involve somewhat more or somewhat less hard coal than the mix that would result if decision cost were zero.

3. At one point in Coase's social cost article (1960, 15–16), Coase notes the possibility that a firm may be substituted for market transactions. He writes:

> Once the costs of carrying out market transactions are taken into account it is clear that such a rearrangement of rights will only be undertaken when the increase in the value of production consequent upon the rearrangement is greater than the costs which would be involved in bringing it about . . .
>
> [When this value is less,] an alternative form of economic organisation which could achieve the same result at less cost than would be incurred by using the market would enable the value of production to be raised. As I explained many years ago, the firm represents such an alternative to organising production through market transactions. Within the firm individual bargains between the various cooperating factors of production are eliminated and for a market transaction is substituted an administrative decision.

Coase's heavy emphasis on transaction cost and his comparative neglect of the incentivizing effects of ownership are, I believe, due to the lingering influence of his earlier classic, "The Nature of the Firm" (1937), in which transaction cost plays a key role in explaining the extent to which firms vertically integrate. This probably explains the phraseology in this quotation, in which he contrasts allocation within the firm to allocation across markets instead of allocation within one firm to allocation in two firms.

4. The ability to exclude nonpayers at zero cost does not imply the ability to execute transactions at no cost. If we continue to assume that people are honorable, a person who does not pay the road's owner to use the road does not surreptitiously use it. Hence, the cost of excluding nonpayers is zero. Yet, there may be a positive cost to collecting fees, a transaction cost, from those who desire to purchase a right to traverse the road. Exclusivity and transferability are not equivalents.

5. This presumption is what, in the terminology of Buchanan and Stubblebine (1962), converts a Pareto-irrelevant interaction into a Pareto-relevant externality.

PART VI

INTRODUCTION

Though the state's legal ability to use force can and does play an important role in the enforcement of private property rights against invasion from others, that same force can threaten the sanctity of private ownership. To the extent that might makes rights (see Haddock, this volume), a mighty government can offset threats from other individuals, groups, or other governments to take property rights. But this raises the age-old question: What stops a mighty government from taking property for itself or redistributing property to others for political gain to itself?

This volume focusing on the efficacy of private property fittingly ends with two chapters considering this question. Certainly America's founding fathers recognized the takings problem inherent in a democratic process. Madison's concerns about the "tyranny of the majority" were basically concerns about how to constrain a democratic government from bowing to the pressure of a majority to take from a minority. His answer in part was to place constitutional limits on the national government's ability to take private property. Hence the takings clause of the Fifth Amendment (and later the Fourteenth) was seen as a bulwark against unwarranted governmental takings, with requirements of just compensation and due process additionally imposed even for takings that were justified.

Of course, there are legitimate reasons for the government to acquire and regulate private property, which both Richard Epstein and William Fischel acknowledge in the next two chapters. Returning to his celebrated work (1985a) on government takings of private property, Epstein considers the need for the state to hold property for public good production. Military bases, the Capitol grounds in Washington, D.C., and some public highways are examples of governmental ownership arguably justified under the economist's rubric of public goods and avoidance of the free rider problem in paying for them. But power is power, Epstein notes. The ability to take appropriately entails the power to try to take inappropriately. Fischel's chapter continues his work (1995; see also Fischel 1985) on regulatory takings. Regulation of private property, especially zoning, is a limitation on private ownership justified by the fact that one person's use of his property can infringe on a neighbor's use of her property.

In general taking property for public goods such as roads or military

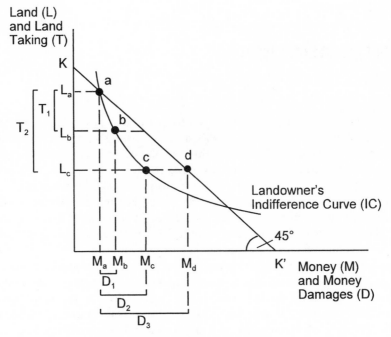

Figure VI.1 Contrasting Concepts of Compensation

bases is compensated while most regulatory takings are not. Unfortunately the very concept of "compensation" is a slippery one. Typical legal definitions include damages that "make the party whole" or that "leave the victim in as good a position as before." But without more, those phrases are inherently ambiguous.[1]

Consider figure VI.1, which employs a standard economic model based on an individual's indifference curve to analyze changes in personal utility as more of one asset is given up for another. To fit the model to the takings situation, let the assets be land (L) and money (M) owned by some person, Trump. Indifference curve IC shows the trade-off landowner Trump attaches to different amounts of land and money under the common economic assumptions. In particular, let relatively little of one asset (e.g., land) be owned, such that its marginal value is high. If some of that asset is taken, Trump will naturally need more of the other asset (money) to compensate him than if he owned much land. Or, if much land is owned relative to money, relatively little money is required to make Trump whole.

Assume that Trump initially is located at point a on IC, owning L_a of land and M_a of money, but that the government is about to take some of the land. A taking of T_1 will move Trump to point b, where he would own only L_b of land. If compensation is defined as that payment in monetary damages which would keep Trump on the same indifference curve ("make him whole"), the damage amount required is D_1, meaning Trump now has monetary assets of M_b.

Figure VI.1 illustrates two initial difficulties associated with compensation in the event of a taking. First, one must know the shape of the indifference curve itself (i.e., the personal utility trade-off to an individual as land is lost and money gained). But these trade-offs are inherently subjective and thus idiosyncratic,[2] particularly with an asset like land. Is the land something that has been in the family for generations (perhaps with Grannie buried up on the hill), or something that was purchased for ordinary investment purposes? Trump's trade-offs are not the same as some other landowner's. In general, the amounts that will truly compensate must be tailored to each landowner's subjective values.

The need to know individual indifference curves to ensure that damage awards are truly compensatory can be seen by comparing T_1 to a larger taking, T_2, that would leave Trump with only L_c of land. Taking T_2 is exactly double taking T_1, but with the owner's diminishing marginal utility the appropriate compensation, D_2, is more than double D_1. As more land is lost, its marginal value increases, requiring disproportionately higher damage payments if true compensation is to be paid. What that true compensatory amount is can only be known if the shape of the individual's indifference curve is known. Only in the most unusual circumstances could the taker divine the shape of the curve, and the landowner has every incentive to misrepresent its shape so as to justify a larger amount for the property taken.

There is yet another complication. Indifference curve IC measures only an individual's subjective valuations of various combinations of the two assets. To compensate in an amount that just makes the owner whole is to protect the owner with what Calabresi and Melamed (1972) call a "liability rule." But other forms of compensation may be more appropriate. Calabresi and Melamed contrast liability rules with "property rules."

Under a property rule, an individual is compensated, not by an amount that would make him whole in the sense of maintaining the same level of utility, but in an amount that mirrors what he would have obtained in a freely negotiated transfer of his property in lieu of a forced taking.[3] To return to figure VI.1, suppose that a market for the taken asset (L) exists. For simplicity, assume that in the market one unit of L sells for one unit of M (e.g., \$1 per square foot). The prices for different levels of L transferred are shown by KK', intersecting the axes at 45-degree angles to reflect the one-for-one market price of land for money. If compensation is based on market price, a taking of T_2 would require a payment of D_3 (not just D_2), putting Trump at point d on KK' instead of point c on IC.

Three important points follow. First, not all assets trade at a single "market price," in part because not all goods are fungible. Just as land-owners' subjective valuations of their property are idiosyncratic, so is most land unique. Land, that is, is not like a grande latte at Starbucks or the widgets too often encountered in economics lectures. Voluntary transfers for things like land and houses typically occur by negotiation between individual owners and potential buyers, not by posting a single market price. Consequently, just as discerning an owner's true indifference curve, IC, is all but impossible under a liability rule, the market price-based payment required for a taking protected by a property rule may also be impossible to know when there is no market generating the price one needs to discern line KK'.

Second, even if a true KK' exists, such that one can know that a unit of M purchases a unit of L in the market, that does not mean that a payment of D_3 would compensate Trump for a taking of T_2. After all, faced with the availability of D_3 in the market, Trump has chosen not to sell amount T_2 of his asset L. The market offers the possibility to move from point a to point d, but Trump has shown his preference not to trade at the going market price, judging himself better off at point a. Property rule protection based on market price, while more compensatory than a liability rule that would require only D_2 of damages, still does not compensate Trump for the full value of his land as he reckons it.

Finally, and perhaps most important, the distinction between liability and property rules creates an incentive for those who want an asset to take it rather than negotiate for it (Haddock, McChesney, and Spiegel 1990). Someone desiring Trump's land would rather take and pay compensation D_2 for taking T_2 than have to negotiate. Even a taking with payment of D_3, based on market price, is preferable to actual negotiation, since Trump has shown that D_3 is not enough to induce him to sell. A government seeking more of Trump's assets will concoct reasons to take rather than negotiate. And thus our constitutional wariness about government taking when it can negotiate, reflected in the Fifth Amendment's requirement of a proper purpose for taking.

Taking without full compensation in either the property- or liability-rule sense naturally would be preferable to a taker. Paying no compensation whatsoever would suit the taker best of all. If that taker is the government, with a monopoly on the use of force, the ease of under-compensated and uncompensated takings naturally increases. Importantly, both Epstein and Fischel emphasize that uncompensated takings of private property lead to excessive use and occupation of private property. At a zero price facing government actors in uncompensated takings, too much property would be taken by governments for public highways or parks and too many takings-like regulations would be imposed on private property owners. In the latter case, for example, private property advocates contend that, because regulators can regulate land use to provide endangered species habitat without paying, the regulations should proceed to the point that prove costly to landowners but do little to enhance habitat.

Epstein confronts the takings issue generally by examining several potential sources of abuse. The fact that the government with its monopoly on legitimate coercion can use duress without worrying about negative reputational fallout or about the targeted parties easily moving to other jurisdictions means that government can play negative-sum games. For example, in the case of inheld land (private land surrounded by governmental land), the government can exact economic rents from the inholder, and the locked-in inholder can do little about it.

Even if payment redress is obtained through legal action, determining what constitutes just compensation is complicated in light of subjective costs. Suppose that a person is required to move from the family farm to which he has strong sentimental attachment so that the land can be used for a public park. Will the owner be compensated for the subjective value of his sentiment? Epstein appropriately concludes that "people who follow the good government model of behavior may take pride in republican virtue as a sufficient safeguard against political misbehavior" (this volume). But once we "recognize that public virtue is a scarce commodity," constitutional limits on governmental taking become all the more important.

Fischel addresses the takings issue in the context of zoning, perhaps one of the more controversial regulatory mechanisms of our time regarding private property. He explains how zoning can create public goods that enhance overall property values. For example, a limit on commercial building in a residential area can make the residential property more valuable though it reduces the value of the specific parcels that can no longer be used for commercial purposes. In small, homogeneous communities where the benefits and costs of zoning are transparent, there is a greater possibility that only positive-sum regulations will result. Fischel also notes that the ability of citizens to vote with their feet by moving to competing political jurisdictions (known as the Tiebout (1956) effect) mitigates against negative-sum zoning regulations.

In the case of real property such as land, which is difficult to move with you, however, the potential for governmental zoning mischief is great. Fischel considers the case of open-space zoning promulgated by majority-faction urban residents who require their rural neighbors to keep their land in agricultural uses. Clearly rural landowners lose because their land's value is reduced by such zoning while urban landowners gain. But in the absence of required compensation to the former from the latter, what is the guarantee that the gains exceed the losses? And even if there is some guarantee that the gains do exceed losses, what are the implications for a civil society if zoning can be used to redistribute wealth?

In conclusion, Fischel calls for a standard of "normal behavior" to evaluate zoning regulations. By this Fischel means that "'harm prevention' ought not to be compensated, but that 'benefit extraction' generally should." Normal behavior would discipline the private landowner against creating nuisance-type harms because he would know that uncompensated regulations would be forthcoming. It would also discipline the zoning community against "majoritarian rent seeking" because taxes would have to be raised to compensate the losers who provide the rents.

A reading of Epstein and Fischel and the vast literature on takings can only lead to the conclusion that private property rights are only as secure as the underlying social ethos and legal constitutional rules regarding the sanctity of private property make them. Though it is common to think of property rights as emanating from government authority, several of the earlier chapters in this volume point out that property rights can evolve from individuals agreeing on who should have access to valuable assets. To be sure, such rights are often codified by sovereign governments that have coercive power to enforce property rights, but that same coercive power also threatens the sanctity of property rights it is designed to bolster. Constitutional rules, checks and balances, federalism, and so on can limit the threat of governmental takings. Such constraints, however, are unlikely to be effective in the long run unless there is a broad understanding and acceptance by the polity that private property rights are equitable as well as efficacious.

Endnotes

1. The discussion here distills a small part of a large literature that begins with the important article by Calabresi and Melamed (1972). For applications and citations to much of the literature, see Haddock, McChesney, and Spiegel (1990).

2. The situation would be different if the good taken were traded in a thick, liquid market, one in which there was a "going" market price. That situation is considered later in this essay.

3. In effect, a liability rule compensates owners for the use value they attach to their property, while a property rule compensates for exchange value.

CHAPTER TWELVE

IN AND OUT OF PUBLIC SOLUTION

The Hidden Perils of Forced
and Unforced Property Transfer

Richard A. Epstein

BACKGROUND

Several previous chapters have considered the interplay between individual and government actions in the creation of property rights. The discussion of the role of government in the creation of property found in chapter 9 is one such example. This chapter focuses on the fate of these property rights once they have been created, whether by government or by custom. The government enjoys the position as the sole possessor of the legitimate use of force within society. That power may be used in two distinct ways.

First, that power may be used to take private property for public use, for such purposes as military defense, the construction of public roads and works, and in the eyes of many, for urban renewal projects. In some situations, these takings may be desirable because they increase overall wealth, without disadvantaging their previous owners who receive compensation for their losses. But other takings are not; instead they are motivated by rent-seeking efforts to transfer wealth from one group of citizens to another, without any overall beneficial effect.

The main objective of government is to weed out the desirable from the undesirable uses of government power. The classic solution to this problem is embodied in the Fifth Amendment's guarantee against taking private property for public use, without just compensation. Ideally the protection of this rule works along two margins. The first is to identify which takings are for a public use, so that government power is not used just to take property from A in order to give it to B. The second is to specify the proper level of just compensation to property owners. These should not be set so high as to discourage needed takings; nor so low as to invite partial confiscation by the exercise of government power.

In addition, the government has acquired by various means huge tracts of property of its own, which must be protected and managed, and sometimes disposed of. In these cases, too, the same questions of public choice arise, as we seek sensible solutions to govern the use and disposition of this property. In dealing with these issues, the U.S. Constitution, at least in its original conception, had a clear and articulated vision of the proper role of government. Although the drafters of the Constitution had not read Buchanan and Tullock's *The Calculus of Consent* (1962), they were fully cognizant of the dangers that factions posed to the operation of the political system. James Madison defined faction to cover "a number of citizens, whether amounting to a majority or minority of the whole, who are united and actuated by some common impulse of passion or interest, adverse to the rights of the citizens, or to the permanent and aggregate interests of the community" (Earle [1787] 1937, 54).

This definition, in concise yet artful language, reveals the massive challenge posed to any political order intent on combating these dangers. Madison rightly concluded that factions could constitute either a majority or minority of the population, such that they continue to operate no matter what the alignment of forces within the political community. In more operational terms, Madison's definition implies that factions arise whenever any group will maximize its own position by adopting a plan of political action at cross-purposes with the needs of the larger society of which it is a part.

Once he sets out the problem, however, Madison fails to propose a cure equal to its pervasive magnitude, relying lamely on the extended republic to eliminate the pettiness and parochialism of local politics. He takes that position because the original Constitution relied largely on structural protections (separation of powers, checks and balances, federalism) to counter the risks of faction. A better approach to counter the risk of faction lies in the creation and protection of property rights, of which the only hint in the unamended Constitution is found in the Contracts Clause.[1] Only the adoption of the Bill of Rights, binding on the federal government, and of the Reconstruction Amendments, binding on the states, used explicit constitutional guarantees to protect private property against political expropriation. Thus, we have the Fifth Amendment guarantee that "nor shall private property be taken for public use, without just compensation" and the due process guarantee of the Fourteenth Amendment that no state shall "deprive any person of life, liberty and property, without due process of law."

The creation of strong property rights limits the options available to government, thereby constraining the potential running-room for factions. Property rights are thus good not only for the incentives that they give to individuals to develop the resources under their command—"only those who sow should reap" is an agricultural metaphor on the internalization of gain that does not lose its luster in an Internet economy—but also for the salutary effect of limiting the range of political action and, thus, the range of political intrigue. As ever, the task is one of social improvement, not of social perfection. Constitutional guarantees of property rights do not negate use of legislative power, but only strip away at its excesses. The acid test is whether these property-based guarantees improve the ratio of well-designed legislative actions to misguided ones.

Toward that end, these guarantees prohibit egregious forms of public misconduct that might prove politically unsalable in any event. These include the outright confiscation of land by government officials and the total invalidation of private debt by government decree. The imposition of protections confined to these extreme cases only invites the substitution of more subtle forms of political action that achieve large portions of the factional enterprise while insulating legislators and regulators from any constitutional check. A property owner may be left in possession of his land, but required to grant an easement over the property to another person or group in order to build an ordinary home;[2] or he may be subject to novel limitations on uses that might disturb the habitat of an endangered species. The debtor may be required to pay the debt, but allowed an extension of time in which to pay off the obligation.[3] The task of constitutional regulation is not systematic unless some effort is made to control the close substitutes to which a crafty legislature may turn if the direct path to property confiscation or debt repudiation is blocked.

The problem here is a familiar one, for often the shoe is on the other foot. Many state prohibitions on individual conduct make sense. Yet the individuals who chafe under these restrictions will resort to clever stratagems to defeat sensible systems of regulation. The early law of torts started with prohibitions against the direct use of force. It has always been illegal to kill a person by beating him with a club. Yet both Roman and common law found it necessary to amend the basic prohibition on killing to cover those close substitutes that fell, as it was called, within the "equity" of the statute. In functional terms, anyone who was barred from killing with sticks, knives, and guns had to be barred as well from setting traps or poisoning their victims.[4]

A similar quandary is found in the law of patents, which deals with the creation and protection of intellectual property rights. The patent application covers at least the invention properly described within the patent. But the so-called doctrine of equivalents was developed to protect patent holders against erosion from a wide range of small, easily engineered modifications of the basic design that resourceful new entrants would make to evade the reach of the patent.[5]

In both these instances, the critical question is what sort of substitute counts as close. Let the substitutes be imperfect and far removed, and the cost of preventing abuse cuts too deeply into legitimate transactions. Let the close substitutes be defined too narrowly and resourceful individuals can camp out at their edges. A priori, it is never quite clear how close the legal system can inch toward the ideal margin. The modern legal realist does not think that any coherent rules underlie the articulation of proximate cause rules once we move beyond the clear case of trespasses (Malone 1956), a conclusion with which I disagree (Epstein 2000, §10.11).

What is true of private individuals facing state regulation is equally true of governments facing constitutional restraint. Some legislation does improve the state of the world, measured against a baseline that looks to either the state of nature (and the war of all against all), or even to the distribution of rights as articulated and defined, not by nature, but by common law courts that follow the natural law theories of John Locke. Therefore, it is useful to begin by showing how a well-ordered state could use legislation to improve overall social welfare and then to indicate when that mission is likely to founder.

In dealing with these issues, we have to consider two separate types of property regimes, each with its own structural weakness. Crudely speaking, we can divide property into two classes. Private property is owned and held by one or more individuals for his (or their) exclusive benefit and use. Public property is held by the government for the benefit of the public it both governs and serves: the government entity could be a town, a state, or the national government, each with its own special constituency. In both of these settings, government can introduce legal rules to alter the underlying patterns of use, either individual or collective. The most obvious target for government use and regulation are public lands, such as highways and parks. It is easy for the state to open up some roads to general use or to close them down; to allow for camping, while precluding hunting and fishing. Assets in the public domain include intellectual property once the protection of the patent and copyright laws have run out.

To understand the difficulties in controlling faction, it is useful to examine how government acquires and regulates both private and public property. It is also critical to pay special attention to the legal mechanisms used to secure the transition of property from private to public hands, or the reverse.

STATE REGULATION OF PRIVATE PROPERTY

In analyzing the role of private property, I shall take an unabashed consequentialist attitude, which asks whether government action or intervention improves the overall level of social utility by combating factional behavior. Stating the proposition in this form, however, raises one of the thorniest problems of property law, for societies, as complex aggregates of individuals, do not have utility as such. Utility is a measurement that can be attached solely to the well-being of human (or perhaps other sentient) beings. The only safe way to advance social welfare is by adopting government projects that advance the overall position of each group member, where utility is determined by his own estimation of the situation and not by the estimation of some outsider.

But what of the distribution of the gains through collective social action? Two variations on the basic theme come quickly to mind. In the first, the government uses coercion to produce all winners and no losers in settings where private transactions could not achieve the same outcome. The intellectual case for consequentialism rests on one proposition: no one could object in principle to using force to obtain that new state of affairs even if the government practice did violate some libertarian norm of autonomy or property. One manifestation of this proposition relates to basic social contract theory that improves upon the state of nature. The legal regime requires everyone to surrender some liberty of action, but imposes like restrictions on the actions of others. All persons value the increased (bodily) security more than the loss of initial liberty. I willingly accede to a law against murder, which admittedly limits acts I can perform with impunity, because that law prohibits others from murdering me.

If their initial positions are identical, then no cash compensation is required, which now becomes the source of administrative waste. Properly executed, this system moves to a higher state of utility by overcoming the full panoply of holdout and bargaining problems that frequently thwart voluntary exchanges. The conceptual problems set in when different individuals receive differential gains, such that while all are better off than before, some are more so than others. In these non–pro rata situations, the hard question asks whether it is appropriate to seek to equalize the gains from the government action or better simply to let matters lie.[6]

The second situation arises when government action in and of itself generates an outcome with some winners and some losers. Now the soil is ripe for factional discord. For example, a given plot of land is taken from one person for a highway that operates for the benefit of all. Although the state action produces many winners, it still leaves one loser — the owner of the taken parcel — even if he shares in the benefits the road provides. Converting a "most win-one loses" into an "all-win" situation ideally requires a side payment from general revenues. Those called upon to pay are better off with access to the public improvement less their fractional tax burden. The individual whose property is taken is better off with the compensation received for the loss of the property, plus his pro rata share of the gain from access to the improvement in question. The key point is that side payments are meant to ensure that the overall gains are now evenly distributed throughout the group. Ideally, we seek a program of government exactions and private payments that results in some level of lockstep improvement for all persons involved in the system. The execution of the program offers an effective antidote to the risks of faction. No one will propose a program that has overall negative consequences, because the putative winners would not pay the exactions needed to leave the losers at least indifferent to the adoption of the new project.

It is useful to analyze these issues as if the world contained two pies. The inner pie contains the rights that all individuals have to their liberty and property in a world in which the state imposes no collective exactions to preserve entitlements. The larger circle arises when taxation and regulation, imposed at some cost, enables government to help prevent private incursions by one citizen on his neighbor. Ideally, all uses of government force should try, within the limits of the possible, to expand each piece of the pie without altering the relative share from the prior distribution. That condition is imposed in order to supply a focal point that limits the potential scope of faction. The prospect of a non–pro rata division of gain could invite factional competition over surplus sufficient to dissipate the surplus created by government action.

Obstacles to a Coherent Takings Law

The major challenge to this system stems from the high administrative costs needed to make it work. In the worst scenario, the administrative costs of arranging forced exchanges exceed the potential gains. In those circumstances, any effort to achieve a stable distribution of gains makes it unwise to undertake the project in the first place. Yet, ignoring the compensation requirement has the unfortunate effect of inviting government initiatives that do not meet even the hypothetical compensation requirement. The hard task, therefore, is to fashion rules of eminent domain that work their way between the horns of this dilemma. I am sufficiently skeptical about the practical success of the constitutional program of forced exchanges to favor a sharp curtailment of the eminent domain process, even when full compensation is paid. A complete analysis of the problem identifies three potential sources of government abuse. The first concerns occasions on which state coercion is exercised. The second concerns the level of compensation paid for the loss of a private right. The third, and novel concern, examines the use of the taking power that removes the property holder from the community altogether. I take these up in order.

The Uses and Dangers of Government Coercion

The standard constitutional model allows government to proceed in two separate ways in dealing with its citizens. First, it may enter into the voluntary market whereby it purchases the inputs it needs from various suppliers by contract. If the government needs to acquire land for new construction or to buy or lease existing facilities, it may do so by entering the voluntary market like anyone else. Indeed, most of the specific assets needed for government operations are acquired in just this fashion, for usually it is easier and cheaper to buy property than to unleash the coercive power of the state. Eminent domain proceedings take time; litigation is costly, even for government. Why fight a legal war if a voluntary transaction reaches the appropriate outcome more quickly and cheaply?

Frequently, however, voluntary markets fail. A highway cuts through the land of multiple landowners, any one of whom could block its completion. Here the coercive power of eminent domain meets the holdout problem that would allow a single landowner to stop the transcontinental railroad. Just this prospect militates against abolishing the eminent domain power altogether. Given this objective of the Takings Clause, a proper compensation formula could not award the landowner the holdout value derivable from the proposed railroad use: why then have the clause at all?

Analytically, it is helpful to distinguish between two components of the increments beyond market value: subjective or unique values to this landowner and holdout value. In principle, all subjective values from current use should be compensable in order to improve the odds that the use of government coercion will result only in win-win treatment.[7] In contrast, the proper response to the holdout values is more problematic. The mere implementation of a takings program has as its raison d'être the elimination of the holdout position. It follows, therefore, that no sensible system of takings law could allocate all the surplus from condemnation to the private owner. It hardly follows, however, that none of it should be so allocated after all subjective and nonmarket values are taken into account. But the effort to figure out how much of that surplus should be so allocated requires some judicial determination of what that surplus is—no mean feat when multiple plots of land must be assembled to complete a single project. On balance, therefore, a respectable case supports the conclusion that all surplus over highest subjective or use value goes to the government.

Once subjective values are ignored, however, then institutionally, government behavior will take advantage of the background legal rules. The eminent domain power thus allows the state to push hard so that the landowner will take a price which is greater than he would have gotten through condemnation (net of expenses) but lower than he would have taken in voluntary exchange. The risk of faction remains evident. Yet the law offers no obvious doctrinal protection that allows landowners to push back against these government threats.

At this point, it is useful to identify a second possible source of government abuse in dealing with voluntary transactions: coercion that combines the implicit threat of condemnation with breach of existing obligations to the targeted landowner. Once again, the same analytical framework applies to both public and private forms of coercion. As a general matter of contract law, the opportunities for coercion are greater when two parties are linked in some ongoing relationship than when they deal as strangers. To be sure, naked coercion, such as guns, could be used to obtain promises, property, or both, in either type of setting. But one stratagem, which cannot be invoked in stranger cases, is available in the context of ongoing relationships: the calculated refusal to perform obligations that have already been undertaken. The point has been well understood since Roman times in connection with a doctrine known, then as now, as duress of goods.[8]

Let us suppose that I leave my clothes to be cleaned with the dry cleaner for an agreed upon price of $10. It is also understood that the value to me of getting back the clean garments on time is $100 because of an important social engagement. What should I do if the cleaner refuses to return the clean garments unless I pay a $50 charge (perhaps dressed up, falsely, as a claim for additional unanticipated expenses). If the cleaner had demanded that $50 upfront, I could have taken my business elsewhere. But now that he possesses the goods, a competitive situation has been transformed into a monopoly holdout problem, where my cleaner tailor holds all the cards. Given the value of the garments, there is little if anything that I could do to persuade him to accept less than the inflated charges since he can simply hold on and, in the end, resell the garments which are worth more than the $50 he demands.

If this scenario is correct, however, then why do we not see it played out all the time? One reason is that the law offers a remedy so that the extra money could be paid over and then recovered in suit, no matter what disclaimers have been provided. But, in most cases, the surer protection comes from social context. The cleaner has multiple customers and depends on repeat business. Pull a stunt like this a single time, and those continuing relations will vanish like smoke into thin air. The cleaner knows this risk, so that this ploy will be tried, if at all, sparingly, and often in disguise. But, once again, the amounts in question are usually too small to justify the effort necessary to pull off a scheme of this sort.

The ability to use this form of duress, then, depends on (1) the negative reputational fallout to third parties, (2) the potential gains from the maneuver, (3) the potential for retaliation by other parties similarly situated with the target, and (4) the ability of potential targets to obtain relief through the legal system. In repeat commercial settings, factors (1) and (3) militate against the practice, and they are supported in large transactions by the legal system.[9] The risks of these holdout games are, moreover, greater in contexts without repeat dealing and the reputational constraints that come from dealing with multiple customers. It is not surprising, therefore, that holdout games of this sort can be played, for example, at some peril by small landowners who own that single plot of land necessary to complete the site for a large office building.[10] (All this does not guarantee that the strategy will work: go one step too far and the entire project can be canceled or relocated, at which point the gains from holding out plummet to zero, while the considerable costs of negotiation remain.)

The great danger of government coercion comes precisely because the threat of breach is not effectively constrained by market forces. The danger is well illustrated when privately held land is surrounded by government lands. Access to private inholdings has to take place over government lands. In the analogous private context, the courts will sometimes create easements by implication or necessity for the benefit of the landlocked parcel.[11] But in virtually all voluntary transactions, the inholders can protect themselves from blockade by acquiring explicit rights of way over the surrounding property.

Nonetheless, many complications lurk when goodwill toward inholders does not lubricate these transactions. The protection of rights of way and other forms of easements (such as those needed to install and maintain phone lines or electrical wires) looks easy only from a distance. It becomes complex when observed up close. Defining and enforcing the content of these rights is never easy, even for parties who act in good faith. What looks like an easement ends up being an incomplete treaty between two warring tribes. Suppose that the easement calls for the use of a dirt road. Exactly what kind of vehicles can be brought over the road? If the inholder needs to haul in heavy equipment to construct a house on the inholding, does that fall within or beyond the scope of the easement? If the inholder occasionally deviates from the easement, does that allow the government to shut it down or to collect damages? If the inholder needs to repair a wash in the road from a summer storm, to cut down weeds that have overgrown the path, or to remove snow and ice during winter, is he allowed to do so? Or must he request that the government take action, and sue if it does not? If allowed to take action, at what time and under what government supervision? What should be done if the same easement services several inholders who need to coordinate their activities? If the government needs to take out one road for one of its own improvements, can it require the inholder to take a more circuitous and bumpy route in exchange?

These examples can be multiplied *ad infinitum*, but the analytics of each of these examples boils down to one critical issue. The inholder is in the position of the customer without the reputational protection; the government is in the position of the cleaner without the reputational constraints. It may be impossible for the government to condemn the easement (without having to pay for the loss of value of the inholding), but it is certainly possible to make life miserable for the inholder in the day-to-day use of the easement. Squabbles over every one of these and other issues can take place daily, where the government takes the position that any violation of its conditions makes the inholder into a trespasser, subject to damage actions and injunctions. Here, the government has little reason to worry about reputational concerns and, indeed, its tough-nosed attitude could win the favor of many environmentalists who disfavor the expansion of private inholdings. The stakes could be large, and the ability to retaliate limited since the government typically does not hold easements over the private inholdings in question.

The upshot is that the government can use low-level forms of coercion — that is low-level continuous breach of the express and implied conditions associated with the right of way — to wear down the resistance of the individual inholder. Once that softening-up takes place, it becomes possible to acquire the land in a voluntary transaction for a fraction of the value that it would have commanded if the rights of way and other easements had been scrupulously respected. The inholdings become the focal point of a war between inholders and government, where the latter holds most of the heavy firepower.

At this point, the line between voluntary and coercive transactions becomes murky. Litigation, like drama, works best when there is one defining incident (an accident, a bankruptcy), but less well with a long and sinuous set of low-level events, each of which lends itself to conflicting interpretations. To give but one example, it may be possible to prevent a township from downzoning land that it promptly condemns based on its reduced value.[12] The one discrete act becomes a sensible focal point for litigation. Yet, just as guerrilla wars rarely feature decisive confrontations, so too it is hard to bring these skirmishes between government and inholders to closure given the stream of continuous incursions by both sides. In these cases, therefore, the precarious nature of the inholder's rights leads to a major inroad (no pun intended) to the constitutional protections afforded to private property, for which I see no obvious constitutional, legislative, or judicial fix. The private, voluntary sales reflect the reduced values of the current holdings and the bleak prospects in a condemnation proceeding.

This gap in the enforcement mechanism translates itself into a degradation of constitutional rights.[13] Any systematic effort to contain the abuse cuts too deeply into the system of ordinary ownership. First, even a prohibition against forced exchanges would not respond to the difficulties involved here. Nor would prohibition against government purchases work for the close substitutes remain: the pressure can be placed on the inholder until the land is sold to a third party that shares the government's vision of how the inholding should be used. Yet to prevent the sale of private inholdings categorically will ensure that, with time, all these interests will be abandoned. So the problem remains an open wound at the boundary between public and private property, one that increases the likelihood that government coercion will produce the factional gain that Madison feared.

Calculating Just Compensation

The second source of concern with the current takings model is that the just compensation owed in a takings case is not correctly computed. Here, the point matters not only for litigated cases, but also for cases settled in the shadow of the law. At this point, the problem is not one of the asymmetric risk of incremental confiscation; rather, it is in the choice of improper legal standards by which the just compensation is determined.

The nub of the difficulty comes in an unexpected place, the ostensibly exacting requirement, first announced in *Monongahela Navigation Co. v. United States* (1893), in which lavish praise for the Takings Clause was followed by its narrow interpretation. On the former issue, the Court made clear that one of the key uses of the clause was that

> it prevents the public from loading upon one individual more than his just share of the burdens of government, and says that when he surrenders to the public something more and different from that which is exacted from other members of the public, a full and just equivalent shall be returned to him. (*Monongahela* 1893, 325–26)

But the judicial follow-through falls short:

> There can, in view of the combination of those two words [just compensation], be no doubt that the compensation must be a full and perfect equivalent for the property taken. And this just compensation, it will be noticed, is for the property, and not to the owner. (*Monongahela* 1893, 326)[14]

As explicated, the object of compensation is to put the owner of condemned property "in as good a position pecuniarily as if his property had not been taken" (*Olson v. United States* 1934, 255). In principle, that measure might allow (depending on the reading of "pecuniarily") compensation for subjective values associated with the property, but these are difficult to measure. As a corrective against possible abuse, hornbook law provides that "the owner is entitled to receive 'what a willing buyer would pay in cash to a willing seller' at the time of the taking."[15] As such, it does not provide any scheduled bonus value to condemnees for any subjective use value (Ellickson 1973). It does, however, allow for the possibility of compensation for future use values, which the landowner is under a burden to establish.[16]

These legal standards are symptomatic of a larger ill. *Monongahela*'s use of the phrase "property taken" narrows compensation in light of what follows, that the compensation is only for the property taken, not for the loss to the owner consequent on that taking. In its restrictive formulation, the compensation rule does not make sufficient accommodation for the collateral or consequential losses that government action imposes on private landowners. To see why, compare that formula with the objective for compensation identified by Blackstone in explaining how the state takes private land for public use: "Not by absolutely stripping the subject of his property in an arbitrary manner; but by giving him a full indemnification and equivalent of the injury thereby sustained" (Blackstone 1765, Book 1, 135).

Monongahela ignored this element of subjective value (i.e. the amount above market value attached to the subject property). There is a good reason why "for sale" signs do not sprout from every front lawn in the United States. In a well-ordered society, most individuals are content with their personal living or business situations. They do not put their property up for sale because they do not think that there is any other person out there who is likely to value it for a sum greater than they do. In the normal case, use value is greater than exchange value, so the property is kept off the market.[17] The use of the market value standard therefore results in a situation in which the party who owns the property, even if he shares in the social gain generated by the project, is still left worse off than his peers. He is forced to sacrifice the subjective values associated with his property, values which almost by definition he could not recreate through his next best use of the funds received, even if he could afford a second set of transaction costs. In contrast, the Blackstone definition seems to include loss of subjective value as part of "the injury thereby sustained."

The current law, however, follows *Monongahela*. In *Kimball Laundry Co. v. United States* (1949, 5), Justice Frankfurter offered this rationale:

The value of property springs from subjective needs and attitudes; its value to the owner may therefore differ widely from its value to the taker. Most things, however, have a general demand which gives them a value transferable from one owner to another. As opposed to such personal and variant standards as value to the particular owner whose property has been taken, this transferable value has an external validity which makes it a fair measure of public obligation to compensate the loss incurred by an owner as a result of the taking of his property for public use. In view, however, of the liability of all property to condemnation for the common good, loss to the owner of nontransferable values deriving from his unique need for property or idiosyncratic attachment to it, like loss due to an exercise of the police power, is properly treated as part of the burden of common citizenship.

Frankfurter thus takes the view that the questions of valuation are always more difficult than the dangers from inappropriate government behaviors. His position presupposes that, in all cases, the subjective value depends on some peculiar and obscure landowner preference.

But in many cases, the subjective value attaches to a well-documented idiosyncratic use that cannot be replicated by others because they lack, for example, a special license or connection to engage in the task. At this point, the unwillingness to sell provides in itself powerful evidence that current use value exceeds transferable value, often in ways that can be objectively measured. Yet the bias in favor of government action, all in the name of the duties of common citizenship, could lead to erroneous but easily monitored decisions. Note that the *Kimball Laundry* decision involved the temporary condemnation of the owner's laundry facilities that resulted in the dissipation of his goodwill, which was held not to be a taking and was not compensable because it was not transferred to the United States. The explicit undercompensation leads to excessive government use and occupation of private property.

Similar shortfalls can be detected with consequential damages and collateral losses.[18] The individual who is forced to surrender property has to enter into an involuntary transaction with the government, one that requires him to expend resources to contest the condemnation (or valuation) itself; to move his personal belongings off his property; and to reestablish his personal relationships or business goodwill after the move has taken place. Thus in one case, state safety regulations prohibited the physical transfer of prescription drugs from one location to another unless they were reinspected for purity. The required tests cost more than the drugs themselves were worth (*Community Redevelopment Agency of Los Angeles v. Abrams* 1975).

Blackstone's test requires full compensation for the losses sustained when the drugs were rendered worthless. But the California State Supreme Court denied compensation under the *Monongahela* formulation because the government had not "taken" the drugs, but had only "destroyed" their value by regulation. The cleavage between what the state has gained and the individual has lost is thus enormous. In the usual private law case, the innocent tort plaintiff always recovers his loss, even if it is greater than the cost to the wrongdoer. But the takings law, which supposedly seeks to put the plaintiff back in the position that he enjoyed before the taking, does not.

The same difficulties attach to the loss of locational goodwill generally, as in *Kimball Laundry*. The government wants the land, but it cannot use the goodwill, which the previous owner is free to take to the next location. But in some cases, it is not possible reestablish the business at all; in other cases, it will require additional expenditures of cash to inform customers of the change in location, and even then some fraction of them will decide to change businesses because of the inconvenience of the new location.

A similar critique applies to the nebulous issue of expectations. A tenant on a short-term lease that has been renewed countless times in the past has the positive expectation (say, 0.95) that the lease will be renewed on attractive terms at the end of the next period, twelve months away. The potential surplus from this lease, given his site-specific investments could be substantial. No matter, the case law is clear that his renewal right only counts as a mere expectation for which no compensation is required when the government condemns the landlord's interest (*United States v. Petty Motors* 1946). The expected value of the prospective relationship with the landlord was positive, precisely because the ongoing relationship itself had proved sturdy on multiple past occasions. The legal value attached to that relationship in condemnation proceedings is, however, rounded off to zero.

Unfortunately, by refusing to compensate all those losses that flow from government action, the takings ignores this fundamental precept: that the compensation in question should leave the owner indifferent between the property once possessed and the compensation tendered thereafter for its use. The inequitable treatment leads to profound allocative distortions: the lower prices stipulated by the government lead to an excessive level of takings, which in turn increase the size of government relative to what it should be, and thereby alters for the worse the balance between public and private control. And these problems remain even if (as per our general formulation) the individual whose property has been taken shares in the public benefits generated by the improvement in question. Following Blackstone, the level of compensation should be beefed up to cover subjective value and consequential damages except in those few cases where the problems of proof are genuinely daunting. But in light of the determined judicial resistance to that position, it is not likely that this reform will be achieved quickly.

Division of the Surplus

The third question associated with governmental takings is more subtle, but of greater importance in some important institutional settings. One categorical proposal is that the government just ought to stay out of the takings business altogether: the danger of abuse is so great that we are in effect better off without a clear response to the holdout problem (Paul 1987). Constitutionally, that position has a faint echo in the public use provision of the Takings Clause which in effect delineates a class of takings (those for private use) for which the government power cannot be exercised at all. It is easy to see why it is regarded it as an abuse of power for the state to take land from A to convey it to B, where both A and B are ordinary private parties.

Unfortunately, even this strategy is routinely tolerated by the United States Supreme Court. In *Hawaiian Housing Authority v. Midkiff* (1984), the Supreme Court sustained a scheme whereby the Hawaiian Housing Authority would purchase leasehold reversions from their owners and then, by prearrangement, resell them to the tenant in possession (and even here, there was some monkey business in the valuation of the reversions). But before the state would engage in the condemnation, it required the acquiring landowner to place the needed funds in escrow so that it could not be caught in a bind. The state thus took no business risk at all, but simply acted as a purchasing agent for the private holder of the property. It was not as though the land afterward was devoted to public use. It did not go into public hands, and the landowner did not (as is the case with common carriers and many public establishments) allow the public to use it as it would. The property was as private in the hands of the new owners as it had been in the hands of the old ones.

The transaction represents a close substitute for the private taking that cries out for judicial nullification. Yet the Supreme Court upheld this transparent piece of derring-do on the ground that any "conceivable public use" would do, thus implying the low scrutiny of the rational basis test to yet another constitutional provision. It then held that the oligopolistic structure of the land market justified the use of state power, even though most of Hawaiian lands are zoned to prevent any real estate development. Even if the land were not taken for a public use, the entire scheme was designed for some public purpose, albeit one that bears no relation to Madison's antifactional program. It is doubtful, however, that the two particularistic features of this case (the holding of the reversion and the large concentration of ownership in the

Hawaiian Bishop Estate) count in any sense as rigorous preconditions for the use of state power. Any politically charged action carries with it multiple consequences — some good, some bad — and it takes only a little imagination to point to one public consequence that could "conceivably" justify the use of legislative power. The broad use of the takings power certainly leads to a deviation from the social ideal to which forced exchanges should be addressed.

The larger question with regard to the public use requirement raises more profound difficulties because it arises with takings that meet any sensible definition of the public use test: the taking of lands for uses made available to everyone in the world. Here the problem is illustrated by contrasting two takings for public use. In the first, A owns a piece of land which is taken in its entirety for inclusion in the public park. In the second, B owns a piece of land, a strip of which is taken for use as a public highway that abuts his property. In both cases, the state pays full and fair compensation for the land, taking into account subject value and collateral losses, just as Blackstone would have it. Under the current takings law, these two situations are treated alike: the state has met the full constitutional obligations in a world with forced exchanges.

Under the basic model set out above, the social and economic consequences of these two takings differ profoundly. In the highway case, there are no economic forebodings about the constitutional regime that is put into place. The owner gets both direct losses and shares in the social gains from the public project. Indeed, the increased value from the retained lands often proves far greater than the value of original plot (without road access). The owner who surrenders the strip to the public free of charge is better off, so long as the state would commit itself to the extensive resources it takes to erect, maintain, and police a public road. It is for that reason that local communities often go into competition with each other to have state or national roads located near enough to them to secure favorable access, even if they would like, at least for residential properties in some urban settings, to have a narrow buffer zone to insulate themselves from the noise and congestion associated with their operation.[19] We can therefore be confident that, even in the best of circumstances, some of the benefits of public roads will be competed away as parties vie to secure the optimal placement of these roads from their own local perspective. Once again, we see the risk of faction. Yet it seems that no manipulation of the compensation requirements could eliminate this source of social loss.

The first situation, with the wholesale condemnation of land for public parks, however, carries with it more dire consequences. The standard model of eminent domain indicates that the landowner receives two sources of benefit from the taking: the direct compensation for the land taken (which as noted, is usually calculated too low) and his pro rata share of the overall gains from the public project undertaken with the property acquired. But once state expropriation extends to the entire property of a given landowner, the second element of value is completely eliminated. All other individuals who remain in that community (or perhaps who enter thereafter) share pro rata in the gains. The party who loses his full holdings to the taking, however, loses both ways relative to his peers: inadequate compensation and no share of the social surplus.

It is for just this reason that the land acquisition battles that take place in the West are fought at such a pitched level. On the one side stand the conservationists who claim that large public appropriations should be directed to the acquisition of sensitive parcels of land (including inholdings) to preserve the natural condition of the land forever. On the other side lie the outnumbered members of small farming and ranching communities, who see in the appropriation of public moneys for land acquisition a plot to destroy their lives and their livelihoods. The battle here is not dissimilar in form to those extensive urban renewal programs[20] that led to the wholesale destruction of neighborhoods, where most renewal never quite took place.

A parallel struggle took place over the *Conservation and Reinvestment Act* (CARA)[21] a bill that proposes to take some royalty revenues the Land and Water Conservation Fund and direct them toward the acquisition of public lands. As might be expected, the political battles over this appropriation legislation were fierce. Yet, if the benign version of the eminent domain paradigm worked, then one should see little, if any, concentrated opposition to the proposed expansion. If the level of compensation made the condemnees indifferent between the lands that they held and the compensation that they received, why would they spend huge private resources to ward off a set of takings whose consequences they dread? From the ground level, they have made the considered judgment that they would be worse off by far from the takings with compensation. The explanation of their resistance lies, I think, in the three factors outlined above: Many of the voluntary purchases have been brought about by the constant tussles over rights of way and similar easements; the level of compensation offered is below the true costs of losing the land; and the public benefits, however defined, are not shared by the individuals who are forced out of the communities in which they live.

The consequences are sobering. Whatever the theoretical promise of the taking of property only with compensation, that gain has been nullified in large measure by the troubled circumstances of its application. It is difficult to know how to fix the situation, although it seems clear that we should try to limit the incidence of forced exchanges to those hold-out situations that justify its application. Here again, the question of what counts as a holdout or blockade is more difficult to determine in practice than it is in theory, once we move away from the single foot of land that blocks the completion of a railroad between two towns. Does the typical inholder, for example, stand as a holdout against the govern-ment control of certain undeveloped lands? Surely if the goal is to keep public ownership of all contiguous property, each inholder counts a po-tential holdout. But if it is asked what gains the government obtains from acquisition, one would be hard pressed to find gains comparable to those of the completed railroad. The basic insight is that the takings power works best to weave the threads of infrastructure—highways, railroads, telephone easements, rivers, and the like—and not for squar-ish plots of land used for other purposes. But what ratio and what set of uses determines what counts as a thread and what as a square? It is a hard question, for which there is no easily administrable answer. The upshot is that all distortions cut in the same direction, so that in equilib-rium there is too much public land and too little private land.

THE REGULATION OF PUBLIC PROPERTY

The second half of the governance problem is as intractable as the first, and perhaps more so. A well-ordered society does not have only private property. Rather, it will contain certain elements that are regarded by the public as held in common, so much so that these elements cannot be reduced to private ownership by either occupation or capture.[22] From the earliest times, the air and the sea have been regarded as part of the *ius communis*, which meant they were open to all. In addition, the state routinely used its eminent domain power or ordinary market transac-tions to acquire private property for use in roads and other forms of public works.

With that thumbnail sketch in place, it is possible to identify discor-dant rationales for treating certain resources as publicly owned. Certain things are treated as public property in the initial position in order to mount an effective social response to a holdout problem. In riparian systems, the privatization of waterways ends their use for transporta-tion and destroys the aesthetic amenities of running water. The custom-ary practice of keeping these waters open to all yields, on average, higher values than any decision to allow their partition under the rule of cap-ture. The decision to treat these resources as part of the commons, therefore, represents a good effort to minimize the sum of the costs of exclusion and coordination. No one has exclusive ownership, but every-one has (a right of) access to the veins and arteries that link separate plots of (privately owned) land — or for that matter, water[23] — together. That same approach requires some modification for highways, for unlike water, their location is not given in nature, but requires collective human choice. In contrast, when the road has to be created out of privately held lands, compensation (in cash or kind) is supplied to limit and, perhaps, to prevent the arbitrary use of state power.

The second class of public property covers resources that are not part of a complex network. The lands in question may be operated, for example, as a public park. As noted earlier, that land may have been successfully owned in private hands, so that its public acquisition cannot be justified as part of a plan to complete some transportation or communication network. How should individual rights, if any, be assigned to property of this sort?

Concurrent Ownership as the Analogue to Public Property

The first point to note is that this problem is not unique to property that is held in common in the public sphere. One common institution in the private law is that property may be held by multiple owners in common, with or without rights of survivorship. The practical difficulty arises because all of the tenants, taken together, do have exclusive rights to the property as against the rest of the world, but none of the tenants individually have exclusive rights against their cotenants. The problems of internal governance are at least as important as the right to exclude, which the cotenants taken together hold as against the rest of the world.[24]

The institution of joint ownership usually works best between husband and wife because of the close parallelism of their objectives. But this body of private law does not respond well to non-pro rata shifts in the patterns of land use which redistribute wealth between the parties. Thus, when jointly owned land is leased to a single tenant, it is easy to divide the net rentals between the cotenants, both of whom are out of possession. But matters grow more difficult when the two tenants no longer have pro rata stakes in the management and control of the property.

Thus, a constant source of tension arises when one of two joint tenants takes sole possession of the property, which in general he is allowed to do on a rent-free basis.[25] The party out of possession is relegated to the costly choice of seeking either partition or judicial sale. Likewise, the rules of joint tenancy have certain slack when one of two joint tenants in possession wishes to change the character of part of the premises, add improvements, or to lease part of them to someone who will.[26] The vast shifts of internal wealth undertaken by unilateral action are hard to cope with in any systematic fashion, even by a system that seeks in general to honor and enforce the respective shares of the parties.

Unavoidable redistributions among cotenants thus take place within the private sector, even when courts treat each cotenant as owning an aliquot portion of the whole. To respond to these difficulties, the law often provides for some general accounting to take place at the termination of the joint tenancy. The logic behind that decision is straightforward. It is costly for courts to intervene with the small decisions in an ongoing relationship in which it is possible that the imbalance in one transaction is offset by an opposite imbalance in another. But once the relationship is terminated, the stakes become higher, and the prospects of reciprocal offsets diminish. At this point a once-and-for-all accounting may redress some interim imbalance (as when the improvements paid for by one are enjoyed by both), so that judicial interference becomes cost-justified.

The legal position becomes only more attenuated when attention turns to public or common property. To the extent that private property analogies govern, public property should be treated as property held in common whereby the people of the locality, state, or nation have the collective right to exclude the outsider, but share among themselves the rights in property as *res communis*. Using this approach would require a court to work out in the constitutional realm the nature of these shared access and use rights in ways that maximized the internal coherence and minimized the indefiniteness of the multiple ownership claims. The minimum condition for this venture is a rejection of the idea that individual members of the public have no access or use rights to public property at all. And in line with the joint tenancy, it would tend to focus judicial intervention to transitional situations when publicly held property is transferred to private hands. Yet judicial thinking takes just the opposite view, chiefly by washing its hands of any supervision over public property. Justice Scalia penned a forceful, but misguided, statement of the basic proposition in *College Savings Bank v. Florida Prepaid Postsecondary Education Expense Board* (1999):

> The hallmark of a protected property interest is the right to exclude others. That is "one of the most essential sticks in the bundle of rights that are commonly characterized as property." That is why the right we all possess to the use of the public lands is not the "property" right of anyone—hence the sardonic maxim, explaining what economists call the "tragedy of the commons," *res publica, res nullius.* (quoting *Kaiser Aetna v. United States* 1979)

The more accurate rendition of the point at hand should be *res publica, res communis*. Unfortunately, consequences attach to the inapt choice of Latin adjectives. The use of the term "*nullius*" literally implies that the thing is the property of no one. One implication of this rule is that it would allow any person to take possession of the property in question, as with any other *res nullius*. The prohibition of such actions shows that the term *res nullius* is applied in an opportunistic fashion. More to the point, if public lands are (selectively) conceived as *res nullius*, then alteration or elimination of the access rights of ordinary individuals may be done at will. So long as no legal rights are taken, no compensation need be tendered. But let these rights be held in common, then their alteration could count as bona fide losses that could easily trigger the operation of legal remedies.

RES NULLIUS VERSUS RES COMMUNIS

How then do we decide which of these conceptions makes sense for common property? Here we can take a leaf from the standard judicial methodology of determining what counts as private property under the Takings Clause. One possible approach is to allow judges to determine what is meant by private property in interpreting that clause. But that approach necessarily guts the Takings Clause by allowing the Supreme Court to deny the honorific title of property to whatever private interest it chooses not to protect. The only way to avoid this trap is to look outside the Constitution, typically to state law, so as to piggyback on definitions of property that the justices did not invent for the occasion.[27] In general, the Supreme Court has been aware of the dangers of its excessive role, by taking the role of finder and not inventor of property rights:

> Property interests, of course, are not created by the Constitution. Rather they are created and their dimensions are defined by existing rules or understandings that stem from an independent source such as state law — rules or understandings that secure certain benefits and that support claims of entitlements to those benefits.[28]

These are not idle words. In a wide variety of contexts dealing with asserted claims to private property, the Supreme Court will look to traditional bodies of state law, particularly to longstanding common law rules that do not present the prospect of legislative intrigue. To give but one example, in *Ruckelshaus v. Monsanto* (1984), the court found that trade secrets were protectable property under the Takings Clause, adopting verbatim their definition in Section 757 of the *Restatement of the Law of Torts* (American Law Institute 1934).[29] What is striking is that this methodology is totally abandoned in working out the definitions of common property under the Constitution. Two types of cases illustrate the basic problem: water rights and public lands.

First, the common law of water rights has always involved a complex division of rights among claimants to the water.[30] Riparians have rights of access from the riverbanks and limited rights to use the water in question. The public has the right to travel on navigable rivers. Different legal regimes govern the capture of fish that swim in the river and mussels, clams, and other forms of life that burrow in the sand. Once these usufructuary rights are established by custom, individuals receive legal protection against those who would exclude them from the river or otherwise impair their rights. The fact that rights are held in common in complex ways has never precluded the recognition of private rights along the river. "For water is a moveable, wandering thing, and must of necessity continue common by the law of nature; so that I can only have a temporary, transient, usufructuary property therein . . ." (Blackstone 1766, Book 2, 18). That said, the riparian system guaranteed all riparians rights of access to the river (just as landowners have rights of access to public roads).

Yet a uniform line of Supreme Court decisions has held that the all-consuming navigation servitude allows the government to wipe out access rights without compensation.[31] The traditional versions of riparian rights give some relief against (unreasonable) interferences with the operation of established dams, but numerous Supreme Court cases hold that the heads of mills and power plants are not protected against government action even though they are protected against the like action of other riparians.[32] The same attitude toward rights has been expressed in relationship with public lands. Thus in *Lyng v. Northwest Indian Cemetery Protective Ass'n* (1985), the Supreme Court gave its blessing to a decision of the U.S. Forest Service to build a road that cut through the sacred sites and burial grounds of three Indian tribes (the Yurok, Karok, and Tolowa). The explanation was simple: "Whatever rights the Indians may have to the use of the area, however, those rights do not divest the Government of its right to use what is, after all, *its* land" (*Lyng v. Northwest Indian Cemetery Protective Ass'n* 1985, 453). The counterargument rests on the view that customary practices that can create group rights even on private lands — in this case easements and other prescriptive rights — could be applied in accordance with the ordinary common law definitions.[33]

It is possible to identify two discordant principles for the constitutional superintendence of public property. The first carries over the private rules of joint ownership to government resources and uses them as a means to constrain political action. The second treats public property as a *res nullius* and thus sees no way to import constitutional constraints on political behavior. The total withdrawal of constitutional principle from regulation of public property does much to simplify the administrative burdens thrown on the judicial system. At the same time, it does much to unleash a wide range of destructive political forces.

The successful operation of joint ventures in the private sphere rests only in part on the legal rules that govern conflicts of interest. More depends on the ability of individuals to choose their business partners. That power of selection allows people to choose partners whom they trust and partners who have the same basic preference set. The first reduces the likelihood of illicit appropriation of common assets. The second reduces the likelihood of major standoffs on collective choice.

Neither of these protective mechanisms is available, however, with respect to property that is held in public hands, for here the joint tenants are, as it were, the citizens of a city, county, state or nation, as the case may be. They are thrown together against their will and operate in large and anonymous settings. The element of trust among them may prove nonexistent, and their preference sets are likely to diverge wildly. Yet they must choose from a broad spectrum of potential land uses, which can be mixed and matched.

By way of contrast, highways have a single use that is compatible with the need to maintain the transportation network, and the prohibition on private use is driven by that one dominant objective. No one may, for example, construct a permanent private improvement on public highways or waterways. Beaches, in contrast, have a broader spectrum of uses, and there the usual rule, for public beaches at least, is that private individuals may claim the exclusive right to a limited portion of beach only for a short period of time, say between sunrise and sunset. The beach chairs that mark a preferred location in the morning must be removed come evening. The next day, the cycle starts anew on a beach that by design has no history.

On the Michigan beach that I frequent, the basic norm, unspoken but strictly observed, is that only the owner of the adjacent land may sit on his private portion of beach. Others may walk across the beach and collect seashells, but they cannot stop and camp out in front of someone's home without his permission, which is usually denied to strangers. In effect, the beach is a form of mixed property — it is treated as common property with respect to movement, but remains a form of limited private property with respect to occupation, which itself is carefully circumscribed to beachfront owners. This partial commons works because the mixed set of allowable uses generates maximum value at that location. And no unilateral deviation in use patterns is tolerated which might upset the initial equilibrium once it is obtained.

The moment the state takes over the operation of a public park, however, the problem of choosing the use or mix of uses intensifies. In this context, the situation is more perilous than it is with private property because the class of citizen owners is likely to have divergent tastes which must be reconciled over a broad class of potential uses. In this context, the blockage of permanent improvements can no longer be rationalized as a way to keep open the arteries of transportation. If private owners may erect extensive improvements on their lands, then why not a similar range of activities on public property? The government is thus put into the position of having to decide who can make what kinds of uses of public lands, and whether to sell or lease all or part of these lands to private individuals. The state can allow the removal of minerals or oil and gas from private lands—through open bids or sweetheart deals. It can dispose of certain lands that it does not need to ordinary citizens—at public auction, or at bargain prices to the well connected.

Constitutional Oversight of Public Property

These government powers to regulate the use and disposition of public lands are subject to little explicit constitutional constraint. That indefiniteness of rights with respect to these assets greatly influences the political behavior in disputes involving public lands and waters. Large shifts in use patterns produce enormous shifts in implicit wealth. But since the underlying assets stay in public solution both before and after the shift takes place, no compensation is payable by any winner to any loser, which necessarily blocks the standard technique for making win-lose transactions into win-win transactions.

The gaps in the current institutional arrangements become clear when we apply the framework of analysis for private property to public property. In both settings, we ask two questions about any shift in either the ownership or use patterns of public resources. The first is, Does the shift result in some overall net social gain in the value of the resources in question? The second is, Are the net gains distributed in a fashion all citizens share in these public improvements? Neither condition is frequently satisfied.

Let us start with the question of the shift in uses of public lands. Suppose, for example, that certain public lands have been left open for hunting and fishing. A new administration comes into power and decides to ban these traditional uses, to erect public roads that reduce the game available, to construct dams that alter or reduce the number of fish available, or, as in *Lyng*, to build roads that cut through the sacred grounds of an Indian tribe. Each of these changes will benefit powerful groups and harm less powerful groups. Yet the usual method for dealing with massive distributional imbalances introduced by government is not available, because no provision of any constitution, state or federal, requires that any compensation be paid by winners to losers for the shift in legislative programs. The upshot is that compensation, when it comes, does so solely out of political compromise, where its amount is at best imperfectly correlated with any sensible social objective.

This omission of compensation is understandable from an administrative perspective. Over a quarter of a billion people in the United States have at least some rights of access with respect to the properties in public possession. Any change in land use patterns will have no effect on large fractions of them, but profound effects, both positive and negative, on substantial minorities. Who, then, can determine who should pay how much to whom? To make matters worse, public management decisions run into a baseline problem. Let us suppose that the current regime of land uses allows extensive fishing and hunting. Once these are curtailed or eliminated by public edict, Coase (see Yandle, this volume) teaches us to ask: Should we characterize that action as the rectification of a wrong done by some private actors (the destruction of wildlife or its habitat), or should we treat it as though it were the restriction on the common law rights of all individuals to reduce fish and wildlife to possession?

Answers to these questions depend on some prior account of rights, such as the rule of capture for wild animals. But once the capture takes place on public lands, it becomes less clear whether the landowner (the state) or the individual entrant owns the animal upon capture. In part, the difficulty stems from the analogous dispute within private law. The basic English rule is that the owner of the soil is entitled to the ownership of any wild animal that a trespasser captures on his property (*Blade v. Higgs* 1865). Yet the Roman law awarded ownership to the trespasser, even if the landowner was entitled to bar his entrance (*Digest of Justinian*, 41.1.3.1). But that private analogy does not work given that the state ordinarily cannot exclude an individual from public property on a whim, but must show cause for its decision. Again the indefiniteness of the system of rights leads to enormous amounts of jockeying. The epic battles that one witnesses between the environmentalists and the western landowners do not stop when private lands are subject to public appropriation. They continue unabated with each management decision of what forms of land use should be allowed and what should be prohibited.

To make matters worse, resources subject to public control are subject to more than simple decisions about use. The question always arises whether the government can, or should, charge for the use of facilities. In this context, the political dynamic favors the emergence of queues, as government officials are reluctant for political reasons to charge anything close to a market-clearing price for use of public resources. It is better for individuals to wait outside Yellowstone Park campgrounds for hours than to raise the price to a market level, because the price might exclude someone who does not have sufficient wealth to back his utility preferences. The upshot is that individuals able to finance their use of public parks now, by queuing, must pay with time instead of cash, which, in the effort to favor individuals of relatively low income, creates all the imbalance of any system that does not allow price to rise to clear queues. Yet because the land is within the public domain, no constitutional device can force the government to deal with its property as a rational private owner — to raise the price until the queues disappear.

The situation here is representative of a larger difficulty in obtaining balance on public lands. At present, it is easier to appropriate funds for the acquisition of public lands (often at bargain prices) than it is to appropriate public funds for the maintenance of lands already acquired. Thus there is a constant chorus of complaints about the rundown nature of public facilities and the erratic level of management on public lands (see Fretwell 2000). The ideal program matches acquisition with management, which requires that we either cut back on the acquisitions or improve the management, or do both in some combination. As between the two, I have little doubt that in the present situation, scaling back on acquisitions, or even divesting public lands, is the preferred approach. The current pattern of acquisitions is spurred by compensation rules that do not take into account the full losses of condemnation, both on the condemnee and other members of his community. Yet the process removes lands from the tax rolls and invites a continuation of the erratic management practices which political concerns make it difficult to correct.

Transfers of Resources from Public to Private Hands

One remaining question is, What constitutional constraints, if any, apply to the transfer of public to private property? At this point, the possibility of imposing effective judicial oversight improves. To begin with the private analogy, courts are rightly reluctant to order an accounting between cotenants for every expenditure that each makes during the period in which the property is jointly held. The administrative costs are high, and the dangers of making serious mistakes is large. But on the termination of the concurrent interests, it becomes feasible to make a once-and-for-all assessment of the various contributions; this is commonly done by giving each joint tenant credit for the cost or the value (or perhaps, whichever is lower).[34]

A similar set of rules could be adapted to dispositions of public lands to private parties. Ideally, these transfers should follow the same norms applicable to takings transactions: No one should be left worse off, and the public at large should be left better off.[35] One possible way to achieve that result is to conduct an auction so that public resources end up in the hands of the highest bidder, with the wealth in question coming to the government. Thus, all individuals who have lost their share in a specific asset at least will receive in its place a pro rata share of the proceeds of sale (Anderson, Smith, and Simmons 1999). Even this strategy does not deal with differential intensities of preferences with respect to the lands moving out of public ownership. If certain hunting land is sold off at bid, the environmentalists may be pleased by the identity of the ultimate purchaser, and thus gain two ways: a portion of the public funds and ownership of the land by their preferred party. Or the distribution of benefits and burdens from the transaction could run in reverse. The sad truth is that even market-value sales will result in substantial wealth transfers from one group to another, and that fact alone is sufficient to set up the usual incentives for seeking political advantage.

The problem here is not confined to public lands, and currently the issue has been squarely raised with government distribution of two kinds of assets once located within the public domain. The first is the radio spectrum, which conceivably could be allocated in one of three ways. A first possession rule could allocate it to the party who first uses it (Lueck, this volume). That system might have worked well at the onset of radio when the rate of occupation was relatively slow, but it could not function well in the current setting where sophisticated parties could occupy the entire spectrum in the twinkling of an eye. The trivial gaps in time are too small to justify the absolute priorities they create. An auction works better than with land because no one can identify those groups who made more intense use of the spectrum before it was sold to private parties. Yet even in the recent auctions of the broadband spectrum for high speed telecommunications, distributional objectives were allowed to creep into the process, namely, to ensure some level of minority ownership in the successful bids.[36] Aside from the traditional allocation of broadcast frequencies, the spectrum is allocated through comparative hearings that invite large amounts of rent dissipation.[37] Here, the object of the massive expenditures is often to gain the right to a license which the lucky recipient can then (after one year's wait) sell to the highest bidder. Rent dissipation is followed by a private auction that puts not a single dollar in the public purse.

A second giveaway of public resources applies to intellectual property, which often falls in the public domain. Thus the *Sonny Bono Copyright Term Extension Act of 1998* (CTEA) has extended the terms of existing copyrights for twenty years without exacting a corresponding quid pro quo from their holders. Copyright does not count as a natural right, but necessarily requires the power of the state to secure it, which is done under the United States Constitution by Art. I, § 8, cl. 8: "To promote the Progress of Science and useful Arts, by securing for limited Times to Authors and Inventors the exclusive Right to their respective

Writings and Discoveries."[38] A world that denies all protection for writings and inventions directs labor toward other, less productive endeavors. Yet a perpetual copyright or patent has the offsetting inconvenience of blocking the use of these writings and inventions, even though the marginal cost of their additional use is zero or close to it.

It is no easy task in the abstract to determine the optimal tradeoffs between the incentive to create and the rate of dissemination of works once created. But it is tolerably clear that writings and other works of art are distinctive in ways inventions are not. The former tend to be unique creations, while the latter will usually be discovered in light of general knowledge and the prior art. Accordingly, the optimal term of years for patentable inventions should be, and is, far shorter (twenty years for a utility patent) than for copyrights (life plus seventy years). It is hard to see how any form of constitutional inquiry dictates the precise term of either.

That global structural judgment, however, hardly justifies the retroactive extension of a copyright term for writings that are about to go out from copyright. Now one side of the traditional copyright bargain has vanished because the additional term adds no incentive to create new works, yet the longer term restricts from treating the work as part of the public domain. Congress cannot grant copyright protection to works that have fallen into the public domain.[39] It is hard to distinguish this case from one which extends a copyright that has only a single day to run. The analogy to the common law doctrine of estates gives, as it were, the public (which here means each member thereof) a remainder interest in the copyrighted material that falls into possession upon the expiration of the copyright term.[40] Once the bargain has been struck, it should be as impermissible to lengthen the term of an existing copyright as it is to shorten it.

To see why, compare this transaction with other dispositions of public property. Suppose the state has an easement over some private property that allows members of the public to reach a public beach. Should the state be able to surrender this easement to the servient tenant for nothing when the easement has value to its regular users? To take a corporate analogy, shareholders should be able to block a giveaway of corporate assets to insiders when nothing is received in return.

Unfortunately, our citizen-shareholders do not have comparable rights to block unilateral transfers of public assets to private parties when no adequate quid pro quo has been received in return. One clear obstacle to legal protection comes from the doctrine of standing, which insulates government decisions over public assets from judicial scrutiny. It is another version of *res publica res nullius*. Since no one has a large enough stake in the process, no one has standing to challenge it,[41] as the law now precludes citizen or taxpayer suits attacking some "generalized grievance" shared in substantially equal measure by all or a large class of citizens" (*Warth v. Seldin* 1975, 499). The standing rule thus blocks the public equivalent of the corporate derivative suit.[42]

The argument seems misguided, for no one has satisfactorily explained the standing doctrine on either textual or structural grounds. The word "standing" does not appear in Article III of the Constitution, which notes that the judicial Power "shall extend to all Cases, in Law and Equity, arising under the Constitution, the Law of the United States, and Treaties made." That language clearly excludes advisory opinions on the validity of legislation before it has been challenged. But a claim of both citizen and taxpayer is adverse to the state and, thus, raises a "case" within the meaning of Art. III, sec. 2. The pragmatic justification offered in response asserts that the floodgates will open if the standing barriers are removed. But as with derivative suits, the real peril is the opposite, because individual litigants often lack the large stake needed to pursue such difficult litigation. The standing barrier only aggravates this problem, for what is needed are rules to coordinate separate suits, or to allow class actions or permissive joinder (as with derivative suits). Once again, sensible private analogies give the best guidance to the needed legal rules in the public realm. Standing is little more than an arbitrary barrier to immunize legislative action over the use of public resources from constitutional oversight.

A Revival of the Public Trust Doctrine

Some years ago I suggested that the flip side to the Takings Clause provided "Nor shall public property be transferred to private use, without just compensation" (Epstein 1987). Inserting "transferred" for "taken" reflects the fact that the government cannot be compelled to surrender public property to private parties. That said, the parallel seems striking and does receive some Constitutional backing in *Illinois Central Railroad Co. v. Illinois* (1892), which authorized setting aside the transfer of submerged lands from the state to private parties on grounds that no one can quite articulate. The public trust doctrine lacks a secure constitutional base over government-owned property. As is the case in *Eldred v. Ashford* (1999),[43] that textual gap has led courts to confine the public use doctrine to the submerged lands.

That judicial reticence is misguided for several reasons. First, in the analogous Takings Clause, the phrase "private property" has been consistently applied to cover all forms of property, not only land. Most specifically, trade secrets, patents, and copyrights are all forms of property that cannot be taken from their owners without just compensation.[44]

In addition, this case is still stronger than the land case. The decision to protect writings as copyrighted material necessarily takes away not only the undivided public interest in the property as such, it also infringes on the individuals' common law liberty to speak as they please. The Constitution not only has property protection, it also has speech protections, which are normally subjected to a higher standard of judicial scrutiny. The initial protection of copyright counts as that interest because, in part, it spurs public discourse and debate by offering incentives for parties to speak on matters of public interest and concern. But no such interest can be identified for the extension of protection to speech that has already been generated.

The pattern of litigation in *Eldred* shows how the government has managed to wriggle out of this standard speech power. In effect, it skirts the question of serious justification by holding that the jurisdictional grant over copyright subjects the government to, at most, rational basis review: so long as any interest could be advanced on behalf of the statute, the copyright interest prevails. Deference to congressional decisions becomes the order of the day.[45] The government has been allowed to argue that removing copyrights from the public domain aids in their dissemination when in fact higher prices reduce public utilization.[46] In the absence of discernible quid pro quo, the CTEA is a giveaway of public assets, cloaked in a set of excuses that only extreme judicial deference would tolerate.

CONCLUSION

One of the missions of a sound system of governance—be it public or private—is to facilitate transfers of resources, both tangible and intangible, to higher-valued users. Frequently, voluntary contract encourages those exchanges even for assets that are owned collectively. Often, government is a party to these exchanges, either by coercion, as through eminent domain, or by voluntary transaction. In both contexts, the task is to create positive-sum transactions where all members of the public to the extent possible share pro rata in the distribution of the gains. Not only does that norm respond to a sense of fairness, it also holds out the possibility of maximizing the gains from these transactions over the long run.

Equally clear is the somber proposition that this regime cannot sustain itself. Transitions always spark danger, whether we speak of getting out of an automobile or changing property rights regimes. Transitions require the highest diligence, both legislative and judicial. Some knaves may slip through a well-constructed net, but those risks are multiplied when lax constitutional standards allow factional behavior to flourish.

As Madison noted, transitions are difficult enough to counteract when legislative and judicial officials are conscious of the perils they pose. They become well-nigh impossible to counteract when these same officials refusal to acknowledge the perils they face.

Yet slippage in the joints is not an inevitable fact of nature. In dealing with these issues, the basic attitudes toward government and property count for far more than the particulars of any system of property rights, public or private, tangible or intellectual. People who follow the good government model of behavior may take pride in republican virtue as a sufficient safeguard against political misbehavior. In so doing, they could endorse a low (or rational basis) standard of review under which almost anything goes. But those who recognize that public virtue is a scarce commodity should favor a higher level of judicial scrutiny of legislative action to improve the odds of securing limited government by constitutional means.

ENDNOTES

My thanks to the participants of the Work-in-Progress Workshop at the University of Chicago for helpful comments, and to Robert Alt and Justin Herring for their research assistance.

1. "No state shall . . . pass any . . . law impairing the obligation of contracts" (U.S. Const. Art. I., § 10). Madison took a strong view that this clause operated as a bulwark against the abuse of private rights. "The sober people of America are weary of the fluctuating policy which has directed the public councils. They have seen with regret and indignation that sudden changes and legislative interferences, in cases involving personal rights, become jobs in the hands of enterprising and influential speculators, and snares to the more-industrious and less-informed part of the community" (Earle 1937 [1787], 291). For my views on that subject, see Epstein (1984).

2. See *Nollan v. California Coastal Commission* (1987) (striking down an ordinance that required the surrender of a lateral easement across land in exchange for the right to build an ordinary beachfront home).

3. On mortgage moratoria, see *Home Building & Loan Ass'n v. Blaisdell* (1934).

4. See, for example, the explication of the *Lex Aquilia* (*Justinian's Digest*, IX, 2), found in Lawson (1950). For an argument about how the same techniques carry over to constitutional interpretation, see Epstein (1992a).

5. For the classical exposition of the doctrine of equivalents, see *Graver Tank & Mfg. Co. v. Linde Air Products Co.* (1950): "To temper unsparing logic and prevent an infringer from stealing the benefit of the invention," a patentee may invoke the doctrine of equivalents against the producer of a device "if it performs substantially the same function in substantially the same way to obtain the same result." For an update, see *Warner-Jenkinson Co. v. Hilton Davis Chemical Co.* (1997).

6. For more detailed discussion of this issue, see Epstein (1993), which examines the distribution of gains from projects that government ought to undertake.

7. For discussion, see Epstein (1998) at 15–19.

8. For one class account, see Dawson (1947); for my views, see Epstein (1975). See also Klein, Crawford, and Alchian (1978).

9. *Austin Instrument, Inc. v. Loral Corp.* (1971) (holdup on delivery of components needed to fulfill navy procurement contract).

10. For a discussion of the risks, see Cohen (1991).

11. The basic problem is apparent even when the surrounding land is owned by another private party. See, for example, *Othen v. Rosier* (1950).

12. See, for example, *Riggs v. Township of Long Beach* (1988). The defendant, Township, which had long been desirous of purchasing Riggs' land, downzoned the property by increasing the minimum lot size for building from 5,000 square feet to 10,000 square feet. It purported to justify this amendment by the need to preserve open space, control population density, and prevent urban sprawl. Even though the New Jersey Court gave that zoning ordinance a presumption of validity, it looked through the township's ostensible police power objectives and struck down the ordinance saying: "The purpose of the zoning amendment was not to fulfill the master plan, but to enable the municipality to pay the property owner less than fair market value under the preexisting zoning ordinance" (815). That approach is in principle available in the inholding case, but harder to achieve because of the absence of a precipitating event like the down-zoning in *Riggs*.

13. Note that in principle, it is possible for the exploitation to run in the opposite direction, whereby landowners make successive low-level incursions onto public lands. But to that point, there are several responses. The first, and most obvious, is that two wrongs do not make a right. Individuals who violate these laws should be prosecuted for their offenses. Yet even here, it is not clear that the inholders are the violators. It is clear that the government is in a far better position to prosecute violations of public lands against an ordinary citizen, than the citizen is in suing the government under the *Federal Tort Claims Act*, 28 U.S.C. § 2671 et seq. or its state law counterpart, which supplies substantial protection for government actions including the exercise of discretionary functions, applicable "whether or not the discretion be abused" 28 U.S.C. § 2680(a).

14. See also *United States v. Miller* (1943).

15. *United States v. 564.54 Acres of Land* (1979) (quoting *United States v. Miller* [1943]).

16. See Laitos (1998, § 17.03[C]), noting that both present and future uses can be considered, with the presumption set so that the owner must establish the value of some future use, which might involve the removal of some current valid land use regulation.

17. All prospective buyers have the option to buy from those individuals who do wish to sell; that is, from the small segment which finds use value lower than sale value. As sale prices move upward, the fraction of owners who cross this line may increase, just as the number of buyers may be similarly reduced until the market comes back into equilibrium. In this connection, it is useful to note

that it is often regarded as bizarre behavior to knock on someone's door and to offer him a price far in excess of market value, although that does happen in some overheated markets.

18. For my more extensive treatment of this subject, see Epstein (1985a).

19. Here, the usual pattern is that the negative externalities from nearby highways decline rapidly with an increase in distance, while the positive externality of good access declines more slowly. It is possible, therefore, that communities would seek to block the construction of roads that are close, but welcome them if located a mile away. Thus in Los Angeles, the Santa Monica and San Diego freeways are both located near but not in Beverly Hills.

20. See, for example, *Berman v. Parker* (1954); *Poletown Neighborhood Council v. City of Detroit* (1981). The actual consequences of the urban renewal plan after *Berman* contrast sharply with Justice Douglas' optimistic rhetoric about government land use planning that led to the expansion of the public use requirement.

21. *Conservation and Reinvestment Act of 1999* (CARA), 107th Cong. (1st sess. H.R. 901); 107th Cong. (1st Sess. S. 1328).

22. For a discussion of the commons questions, see Epstein (1998, 251–78). The historical rules are set out with clarity in Justinian's *Institutes* (2.1).

23. See, for example, *Kaiser Aetna v. United States* (1979) (finding a taking where the United States demanded public access to a private marina as a condition for allowing access from the marina to public waters).

24. For a recent academic defense of the right to exclude as the central notion of property law, see Merrill (1998).

25. See, for example, *Spiller v. Mackereth* (1976) for a case that requires a complete ouster before the cotenant out of possession has a remedy short of partition against the party in possession.

26. *Swartzbaugh v. Sampson* (1936) (sustaining the cutting down of walnut trees on the leased portion of common premises).

27. For a discussion of this approach, see Merrill (n.d.).

28. *Bd. of Regents v. Roth* (1972) (finding no property interest for renewal of one-year term contract).

29.

b. Definition of a trade secret. A trade secret may consist of any formula, pattern, device, or compilation of information which is used in one's business, and which gives him an opportunity to obtain an advantage over competitors who do not know it. It may be a chemical compound, a process of manufacturing, treating or preserving materials, a pattern for a machine or other device or a list of customers. (Restatement (Torts) §757, comment *b*)

The topic of trade secrets was dropped from subsequent editions of the *Restatement (Second) of the Law of Torts*. The newer definition is found in *Restatement of the Law: Unfair Competition* (American Law Institute 1995): "A trade secret is an information that can be used in the operation of a business or other enterprise and that is sufficiently valuable and secret to afford an actual or potential economic advantage over others." It seems clear that this definition was not meant to alter the earlier law, or to exclude from the coverage of trade secrets any of the items listed in comment *b* of *Restatement of the Law of Torts* §757.

30. For a convenient summary of the basic rules, see 4 *Restatement (Second) of Torts*, 209–12 (1979).

31. See, for example, *Scranton v. Wheeler* (1900); *United States v. Commodore Park Inc.* (1945); *United States v. Rands* (1967). For my more exhaustive critique, see Epstein (1985a, 67–73).

32. See, for example, *United States v. Chandler-Dunbar Water Power Co.* (1913) (power plant on navigable river); *United States v. Willow River Power Co.* (1944) (power plant at junction of navigable and nonnavigable rivers).

33. As suggested in Lupu (1989). It is no accident that Lupu uses the same test that I have adopted in analyzing takings: "Whenever religious activity is met by intentional government action analogous to that which, if committed by a private party, would be actionable under general principles of law, a legally cognizable burden on religion is present" (Lupu 1989, 966). Compare his statement with the position I took in *Takings*:

> On Lockean principles the government stands no better than the citizens it represents on whether property has been taken, so a simple test determines, not the ultimate liability of the government, but whether its actions are brought within the purview of the eminent domain clause. Would the government action be treated as a taking of private property if it had been performed by some private party? (Epstein 1985a, 36)

34. For a more detailed statement of the rules, see Casner (1952, 2:§6).

35. For my earlier development of this position, see Epstein (1987).

36. Congress ordered the Federal Communications Commission to act to "ensure that . . . businesses owned by members of minority groups and women are given the opportunity to participate in the provision of spectrum-based services, and, for such purposes, consider the use of tax certificates, bidding preferences, and other procedures" 47 U.S.C. 309(j)(4)(D). For a defense of the system, see Ayres and Cramton (1996). The argument seems odd, for it is unclear whether the objective is higher revenues or more minority participation. It is wishful thinking to believe that the process can do both. The process can to some extent increase the price at which the asset is sold, by forcing the winning bidder closer to his reservation price. But in other cases, the subsidized bidder will win, reducing the money paid into public coffers. In addition, minority bidders often delegate in advance corporate control to the larger players with whom they team up in the bidding process. And, the entire scheme depends on the untested hypothesis that minority owners (as opposed to owners that can hire skilled marketers) are better able to reach certain portions of the population. An outright sale of frequencies, with the time-brokering by some network owners that did not care to supervise their content, would work better. Naturally, time-brokering is explicitly banned under the current statute. See *Cosmopolitan Broadcasting Co. v. FCC* (1978).

37. On which, see Ronald H. Coase (1959); and Thomas Hazlett (1990).

38. The use of federal power came out of recognition of the inability to find a distinct locus for intellectual property. The national protection obviated the need for different and overlapping state regimes. That problem is not, however, on the international scene. For the denial of the natural right approach in the context of patents, see *Graham v. John Deere Co.* (1966): "The patent monopoly was not designed to secure to the inventor his natural right in his discov-

eries. Rather, it was a reward, an inducement, to bring forth new knowledge." No less an authority than Thomas Jefferson agreed. See Jefferson (1861, 5:180–81). The point extends to copyrights, which are yoked to patents in the same constitutional clause.

39. See *Bridge Publications, Inc. v. F.A.C.T. Net, Inc.* (1998) "Once a work enters the public domain, it remains there irrevocably." This statement is perhaps too strong, but if it leaves the public domain, then the public should at the very least receive a quid pro quo in exchange.

40. For a succinct and powerful statement of the arguments on copyright, see Plaintiff's Brief at 52–62, *Eldred v. Reno* (1999), as prepared by Professor Lawrence Lessig.

41. For a general statement of the standing doctrine, see *Warth v. Seldin* (1975).

42. *Massachusetts v. Mellon* (1923) (disallowing taxpayer suits to challenge public expenditures). The *Mellon* rule is subject to a narrow, if somewhat unprincipled exception for the case of transfers to religious organizations challenged under the establishment clause. See *Flast v. Cohen* (1968). There is good reason for the exception to become the rule as a means to combat sweetheart deals between government and favored organizations. The fear is often expressed that the frequency of such suits will paralyze the courts. I suspect the real risk is that too few people will have the incentive to bear the private costs needed to stop such a transfer.

43. *Eldred v. Reno*, 239 F.3d 372 (D.C. Cir.), rehearing denied, sub nom. Eldred v. Ashcroft, 255 F.3d 849 (D.C. 2001), cert. granted, _____ U.S. _____, 122 S. Ct. 1062 (2002).

44. See, for example, *Ruckelshaus v. Monsanto Co.* (1984).

45. See, for example *Sony Corporation of America v. Universal City Studios* (1984, 431):

> Sound policy, as well as history, supports our consistent deference to Congress when major technological innovations alter the market for copyrighted materials. Congress has the constitutional authority and the institutional ability to accommodate fully the varied permutations of competing interests that are inevitably implicated by such new technology.

46. The other justifications offered fare no better (U.S. Senate 1996, 11). For example, the committee report denies that the act amounts to a perpetual term, but does not preclude a subsequent term extension. The twenty-year extension, we are told, is meant to preserve the older objective to protect "the author and at least one generation of heirs." Thus the CTEA "merely modifies the length of protection in nominal terms to reflect the scientific and demographic changes that have rendered the life-plus-50 term insufficient to meet this end." But longer life expectancy (even with later marriage) means that the writer who dies in his 80s leaves children in their 50s. Longer life already offers greater copyright protection.

CHAPTER THIRTEEN

PUBLIC GOODS
AND PROPERTY RIGHTS

Of Coase, Tiebout, and Just Compensation

William A. Fischel

THE LIGHTHOUSE

Any comprehensive discussion of private property and government must include consideration of public goods. That phrase refers to goods that either cannot be produced optimally by private producers, or perhaps cannot be privately produced at all. National defense is the classic public good. Citizens presumably want to be defended, but because of prisoner's dilemma and hold-out problems, armies require government financing through taxation, and most often are governmentally created and operated as well.

Production of public goods often raises issues concerning the taking of property. Public highways, for example, typically entail a government taking for the right of way. Land use, including zoning, usually involves a regulatory taking, meaning that government asserts rights over certain sticks in the bundle of otherwise private rights. (On both takings and regulatory takings, see Epstein, this volume.) This chapter explores the interplay between production of public goods and maintenance of private property rights. As will be seen, this is a subject whose complexities economists have not well understood.

William Safire, a political columnist for the *New York Times*, writes a weekly column on language for its Sunday magazine. When he makes a linguistic error in his column, a cadre of regular readers eagerly points it out. Safire calls his regulars "the gotcha gang."

If economics had a "gotcha gang," one of its founding documents would be Ronald Coase's 1974 article, "The Lighthouse in Economics." Coase starts off by quoting famous economists—J. S. Mill, Sidgewick, Pigou, and Samuelson—who use the lighthouse as an example of a public good. A lighthouse casts its warning signal to all ships at sea, regardless of whether they have paid for its services. But charging for the services of a lighthouse is, according to these famous economists, an improbable proposition. Coase quotes a footnote from Samuelson's influential textbook in which Samuelson (1964, 45) refers to "a man odd enough to try to make his fortune running a lighthouse." The reason it is odd, Samuelson says in the same place, is that "lighthouse keepers cannot reach out to collect fees from skippers." That is as much analysis of actual lighthouses as one gets from Samuelson's example.

But Coase went beyond theory to the facts. He investigated the British lighthouse system, reading its history and learning about its contemporary operation. He found that the system had been developed in large part by shipping interests, and they had for much of its history arranged to levy a charge upon ships to cover the cost of erecting and maintaining lighthouses. There were actually privately owned lighthouses in this system, and some of their owners did well, especially when they sold their assets to the government-chartered monopoly, Trinity House. Coase (1974, 368) points out dryly that "thus we find examples of men who were not only, in Samuelson's words, 'odd enough to try to make a fortune running a lighthouse business,' but actually succeeded in doing so." Gotcha.

There is much more than "gotcha" in this tale. Coase's account of how lighthouses were actually financed (up to 1830 in Britain) and his defense of this system constitutes a profound inquiry into the nature of what economists call public goods. A public good is said to have two characteristics that distinguish it from a private good. Public goods are nonexclusive and nonrival in their consumption.

Nonexclusive means that it is too costly for the providers of the public good to collect a payment from those who benefit from it. Nonexclusiveness gives rise to the free rider problem. Entrepreneurs who propose to provide a good from which consumers cannot be excluded will underprovide it, because it is too difficult to exclude those who do not pay (Musgrave 1939). In most discussions of nonexclusivity, how difficult is too difficult is usually inferred from an example, such as national defense or lighthouses. The subject of transaction costs is usually left for advanced treatments or later chapters, if it is brought up at all, even though it is the heart of the exclusion problem.

Nonrival means that the enjoyment of the good by one consumer does not diminish its availability for other consumers to enjoy. If you eat a particular burger, then I cannot eat it. Overhead fireworks, whether for the nation's anti-missile defense system or for the local Fourth of July celebration, are a nonrival good. Another person's enjoyment of the fireworks does not subtract from that of those already viewing it (unless there is crowding in getting a good view). Most nonrival goods are also nonexclusive, but there are examples of nonexclusive but rival goods, such as ocean fish, and nonrival goods from which exclusion is simple, such as television signals. For a nuanced discussion of such distinctions, see Vincent Ostrom (1991, 168).

Nonrivalry is at the heart of Samuelson's (1954) economic analysis of public goods. Because, as Coase found, lighthouses were financed by a charge that varied in part by the number of a company's ships that enjoyed their services, at least some voyages would be discouraged by the charge. Samuelson pointed out that this violated the price equals marginal cost condition that undergraduates are taught is the basis for the efficient allocation of resources. The cost of shining a light upon ship B after ship A has financed the light is zero, so the price charged to ship B or any other beneficiary of the light should be zero.

Coase did not disagree with the price-equals-marginal-cost principle, but he was more interested in the reality of how best to provide lighthouses. Coase inferred that Samuelson's answer was that the lighthouse should be provided out of general government funds, raised by taxes on the public in general. This would be the least distorting method of taxation, if one were choosing among taxes alone. Although there is some efficiency loss from all taxation, at least the broader fiscal mechanism would not deter ships from taking a voyage, as the lighthouse toll might.

By studying the details of lighthouse provision, Coase discovered that Samuelson's fixation on the price-equals-marginal-cost principle was unfounded. Shipping companies were charged according to how many ships were likely to pass lighthouses, but this schedule involved an easily-reached ceiling on the number of voyages. Thus a company with many ships would be charged more, but the marginal ship—the voyage that would be undertaken just at the point at which its marginal revenue would just exceed marginal cost—in most cases would not increase the shipping company's lighthouse fees. Of course, there might be other margins that the lighthouse payment might affect, such as how many ships to add to a fleet, if the additional ships would boost the company into the higher toll bracket.

Moreover, Coase found another efficiency advantage of the earmarked lighthouse payment, one which Samuelson and most other public finance economists of the time neglected. By financing lighthouses from payments charged by shipping companies rather than the general public, ship owners had an interest in seeing to it that lighthouses were managed efficiently. Having lighthouses financed by general tax revenues would make the shipping owners less concerned with inefficiencies in lighthouse operation. A national lighthouse bureau would more likely become a source of political patronage, as suggested by Ambrose Bierces' famous definition, which applied to the American system: Lighthouse: "A tall building on the seashore in which the government maintains a lamp and the friend of a politician" (quoted in Coase 1974, 376).

I have given only the faintest flavor of Coase's examination of the actual operation of the British lighthouse industry. After Coase, David

Van Zandt (1993) probed even more deeply into the history of British lighthouses. He found evidence of more government activity in the provision of lighthouse services than Coase's article had suggested. Van Zandt concluded that lighthouses were provided on a continuum between private and government provision, with the government in many cases providing a more directed set of arrangements such as local monopolies and regulated fees, than one would expect in other arrangements we regard as private enterprise.

Although Van Zandt's conclusion is somewhat different from Coase's, Van Zandt actually did study the institution involved, and the undertaking of such investigations is what Coase wanted to impress upon his readers. Coase's criticism of economists' rationale for government intervention is not the deductive logic by which they arrive at their conclusions, but rather the inductive logic from examples that do not conform to the data. Coase describes what a positive empirical program would look like (1974, 375):

> I think we should try to develop generalizations which would give us guidance as to how various activities should best be organized and financed. . . . But such generalizations are not likely to be helpful unless they are derived from studies of how such activities are actually carried out within different institutional frameworks. Such studies would enable us to discover which factors are important and which are not in determining the outcome, and they would lead to generalizations which have a solid base. They are also likely to serve another purpose by showing us the richness of the social alternatives among which we can choose.

Note that Coase does not say public goods, just various activities, in which publicness may or may not be discovered.

Coase and Van Zandt's investigations of lighthouse provision reveal the power of a property rights approach to a set of economic problems in which the very notion of property is ordinarily disregarded. In most expositions of the theory of public goods, the conclusory principle of nonexclusion diverts attention from the possibility of ownership. How could one have property in something from which beneficiaries cannot be excluded? Traditional rationales for public goods assumed property rights could not be established in lighthouses or other goods usually provided by the public sector.

The possibility of property rights underlies the "social alternatives" of which Coase spoke. The difficulties of excluding beneficiaries should not obscure the fact that lighthouses could be owned and that a system of payments could be invented that rewarded their owners for providing their nonexcludable services. Ownership of lighthouses themselves and the obligation to pay port duties to fund their services were important means by which entrepreneurial capital was invested in this critical service. The prospect of reward and the ability to capitalize lighthouse investments by bequeathing or selling them to others, including the state, appear to have produced lighthouse services at least as well as a program that relied exclusively on government provision and general taxation to fund them. As Professor Van Zandt rightly emphasizes, purely private ownership is not the only area in which the concept of property rights can shed its light. That is the focus of this chapter.

The Tiebout Model for Local Public Goods

In this and subsequent sections, I describe how economists have uncovered a more systematic approach to balancing the multiple issues of public goods for a large class of them. The system is named for Charles Tiebout (1956), who first identified the possibility of migration and local government as a means of dealing with the problem of a particular type of public goods.[1]

The type of public goods Tiebout had in mind are those that are nonexcludable and nonrival only within a limited geographic area. The services of roads, parks, watersheds, and similar residential amenities are public goods only within a localized area. Exclusion of free riders is possible within the area, but the costs of doing so are high. Rivalrous consumption—congestion of the local amenity—does not set in until the number of those enjoying the good becomes large. Given that this class of goods accounts for about half of total governmental domestic spending (Fisher 1988, 4–5), we return to the question of how such goods should be provided.

The conventional wisdom among economists before Tiebout was that the problem of providing these goods was no different from that of providing national defense. The free rider problem engendered by non-exclusiveness of goods required that the only mechanism of providing the good was political. While economists from Erik Lindahl ([1919], 1964) onward have discussed how voting shares might be reconciled with tax shares, the default answer for public goods invariably was that elected officials would have to somehow divine the public's will (Musgrave 1959; Samuelson 1954). They would set expenditures and raise tax monies to fund them at the levels that private citizens would have found optimal themselves. The political connection between taxes and revenues was impossible to maintain in the same way that the market price paid for hamburgers is connected to the demand and supply of hamburgers. State paternalism seemed the best solution to public good provision because no one saw an opportunity to establish property rights for the provision of such goods.

Because the free rider problem seemed to be no different at the local level than at the state or national level, mainstream public finance theory before Tiebout had no reason to explain the existence of local government, let alone prefer it to more centralized governments. Larger units of government actually seem preferable under such conditions. They have larger staffs with more expertise; their outlooks are global rather than parochial; and their tax bases are less likely to migrate in response to an increase in rates because there are fewer alternative jurisdictions. From this vantage point, local government seemed to be an anachronism, suitable perhaps as an administrative unit of the state, but hardly an appropriate decision-making body.

Tiebout (1956) argued, however, that the existence of many local governments within a metropolitan area — a common condition in the United States — might provide an alternative solution to the Musgrave-Samuelson free-rider problem. For local public goods, the mechanism to determine the efficient level might not have to be voting at the ballot box (for elected officials), but voting with one's feet among communities.

As Tiebout envisioned the process, municipal managers would offer a menu of public services, and potential residents would choose their residence from among competing communities. By doing so, residents would reveal their demand for local public goods. Municipal managers might act like firms, but even if they were not governed by the profit motive, Darwinian selection (as suggested by Armen Alchian 1950) could winnow out those who did not give potential immigrants what they wanted.

Tiebout's model was a brilliant insight, but it was also incomplete. It lacked a credible supply side; it did not explain how local public goods were financed, nor did it explain how community interlopers — local free riders — were dealt with. As a result, Tiebout's theory got little attention from economists until Wallace Oates (1969) pointed out that most local governments financed their public services with property taxes, and these taxes and the activities they financed provided a guide of the fiscal benefits of each community to potential residents.

Oates' empirical research found that differences in property taxes and public services were reflected in home values: Home buyers purchase a community along with a home. Communities with better schools and lower taxes have higher home values (Dee 2000). This relationship indicates that potential residents do indeed value local public goods when selecting a place to live. As Caroline Hoxby (1999) has most recently demonstrated, the effect of locally financed services on home values provides information and incentives for local officials to provide the efficient level of spending and taxation at a cost lower than any centralized planner could hope to achieve.

Zoning Establishes De Facto Municipal Property Rights

Oates' contribution breathed life into Tiebout's model by showing that a community's local public goods made a difference, but Oates did not address how free riders might be dealt with. Free riders in the Tiebout model would be households that see an attractive community, vote with their feet to go there, but build a small home to avoid paying the high property taxes. The Tiebout–Oates model was, in other words, unstable. Households could still free ride by building a smaller home and getting more in local public goods than they paid in local property taxes. As Buchanan and Goetz (1972) pointed out, mobility has two faces. People can select a community that they prefer, but others can move in afterward and free ride by paying less in taxes than the cost of providing services.

Bruce Hamilton (1975, 1976) was the first to propose (for the benefit of academic economists) that local land use regulations could be used to exclude free riders in the Tiebout–Oates system. Zoning laws could be used to specify the minimum amount of property that people had to buy to get into the community. Thus a family that valued local public goods but tried to build a smaller-than-average home would be prevented from doing so by zoning laws. These laws could require such things as minimum lot size, setbacks, road frontage, and building quality. By adopting a comprehensive zoning system, communities could specify how much in taxes all prospective development would have to pay. In effect, Hamilton suggested that zoning created municipal property rights, rights that were vested in the existing residents of the community. It was this insight that led me, in my 1985 book, *The Economics of Zoning Laws*, to add as subtitle *A Property Rights Approach to American Land Use Controls*.

From a property rights perspective, the property tax becomes a fee for service. Property taxes can be supplemented by discretionary land-use exactions and impact fees in instances in which additional property tax liabilities are less than the average of the rest of the community (Altshuler and Gómez-Ibáñez 1993). Because homebuyers cannot shirk from the required minimum home value, they must reveal their preference for housing and public goods simultaneously. As long as there are numerous communities, mobile homebuyers can find a community whose level of public services and minimum housing levels correspond to their preferences. The problem of public goods is thereby resolved, at least for goods that can be geographically confined, without the political solution that Samuelson and Musgrave, among countless other economists, had assumed was necessary.

The key question for the applicability of the Tiebout model is the extent to which zoning and related land use controls can, in fact, exclude free riders. The answer is that zoning is at least as effective as other forms of exclusion of free riders. From a Coasian perspective,[2] zoning constitutes a de facto collective property right (Fischel 1978).[3] The collectivity that owns zoning and the right to change it is the politically influential group in the municipality. In most American municipalities, homeowners are the most influential group and they can be thought of as the stockholders, whose interests are in maximizing the value of their homes (Sonstelie and Portney 1978; Fischel 2000).[4]

Zoning is best viewed as a means by which existing homeowners control entry into their municipal corporation. Developers of new housing and of other types of property must satisfy existing homeowners that their proposed use will not make them worse off. Like other clubs, municipalities jealously guard their property rights. Scores of econometric studies (reviewed and summarized in Yinger et al. 1988; Dowding, John, and Biggs 1994) find that the quality and cost of local public goods systematically influence local housing values. Zoning provides one mechanism where the benefits of owning real estate in a municipality can be protected from opportunistic entrants.

Rezonings and Majoritarian Rent Seeking

Zoning can be thought of as creating benefits for the existing residents of a municipality, but these benefits do not come without an economic cost. Owners of property whose land is restricted by zoning bear this cost. The economic issue this raises is whether the people who change zoning rules actually perceive this cost and whether the costs of a zoning change exceed the benefits.[5] In this context, a zoning change is excessively restrictive if the total loss in land values by those property owners who are restricted by zoning exceeds the total gain by property owners who are the beneficiaries of zoning (McMillen and McDonald 1993; Pines and Weiss 1976). When this rule is not followed (and it commonly is not), the process of rezoning usually results in communities that have an inefficiently low density of homes (Pollakowski and Wachter 1990). This results in metropolitan areas in the United States that are too spread out. I illustrate this with a concrete example, but the sources I cite indicate that the problem is ubiquitous.

The township of Damwell,[6] New Jersey, is a semi-rural community in the west-central part of the state. Its population is about 4,000. Its older housing stock is located in a few small hamlets and farmsteads spread over its twenty-four square miles. Newer development is on larger lots in small subdivisions and estate-sized parcels scattered along the rural roads. Although the dominant land use in the township is farming, the farmers are now outnumbered by more recent arrivals who work elsewhere (if at all) in central New Jersey.

Although called a township, Damwell has full municipal powers, including a planning and zoning board appointed by a five-member Township Committee. Committee members are elected at large for three-year terms. From their ranks, committee members annually select a mayor and deputy mayor, who perform most executive functions with the help of a small staff. The township, like thousands of other suburban local governments, is a municipal corporation. It is governed more like a corporation, with its elected board of directors and hired executive, than like the state or national governments, with their bicameral legislatures and independently elected executives (Fischel 2000).

The problem with the corporate analogy, though, is that Damwell's board of directors is elected on the one-person one-vote principle, in contrast to business corporations which normally choose to allocate votes among their shareholders by the number of shares they hold, so that the rule is closer to one-dollar one-vote.

The municipal allocation encourages rent-seeking activity of exactly the sort that James Madison worried about in *The Federalist no. 10*. The difficulty is not one of special interest dominance or bureaucratic influence. It is majority rule in one of its most straightforward manifestations. Without some constraints on the majority's decisions, they may use their powers of regulation to transfer economic resources from the minority.

This is apparently what happened in Damwell. Up to the late 1990s, most of the rural land in the township was zoned for three-acre minimum lots. Arguably, this size lot might be economically appropriate for rural residential areas, where water must usually be obtained from an onsite well and sewage disposal requires a septic system. Onsite sewer and water can often be done safely for the new home without jeopardizing the health of its neighbors on even smaller lots, but having three acres could be argued to preserve a margin of error in a world in which water and sewerage are critical to home values nearby. Three-acre minimums are, at any rate, a fairly common norm for rural-residential zoning. But even this large minimum was apparently not enough for the nonfarming residents of Damwell.

In the later 1990s, Damwell rezoned its rural residential area to a ten-acre minimum lot size. The rezoning took away two-thirds of the development rights that owners of rural land formerly held. The rationale for the rezoning was that it was necessary to preserve farmland. The majority of full-time farmers in Damwell, however, opposed the rezoning. While few of them wish to quit farming and sell their land to developers in the near future, the option to do so is, for most of them, their major source of wealth.

Aside from the wipeout of two-thirds of their land's value, the down-zoning actually makes it more difficult for the farmers to continue to operate even in the near term. Most true farmers (as opposed to hobby farmers, some of whom in Damwell support the new regulations) need to borrow money to finance their annual operation cycle. The chief asset against which they can borrow is their land. The banks appraise their land based largely on its development potential. By reducing the development potential, the rezoning makes it riskier to lend money to farmers, which makes them less likely to continue in farming.

The intent of this rezoning was to preserve the amenity value of farm-land and open space for the benefit of the majority of residents who themselves are not farmers (Kline and Wichelns 1994). This is evident from newspaper reports of how the down-zoning came about. When the planning commission first proposed the new restrictions, the town-ship committee held hearings (as required by state law). All of the oppo-nents were farmland owners. The committee voted in 1997 not to un-dertake the down-zoning.

In the next election, committee members who had opposed the rezon-ing were defeated by candidates who ran with the avowed intent to adopt the rejected plan. Because by now farmers and other owners of developable land were in the minority, they were unable to politically resist the rezoning majority. Although the new zoning plan threw some concessions to the farmers in the form of "right to farm" laws, it is safe to infer from the many econometric studies of the effect of large-lot zoning effect on land values that the farmland owners got the short end of the stick (Brownstone and DeVany 1991).

Efficiency and Compensation

It is also fair to say, though with slightly less confidence, that the rezon-ing in Damwell was inefficient when defined in terms of whether a re-zoning raises the aggregate value of land in the jurisdiction (Pines and Weiss 1976).[7] A rezoning that did meet the efficiency test would not necessarily increase every parcel's value. Some parcels might decline in value while others would increase, but the positive increments would sum to an amount that exceeded the decrements. In such a situation, compensation for those landowners whose land was devalued would promote both fairness and efficiency. The fairness criterion in Damwell would generally call at least for paying compensation to the farmland owners being asked to give up a normal activity, the right to develop homes just like those in the rest of the community, for the benefit of the majority of nonfarmer residents (Michelman 1967).

Compensation would also promote efficiency (Knetsch 1983). The faction of nonfarmers seeking to down-zone the rural land would have to consider the effect of their plan on their own wealth if Damwell had to pay for the development rights. Property taxes would rise in the town to pay compensation. If the benefits of farmland preservation were as large as what proponents implied, then property values in town would rise as homebuyers saw that the town was especially amenable. If this capital gain to the homeowners were greater than the loss in value to the farmland owners, then it would be politically worthwhile to undertake the rezoning, since homeowners would gain from it (Sonstelie and Portney 1980).

If, as is more likely, the ten-acre lot size increased nonfarmers' home values by only a small amount, then the demand for compensation to the farmers would most probably induce the nonfarmer majority to vote against the rezoning. The increase in property taxes needed to compensate the farmland owners would depress home values by more than the benefit that farmland preservation would increase them. Compensation for zoning changes thus amounts to a benefit-cost discipline that guides the governing political faction in the community to choose only those actions that increase aggregate land values.

Some zoning changes that would meet the compensation criterion would not require any out-of-pocket expenditures. A new regulation might provide sufficiently large in-kind compensation to those burdened by it that the landowners are made whole without further payment. For example, a rezoning of a single-family home neighborhood that disallowed certain types of commercial activity might meet this test. The homeowner who complained that she could not now operate a real estate business from her home could be consoled by the fact that her neighbors are likewise constrained. If the reciprocal benefits of doing so were sufficiently large, the new restrictions would not require compensation.

It is important, however, to examine closely the context of claims like this, which are often called "reciprocity of advantage" (Oswald 1997). Often, a regulation that on its face seems to cast its burdens evenly in fact singles people out for special burdens. For example, if Damwell passed a township-wide regulation that imposed a restriction on the keeping of cattle, the equality of burden would be chimerical. Such a regulation would be acceptable and probably efficient if it applied only to zones composed of residences on small lots, but to apply it equally to farm-sized lots would in fact be inefficient.

In sum, the majority-rule political structure of local government makes it likely that a majority faction will at some point disregard the property values of the minority if a strict compensation rule is not enforced. Before discussion of why American land-use jurisprudence fails to do this, an aside about wealth and factionalism is appropriate. The conventional fear about majority rule is that the numerous poor will use the political process to obtain resources from the rich. However, in the Damwell situation, it is likely that the redistribution goes from people with lower wealth to those with higher wealth. The nonfarming residents of the township are generally affluent, measured by income levels. The primary activist promoting the new regulations was the wealthy owner of a thoroughbred horse farm, and she divides her time between dressage and dressing up the ordinances of the town. The majority of farmland owners appear to be poorer.

Of course, some farmland is owned by developers and land speculators, so the losers from the down-zoning are not necessarily all farmers. Nor do I suggest that income and wealth considerations ought to be decisive in local land use issues. Economics teaches that attempts to redistribute income are apt to be perverse unless undertaken on a national level and aimed at income and wealth rather than particular goods or entitlements (Kaplow and Shavell 1994; Oates 1972). But even if one ignores that lesson — as many of the defenders of uncompensated rezonings do — it should be understood that the resulting redistribution of wealth is apt to hurt at least as many lower-income people as it does high-income people.

Compensation and Opportunity Cost

If compensation offers the win-win opportunity so far described, one would expect the rule to be widely adopted. And, in fact, it is adopted in the case of public acquisition or physical invasion of land. If the public seeks to build a new road or a new school, the owner of the land on which the project is placed must be compensated for it. Although the obligation to compensate does create a build-in-the-path-of-bulldozers moral hazard on the part of landowners (Blume and Rubinfeld 1984) — as it does for victims of torts — the extent of that inefficiency in land use appears to be small relative to the political hazards that flow from undercompensation (Burrows 1991; Usher 1995). The great economic virtue of just compensation for takings is that it makes elected officials who make the decisions perceive the opportunity cost of what they do (Cordes and Weisbrod 1979; Stroup 1997).

Indeed, the moral hazard problem seems more likely to apply when compensation is not forthcoming. As several studies have indicated, landowners know that the discovery of an endangered species on their property will result in regulations whose effect is often to reduce the value of their land. In the absence of compensation, landowners have been known to try to dispose of or conceal the existence of the species, thus perversely defeating the purpose of the regulation (Thompson 1997; Lueck and Michael 2000).

The problem with constitutional commands for just compensation is that courts do not generally apply them to regulations that amount to a partial taking (Eagle 1996). Although every state and federal court has been presented with the issue, judges have been reluctant to apply the just compensation rule to land use regulations by local governments. The U.S. Supreme Court standard, which forms a floor under the states' standards, is that compensation for a down-zoning like that of Damwell would not be forthcoming unless it resulted in the land having no viable economic use at all or if there were no palpable public benefit from it (*Agins v. Tiburon* 1980). This standard is generous to municipal authorities and invites a substantial amount of rent seeking. The result is that inefficient rezonings like those in Damwell are not automatically deterred.

Courts' reluctance to award just compensation for down-zonings could be caused by the high transaction costs of awarding damages. It is often argued that it would be too difficult to assess the true damages to the land, that winnowing out false claims would be difficult, and the higher property taxes would be harmful to capital formation in the rest of the community (Kaplow 1986; Sax 1971). While these considerations might apply for regulatory changes undertaken over a wider area, such as air pollution standards, they are not persuasive at the local level.

In the Damwell case, the victims are obvious, and assessing their loss is no more (or less) difficult a task than that presented in traditional eminent-domain takings. Indeed, there is a proven market in development rights in New Jersey, as the state government has funded their voluntary purchase over a wide area. Of course, plaintiffs will seek to get as much in damages as possible, but that is no different than the behavior of landowners whose property is taken for an airport runway.

As for the effect of the higher property tax, that seems misplaced in this instance. Nonfarming residents of Damwell should face higher property taxes, both because it will temper their enthusiasm for regulation and because the benefits of the regulation redound primarily to them. Indeed, precisely because the benefits of the regulation do redound to nearby land, the taxes on that land should not cause excess burden to the taxpayers.

It is sometimes argued that compensation is not necessary to provide the signals of the market about the correct opportunity cost of open space zoning. The story, a version of the Coase theorem, goes like this: If we allowed Damwell free rein with its zoning, it would eventually establish the most stringent possible regime. Rather than ten-acre zoning, it would have a 1,000-acre minimum lot size and allow no development whatsoever. At the same time, Damwell could grant zoning variances for those developers who wanted to build homes and to accept cash (or equivalent goods in kind) for the variances. Trade would ensue. Developers would pay the community for the right to build on the farmland. The community would sell those rights whose value to it exceeded the value of the open views and other public benefits from farmland. The resulting higher-density development would both reflect outsider's willingness to pay to locate in the community and preexisting residents' true demand for open space (Fischel 1978; Nelson 1977).

The troubles with this scheme are two. One is that it discounts entirely the well-being of the owners of farmland. The efficiency of the plan is precisely the source of its unfairness (Fischel 1991). By completely divesting the current owners of their rights, the rezoning transfers the rights to the decision makers — the other residents of Damwell — who now have an incentive to make efficient decisions.

The other trouble is that such a system is inherently unstable. To expropriate all of the development rights and the right to resell them, the courts and legislatures of New Jersey and the United States must throw out hundreds of years of property law (Kayden 1991). Such a radical change in property rights cannot be confined to a single township or a single area of property law (Michelman 1967). Landowners elsewhere would become anxious that their rights would be similarly disregarded, and they might rush to develop at an inefficiently early time (Dana 1995). Owners of other types of property would become anxious. Copyright holders might suspect that they were next and modify their behavior, moving into other lines of work or attempting to protect their works by other, more costly means.

Indeed, it is not even clear that such a scheme would work locally. Developers who were offered the newly expropriated development rights by the township might wonder, what is to stop the township from doing this again? I buy the rights to develop something next year on the land, make my preparations, and then the township changes its mind and down-zones it again. Such a possibility is not an abstract theory, as the experience of New York City with rent control shows (Salins and Mildner 1992). When rent control was phased out in the early 1970s, developers came forth with new units. The city subsequently adopted new rent controls that applied to the newer units, which caught the landlords by surprise. No longer. The story is now legendary among New York area developers, who repeat it with an air of "fool me once, shame on you; fool me twice, shame on me."

Anxiety over regulatory takings may go some distance toward explaining a seeming oddity in the U.S. Supreme Court's takings jurisprudence. The court tolerates down-zonings as long as there is some color-able public purpose to them and as long as they do not result in the property being deprived of all economic use unless otherwise justified by the state's common law of nuisance and related doctrines (*Lucas v. South Carolina Coastal Council* 1992). That standard would not help the farmers in Damwell, New Jersey, since two-thirds but not all of their land's value is removed; a single family home on a ten-acre lot is still a viable economic use.

The Court, however, would clearly frown on a subsequent scheme requiring the landowner to pay most of the incremental value of land to the township in return for a variance to allow, say, five homes on a ten-acre parcel. In such an instance, the court would demand that the payment be earmarked for a project that was related to the purpose of the farmland regulation itself and that the amount of the payment be "roughly proportional" to the cost to the community of allowing the variance (*Dolan v. Tigard* 1994).

Numerous commentators note that the court's rules limiting exactions inhibit exchange between landowners subject to severe regulation and the government agency that has the power to modify the regulation (Fennell 2000; Fischel 1995; Gyourko 1991). To use my farmland example, if the New Jersey courts are willing to accept the ten-acre minimum lot size, it does not help those landowners affected to restrict farmers' ability to repurchase their rights from the township authorities. The court might reason, however, that it should not make down-zonings even more attractive to local governments by allowing them to be sold for cash. Beyond that, the court's constraints may reflect a deeper unease about the total scheme's effect on the fundamental framework of private property law. If it were to allow such trades routinely, the foundations of private property might begin to crack in unexpected places.

PRIVATE GOVERNMENTS

Zoning presents both an expansion and contraction of property rights. In a Tiebout framework, zoning is necessary to protect the local government's tax base and the value of its homes. Yet an open-ended regulatory regime also invites majoritarian rent seeking by homeowners in those local governments. Numerous scholars have suggested that the just compensation principle would go far to reconcile these problems, but courts so far have been reluctant to apply it. This section asks: Why not abolish zoning and replace it with some other institution that would accomplish the same aims with fewer disadvantages?

We need not look far for workable alternatives. Increasingly, substantial residential developments are organized as private community associations (Dilger 1992). Association constitutions are typically set up by the initial landowner-developer, and buyers of homes in the projects must accept the governance rules of these organizations. The associations adopt and enforce regulations even more detailed and, in many people's eyes, more intrusive than municipal zoning (Sterk 1997). They are not controversial, though, since the governance of the community association usually cannot change initial rules — adopt rezonings — without a supermajority of votes from residents (Ellickson 1982). Moreover, most associations do not allocate votes on a per capita basis, as municipalities do. Voting is allocated by unit ownership or some related characteristic (Barzel and Sass 1990). Tenants do not vote, and owners of two units would typically have two votes, regardless of whether they lived in the community or not.

The rapid growth of community associations testifies to their success in providing alternatives to zoning. Several scholars have advocated expanding their role to displace many municipal functions (Ellickson 1998; Liebmann 2000; Nelson 1999). But the strongest testimony is still lacking. No community association has, to my knowledge, induced any local government unit within which it was located to disincorporate and shift the entire burden of municipal services and regulatory authority to the community association. Many community associations have negotiated for tax rebates for the municipal services such as sanitation services that they provide themselves. And the development of community associations in unincorporated parts of counties (a common pattern in the South and West) has possibly deterred the incorporation of municipalities. But, for the most part, the community association movement seems an additional layer of governance, not a one-for-one displacement of local government.

One reason for municipalities' durability is favorable tax treatment by the federal government. Municipalities can issue tax-exempt bonds, and municipal property taxes — but not community association dues and assessments — are deductible for itemizers on the federal income tax. Indeed, several municipalities in the Los Angeles area were founded as private community associations, whose members then incorporated as municipalities to get the tax advantages (Miller 1981).

A less obvious explanation for the persistence of municipal governments where there are plentiful private alternatives may be their role as mediating institutions. In one important dimension, private community associations may be inferior to municipalities because the latter possess the power to displace the state government's powers. Provision of local public goods by the state government is likely to be less efficient.

By hypothesis, private associations could fill the mediating role, but probably less effectively in important ways. A local government with police power can displace the state's police powers. Municipalities need not be simply administrative conduits; their authority is essentially that of the state. Legally, local governments are creatures of the state, so the state can override locals if legislatures want to. In reality, ironically, state legislatures are closer to being creatures of local government (Burns and Gamm 1997; Monkkonen 1988, 1995). All states elect legislatures by districts whose boundaries are almost always contiguous to some aggregation of local governments. Thus, local officials are the candidates most likely to become legislators, and their continuing basis of support is most likely to be local government units. Without those units, the basis for geographic districts and the resulting responsiveness of legislatures to the demand for local control would evaporate.

Private governments would be problematic substitutes for local governments as mediating institutions. They could not assume the local version of the state's powers to tax, regulate, and employ eminent domain, except in the most limited circumstances. If they could do so in general circumstances, they would then become municipalities, possessing zoning and other coercive powers. State-level interest groups such as public employee unions and income-based lobbying groups would determine both state and local policy, often to the detriment of local residents. The baleful educational results of school-finance centralization, mostly induced by state courts hostile to localism, attests to this possibility (Husted and Kenny 2000; Silva and Sonstelie 1995). Indeed, blunting such interest group influence was largely what motivated Judge Thomas M. Cooley's famous constitutional defense of local government autonomy in *People ex rel. Le Roy v. Hurlbut* (1871).

CONCLUSION

The Tiebout model of local government formalizes economically one of the many virtues of local government, apparent to observers at least since the time of Alexis de Tocqueville (1835). I have argued that a necessary condition for the Tiebout model to function is municipal zoning. Zoning's success lies in its ability to manage community development so as to preserve the value of previously developed single-family homes.

Like many other useful institutions, zoning can be pressed to excess. Large-lot zoning has subverted the mechanism by which the demands of outsiders can be felt within a locality. Owners of land upon which development can take place are responsive to the demands of outsiders. The land market responds to future residents because landowners can make money by catering to them. By nullifying this possibility and distributing the right to develop to community authorities, large-lot zoning penalizes would-be residents.

Judicial reluctance to review the content of local zoning laws and award damages is at the heart of this deficiency. Judges might defer because wealthy landowners are well placed in the political marketplace. Whatever merits this argument has at the state or national level, it is surely wrong at the local level. Most observers agree that if the majoritarian principle applies anywhere, it is in the small local governments that, as a group, control most of the land in American metropolitan areas (Komesar 1978; Ellickson 1977).

Although owners of developable land are not widows and orphans, the majority are hardly rich, and the homeowners who gain from this redistribution are typically in the upper ranks of the income distribution. No coherent redistributive goal is advanced by ten-acre minimum lot sizes, even if it has no adverse effects on those outside the community.

Another source of judicial reluctance to intervene in blatant downzonings is the belief that the damages remedy would result in an open-ended assault on all municipal regulation. Even those judges who are inclined to protect property rights worry that a damages remedy would undermine the desirable features of local autonomy. Their anxieties are probably heightened by the scholarly deployment of the regulatory takings doctrine as a broad cudgel against all regulatory institutions, not just local zoning (Epstein 1985a; Paul 1987).

Without disputing or endorsing the merit of the broader use of the takings clauses, I note there is a middle way. The key to a jurisprudence of takings, recognizing both the purposes of the takings clause and the limitations of judicial resources, must acknowledge two aspects of local zoning that makes it different from other levels of government and other types of regulation. First, owners of land do not have the option of exit to discipline the enthusiasms of local governments (Epstein 1992b; Sterk 1992). Even in locales enthusiastic about regulation, attempts to regulate the price of food and clothing are few. The likelihood that store owners would pull out of the jurisdiction stays the regulation. But land cannot be moved. Landowners can, of course, sell and leave, but the capital loss they endure is unavoidable because their land stays put.

Zoning is an object of judicial scrutiny also because the local legislatures enacting it are likely to commit the majoritarian excesses that motivated the takings clause (Rose 1989). Madison's *The Federalist no. 10* warns against the evils of "faction," by which he meant local majoritarianism (Fischel 1995, chapter 3). Local governments are most prone to the tyranny of the majority, and judges ought to pay special attention to local zoning decisions for this reason.

If judges were to invoke the jurisprudence of regulatory takings, how should they balance the virtues of local self-governance with the virtues of private landownership? The most coherent answer was provided by Robert Ellickson (1973, 1977). He argues that both communities and landowners should be judged by a standard of "normal behavior," which is a flexible application of the principle that "harm prevention" ought not to be compensated, but "benefit extraction" generally should (Oswald 1997; Wyeth 1996).

"Normal behavior" is a two-edged standard that disciplines both private landowners and community zoning. The clearest but not only violation of normal behavior by the landowner would be to develop something that fell in or close to the traditional category of nuisance (Kmiec 1988). Segregation of land uses by zoning into residential, commercial, and industrial zones would not violate this norm in most places and should not require compensation. The clearest violation of "normal behavior" by a community within a metropolitan region would be zoning its undeveloped land to achieve densities much lower than those already enjoyed by the majority of residents in the community (Ellickson 1977). Requiring such low densities does nothing to promote the efficiencies of the Tiebout model or any other widely held virtue found in local self-governance.

The normal-behavior standard is best viewed as a temporal application of the golden rule (Fischel 1995). If current residents were themselves outsiders who might want to live in their own community, would they willingly embrace them? That is, if the residents of a community characterized by half-acre lots suddenly became strangers to their own community, would they want the lots zoned for ten-acre minimum lot sizes? The fact that this might preserve open space would then be tempered by the fact that most residents could not afford to live in the community.

If current residents would be willing to pay for a low-density community, compensation can still achieve the efficient result. The virtue of the damages remedy for regulatory takings is that judges do not actually have to get inside the minds of those who make the laws. If residents truly value the remaining land in their township as open space more than outsiders value it as housing lots, judges can let them do it (Kanner 1989). By insisting that the community pay for its preferences by paying damages for excessive land-use easements, they can accomplish that most American of remedies, putting your money where your mouth is.

Application of the normal-behavior rule would still allow for the community specialization that is one of the virtues of the Tiebout model. Many communities would develop as single-family residential enclaves. Zoning would protect homeowners' assets from subnormal interlopers unless they consented to such uses. A few communities might retain large amounts of land in open space or as farms, finding it worthwhile to pay owners of land for their development rights or to purchase the land outright as a nature preserve. Other communities would actively seek a mix of residential types and perhaps mix residences with commerce in a controlled manner. The success of such mixing in privately planned communities such as Celebration, Florida, and Columbia, Maryland, suggests that some suburbs would use zoning to go in that direction even if they were not required to do so (Burkhardt 1981; Frantz and Collins 1999). A virtue of a normal-behavior standard enforced by monetary damages is that it allows the Tiebout model to work by inducing both prospective residents and existing residents to reveal their true preferences.

The lesson of Coase's Lighthouse is that property rights can illuminate the problem of public goods. I have confined myself to a particular area — the local public sector — to convey a sense of how Coase's framework works. Collective entities such as local governments can be thought of as possessing property rights in the quality of life in their communities. Homeowners are the dominant faction in most American municipalities, and they use land-use controls in rational, if not always admirable, ways to advance their interests. The chief problem with local zoning is that it can work too well for existing residents. By taking away development rights from owners of developable land, zoning can unfairly dash legitimate expectations of landowners and, in so doing, disenfranchise would-be members of the community. Insistence by the courts that existing homeowners respect others' right to develop land in ways deemed normal to a larger region reconciles the virtues of a decentralized republic and the institution of private property.

ENDNOTES

1. An influential generalization of Tiebout's approach, called club theory, was proposed by James Buchanan (1965).

2. I came up with the idea in 1975 after rereading Coase's 1960 article.

3. Robert Nelson (1977) had earlier published *Zoning and Property Rights*, but he did not invoke Coase's or related scholarship.

4. Most of America's 25,000 municipalities are small, so that homeowners are not outmaneuvered by special-interest groups. Only about a quarter of all Americans live in municipalities whose population exceeds 100,000 (Monkkonen 1995, 3).

5. I cast the issue in terms of zoning changes because nearly every acre within urban areas is now subject to zoning either by the municipality or the county. Although Houston, Texas, has been a fertile source of studies about landowner behavior and housing markets in the absence of zoning (Siegan 1972; Peiser

1981; Speyrer 1989), there is no perceptible move toward abolition of zoning in any city in the United States (McDonald 1995).

6. I was retained as an economics expert by the attorney for the plaintiff landowners, and, because the case has not been tried at the time of this writing, I have fictionalized the name of the town and rounded off its statistical descriptors.

7. This assumes the jurisdiction itself is not so large as to have market power over developable land in the region. The latter condition would be unusual in American metropolitan areas and almost unthinkable in New Jersey, with its 566 municipal corporations within the state. If the jurisdiction did have market power, however, not all actions that raised aggregate land values would be efficient, since some of the value increase would come at the expense of would-be residents who are priced out of the market (Thorson 1996).

REFERENCES

Abelson, Reed. 2000. Preserving the Forest by Leasing the Trees. *New York Times*, 24 September, sec. III, p. 6.

Acemoglu, Daron, Simon Johnson, and James A. Robinson. 2001. The Colonial Origins of Comparative Development: An Empirical Investigation. *American Economic Review* 91(5): 1369–1401.

Ackerman, Bruce A., ed. 1975. *Economic Foundation of Property Law*. Boston: Little, Brown Publishers.

Agnello, Richard J., and Lawrence P. Donnelley. 1975a. Prices and Property Rights in the Fisheries. *Southern Economics Journal* 42(2): 253–62.

———. 1975b. Property Rights and Efficiency in the Oyster Industry. *Journal of Law and Economics* 18(2): 521–34.

Alchian, Armen A. 1950. Uncertainty, Evolution, and Economic Theory. *Journal of Political Economy* 58(June): 211–21.

———. 1958. Private Property and The Relative Cost of Tenure. In *The Public Stake in Union Power*, ed. Philip D. Bradley. Charlottesville, VA: University Press of Virginia, 350–71.

———. 1961. *Some Economics of Property*. Santa Monica: RAND Corporation.

———. 1965a. The Basis of Some Recent Advances in the Theory of Management of the Firm. *Review of Industrial Economics* 14(November): 30–41.

———. 1965b. Some Economics of Property Rights. *Il Politico* 30(4): 816–29.

———. 1967. How Should Prices Be Set? *Il Politico* 32(2): 369–82.

Alchian, Armen A., and William R. Allen. 1977. *Exchange and Production*. Belmont, CA: Wadsworth.

Alchian, Armen A., and Harold Demsetz. 1972. Production, Information Costs, and Economic Organization. *American Economic Review* 62(December): 777–95.

Allen, Douglas W. 1991. Homesteading and Property Rights: or, "How the West Was Really Won." *Journal of Law and Economics* 34(April): 1–23.

Allen, Douglas W., and Dean Lueck. 1992. Contract Choice in Modern Agriculture: Cropshare Versus Cash Rent. *Journal of Law and Economics* 35(2): 397–426.

Alston, Lee J., Gary D. Libecap, and Bernardo Mueller. 1999a. A Model of Rural Conflict: Violence and Land Reform Policy in Brazil. *Environment and Development Economics* 4: 135–60.

———. 1999b. *Titles, Conflict, and Land Use: The Development of Property Rights and Land Reform on the Brazilian Amazon Frontier*. Ann Arbor: University of Michigan Press.

———. 2000. Land Reform Policies, The Sources of Violent Conflict and Implications for Deforestation in the Brazilian Amazon. *Journal of Environmental Economics and Management* 39: 162–88.

Alston, Lee J., Gary D. Libecap, and Robert Schneider. 1995. Property Rights and the Preconditions for Markets: The Case of the Amazon Frontier. *Journal of Institutional and Theoretical Economics* 151(1): 89–107.

———. 1996. The Determinants and Impact of Property Rights: Land Titles on the Brazilian Frontier. *The Journal of Law, Economics and Organization* 12(1): 25–61.

Altshuler, Alan A., and Jose A. Gómez-Ibáñez, with Arnold M. Howitt. 1993. *Regulation for Revenue: The Political Economy of Land Use Exactions.* Cambridge: Lincoln Institute of Land Policy.

American Law Institute. 1934. *Restatement of the Law of Torts,* §757. Philadelphia: American Law Institute Publishers.

———. 1965–1979. *Restatement (Second) of the Law of Torts.* Philadelphia: American Law Institute Publishers.

———. 1979. 4 *Restatement (Second) of Torts,* 209–12. Philadelphia: American Law Institute Publishers.

Anderson, Terry L. 1987. The First Privatizers. In *Essays on the Economy of the Old Northwest,* ed. Richard K. Vedder and David C. Klingaman. Athens: Ohio University Press.

———. 1995. *Sovereign Nations or Indian Reservations? An Economic History of American Indians.* San Francisco: Pacific Research Institute for Public Policy.

———. 1998. Viewing Wildlife through Coase-Colored Glasses. In *Who Owns the Environment?* ed. Peter J. Hill and Roger E. Meiners. Lanham, MD: Rowman and Littlefield Publishers, 259–82.

Anderson, Terry L., and Peter J. Hill. 1975. The Evolution of Property Rights: A Study of the American West. *Journal of Law and Economics* 18(1): 163–79.

———. 1979. An American Experiment in Anarcho-Capitalism: The *Not* So Wild, Wild West. *Journal of Libertarian Studies* 3(1): 9–29.

———. 1983. Privatizing the Commons: An Improvement? *Southern Economics Journal* 50(2): 438–50.

———. 1990. The Race for Property Rights. *Journal of Law and Economics* 33(April): 177–97.

———. 1994. Rents from Amenity Resources: A Case Study of Yellowstone National Park. In *The Political Economy of the American West,* ed. Terry L. Anderson and Peter J. Hill, Lanham, MD: Rowman and Littlefield Publishers, 113–27.

———. 1996. Rent from Amenity Resources: The Case of Yellowstone Park. *Economic Inquiry* 34(July): 506–18.

———. 2001. *The Technology of Property Rights.* Lanham, MD: Rowman and Littlefield Publishers.

———. 2002. The Evolution of Property Rights. In this volume.

Anderson, Terry L., and Ronald N. Johnson. 1986. The Problem of Instream Flow. *Economic Inquiry* 24(4): 535–54

Anderson, Terry L., and Donald R. Leal. 1991. *Free Market Environmentalism.* San Francisco: Pacific Research Institute for Public Policy.

———. 1997. *Enviro-Capitalists: Doing Good While Doing Well.* Lanham, MD: Rowman and Littlefield Publishers.

Anderson, Terry L., and Dean Lueck. 1992. Land Tenure and Agricultural Productivity on Indian Reservations. *Journal of Law and Economics* 35(2): 427–54.

Anderson, Terry L., and Fred S. McChesney. 1994. Raid or Trade? An Economic Model of Indian–White Relations. *Journal of Law and Economics* 37(1): 39–74.

Anderson, Terry L., Vernon L. Smith, and Emily Simmons. 1999. How and Why to Privatize Federal Lands. *Cato Policy Analysis* 363. 9 December.

Anderson, Terry L., and Pamela S. Snyder. 1997. *Water Markets: Priming the Invisible Pump*. Washington, DC, Cato Institute.

Arnason, Ragnar. 1993. The Icelandic Individual Transferable Quota System: A Descriptive Account. *Marine Resource Economics* 8: 201–18.

———. 1996. Property Rights as an Organizational Framework in Fisheries: The Cases of Six Fishing Nations. In *Taking Ownership: Property Rights and Fishery Management on the Atlantic Coast*, ed. Brian L. Crowley. Halifax, NS, Canada: Atlantic Institute for Market Studies, 99–144.

Atkinson, Charles Milner. 1969. *Jeremy Bentham: His Life and Work*, New York: Augustus M. Kelley.

Axelrod, Robert. 1984. *The Evolution of Cooperation*. New York: Basic Books.

Ayres, Ian, and Peter Cramton. 1996. Deficit Reduction Through Diversity: How Affirmative Action at the FCC Increased Auction Competition. *Stanford Law Review* 48: 761–814.

Baden, John, Richard Stroup, and Walter Thurman. 1981. Myths, Admonitions and Rationality: The American Indian as a Resource Manager. *Economic Inquiry* 19(1): 132–43.

Bain, Joe S. 1947. *The Economics of the Pacific Coast Petroleum Industry*, Part III. Berkeley: University of California Press.

Barde, Jean-Philipe. 1997. Environmental Taxation: Experience in OECD Countries. In *Ecotaxation*, ed. Timothy O'Riordan. New York: St. Martin's Press, 223–45.

Barringer, D. M., and J. S. Adams. 1900. *The Law of Mines and Mining in the United States*. St. Paul: Keefe-Davidson.

Barrington, Linda, ed. 1999. *The Other Side of the Frontier: Economic Explorations into Native American History*. Boulder: Westview Press.

Bartlett, Richard A. 1974. *Nature's Yellowstone*. Tucson: University of Arizona Press.

Barzel, Yoram. 1968. Optimal Timing of Innovations. *Review of Economics and Statistics* 50(August): 348–55.

———. 1974. A Theory of Rationing by Waiting. *Journal of Law and Economics* 17(April): 73–95.

———. 1982. Measurement Cost and Organization of Markets. *Journal of Law and Economics* 25(April): 27–48.

———. 1987. The Entrepreneur's Reward for Self-Policing. *Economic Inquiry* 25(1): 103–16.

———. 1989. *Economic Analysis of Property Rights*. New York: Cambridge University Press.

———. 1992. Confiscation by the Ruler: The Rise and Fall of Jewish Lending in the Middle Ages. *Journal of Law and Economics* 35(1): 1–13.

———. 1994. The Capture of Wealth by Monopolists and the Protection of Property Rights. *International Review of Law and Economics* 14(December): 393–409.

———. 1997. *Economic Analysis of Property Rights*. 2d ed. New York: Cambridge University Press.

———. 2002a. *A Theory of the State: Economic Rights, Legal Rights and the Scope of the State*. New York: Cambridge University Press.

———. 2002b. Property Rights in the Firm. In this volume.

Barzel, Yoram, and Levis A. Kochin. 1992. Ronald Coase on the Nature of Social Cost as a Key to the Problem of the Firm. *Scandinavian Journal of Economics* 94(1): 19–31.

Barzel, Yoram, and Tim R. Sass. 1990. The Allocation of Resources by Voting. *Quarterly Journal of Economics* 105(August): 745–71.

Barzel, Yoram, and Wing Suen. 1995. *Equity as a Guarantee: A Contribution to the Theory of the Firm*. Mimeo. Seattle: University of Washington Press.

Batchelder, Ronald, and Nicolas Sanchez. n.d. The Encomienda and the Optimizing Imperialist: An Interpretation of Spanish Imperialism in the Americas. Unpublished manuscript.

Baumol, William J. 1990. Entrepreneurship: Productive, Unproductive, and Destructive. *Journal of Political Economy* 98 (5,1): 893–921.

Bean, Richard. 1973. War and the Birth of the Nation State. *Journal of Economic History* 33(1): 203–21.

Bell, Frederick W. 1972. Technological Externalities and Common-Property Resources: An Empirical Study of the U.S. Northern Lobster Fishery. *Journal of Political Economy* 80(1): 149–58.

Benson, Bruce L., and David W. Rasmussen. 2000. *The American Drug War: Anatomy of a Futile and Costly Police Action*. Oakland, CA: The Independent Institute.

Bentham, Jeremy. 1882. *Theory of Legislation*. 4th ed. London: Trübner.

Berger, L. 1985. An Analysis of the Doctrine that "First in Time is First in Right." *Nebraska Law Review* 64: 349–88.

Berle, Adolph, and Gardiner Means. 1932. *The Modern Corporation and Private Property*. New York: Commerce Clearing House.

Besley, Timothy. 1995. Property Rights and Investment Incentives: Theory and Evidence from Ghana. *Journal of Political Economy* 103(5): 903–37.

———. 1998. Investment Incentives and Property Rights. In *The New Palgrave Dictionary of Economics and the Law* 2, ed. Peter Newman. New York: Macmillan, 359–65.

Bethell, Tom. 1998. *The Noblest Triumph*. New York: St. Martin's Griffin.

Blackstone, William. 1765–66. *Commentaries on the Laws of England*, 1–2. Oxford: Clarendon Press.

———. [1766] 1979. *Commentaries on the Laws of England, Book II*. Chicago: University of Chicago Press.

Blume, Lawrence E., and Daniel L. Rubinfeld. 1984. Compensation for Takings. *California Law Review* 72(July): 569–628.

Bogue, Allan G. 1963. The Iowa Claims Clubs: Symbol and Substance. In *The Public Lands*, ed. Vernon Carstensen. Madison: University of Wisconsin Press.

Bohn, Henning, and Robert T. Deacon. 2000. Ownership Risk, Investment and the Use of Natural Resources. *American Economic Review* 90: 526–49.

Boorstin, Daniel J. 1958. *The Americans: The Colonial Experience*. New York: Random House.

Borcherding, Thomas E., ed. 1977. *Budgets and Bureaucrats: The Sources of Government Growth*. Durham, NC: Duke University Press.

Bottomley, Anthony. 1963. The Effect of Common Ownership of Land upon Resource Allocation in Tripolitania. *Land Economics* 39(1): 91–95.

Boudreaux, Donald J., and Roger E. Meiners. 1998. Existence Value and Other of Life's Ills. In *Who Owns the Environment?* ed. Peter J. Hill and Roger E. Meiners. Lanham, MD: Rowman and Littlefield Publishers, 153–85.

Bovenberg, A. Lans, and Lawrence H. Goulder. 1997. Costs of Environmentally Motivated Taxes in the Presence of Other Taxes: General Equilibrium Analysis. *National Tax Journal* 50(March): 59–87.

Brady, Rose. 1999. *Kapitalizm: Russia's Struggle to Free its Economy*. New Haven: Yale University Press.

Brannlund, Runar. 1995. Where Have Eco-Taxes Worked? The Swedish Experience. Presentation at the Center for European Policy Studies, Brussels. December.

Brownstone, David, and Arthur DeVany. 1991. Zoning, Returns to Scale, and the Value of Undeveloped Land. *Review of Economics and Statistics* 73(November): 699–704.

Brubaker, Elizabeth. 1998. The Common Law and the Environment: The Canadian Experience. In *Who Owns the Environment?* ed. Peter J. Hill and Roger E. Meiners. Lanham, MD: Rowman and Littlefield Publishers, 87–118.

Buchanan, James M. 1965. An Economic Theory of Clubs. *Economica* 32(February): 1–14.

———. 1975. *The Limits of Liberty: Between Anarchy and Leviathan*. Chicago: University of Chicago Press.

———. 1978. *The Economics of Politics*. Readings No. 18. London: Institute of Economic Affairs.

———. 1979. *What Should Economists Do?* Indianapolis: Liberty Press.

———. 1987a. The Constitution of Economic Policy. *American Economic Review* 87(3): 243–44.

———. 1987b. *Economics: Between Predictive Science and Moral Philosophy*. College Station, TX: Texas A&M Press, 153–68.

———. 1988. Market Failure and Political Failure. *Cato Journal* 8(1): 1–13.

Buchanan, James M., and Charles J. Goetz. 1972. Efficiency Limits of Fiscal Mobility: An Assessment of the Tiebout Model. *Journal of Public Economics* 1(April): 25–43.

Buchanan, James M., and William Craig Stubblebine. 1962. Externality. *Economica* 29(November): 371–84.

Buchanan, James, and Gordon Tullock. 1962. *The Calculus of Consent: Logical Foundations of Constitutional Democracy*. Ann Arbor: University of Michigan Press.

Bull, Martin J., and Mike Ingham, eds. 1998. *Reform of the Socialist System in Central and Eastern Europe*. New York: St. Martin's Press.

Burkhardt, Lynne C. 1981. *Old Values in a New Town*. New York: Praeger.

Burns, Nancy, and Gerald Gamm. 1997. Creatures of the State: State Politics and Local Government, 1871–1921. *Urban Affairs Review* 33(September): 59–96.

Burrows, Paul. 1991. Compensation for Compulsory Acquisition. *Land Economics* 67(February): 49–63.

Calabresi, Guido, and A. Douglas Melamed. 1972. Property Rules, Liability, and Inalienability: One View of the Cathedral. *Harvard Law Review* 85(6): 1089–1128.

Casner, A. James, ed. 1952. *American Law of Property* 2, §6. Boston: Little, Brown & Co.

Chadwick, Edwin. 1859. Results of Different Principles of Legislation and Administration in Europe; of Competition for the Field, as Compared with Competition within the Field of Service. *Journal of the Royal Statistical Society* 22: 381–402.

Chernow, Ron. 1998. *Titan*. New York: Vintage Books.

Cheung, Steven N. S. 1969. *The Theory of Share Tenancy*. Chicago: University of Chicago Press.

———. 1970. The Structure of a Contract and the Theory of a Non-Exclusive Resource. *Journal of Law and Economics* 13(1): 49–70.

———. 1983. The Contractual Nature of the Firm. *Journal of Law and Economics* 26(April): 1–22.

Chisem, D. S., and M. A. Jacobs. 1992. *Understanding Intellectual Property Law*. New York: Matthew Bender.

Christiansen, Gregory B., and Brian C. Gothberg. 2001. The Potential of High Technology for Establishing Tradable Rights to Whales. In *The Technology of Property Rights*, ed. Terry L. Anderson and P. J. Hill. Lanham, MD: Rowman and Littlefield Publishers.

Ciriacy-Wantrup, Sigfried V., and Richard C. Bishop. 1975. Common Property as a Concept in Natural Resource Policy. *Natural Resources Journal* 15: 713–27.

Clark, Colin W. 1973. Profit Maximization and the Extinction of Animal Species. *Journal of Political Economy* 81(4): 950–61.

Clarkson, Kenneth W. 1974. International Law, U.S. Seabeds Policy, and Ocean Resource Development. *Journal of Law and Economics* 17(1): 117–42.

Coase, Ronald H. 1937. The Nature of the Firm. *Economica* 4(3): 386–405.

———. 1959. The Federal Communications Commission. *Journal of Law and Economics* 2 (October): 1–40.

———. 1960. The Problem of Social Cost. *Journal of Law and Economics* 3(October): 1–44.

———. 1974. The Lighthouse in Economics. *Journal of Law and Economics* 17(October): 357–76.

———. 1988. *The Firm, the Law, and the Market*. Chicago: University of Chicago Press.

———. 1994. *Essays on Economics and Economists*. Chicago: University of Chicago Press.

Coelho, Philip R. P. 1985. An Examination Into the Causes of Economic Growth: Status as an Economic Good. *Research in Law and Economics* 7(1): 89–116.

Cohen, Lloyd. 1991. Holdouts and Free Riders. *Journal of Legal Studies* 20: 351–62.

Connell, Evan S. 1984. *Son of Morning Star*. San Francisco: North Point Press.

Cooter, Robert D. 1996. Decentralized Law for a Complex Economy: The Structural Approach for Adjudicating the New Law Merchant. *University of Pennsylvania Law Review* 144 (5): 1643–96.

Cooter, Robert D., and Daniel L. Rubinfeld. 1989. Economic Analysis of Legal Disputes and Their Resolution. *Journal of Economic Literature* 27(3): 1067–97.

Cordes, Joseph J. 1981. The Relative Efficiency of Taxes and Standards. *Public Finance* 36: 339–42.

Cordes, Joseph J., and Burton A. Weisbrod. 1979. Government Behavior in Response to Compensation Requirements. *Journal of Public Economics* 11(February): 47–58.

Costa, Bob. 1996. Golf and the Environment: Initiating Change. *Golf Course Management*. Lawrence, KS: Golf Course Superintendents Association of America. February, 136.

Crain, Mark, and Robert Ekelund. 1976. Chadwick and Demsetz on Competition and Regulation. *Journal of Law and Economics* 19(1): 149–62.

Dana, David A. 1995. Natural Preservation and the Race to Develop. *University of Pennsylvania Law Review* 143(January): 655–708.

Dasgupta, Partha, and Joseph Stiglitz. 1980. Uncertainty, Industrial Structure, and the Speed of R&D. *Bell Journal of Economics* 11: 1–28.

Davis, Lance E., and Douglass C. North. 1971. *Institutional Change and American Economic Growth*. New York: Cambridge University Press.

Davis, Peter N. 1971. Theories of Water Pollution Litigation. *Wisconsin Law Review* 3: 738–81.

Dawkins, Richard. 1989. *The Selfish Gene: New Edition*. Oxford: Oxford University Press.

Dawson, John. 1947. Economic Duress — An Essay In Perspective. *Michigan Law Review* 45: 253–90.

Day, Robert. 1989. "Sooners" or "Goners," They Were Hellbent on Grabbing Free Land. *Smithsonian* 20(8): 192–206.

De Alessi, Louis. 1969. Some Implications of Property Rights for Government Investment Choices. *American Economic Review* 59(1): 16–23.

———. 1975. *The Economics of Regulation in the Oyster Industry*. Unpublished manuscript. Washington, DC: Department of Economics, George Washington University.

———. 1980. The Economics of Property Rights: A Review of the Evidence. *Research in Law and Economics* 2: 1–47.

———. 1983. Property Rights, Transaction Costs, and X-Efficiency: An Essay in Economic Theory. *American Economic Review* 73(1): 64–81.

———. 1988. How Markets Alleviate Scarcity. In *Rethinking Institutional Analysis and Development: Issues, Alternatives, and Choices*, ed. Vincent Ostrom, David Feeny, and Hartmut Picht. San Francisco: International Center for Economic Growth, 339–76.

———. 1992. Efficiency Criteria for Optimal Laws: Objective Standards or Value Judgments? *Constitutional Political Economy* 3(3): 321–42.

―――. 1995. The Public Choice Model of Antitrust Enforcement. In *The Causes and Consequences of Antitrust: The Public-Choice Perspective*, ed. Fred S. McChesney and William F. Shughart II. Chicago: University of Chicago Press, 189–200.

―――. 1998a. Private Property Rights as the Basis for Free Market Environmentalism. In *Who Owns the Environment?* ed. Peter J. Hill and Roger E. Meiners. Lanham, MD: Rowman and Littlefield Publishers, 1–35.

―――. 1998b. Reflections on Coase, Cost, and Efficiency. In *The Economists' Vision: Essays in Modern Economic Perspectives*, ed. James M. Buchanan and Bettina Monissen. Frankfurt: Campus Verlag, 91–114. Reprinted in *Journal des Économistes et des Études Humaines* 1: 5–25.

―――. 2002. Gains from Private Property: The Empirical Evidence. In this volume.

De Alessi, Michael. 1997. Holding Out for Some Local Heroes. *New Scientist* 153(March 8): 46.

―――. 1998. *Fishing for Solutions*. London: Institute for Economic Affairs, Environment Unit.

―――. 1999. *The World's Fisheries: Regulatory Failures and the Promise of Private Conservation*. Washington, DC: Center for Private Conservation, Competitive Enterprise Institute.

―――. 2000. Fishing for Solutions: The State of the World's Fisheries. In *Earth Report 2000: Revisiting the True State of the Planet*, ed. Ronald Bailey. New York: McGraw-Hill, 85–114.

De Soto, Hernando. 1989. *The Other Path*. New York: Harper & Row.

―――. 2000. *Mystery of Capital: Why Capitalism Is Failing Outside the West & Why the Key to Its Success Is Right under Our Noses*. New York: Basic Books.

de Tocqueville, Alexis. 1835. *Democracy in America*. London: Saunders and Otley.

De Vany, Arthur S. 1977. Land Reform and Agricultural Efficiency in Mexico: A General Equilibrium Analysis. *Journal of Monetary Economics* (supplementary series) 6: 123–47.

De Vany, Arthur S., and Nicholas Sanchez. 1979. Land Tenure Structures and Fertility in Mexico. *Review of Economics and Statistics* 61(1): 67–72.

Dean, James M., and A.M.C. Waterman, eds. 1999. *Religion and Economics: Normative Social Theory*. Boston: Kluwer Academic Publishers.

Dee, Thomas S. 2000. The Capitalization of Education Finance Reforms. *Journal of Law and Economics* 43(April): 185–214.

DeLong, James V. 1997. *Property Matters*. New York: The Free Press.

Demsetz, Harold. 1964. The Exchange and Enforcement of Property Rights. *Journal of Law and Economics* 7 (October): 11–26.

―――. 1966. Some Aspects of Property Rights. *Journal of Law and Economics* 9 (October): 61–70.

―――. 1967. Toward a Theory of Property Rights. *American Economic Review: Papers and Proceedings* 57(2): 347–59.

―――. 1968. Why Regulate Utilities? *Journal of Law and Economics* 11 (April): 55–65.

———. 1969. Information and Efficiency: Another Viewpoint. *Journal of Law and Economics* 12(1): 1–22.

———. 1998. Property Rights. In *New Palgrave Dictionary of Economics and the Law*. London: Macmillan.

———. 2002. Ownership and the Externality Problem. In this volume.

Dennen, R. Taylor. 1977. Some Efficiency Effects of Nineteenth-Century Federal Land Policy: A Dynamic Analysis. *Agricultural History* 41: 718–36.

Dharmapala, Dhammika, and Rohan Pitchford. 2002. An Economic Analysis of "Riding to Hounds": *Pierson v. Post* Revisited. *Journal of Law, Economics, and Organization* 18: 39–66.

Dietze, Gottfried. 1971. *In Defence of Property*. Baltimore: Johns Hopkins University Press.

Dilger, Robert J. 1992. *Neighborhood Politics: Residential Community Associations in American Governance*. New York: NYU Press.

Dowding, Keith, Peter John, and Stephen Biggs. 1994. Tiebout: A Survey of the Empirical Literature. *Urban Studies* 31(1994): 767–97.

Dukeminier, Jesse, and James E. Krier. 2002. *Property*. 5th ed. New York: Aspen Law and Business.

Durrenberger, E. P., and G. Palsson. 1987. Ownership at Sea: Fishing Territories and Access to Sea Resources. *American Ethnologist* 14: 508–22.

Eagle, Stephen J. 1996. *Regulatory Takings*. Charlottesville, VA: Michie.

Earle, Edward M., ed. [1787] 1937. *The Federalist*. New York: Modern Library.

Eckert, Ross D. 1973. On the Incentives of Regulators: The Case of Taxicabs. *Public Choice* 14: 83–100.

Edwards, Stephen F. 1994. Ownership of Renewable Ocean Resources. *Marine Resource Economics* 9: 253–73.

Egenhofer, Christian. 1996. *Applying Economic Instruments in EU Environmental Policy: Challenges, Experiences and Prospects*. Business Policy Report No. 2. Brussels: Center for European Policy Studies. September.

Eggertsson, Thráinn. 1990. *Economic Behavior and Institutions*. New York: Cambridge University Press.

———. 1992. Analyzing Institutional Successes and Failures: A Millennium of Common Mountain Pastures in Iceland. *International Review of Law and Economics* 12(4): 423–37.

———. 2002. Open Access versus Common Property. In this volume.

Eig, Jonathan. 2001. Chicago Claim Jumpers Are Likely to Have Their Cars Vandalized. *Wall Street Journal*, 11 January, sec. A1.

Ellickson, Robert C. 1973. Alternatives to Zoning: Covenants, Nuisance Rules, and Fines as Land Use Controls. *University of Chicago Law Review* 40(Summer): 681–782.

———. 1977. Suburban Growth Controls: An Economic and Legal Analysis. *Yale Law Journal* 86(January): 385–511.

———. 1982. Cities and Homeowners Associations. *University of Pennsylvania Law Review* 130(June): 1519–80.

———. 1989. A Hypothesis of Wealth-Maximizing Norms: Evidence from the Whaling Industry. *Journal of Law, Economics, and Organization* 5(1): 83–97.

———. 1991. *Order Without Law: How Neighbors Settle Disputes.* Cambridge: Harvard University Press.

———. 1998. New Institutions for Old Neighborhoods. *Duke Law Journal* 48(October): 75–110.

Enthoven, Alain A. 1963. Economic Analysis in the Department of Defense. *American Economic Review* 53 (May): 422–26.

Epstein, Richard A. 1975. Unconscionability: A Critical Reappraisal. *Journal of Law and Economics* 18(2): 293–315.

———. 1979. Possession as the Root of Title. *Georgia Law Review* 13(4): 1221–43.

———. 1984. Toward a Revitalization of the Contract Clause. *University of Chicago Law Review* 51: 703–51.

———. 1985a. *Takings: Private Property and the Power of Eminent Domain.* Cambridge: Harvard University Press.

———. 1985b. Why Restrain Alienation? *Columbia Law Review* 85: 970–90.

———. 1986, Past and Future: The Temporal Dimension of the Law of Property. *Washington University Quarterly Review* 64: 667–722.

———. 1987. The Public Trust Doctrine. *Cato Journal* 7: 411–30.

———. 1992a. A Common Lawyer Looks at Constitutional Interpretation. *Boston University Law Review* 72: 699–727.

———. 1992b. Exit Rights Under Federalism. *Law and Contemporary Problems* 55(Winter): 147–65.

———. 1993. *Bargaining with the State.* Princeton: Princeton University Press.

———. 1995. *Simple Rules for a Complex World.* Cambridge: Harvard University Press.

———. 1998. *Principles for a Free Society: Reconciling Individual Liberty with the Common Good.* Reading, MA: Perseus Books.

———. 2000. *Torts.* 7th ed. Gaithersburg, MD: Aspen Law & Business.

———. 2002. In and Out of Public Solution: The Hidden Perils of Forced and Unforced Property Transfer. In this volume.

European Council Regulation (EEC). 1992. *Official Journal of the European Communities*, March 23.

Farrington, Brendan. 1999. Gator Hunters Confront Challenges. *The Miami Herald*, 12 September, sec. 6B.

Feder, Gershon, and David Feeny. 1991. Land Tenure and Property Rights: Theory and Implications for Development Policy. *World Bank Economic Review* 3: 135–53.

Feder, Gershon, and Tongroj Onchan. 1987. Land Ownership Security and Farm Investment in Thailand. *American Journal of Agricultural Economics* 69(2): 311–20.

Fennell, Lee Anne. 2000. Hard Bargains and Real Steals: Land Use Exactions Revisited. *Iowa Law Review* 86(October): 1–85.

Field, Barry C. 1984. The Evolution of Individual Property Rights in Massachusetts Agriculture, 17th–19th Centuries. *Northeastern Journal of Agricultural and Resource Economics* 14(2): 97–109.

———. 1989. The Evolution of Property Rights. *Kyklos* 42(3): 319–45.

Filmer, Sir Robert. [1680] 1991. *Patriarcha and Other Writings*, ed. Jóhann P. Sommerville. Cambridge: Cambridge University Press.

Fischel, William A. 1978. A Property Rights Approach to Municipal Zoning. *Land Economics* 54(February): 64–81.

———. 1985. *The Economics of Zoning Laws: A Property Rights Approach to American Land Use Controls*. Baltimore: Johns Hopkins University Press.

———. 1991. Exploring the Kozinski Paradox: Why Is More Efficient Regulation a Taking of Property? *Chicago-Kent Law Review* 67: 865–912.

———. 1995. *Regulatory Takings: Law, Economics, and Politics*. Cambridge: Harvard University Press.

———. 2000. Municipal Corporations, Homeowners, and the Benefit View of the Property Tax. In *Property Taxation and Local Public Finance*, ed. Wallace E. Oates. Cambridge, MA: Lincoln Institute for Land Policy.

———. 2002. Public Goods and Property Rights: Of Coase, Tiebout, and Just Compensation. In this volume.

Fisher, Ronald C. 1988. *State and Local Public Finance*. Glenview, IL: Scott Foresman.

Fletcher, Robert H. 1960. *Free Grass to Fences: The Montana Cattle Range Story*. New York: University Publishers Incorporated.

Fogel, Robert W., and Stanley L. Engerman. 1974. *Time on the Cross: The Economics of American Negro Slavery*. Boston: Little, Brown.

Frantz, Douglas, and Catherine Collins. 1999. *Celebration, U.S.A.* New York: Holt.

Fretwell, Holly Lippke. 2000. *Federal Estate: Is Bigger Better?* Bozeman, MT: Political Economy Research Center.

Friedlin, Jennifer. 2000. 3M Halts Much of Scotchguard Line. TheStreet.com. www.thestreet.com/_yahoo/brknewes/general/940670.html. 16 May.

Friedman, David D. 1973. *The Machinery of Freedom*. New York: Harper Colophon.

———. 1979. Private Creation and Enforcement of Law: A Historical Case. *Journal of Legal Studies* 8(2): 399–415.

———. 2000. *Law's Order: What Economics Has to Do with Law and Why It Matters*. Princeton: Princeton University Press.

Fudenberg, Drew, et al. 1983. Preemption, Leapfrogging, and Competition in Patent Races. *European Economic Review* 22: 3–31.

Fulton, Dan. 1982. *Failure on the Plains: A Rancher's View of the Public Lands Problem*. Bozeman, MT: Big Sky Books, Montana State University.

Furubotn, Eirik G., and Svetozar Pejovich. 1972. Property Rights and Economic Theory: A Survey of Recent Literature. *Journal of Economic Literature* 10(4): 1137–62.

Furubotn, Eirik G., and Rudolf Richter. 1997. *Institutions and Economic Theory: The Contribution of the New Institutional Economics*. Ann Arbor: University of Michigan Press.

Gauvin, John R., John M. Ward, and Edward E. Burgess. 1994. Description and Evaluation of the Wreckfish (*Polyprion Americanus*) Fishery under Individual Transferable Quotas. *Marine Resource Economics* 9: 99–118.

Gerard, David. 1998. The Development of First-Possession Rules in U.S. Mining, 1872–1920: Theory, Evidence, and Policy Implications. *Resources Policy* 24: 251–64.

Getches, David H., Charles F. Wilkinson, and Robert A. Williams, Jr. 1998. *Cases and Materials on Federal Indian Law*, 4th ed. St. Paul: West.

Goklany, Indur M. 1999. *Clearing the Air.* Washington, DC: Cato Institute.

Golf Course Superintendents Association of America. 1996a. *The Audubon Cooperative Sanctuary Program for Golf Courses.* Available on the Internet from www.gcsaa.org. Cited: 8 October 1997.

———. 1996b. Environmental Activists Tee Off. *Golf Course Management* (February): 22–40.

Goodall, Jane. 1971. *In the Shadow of Man.* New York: Dell Publishing.

———. 1992. Order Without Law. In *Law, Biology, and Culture*, 2d ed., ed. Margaret Gruter and Paul Bohannan. New York: McGraw-Hill Primis.

Gordon, H. Scott. 1954. The Economic Theory of a Common Property Resource: The Fishery. *Journal of Political Economy* 62(2): 124–42.

Grady, Mark F., and J. I. Alexander. 1992. Patent Law and Rent Dissipation. *Virginia Law Review* 78: 305–50.

Griswold, Charles L. 1999. *Adam Smith and the Virtues of Enlightenment.* New York: Cambridge University Press.

Grossman, Herschel I., Minseong Kim, and Juan Mendoza. 2001. *Decisiveness and the Viability of Anarchy.* Unpublished manuscript. Providence, RI: Department of Economics, Brown University.

Grossman, Sanford J., and Oliver D. Hart. 1986. The Cost and Benefits of Ownership: A Theory of Vertical and Lateral Integration. *Journal of Political Economy* 94(August): 691–719.

Gwartney, James, Robert Lawson, and Walter Block. 1996. *Economic Freedom of the World: 1975–1995.* Vancouver, BC, Canada: The Fraser Institute.

Gyourko, Joseph. 1991. Impact Fees, Exclusionary Zoning, and the Density of New Development. *Journal of Urban Economics* 30(September): 242–56.

Haddock, David D. 1986. First Possession versus Optimal Timing: Limiting the Dissipation of Economic Value. *Washington University Law Quarterly* 64(3): 775–92.

———. 1994. Foreseeing Confiscation by the Sovereign: Lessons from the American West. In *The Political Economy of the American West*, ed. Terry L. Anderson and Peter J. Hill. Lanham, MD: Rowman and Littlefield Publishers.

———. 1997a. Must Water Regulation Be Centralized? In *Water Marketing— The Next Generation*, ed. Terry L. Anderson and Peter J. Hill. Lanham, MD: Rowman and Littlefield Publishers, 43–61.

———. 1997b. Sizing Up Sovereigns: Federal Systems, Their Origins, Their Decline, Their Prospects. In *Environmental Federalism*, ed. Terry L. Anderson and Peter J. Hill. Lanham, MD: Rowman and Littlefield Publishers, 1–21.

———. 2002. Force, Threat, Negotiation: The Private Enforcement of Rights. In this volume.

Haddock, David D., and L. Lynne Kiesling. 2001. A Model of the Evolution of Property Rights After the Black Death. Paper presented at The Evolution of Property Rights Conference, Northwestern University, Chicago. 21–22 April.

Haddock, David D., Fred S. McChesney, and Menahem Spiegel. 1990. An Ordinary Economic Rationale for Extraordinary Legal Sanctions. *California Law Review* 78(1): 1–51.

Hamilton, Bruce W. 1975. Zoning and Property Taxation in a System of Local Governments. *Urban Studies* 12(June): 205–11.

———. 1976. Capitalization of Intrajurisdictional Differences in Local Tax Prices. *American Economic Review* 66(December): 743–53.

Hardin, Garrett. 1968. The Tragedy of the Commons. *Science* 162(December): 1243–48.

Hardwicke, Robert E. 1935. The Rule of Capture and Its Implications as Applied to Oil and Gas. *Texas Law Review* 13: 391–422.

Harris, Christopher, and John Vickers. 1985. Perfect Equilibrium in a Model of a Race. *Review of Economic Studies* 52: 193–209.

Harsanyi, John G. 1968. Individualistic and Functionalistic Explanations in the Light of Game Theory: The Example of Social Status. In *Problems in the Philosophy of Science*, ed. Imre Lakatos and Alan Musgave. Amsterdam: North Holland, 305–48.

Hayek, F.A. 1945. The Use of Knowledge in Society. *American Economic Review* 35 (September): 519–30.

———. 1969. *Studies in Philosophy, Politics and Economics*. New York: Simon and Schuster.

Hazlett, Thomas W. 1990. The Rationality of U.S. Regulation of the Broadcast Spectrum. *Journal of Law and Economics* 33(1): 133–75.

Head, John G. 1974. *Public Goods and Public Welfare*. Durham, NC: Duke University Press.

Heller, Michael A. 1998. The Tragedy of the Anticommons: Property in the Transition from Marx to Markets. *Harvard Law Review* 11: 621–88.

Herzel, Leo. 1951. "Public Interest" and the Market in Color Television Regulation. *University of Chicago Law Review* 18: 802–16.

Hibbard, Benjamin H. 1939. *A History of the Public Land Policies*. New York: Peter Smith.

Higgs, Robert. 1982. Legally Induced Technical Regress in the Washington Salmon Fishery. *Research in Economic History* 7: 55–86.

———. 1987. *Crisis and Leviathan: Critical Episodes in the Growth of American Government*. New York: Oxford University Press.

Hirschleifer, Jack. 1995. Anarchy and Its Breakdown. *Journal of Political Economy* 103(1): 26–52.

Hirschleifer, Jack, and John G. Riley. 1983. *The Analytics of Uncertainty and Information*. Cambridge: Cambridge University Press.

Hobbes, Thomas. [1651] 1914. *Leviathan*. London: Dent.

Holdaway, Richard R., and Chris Jacomb. 2000. Rapid Extinction of the Moas (*Aves: Dinornithiformes*): Model, Test, and Implications. *Science* 287(March 24): 2250–54.

Holderness, Clifford G. 1985. A Legal Foundation for Exchange. *Journal of Legal Studies* 14(June): 321–44.

———. 2000. Joint Ownership and Alienability. Working paper. SSRN Electronic Paper Collection: http://papers.ssrn.com/paper.taf?abstract.id= 229801.

Holmes, Oliver Wendell. [1881] 1946. *The Common Law*, 40th printing. Boston: Little, Brown.

Hoxby, Caroline M. 1999. The Productivity of Schools and Other Local Public Goods Producers. *Journal of Public Economics* 74(October): 1–30.

Hudson, Richard L. 1990. Tough Bird Laws Mean Little When It's Time for Dinner. *Wall Street Journal*, 18 January, sec. A1.

Hume, David. [1752] 1985. Of Commerce. In *Essay Moral, Political, and Literacy*, ed. Eugene Millar. Indianapolis: Liberty Classics.

Huppert, Daniel, and Gunnar Knapp. 2001. Technology and Property Rights in Fisheries Management. In *The Technology of Property Rights*, ed. Terry L. Anderson and P. J. Hill. Lanham, MD: Rowman and Littlefield Publishers.

Husted, Thomas A., and Lawrence W. Kenny. 2000. Evidence on the Impact of State Government on Primary and Secondary Education and the Equity-Efficiency Tradeoff. *Journal of Law and Economics* 43(April): 285–308.

Jefferson, Thomas. 1861. *Writings of Thomas Jefferson 5*, ed. H. A. Washington. New York: H. W. Derby.

Jensen, Michael C., and William H. Meckling. 1976. Theory of the Firm: Managerial Behavior, Agency Costs and Ownership Structure. *Journal of Financial Economics* 3(October): 305–60.

———. 1979. Rights and Production Functions: An Application to Labor-Managed Firms and Codetermination. *Journal of Business* 52(4): 469–506.

Johannes, R. E. 1992. *Words of the Lagoon: Fishing and Marine Lore in the Palau District of Micronesia*. Berkeley: University of California Press.

Johnsen, D. Bruce. 1999. Property Rights, Salmon Husbandry, and Institutional Change Among the Northwest Coast Tribes. Unpublished manuscript. Arlington, VA: George Mason University School of Law, Working Papers in Law and Economics.

Johnson, Ronald N. 1995. Implications of Taxing Quota Value in an Individual Transferable Quota Fishery. *Marine Resources Economics* 10: 327–40.

———. 1999. Rents and Taxes in an ITQ Fishery. In *Individual Transferable Quotas in Theory and Practice*, ed. Ragnar Arnason and Hannes H. Gissurarson. Reykjavik: University of Iceland Press, 207–14.

Johnson, Ronald N., and Gary D. Libecap. 1982. Contracting Problems and Regulations: The Case of the Fishery. *American Economic Review* 72(5): 1005–22.

Joskow, Paul L. 1988. Asset Specificity and the Structure of Vertical Relationships: Empirical Evidence. *Journal of Law, Economics, and Organization* 4(1): 95–117.

Journal of Law and Economics. 1983. Various articles. June.

Kanazawa, Mark T. 1996. Possession is Nine Points of the Law: The Political Economy of Early Public Land Disposal. *Explorations in Economic History* 33: 227–49.

Kanner, Gideon. 1989. Measure of Damages in Nonphysical Inverse Condemnation Cases. In *Proceedings of the Institute on Planning, Zoning and Eminent Domain*. New York: Matthew Bender and Company.

Kaplow, Louis. 1986. An Economic Analysis of Legal Transitions. *Harvard Law Review* 99(January): 509–617.

Kaplow, Louis, and Steven Shavell. 1994. Why the Legal System Is Less Efficient than the Income Tax in Redistributing Income. *Journal of Legal Studies* 23(June): 667–81.

Karpoff, Jonathan M. 2001. Public Versus Private Initiative in Arctic Exploration: The Effect of Incentives and Organizational Structure. *Journal of Political Economy* 109 (February): 38–78.

Kayden, Jerold S. 1991. Zoning for Dollars: New Rules for an Old Game? Comments on the *Municipal Art Society* and *Nollan* Cases. *Washington University Journal of Urban and Contemporary Law* 39: 3–51.

Keefer, Phillip, and Stephen Knack. 1997. Why Don't Poor Countries Catch Up? A Cross-National Test of an Institutional Explanation. *Economic Inquiry* 35: 590–602.

Kirzner, Israel M. 1973. *Competition and Entrepreneurship*. Chicago: University of Chicago Press.

———. 1976. *The Economic Point of View*. Kansas City: Sheed & Ward.

———. 1985. *Discovery and the Capitalist Process*. Chicago: University of Chicago Press.

Kitch, Edward. 1977. The Nature and Function of the Patent System. *Journal of Law and Economics* 20: 265–90.

Klein, Benjamin, Robert G. Crawford, and Armen A. Alchian. 1978. Vertical Integration, Appropriable Rents, and the Competitive Contracting Process. *Journal of Law and Economics* 21(2): 297–326.

Klein, Benjamin, and Kevin M. Murphy. 1997. Vertical Integration as a Self-Enforcing Contractual Arrangement. *American Economic Review* 87(2): 415–20.

Kline, Jeffrey, and Dennis Wichelns. 1994. Using Referendum Data to Characterize Public Support for Purchasing Development Rights to Farmland. *Land Economics* 70(May): 223–33.

Kmiec, Douglas W. 1988. The Original Understanding of the Taking Clause Is Neither Weak nor Obtuse. *Columbia Law Review* 88(December): 1630–66.

Knetsch, Jack L. 1983. *Property Rights and Compensation: Compulsory Acquisition and Other Losses*. Toronto: Butterworths.

Knight, Frank H. 1924. Fallacies in the Interpretation of Social Cost. *Quarterly Journal of Economics* (November).

———. [1924] 1997. Fallacies in the Interpretation of Social Cost. *The Ethics of Competition*. New York: Harper and Sons, 220–21. Original article published in *Quarterly Journal of Economics*, November 1924.

———. 1935. *The Ethics of Competition*. New York: Harper and Sons.

Komesar, Neil K. 1978. Housing, Zoning, and the Public Interest. In *Public Interest Law*, ed. Burton A. Weisbrod. Berkeley: University of California Press.

Konar, Shameek, and Mark A. Cohen. 1997. Information as Regulation: The Effects of Community Right to Know Laws on Toxic Emissions. *Journal of Environmental Economics and Management* 32: 109–24.

Kramer, Bruce, and Patrick H. Martin. 1989. *The Law of Pooling and Unitization*. 3d ed. New York: Matthew Bender.

Krech, Shepard III. 1999. *The Ecological Indian: Myth and History*. New York: W. W. Norton.

Krueger, Anne O. 1974. The Political Economy of the Rent-Seeking Society. *American Economic Review* 65(June): 291–303.

Laitos, Jan G. 1998. *Law of Property Rights Protection: Limitations on Governmental Powers*. Gaithersburg, MD: Aspen Law and Business.

Landry, Clay J. 1998. *Saving Our Streams through Water Markets: A Practical Guide*. Bozeman, MT: Political Economy Research Center.

Lawson, F. H. 1950. *Negligence in the Civil Law*. Oxford: Clarendon Press.

Lawson, F. H., ed. 1975. *International Encyclopedia of Comparative Law* VI. Paris: J.C.B. Mohr.

Leal, Donald. 1998. Cooperating on the Commons: Case Studies in Community Fisheries. In *Who Owns the Environment?* ed. Peter J. Hill and Roger E. Meiners. Lanham, MD: Rowman and Littlefield Publishers, 283–313.

Leal, Donald R., and Bishop Grewell. 1999. *Hunting for Habitat*. Bozeman, MT: Political Economy Research Center.

Lepage, Henri. 1985. *Pourquoi la Propriété?* Paris: Hachette.

Lerner, Abba P. 1944. *The Economics of Control*. New York: Macmillan.

Lerner, Josh. 1997. An Empirical Exploration of a Technological Race. *RAND Journal of Economics* 28: 228–47.

Leshy, John D. 1987. *The Mining Law*. Washington, DC: Resources for the Future.

Libecap, Gary D. 1978. Economic Variables and the Development of the Law: The Case of Western Mineral Rights. *Journal of Economic History* 38(2): 338–62.

———. 1979. Government Support of Private Claims to Public Minerals: Western Mineral Rights. *Business History Review* 53: 364–85.

———. 1981a. Bureaucratic Opposition to the Assignment of Property Rights: Overgrazing on the Western Range. *Journal of Economic History* 41(1): 151–58.

———. 1981b. *Locking Up the Range: Federal Land Controls and Grazing*. San Francisco: Pacific Institute for Public Policy Research, Ballinger Publishing.

———. 1986. Property Rights in Economic History: Implications for Research. *Explorations in Economic History* 23: 227–52.

———. 1989a. *Contracting for Property Rights*. New York: Cambridge University Press.

———. 1989b. Distributional Issues in Contracting for Property Rights. *Journal of Institutional and Theoretical Economics* 145(1): 6–24.

———. 1998a. Common Property. In *The New Palgrave Dictionary of Economics and The Law* 1, ed. Peter Newman. New York: Macmillan, 317–24.

———. 1998b. Unitization. In *The New Palgrave Dictionary of Economics and The Law* 3, ed. Peter Newman. New York: Macmillan, 641–43.

———. 2002. Contracting for Property Rights. In this volume.

Libecap, Gary D., and Ronald N. Johnson. 1980. Legislating Commons: The Navajo Tribal Council and the Navajo Range. *Economic Inquiry* 18(1): 69–86.

———. 1981. The Navajo and Too Many Sheep: Overgrazing on the Reservation. In *Bureaucracy vs. Environment: The Environmental Costs of Bureaucratic Governance*, ed. John Baden and Richard Stroup. Ann Arbor: University of Michigan Press, 87–107.

Libecap, Gary D., and James L. Smith. 1999. The Self-Enforcing Provisions of Oil and Gas Unit Operating Agreements: Theory and Evidence. *Journal of Law, Economics, and Organization* 15(2): 526–48.

———. 2001. Regulatory Remedies to the Common Pool: The Limits to Oil Field Unitization. *Energy Journal* 22(1): 1–26.

Libecap, Gary D., and Steven N. Wiggins. 1984. Contractual Responses to the Common Pool: Prorationing of Crude Oil Production. *American Economic Review* 74(1): 87–98.

———. 1985. The Influence of Private Contractual Failure on Regulation: The Case of Oil Field Unitization. *Journal of Political Economy* 93(4): 690–714.

Liebmann, George W. 2000. *Solving Problems Without Large Government: Devolution, Fairness, and Equality*. Westport, CT: Praeger.

Lindahl, Erik. [1919] 1964. Just Taxation—A Positive Solution. Translated and reprinted in *Classics in the Theory of Public Finance*, ed. Richard A. Musgrave and Alan T. Peacock. London: Macmillan, 168–76.

Lindley, C. H. 1903. *A Treatise on the American Law Relating to Mines and Mineral Lands*. 2d ed. San Francisco: Bancroft-Whitney Company.

Locke. John. [1690] 1963. *Two Treatises of Government*, ed. P. Laslett. 2d ed. Cambridge: Cambridge University Press.

———. [1690] 1991. *Two Treatises of Government*, ed. P. Laslett. 3d ed. Cambridge: Cambridge University Press.

Loury, Glenn C. 1979. Market Structure and Innovation. *Quarterly Journal of Economics* 93: 395–410.

Lueck, Dean. 1989. The Economic Nature of Wildlife Law. *Journal of Legal Studies* 18(2): 291–324.

———. 1991. Ownership and the Regulation of Wildlife. *Economic Inquiry* 29(2): 249–60.

———. 1994. Common Property as an Egalitarian Share Contract. *Journal of Economic Behavior and Organization* 25: 93–108.

———. 1995. The Rule of First Possession and the Design of the Law. *Journal of Law and Economics* 38(2): 393–436.

———. 1998. First Possession. In *The New Palgrave Dictionary of Economics and the Law*, ed. Peter Newman. London: Macmillan, 132–44.

———. 2001. The Extermination and Conservation of the American Bison. Paper presented at The Evolution of Property Rights Conference, Northwestern University, Chicago, 21–22 April.

———. 2002. First Possession as the Basis of Property. In this volume.

Lueck, Dean, and Jeffrey Michael. 2000. *Preemptive Habitat Destruction under the Endangered Species Act*. Working Paper. Bozeman, MT: Department of Agricultural Economics and Economics, Montana State University.

Lueck, Dean, and Philip Schenewerk. 1996. An Economic Analysis of Unitized and Non-unitized Production. *Proceedings of the 1996 Society of Petroleum Engineers Annual Technical Conference*, 67–76.

Lueck, Dean, and Jonathan Yoder. 1997. Federalism and Wildlife Conservation in the West. In *Environmental Federalism in the West*, ed. Terry L. Anderson and Peter J. Hill. Lanham, MD: Rowman and Littlefield Publishers, 89–131.

Lupu, Ira C. 1989. Where Rights Begin: The Problem of Burdens on the Free Exercise of Religion. *Harvard Law Review* 102: 933–90.

Macaulay, Hugh H. 1972. Environmental Quality, the Market, and Public Finance. In *Modern Fiscal Issues*, ed. Richard Bird and John G. Head. Toronto: University of Toronto Press, 187–224.

Macey, Jonathan. 1994. Property Rights, Innovation, And Constitutional Structure. In *Property Rights*, ed. Ellen Paul Frankel, Fred D. Miller Jr., and Jeffrey Paul. Social Philosophy and Policy Series. Cambridge: Cambridge University Press.

Malone, Michael P., and Richard B. Roeder. 1976. *Montana: A History of Two Centuries*. Seattle: University of Washington Press.

Malone, Wex. 1956. Ruminations on Cause-in-Fact. *Stanford Law Review* 9: 60–99.

Malthus, Thomas R. [1836] 1951. *Principles of Political Economy*. 2d ed. New York: Augustus M. Kelley.

Martin, P. S., and C. R. Szuter. 1999. War Zones and Game Sinks in Lewis and Clark's West. *Conservation Biology* 13: 36–45.

Marx, Karl. [1844] 1959. *Economic and Philosophic Manuscripts of 1844*, trans. Martin Milligan. Moscow: Foreign Languages Publishing House.

Marx, Karl, and Friedrich Engels. [1848] 1962. *Selected Works*, ed. V. Adorakskyl. Prepared by the Marx/Engels Institute, Moscow. New York: International Publishers.

Marzulla, Nancie G., and Roger J. Marzulla. 1997. *Property Rights*. Rockville, MD: Government Institutes.

McChesney, Fred S. 1986. Government Prohibitions on Volunteer Fire Fighting in Nineteenth-Century America: A Property Rights Perspective. *Journal of Legal Studies* 15(1): 69–92.

———. 1988. Intellectual Attitudes and Regulatory Change: Legal Scholars in the Depression. *Journal of Legal Education* 38: 211–41.

———. 1990. Government as Definer of Property Rights: Indian Lands, Ethnic Externalities, and Bureaucratic Budgets. *Journal of Legal Studies* 19(2): 297–335.

———. 1997. *Money for Nothing: Politicians, Rent Extraction, and Political Extortion*. Cambridge: Harvard University Press.

———. 2002. Government as Definer of Property Rights: Tragedy Exiting the Commons? In this volume.

McDonald, John F. 1995. Houston Remains Unzoned. *Land Economics* 71(February): 137–40.

McEvoy, A. F. 1986. *The Fisherman's Problem*. Cambridge: Cambridge University Press.

McGrath, Roger D. 1984. *Gunfighters, Highwaymen & Vigilantes*. Berkeley: University of California Press.

McKay, Bonnie J., and James M. Acheson. 1987. *The Question of the Commons*. Tucson: University of Arizona Press.

McKean, Margaret A. 1986. Management of Traditional Common Lands (*Iriaichi*) in Japan. In *Proceedings of the Conference on Common Property Resource Management, April 21–26, 1985*. Washington, DC: National Academy Press, 533–89.

———. 1992. Success on the Commons: A Comparative Examination of Institutions for Common Property Resource Management. *Journal of Theoretical Politics* 43: 247–81.

McKean, Roland N. 1964. Divergences between Individual and Total Costs within Government. *American Economic Review* 54(2): 243–49.

McMillan, John. 1994. Selling Spectrum Rights. *Journal of Economic Perspectives* 8: 145–62.

McMillen, Daniel P., and John F. McDonald. 1993. Could Zoning Have Increased Land Values in Chicago? *Journal of Urban Economics* 33(March): 167–88.

Meiners, Roger E., and Bruce Yandle. 1998. The Common Law: How It Protects the Environment. *PERC Policy Series* No. 13. Bozeman, MT: Political Economy Research Center.

———. 1999. Common Law and the Conceit of Modern Environmental Policy. *George Mason University Law Review* 7(Summer): 923–63.

Meiners, Roger E., Stacie Thomas, and Bruce Yandle. 2000. Burning Rivers, Property Rights, and Common Law. In *Common Law and the Environment*, ed. Roger E. Meiners and Andrew Morriss. Lanham, MD: Rowman and Littlefield Publishers, 54–85.

Meltzer, Allan H. 1991. The Growth of Government Revisited. In *Perspectives on an Economic Future: Forms, Reforms, and Evaluations*, ed. Shripad G. Pendse. New York: Greenwood Press, 131–43.

Merrill, Thomas W. n.d. *Constitutional Property*. Duplicated.

———. 1998. Property and the Right to Exclude. *Nebraska Law Review* 77: 730–55.

Merrill, Thomas W., ed. 1986. Roundtable Discussion: Symposium on Time, Property Rights, and the Common Law. *Washington University Law Quarterly* 64: 793–865.

Miceli, Thomas J., and C. F. Sirmans. 1995. An Economic Theory of Adverse Possession. *International Review of Law and Economics* 15: 161–73.

Michalak, Anna M. 2001. Feasibility of Contaminant Source Identification for Property Rights Enforcement. In *The Technology of Property Rights*, ed. Terry L. Anderson and P. J. Hill. Lanham, MD: Rowman and Littlefield Publishers.

Michelman, Frank I. 1967. Property, Utility, and Fairness: Comments on the Ethical Foundations of "Just Compensation" Law. *Harvard Law Review* 80(April): 1165–1258.

Mill, John Stuart. [1848] 1969. *Principles of Political Economy*, ed. Sir William Ashley. New York: Augustus M. Kelly.

Miller, Gary J. 1981. *Cities by Contract: The Politics of Municipal Incorporation*. Cambridge: MIT Press.

Mokyr, Joel. 1983. *Why Ireland Starved*. London: Allen and Unwin.

Mommsen, T., P. Krueger, and A. Watson, eds. 1985. *The Digest of Justinian*. Philadelphia: University of Pennsylvania Press.

Monkkonen, Eric H. 1988. *America Becomes Urban: The Development of United States Cities and Towns, 1780–1980*. Berkeley: University of California Press.

———. 1995. *The Local State: Public Money and American Cities.* Stanford: Stanford University Press.

Mortensen, Dale T. 1982. Property Rights and Efficiency in Mating, Racing, and Related Games. *American Economic Review* 72: 968–79.

Musgrave, Richard A. 1939. The Voluntary Exchange Theory of Public Economy. *Quarterly Journal of Economics* 53(February): 213–37.

———. 1959. *The Theory of Public Finance.* New York: McGraw-Hill.

Narveson, Jan. 1991. Property Rights: Original Acquisition and Lockean Provisos. Unpublished monograph. Waterloo, ON, Canada: University of Waterloo.

National Research Council. 1986. *Proceedings of the Conference on Common Property Resource Management.* Washington, DC: National Academy Press.

Nelson, Robert H. 1977. *Zoning and Property Rights.* Cambridge: MIT Press.

———. 1995. *Public Lands and Private Rights: The Failure of Scientific Management.* Lanham, MD: Rowman and Littlefield Publishers.

———. 1999. Privatizing the Neighborhood: A Proposal to Replace Zoning with Private Collective Property Rights to Existing Neighborhoods. *George Mason Law Review* 7(Summer): 827–80.

Netter, J. M., P. L. Hersch, and W. D. Manson. 1986. An Economic Analysis of Adverse Possession Statutes. *International Review of Law and Economics* 6: 217–27.

Njal's Saga. 1960. Translation of medieval text with an introduction by Magnus Magnusson and Herman Pálsson. New York: Penguin Books.

North, Douglass C. 1981. *Structure and Change in Economic History.* New York: W. W. Norton.

———. 1989. Institutional Change and Economic History. *Journal of Institutional and Theoretical Economics* 145(1): 238–45.

———. 1990. *Institutions, Institutional Change and Economic Performance.* Cambridge: Cambridge University Press.

North, Douglass C., and Robert P. Thomas. 1973. *The Rise of the Western World.* Cambridge: Cambridge University Press.

———. 1977. The First Economic Revolution. *Economic History Review* Second Series 30(2): 229–41.

Norton, Seth W. 1998. Property Rights, the Environment, and Economic Well-Being. In *Who Owns the Environment?* ed. Terry L. Anderson and Peter J. Hill. Lanham, MD: Rowman and Littlefield Publishers, 37–54.

Nozick, Robert. 1974. *Anarchy, State, and Utopia.* New York: Basic Books.

O'Riordan, Timothy. 1997. *Ecotaxation.* New York: St. Martin's Press.

Oates, Wallace E. 1969. The Effects of Property Taxes and Local Public Spending on Property Values: An Empirical Study of Tax Capitalization and the Tiebout Hypothesis. *Journal of Political Economy* 77(November): 957–71.

———. 1972. *Fiscal Federalism.* New York: Harcourt Brace Jovanovich.

Olson, Mancur. 1965. *The Logic of Collective Action.* Cambridge: Harvard University Press.

Ostrom, Elinor. 1986. An Agenda for the Study of Institutions. *Public Choice* 48(1): 3–25.

———. 1990. *Governing the Commons: The Evolution of Institutions for Collective Action.* Cambridge: Cambridge University Press.

———. 1997. Private and Common Property Rights. In *Encyclopedia of Law and Economics*, ed. Boudewijn Bouckaert and Gerrit De Geest. Available on the Internet from www.encyclo.findlaw.com.

———. 1998. Self-Governance of Common Pool Resources. In *The New Palgrave Dictionary of Economics and The Law*. London: Macmillan.

Ostrom, Vincent. 1991. *The Meaning of Federalism: Constituting a Self-governing Society*. San Francisco: Institute for Contemporary Studies Press.

Oswald, Lynda J. 1997. The Role of the "Harm/Benefit" and "Average Reciprocity of Advantage" Rules in a Comprehensive Takings Analysis. *Vanderbilt Law Review* 50(November): 1449–1524.

Paul, Ellen Frankel. 1979. *Moral Revolution and Economic Science*. London: Greenwood Press.

———. 1987. *Property Rights and Eminent Domain*. New Brunswick: Transaction Press.

Pauly, Mark, and Michael Redisch. 1973. The Not-for-Profit Hospital as a Physicians' Cooperative. *American Economic Review* 61(1): 87–99.

Peiser, Richard B. 1981. Land Development Regulation: A Case Study of Dallas and Houston, Texas. *AREUEA Journal* 9(Winter): 397–417.

Pejovich, Svetozar. 1972. Towards an Economic Theory of The Creation of Property Rights. *Review of Social Economics* 30: 309–25.

Pigou, A. C. 1920. *The Economics of Welfare*. London: Macmillan.

———. 1932. *The Economics of Welfare*. 4th ed. London: Macmillan.

Pines, David, and Yoram Weiss. 1976. Land Improvement Projects and Land Values. *Journal of Urban Economics* 3(January): 1–13.

Pipes, Richard. 1999. *Property and Freedom*. New York: Alfred A. Knopf.

Plato. 1955. *The Republic*. Baltimore: Penguin Books.

Polinsky, A. Mitchell, and Steven Shavell. 2000. The Economic Theory of Public Enforcement of Law. *Journal of Economic Literature* 38(1): 45–76.

Pollakowski, Henry, and Susan M. Wachter. 1990. The Effects of Land Use Constraints on Land Values. *Land Economics* 66(August): 315–24.

Porter, Bruce D. 1994. *War and the Rise of the State*. New York: Macmillan.

Posner, Eric. 1996. Law, Economics, and Inefficient Norms. *University of Pennsylvania Law Review* 144(5): 1697–1744.

Proudhon, Pierre-Joseph. [1840] 1994. *What Is Property?* ed. and trans. D. R. Kelley and B. G. Smith. Cambridge: Cambridge University Press.

Ramseyer, J. Mark. 1989. Water Law in Imperial Japan: Public Goods, Private Claims, and Legal Convergence. *Journal of Legal Studies* 18: 51–78.

Reinganum, Jennifer F. 1989. The Timing of Innovation: Research, Development, and Diffusion. In *Handbook of Industrial Organization*, ed. R. Schmalensee and R. D. Willig. Amsterdam: North-Holland.

Ridley, Matt. 1996. *The Origins of Virtue*. New York: Penguin Books.

Rinehart, James R., and Jeffrey J. Pompe. 1997. Entrepreneurship and Coast Resource Management. *Independent Review* 1(Spring): 543–59.

Robbins, Lionel. 1935. *An Essay on the Nature and Significance of Economic Science*. London: Macmillan & Co.

———. 1952. *The Theory of Economic Policy in English Classical Political Economy*. London: Macmillan & Co.

Roberts, Paul Craig, and Lawrence M. Stratton. 2000. *The Tyranny of Good Intentions*. Roseville, CA: Forum.

Rose, Carol M. 1985. Possession as the Origin of Property. *University of Chicago Law Review* 53: 73–88.

———. 1986. The Comedy of the Commons: Custom, Commerce, and Inherently Public Property. *University of Chicago Law Review* 53: 711–81.

———. 1989. The Ancient Constitution vs. the Federalist Empire: Anti-Federalism from the Attack on "Monarchism" to Modern Localism. *Northwestern University Law Review* 84(Fall): 74–105.

———. 1990. Energy and Efficiency in the Realignment of Common-law Water Rights. *Journal of Legal Studies* 19: 261–96.

Rose-Ackerman, Susan. 1985. Inalienability and the Theory of Property Rights. *Columbia Law Review* 85: 931–69.

Runolfsson, B. 1997. Fencing the Oceans. *Regulation* (Summer): 57–62.

Runte, Alfred. 1979. *National Parks: The American Experience*. Lincoln: University of Nebraska Press.

———. 1990. *Trains of Discovery*. Niwot, CO: Roberts Rinehart.

Rutherford, Malcolm. 1994. *Institutions in Economics: The Old and the New Institutionalism*. Cambridge: Cambridge University Press.

Ryan, Alan. 1989. Property. In *The New Palgrave: The Invisible Hand*, ed. John Eatwell, Murray Milgate, and Peter Newman. London, New York: W. W. Norton.

Salins, Peter D., and Gerald C. S. Mildner. 1992. *Scarcity by Design: The Legacy of New York City's Housing Policies*. Cambridge: Harvard University Press.

Samuelson, Paul A. 1954. The Pure Theory of Public Expenditures. *Review of Economics and Statistics* 36(November): 387–89.

———. 1964. *Economics: An Introductory Analysis*. 6th ed. New York: McGraw-Hill.

Sanera, Michael, and Jane S. Shaw. 1996. *Facts, Not Fear: A Parent's Guide to Teaching Children About the Environment*. Washington, DC: Regnery.

Sax, Joseph. 1971. Takings, Private Property and Public Rights. *Yale Law Journal* 81(December): 149–86.

Schlager, Edella, and Elinor Ostrom. 1992. Property Rights to Natural Resources: A Conceptual Analysis. *Land Economics* 68: 249–62.

Schmalensee, Richard, 1987. Competitive Advantage and Collusive Optima. *International Journal of Industrial Organization* 5: 351–67.

Schoenbaum, T. J. 1987. *Admiralty and Maritime Law*. St. Paul, MN: West Publishing.

Schumpeter, Joseph A. 1934. *The Theory of Economic Development*. Cambridge: Harvard University Press.

Scott, Anthony D. 1955. The Fishery: The Objectives of Sole Ownership. *Journal of Political Economy* 63(2): 116–24.

———. 1996. The ITQ as a Property Right: Where It Came From, How It Works, and Where It Is Going. In *Taking Ownership: Property Rights and Fishery Management on the Atlantic Coast*, ed. Brian L. Crowley. Halifax, NS, Canada: Atlantic Institute for Market Studies, 31–98.

Scott, Anthony D., and Georgina Coustalin. 1995. The Evolution of Water Rights. *Natural Resources Journal* 35(4): 821–979.

Siegan, Bernard H. 1972. *Land Use without Zoning.* Lexington, MA: Lexington Books.

Silva, Fabio, and Jon C. Sonstelie. 1995. Did *Serrano* Cause a Decline in School Spending? *National Tax Journal* 48(June): 199–215.

Simmons, N. E. 1989. Natural Law. *The New Palgrave:* In *The Invisible Hand,* ed. John Eatwell, Murray Milgate, and Peter Newman. London, New York: W. W. Norton.

Skogh, Göran, and Charles Stuart. 1982. A Contractarian Theory of Property Rights and Crime. *Scandinavian Journal of Economics* 84(1): 27–40.

Slocum, Ken. 1987. The Game Is at Stake as Wardens Combat a Plague of Poachers. *Wall Street Journal,* 4 May, sec. A, p. 1.

Smith, Adam. 1896. *Lectures on Justice, Police, Revenue and Arms. Delivered in the University of Glasgow by Adam Smith, reported by a student in 1763,* ed. Edwin Cannan. Oxford: Clarendon Press.

———. [1776] 1976a. *An Inquiry into the Nature and Causes of the Wealth of Nations,* ed. R. H. Campbell, A. S. Skinner, and W. B. Todd. Reprinted in two volumes. Oxford: Clarendon Press.

———. [1759] 1976b. *The Theory of Moral Sentiments,* ed. D. D. Raphael and A. L. Macfie. Oxford: Clarendon Press.

Smith, James L. 1987. The Common Pool, Bargaining, and the Rule of Capture. *Economic Inquiry* 25(4): 631–44.

Smith, John Maynard. 1982. *Evolution and the Theory of Games.* Cambridge: Cambridge University Press.

Smith, Vernon L. 1968. Economics of Production from Natural Resources. *American Economic Review* 58 (June): 409–31.

———. 1975. The Primitive Hunter Culture, Pleistocene Extinction, and the Rise of Agriculture. *Journal of Political Economy* 82(4): 727–55.

Sonstelie, Jon C., and Paul R. Portney. 1978. Profit Maximizing Communities and the Theory of Local Public Expenditures. *Journal of Urban Economics* 5(April): 263–77.

———. 1980. Take the Money and Run: A Theory of Voting in Local Referenda. *Journal of Urban Economics* 8(September): 187–95.

Sowell, Thomas. 1987. *A Conflict of Visions.* New York: William Morrow and Company.

Speyrer, Janet Furman. 1989. The Effect of Land Use Restrictions on the Market Value of Single Family Homes in Houston. *Journal of Real Estate Finance and Economics* 2(June): 117–30.

Spiegel, Henry William. 1971. *The Growth of Economic Thought.* Englewood Cliffs, NJ: Prentice-Hall.

State Environmental Monitor. 1997. USEPA Gives Eight States ISO 14000 "Management System" Grants. Washington, DC: *Inside Washington,* 5 May, 19–20.

Stavins, Robert N. 1995. Transaction Costs and Tradeable Permits. *Journal of Environmental Economics and Management* 29: 133–48.

Stephan, P. 1996. The Economics of Science. *Journal of Economic Literature* 34: 1199–1262.

Sterk, Stewart E. 1992. Competition Among Municipalities as a Constraint on Land Use Exactions. *Vanderbilt Law Review* 45(May): 831–67.

———. 1997. Minority Protection in Residential Private Governments. *Boston University Law Review* 77(April): 273–341.

Stigler, George J. 1968. *The Organization of Industry*. Homewood, IL: Richard D. Irwin.

Stroup, Richard L. 1997. The Economics of Compensating Property Owners. *Contemporary Economic Policy* 15(October): 55–65.

Suen, Wing. 1989. Rationing and Rent Dissipation in the Presence of Heterogeneous Individuals. *Journal of Political Economy* 97: 1384–94.

Swierenga, Robert P. 1968. *Pioneers and Profits: Land Speculation on the Iowa Frontier*. Ames: Iowa State University Press.

Tang, S. Y. 1992. *Institutions and Collective Actions: Self-Governance in Irrigation*. San Francisco: Institute for Contemporary Studies Press.

Tarlock, A. Daniel, J. N. Corbridge, and David H. Getches. 1993. *Water Resource Management*. 4th ed. Westbury, NY: Foundation Press.

Thomas, Elizabeth Marshall. 1958. *The Harmless People*. New York: Alfred A. Knopf.

Thomas, Stacie. 1999. Eco-Seals. In *The Market Meets the Environment*, ed. Bruce Yandle. Lanham, MD: Rowman and Littlefield Publishers, 125–65.

Thomas, Stacie, and Bruce Yandle. 1998. American Heritage Rivers: Another Property Rights Battle. *Journal of the James Madison Institute* 3(September/October): 20–23.

Thompson, Barton H. Jr. 1997. The Endangered Species Act: A Case Study in Takings and Incentives. *Stanford Law Review* 49: 601–76.

Thorson, James A. 1996. An Examination of the Monopoly Zoning Hypothesis. *Land Economics* 72(February): 43–55.

Tiebout, Charles M. 1956. A Pure Theory of Local Expenditures. *Journal of Political Economy* 64(October): 416–24.

Tietenberg, Tom. 1992. *Environmental and Natural Resources Economics*. New York: HarperCollins.

Trefil, James. 1989. *Reading the Mind of God: In Search of the Principle of Universality*. New York: Anchor Books.

Trelease, Frank J., and G. A. Gould. 1986. *Water Law: Cases and Materials*. 4th ed. St. Paul, MN: West Publishing.

Trosper, Ronald L. 1978. American Indian Relative Ranching Efficiency. *American Economic Review* 68(4): 503–16.

Tullock, Gordon. 1967. The Welfare Costs of Tariffs, Monopolies, and Theft. *Western Economic Journal* 5(June): 224–32.

———. 1987. *Autocracy*. Dordrecht, The Netherlands: Kluwer.

———. 1993. *Rent Seeking*. Aldershot, England: Edward Elgar and the Locke Institute.

Turnbull, Colin M. 1972. *The Mountain People*. New York: Simon and Schuster.

Turvey, Ralph. 1963. On Divergences between Social Cost and Private Cost. *Economica* 30(August): 309–13.

Umbeck, John. 1977a. A Theory of Contract Choice and the California Gold Rush. *Journal of Law and Economics* 20(2): 421–37.

———. 1977b. The California Gold Rush: A Study of Emerging Property Rights. *Explorations in Economic History* 14(3): 197–226.

———. 1981. Might Makes Rights: A Theory of the Formation and Initial Distribution of Property Rights. *Economic Inquiry* 19(1): 38–59.

Usher, Dan. 1995. Victimization, Rent-Seeking and Just Compensation. *Public Choice* 83(April): 1–20.

Valcke, Catherine. 1989. Locke on Property: A Deontological Interpretation. *Harvard Journal of Law and Public Policy* 12(3): 941–1008.

Van Zandt, David E. 1993. The Lessons of the Lighthouse: "Government" or "Private" Provision of Goods. *Journal of Legal Studies* 22(January): 47–72.

Viner, Jacob. 1958. *The Long View and the Short: Studies in Economic Theory.* Glencoe, IL: The Freeman Press.

———. 1965. *Guide to John Rae's Life of Adam Smith.* New York: Augustus M. Kelly.

Wahl, Richard W. 1989. *Markets for Federal Water: Subsidies, Property Rights, and the Bureau of Reclamation.* Washington, DC: Resources for the Future.

Waldron, Jeremy. 1994. The Advantages and Difficulties of the Human Theory of Property. In *Property Rights*, ed. Ellen Frankel Paul, Fred D. Miller Jr., and Jeffrey Paul. Social Philosophy and Policy Series. Cambridge: Cambridge University Press.

Walras, León. [1874, Part I; 1877, Part II] 1954. *Elements of Pure Economics.* Originally published in French. Trans. William Jaffé. Homewood, IL: Richard D. Irwin.

Watson, Alec. 1999. An Economic Analysis of the Interaction between Golf Courses and the Environment. In *The Market Meets the Environment*, ed. Bruce Yandle. Lanham, MD: Rowman and Littlefield Publishers, 231–58.

Watson, James D. 1968. *The Double Helix: A Personal Account of the Discovery of the Structure of DNA.* New York: Antheneum.

Webb, Walter Prescott. 1931. *The Great Plains.* New York: Grossett and Dunlap.

Weber, Joseph. 2000. 3M's Big Cleanup. *Business Week*, June 5, 96–98.

West, Edwin G. 2002. Property Rights in the History of Economic Thought: From Locke to J. S. Mill. In this volume.

Wellman, Paul I. [1939] 1967. *The Trampling Herd: The Story of the Cattle Range in America.* Lincoln: University of Nebraska Press.

Whitcomb, David K. 1972. *Externalities and Welfare.* New York: Columbia University Press.

White, Helen E. 1987. Death in Bangkok: Competition Comes to the Body Business, *Wall Street Journal*, 7 January, p. 1.

Wiggins, Steven N., and Gary D. Libecap. 1985. Oil Field Unitization: Contractual Failure in the Presence of Imperfect Information. *American Economic Review* 75(3): 376–85.

Wilkinson, Charles F. 1992. *Crossing the Next Meridian: Land, Water and the Future of the West.* Washington, DC: Island Press.

Williams, Stephen F. 1983. The Requirement of Beneficial Use as a Cause of Waste in Water Resource Development. *Natural Resources Journal* 23: 7–22.

Williamson, Oliver E. 1975. *Markets and Hierarchies: Analysis and Antitrust*

Implications. A Study in the Economics of Internal Organization. New York: Basic Books.

———. 1979. Transaction-Cost Economics: The Governance of Contractual Relations. *Journal of Law and Economics* 22(2): 233–61.

———. 1981. The Modern Corporation: Origins, Evolutions, Attributes. *Journal of Economic Literature* 19: 1537–68.

———. 1985. *The Economic Institutions of Capitalism: Firms, Markets, Relational Contracting.* New York: The Free Press.

———. 1996. *The Mechanisms of Governance.* New York: Oxford University Press.

Wolfson, Nicholas. 1984. *The Modern Corporation: Free Markets vs. Regulation.* New York: The Free Press.

Woodham-Smith, Cecil. 1968. *The Great Hunger: Ireland 1845–1849.* London: Hamish Hamilton.

World Bank. 1996. *Market Based Instruments for Environmental Policymaking in Latin American and the Caribbean: Lessons from Eleven Countries.* Washington, DC: World Bank.

Wright, Brian W. 1983. The Economics of Invention Incentives: Patents, Prizes, and Research Contracts. *American Economic Review* 73: 691–707.

Wyeth, George. 1996. Regulatory Competition and the Takings Clause. *Northwestern University Law Review* 91(Fall): 87–143.

Yandle, Bruce. 1997. *Common Sense and Common Law for the Environment: Creating Wealth in Hummingbird Economies.* Lanham, MD: Rowman and Littlefield Publishers.

———. 1998. Coase, Pigou and Environmental Rights. In *Who Owns the Environment?* ed. Peter J. Hill and Roger E. Meiners. Lanham, MD: Rowman and Littlefield Publishers, 119–52.

———. 1999. Public Choice at the Intersection of Environmental Law and Economics. *European Journal of Law and Economics* 8: 5–27.

———. 2002. Property Rights or Externalities? In this volume.

Yandle, Bruce, ed. 1995. *Land Rights: The 1990's Property Rights Rebellion.* Lanham, MD: Rowman and Littlefield Publishers.

Yinger, John et al. 1988. *Property Taxes and Housing Values: The Theory and Estimation of Intrajurisdictional Property Tax Capitalization.* Boston: Academic Press.

CASES CITED

Acton v. Blundell, 152 Eng. Rep. 1223 (Ex. 1843)

Agins v. Tiburon, 447 U.S. 255 (1980)

Armory v. Delamirie, King's Bench, 1722, 1 Strange 505.

Austin Instrument, Inc. v. Loral Corp., 272 N.E.2d 533 (N.Y. 1971)

Bd. of Regents v. Roth, 408 U.S. 564 (1972)

Berman v. Parker, 348 U.S. 26 (1954)

Blade v. Higgs, 11 H.L. Cases 621, 11 Eng. Rep. 1474 (1865)

Bridge Publications, Inc. v. F.A.C.T. Net, Inc., 183 F.R.D. 254, 262 (D. Colo. 1998)

Coffin v. Left Hand Ditch Co., 6 Colo.443 (1882)

College Savings Bank v. Florida Prepaid Postsecondary Education Expense Bd., 119 S. Ct. 2219 (1999)

Columbus-America Discovery Group, Inc. v. Atlantic Mutual Ins. Co., 974 F.2d 450 (4th Cir. 1992)

Community Redevelopment Agency of Los Angeles v. Abrams, 15 Cal. 3d 813, 543 P.2d 905, 126 Cal. Rptr. 473 (1975)

Cosmopolitan Broadcasting Co. v. FCC, 581 F.2d 917 (D.C. Cir. 1978)

Dolan v. Tigard, 512 U.S. 687 (1994)

Del Monte Mining & Milling Co. v. Last Chance Mining & Milling Co., 171 U.S. 55; 18 S. Ct. 895 (1898)

Eldred v. Reno, 239 F.3d 372 (D.C. Cir.), rehearing denied, sub nom. Eldred v. Ashcroft, 255 F.3d 849 (D.C. 2001), cert. granted, _____ U.S. _____, 122 S. Ct. 1062 (2002).

Flast v. Cohen, 392 U.S. 83 (1968)

Ghen v. Rich, 8 F. 159 (D. Mass) (1881)

Graham v. John Deere Co., 383 U.S. 1 (1966)

Graver Tank & Mfg. Co. v. Linde Air Products Co., 339 U.S. 605 (1950)

Haslem v. Lockwood, 37 Conn. 500 (1871)

Hawaiian Housing Authority v. Midkiff, 467 U.S. 229 (1984)

Home Building & Loan Ass'n v. Blaisdell, 290 U.S. 398 (1934)

Illinois Central Railroad Co. v. Illinois, 146 U.S. 387 (1892)

Johnson v. M'Intosh, 21 U.S. (8 Wheat.) 543 (1823)

Kaiser Aetna v. United States, 444 U.S. 164 (1979)

Kimball Laundry Co. v. United States, 338 U.S. 1 (1949)

Kirwin v. Mexican Petroleum Co., 267 F. 460 (D. R.I., 1920)

Lone Wolf v. Hitchcock, 187 U.S. 553 (1903)

Lucas v. South Carolina Coastal Council, 505 U.S. 1003 (1992)

Lyng v. Northwest Indian Cemetery Protective Ass'n, 485 U.S. 439 (1985)

Massachusetts v. Mellon, 262 U.S. 447 (1923)

McKee v. Gratz, 260 U.S. 127 (1922)

Monongahela Navigation Co. v. United States, 148 U.S. 312 (1893)

ABOUT THE EDITORS AND AUTHORS

Terry L. Anderson is executive director of PERC — The Center for Free Market Environmentalism — in Bozeman, Montana, senior fellow at the Hoover Institution at Stanford University, and professor emeritus at Montana State University. He has published widely on property rights, especially as they relate to environmental policy.

Fred S. McChesney teaches at Northwestern University, where he is the Class of 1967/James B. Haddad Professor of Law, and Professor, Department of Management & Strategy, Kellogg School of Management. Previously, he was a member of the faculties of Cornell University and Emory University, and has also taught at the University of Chicago and Université d'Aix-Marseille III. He serves on the editorial boards of three journals: *Public Choice, Managerial and Decision Economics*, and the *Journal des Économistes et des Études Humaines*.

Yoram Barzel is a professor of economics at the University of Washington and past president of the Western Economic Association. He is the author of numerous articles in applied price theory, and of *Economic Analysis of Property Rights* and *A Theory of the State: Economic Rights, Legal Rights and the Scope of the State*, both published by Cambridge University Press.

Louis De Alessi is professor emeritus of economics at the University of Miami. He has published extensively on economic theory and its application to alternative systems of property rights.

Harold Demsetz is professor emeritus of business economics at the University of California-Los Angeles. He is counted among the great economists by Mark Blaugh in his book *Great Economists Since Keynes* and he has recently been ranked among the top ten economists whose work is most frequently cited.

Thráinn Eggertsson is professor of economics at the University of Iceland, Reykjavík, and visiting scholar at Columbia University. He was a senior fellow with the Max Planck Institute for Research into Economic Systems in Jena, and for two years a visiting fellow at the Hoover Institution, Stanford University. Eggertsson writes on the economics of institutions.

Richard A. Epstein is the James Parker Hall Distinguished Service Professor of Law at the University of Chicago, and the Peter and Kristin Bedford Senior Fellow at the Hoover Institution. He has written extensively on the constitutional and economic aspects of property.

William A. Fischel is professor of economics at Dartmouth College. He specializes in the law and economics of local government, property taxation, and land-use regulation. Fischel is author of *The Economics of Zoning Laws* (Johns Hopkins 1985), *Regulatory Takings* (Harvard 1995), and *The Homevoter Hypothesis* (Harvard 2001).

David D. Haddock is a professor in the law school and the economics department at Northwestern University and a senior associate at PERC in Bozeman, Montana. His research has covered law and economics broadly, including a number of articles and book chapters that discuss the theory of property rights economics.

Peter J. Hill is the George F. Bennett Professor of Economics at Wheaton College, Illinois, and a senior associate at PERC in Bozeman, Montana. He has published articles and books on the evolution of property rights in the American West, US constitutional history, and environmental issues.

Gary D. Libecap is the Anheuser Busch Professor of Entrepreneurial Studies, Economics, and Law and director of the Karl Eller Center at the University of Arizona, Tucson. He is also a research associate with the National Bureau of Economic Research. Libecap has published extensively on property rights and regulation as they relate to natural resources, the environment, and agriculture. He has been coeditor of the *Journal of Economic History* and member of the Economics Panel of the National Science Foundation.

Dean Lueck is professor of economics at Montana State University and visiting professor of law at the University of Virginia. He has published widely in law and economics and contract economics with emphasis on applications in agriculture and natural resources, and is author of *The Nature of the Farm* (MIT Press).

Edwin West (1922–2001) was professor of economics at Carleton University, Ottawa, Canada. He was the author of several publications on the history of economic thought, as well as public finance and the economic analysis of education.

Bruce Yandle is professor emeritus of economics at Clemson University, a senior associate at PERC in Bozeman, Montana, and a faculty member with George Mason University's Mercatus Center. His books include *Land Rights: The 1990s' Property Rights Rebellion*, *Common Sense and Common Law for the Environment*, and *The Environment Meets the Market* published by Rowman and Littlefield Publishers.

INDEX